General Idea

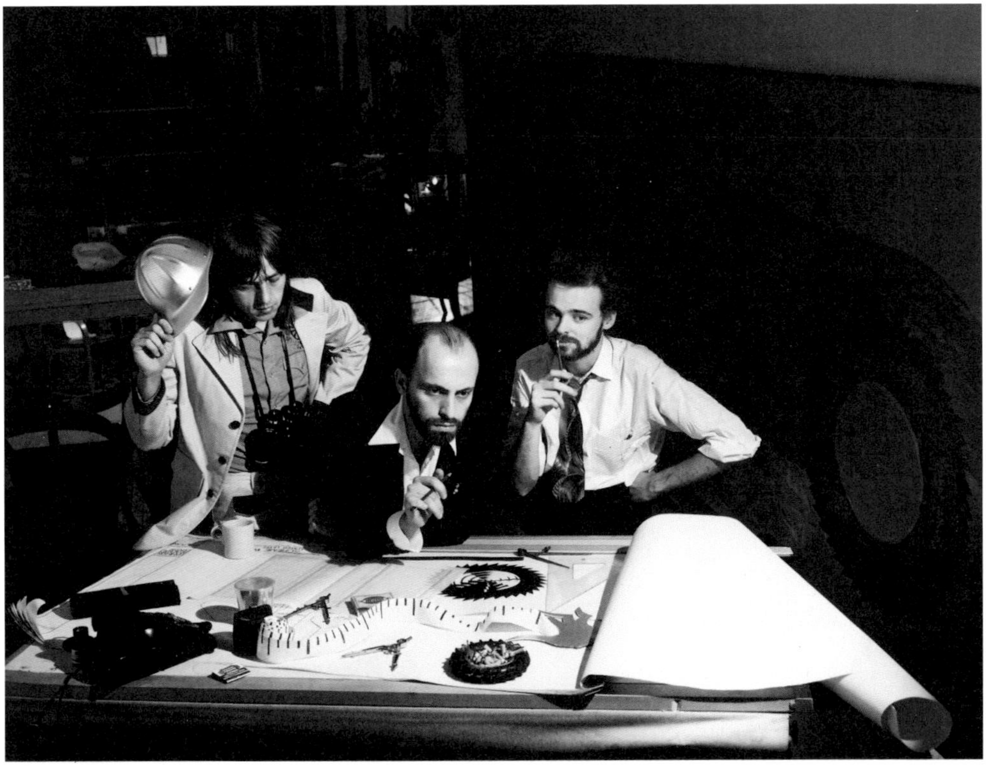

General Idea

Haute Culture
A Retrospective, 1969–1994

ARC/Musée d'Art moderne de la Ville de Paris
Art Gallery of Ontario, Toronto

jrp|ringier

Table of Contents

The inserts are a retranscription of selected Showcards, a series of works realized by General Idea between 1975 and 1979.

Foreword

Certain works produce an immediate echo by their presence, while others induce a more complex resonance: we come to hear them with extra clarity through a more gradual and repetitive absorption.

The works of General Idea, the Canadian collective founded

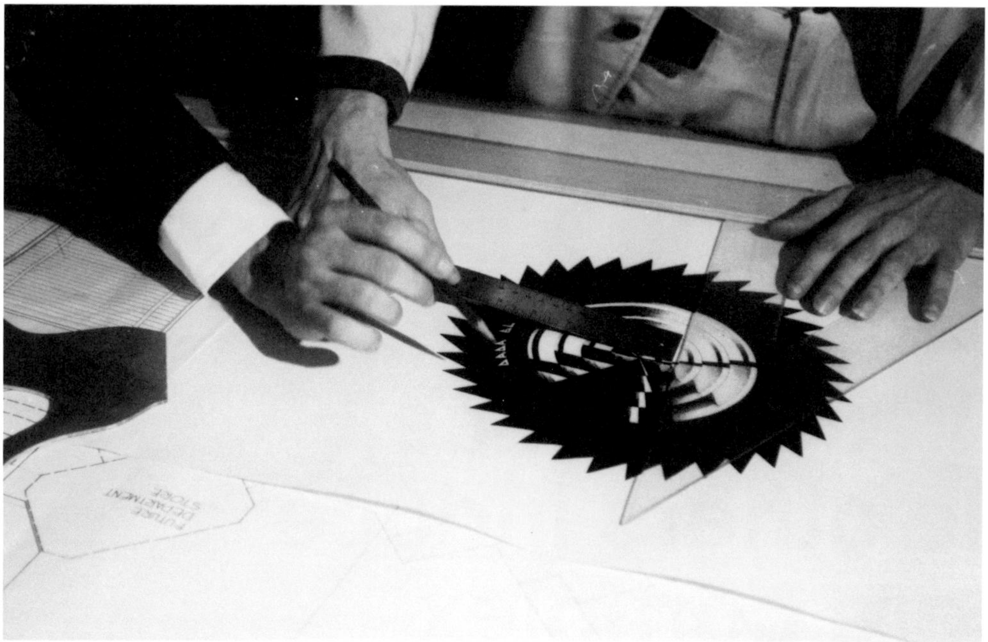

in the late 1960s and active until the early 1990s, belong in both categories. Projects like *FILE Megazine*, seen within the counterculture of the 1970s, and *AIDS*, within the socio-political context of the 1980s, immediately provoked interest, discussion, reaction, and interpretation. But "Miss General Idea," their pseudo-mythological muse, teacher, and guardian angel, around whom so many works revolve; their pseudo-archaeological narratives, peculiar to the 1970s, describing an improbable "Pavillion" set in the year 1984; or their constant tripling of image and language as a collective identity—all these take on new significance as the decades go by.

Thus, since the end of the 1980s, we have related the work of General Idea to artistic activism (Group Material, Gran Fury, etc.); we have noted the subtlety of the group's identity-based appropriation and authorship's delegation strategies (echoing the appropriation of Sherrie Levine or the self-representations of Jeff Koons, for example); and measured the impact of General Idea's invention of exhibition devices and formats (explicit traces can be found in both Philippe Parreno and Liam Gillick, to mention only two).

Does this mean that General Idea was ahead of its time while also being at the heart of the preoccupations of its day? Can its practices be unraveled in so many different ways, and in so many new contexts, that under each level of meaning we find only another level, and beneath that another, and so on? Yes, all that and much more.

Multiple interpretations jostle for dominance in this publication: in General Idea's work we find a model derived from the 1970s, centered on performance, printed matter (or multiples), and exchange; the work uses the appropriation of motifs and logos in order to inject images, as viruses, into the mainstream culture; Elisabeth Lebovici discovers General Idea's "trouple," transported into the genre of artistic utterance; and of course we must include General Idea's symbiotic relationship to the mass media, and particularly press and television.

It is a safe bet that this analysis will prompt subsequent interpreters to have another look at the major stages of an aesthetic project, which we can already anticipate will give rise to future retrospectives in 2020, 2030, or 2050 …

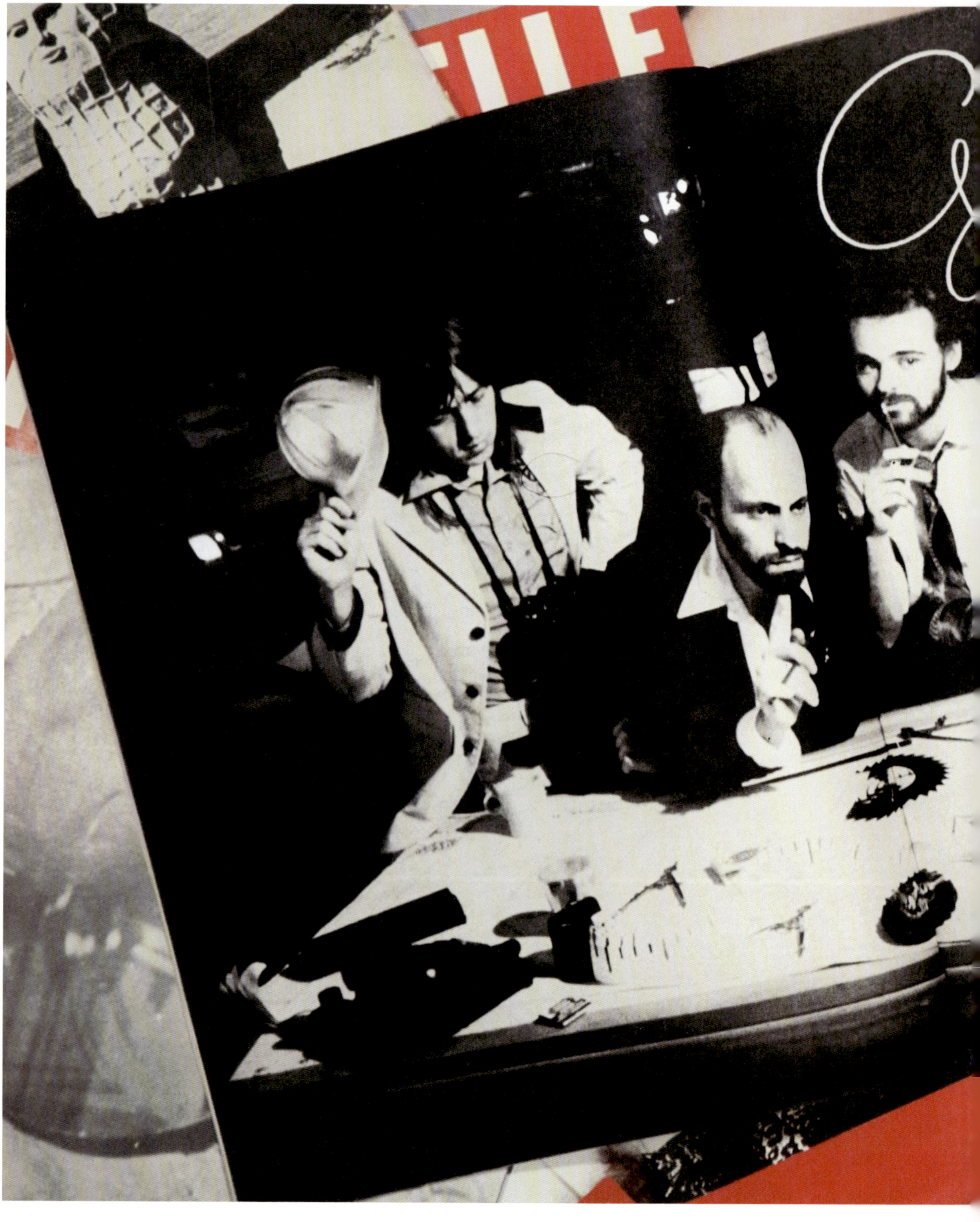

"Glamour," FILE Megazine, 1975, p. 20-21

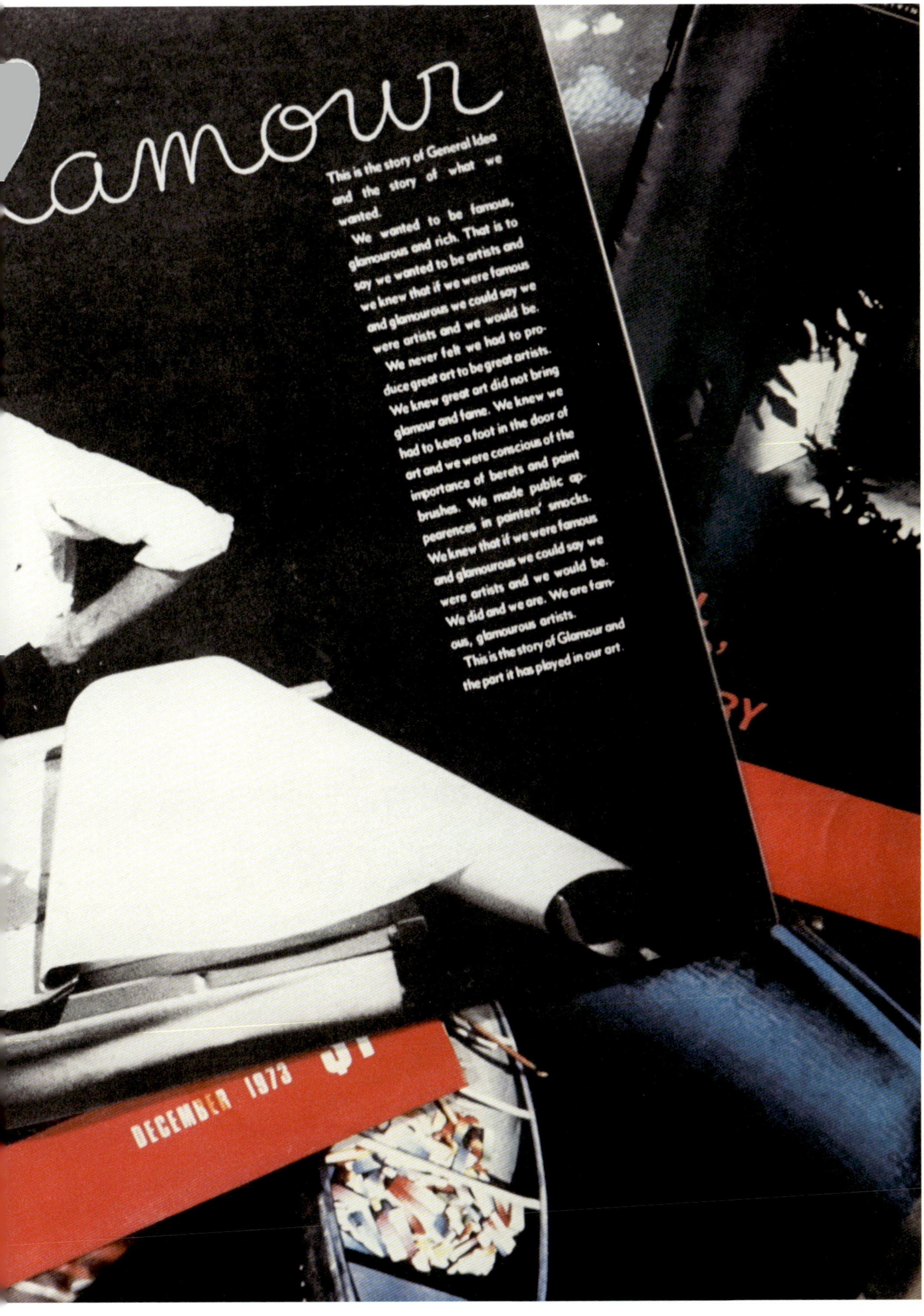

Glamour
This is the story of General Idea and the story of what we wanted.
We wanted to be famous, glamourous and rich. That is to say we wanted to be artists and we knew that if we were famous and glamourous we could say we were artists and we would be.
We never felt we had to produce great art to be great artists. We knew great art did not bring glamour and fame. We knew we had to keep a foot in the door of art and we were conscious of the importance of berets and paint brushes. We made public appearences in painters' smocks.
We knew that if we were famous and glamourous we could say we were artists and we would be. We did and we are. We are famous, glamourous artists.
This is the story of Glamour and the part it has played in our art.
DECEMBER 1973

Setting the Stage: Back to Reality!

Frédéric Bonnet

New York, November 1987: Strange posters pop up in Lower Manhattan, bearing a highly familiar but weirdly subverted image. The health crisis triggered by AIDS, a major epidemic that was only given a definitive name in

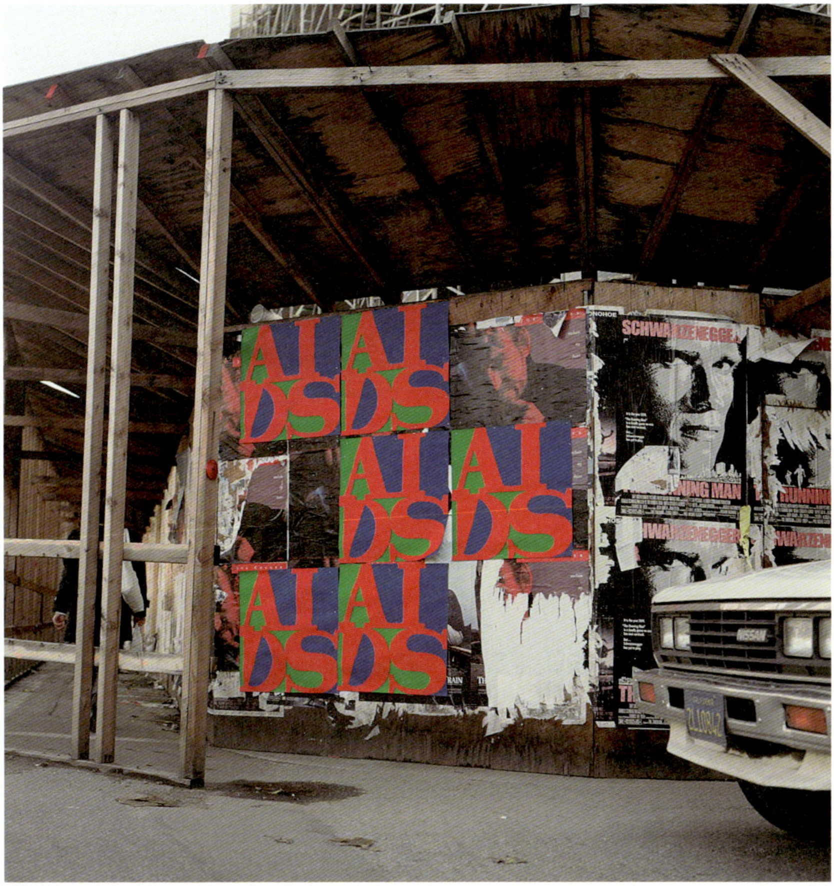

AIDS, San Francisco, 1988

1986 (Acquired Immune Deficiency Syndrome), thus acquired an internationally recognizable visual expression: this AIDS logo was created by General Idea's appropriation of the shape and colors—red, green, blue—of Robert Indiana's famous *LOVE* image of 1964. Indiana's work, the graphic symbol of an entire generation, had become hackneyed through overuse, appearing on too many spin-offs. The Canadian trio of General Idea, being good PR men, behaved as though the visual impact of Indiana's icon had fallen into the public domain, rather like some drug patent, so that they could create and manufacture generic versions of it in all available media.

In fact, the image that would give birth to the vast, tentacular AIDS Project had first appeared several weeks earlier as a painting [*AIDS*, 1987] exhibited in New York in June as part of a series of shows to benefit the fight against AIDS.[1] Like the virus targeted by this work, the project spread swiftly throughout the entire world in various forms. In January 1988 the posters surfaced in San Francisco, simultaneously appearing in clusters on city walls, on a large billboard, and within an exhibition venue—Artspace—where one room was entirely covered with wallpaper that bore the silkscreened logo.[2] The posters were soon being plastered across the planet—Toronto (Canada), Hartford (Connecticut), Tourcoing (France), Berlin (Germany), and so on. In September 1989, a huge lighted sign in New York's Time Square flashed a 30-second message that alternated "LOVE/AIDS" once a minute for a month. In December of that year, still in New York, the subway was invaded when a poster appeared in every train. In 1990 the posters spread to Amsterdam's tram system. In the meantime, the image had mutated and adopted various forms such as lottery ticket, ring, and sheet of stamps, among others.

Geneva, March 1984: General Idea gives a performance at the Centre d'Art Contemporain.[3] Three huge unstretched canvases, set high on one wall, roll down onto the floor. In front are three stuffed white poodles. The artists grab the poodles, half-dip them in tubs of blue paint—a variant on International Klein Blue (IKB)—then drag them across each canvas in the pattern of a giant X.

Titled *XXX (bleu)*, this performance was an ironic take on a kind of gestural, deliberately "aggressive" painting that significantly marked the early 1980s, and was inspired by a 1962 film, *Mondo Cane*, by Paolo Cavara, Gualtiero Jacopetti, and Franco Prosperi. The movie adopted the tone of an anthropological documentary to present cultural practices around the world in the guise of a "museum of horrors" that would shock Western opinion. At the filmmakers' request, Yves Klein organized a performance of live models making his "anthropometries" on a funeral shroud; given the way this footage was used in the final film, Klein left the screening at the Cannes Film Festival feeling fairly humiliated. Rushes of Klein's performance, for that matter, surfaced in General Idea's 1985 video *Shut the Fuck Up*, intercut with excerpts from its own performance, to which were added highly ironic scenes from the 1966 film *Batman*, in which the Joker wins a

XXX (bleu), 1984

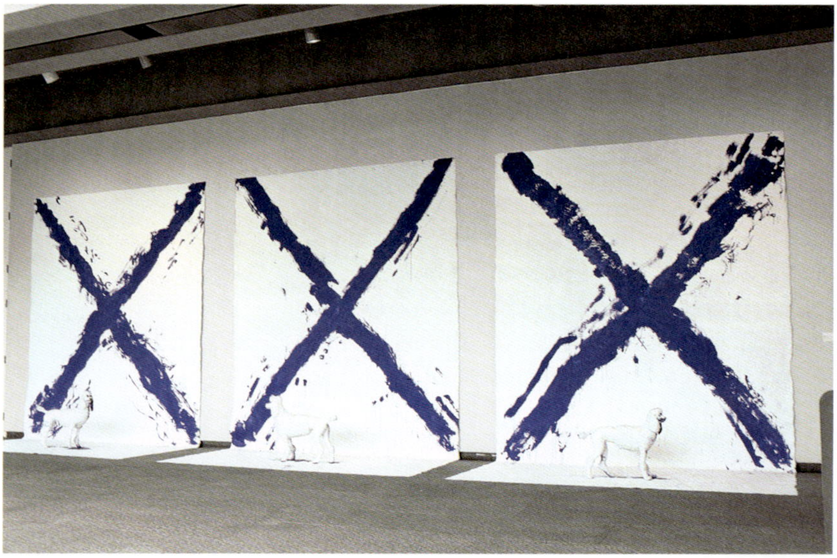

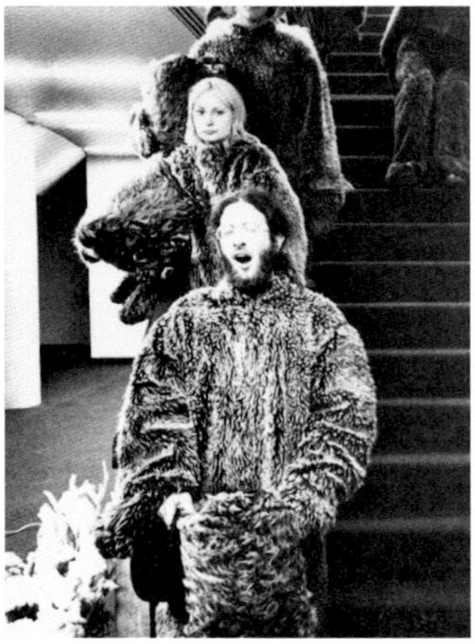

The 1970 Miss General Idea Pageant, 1970

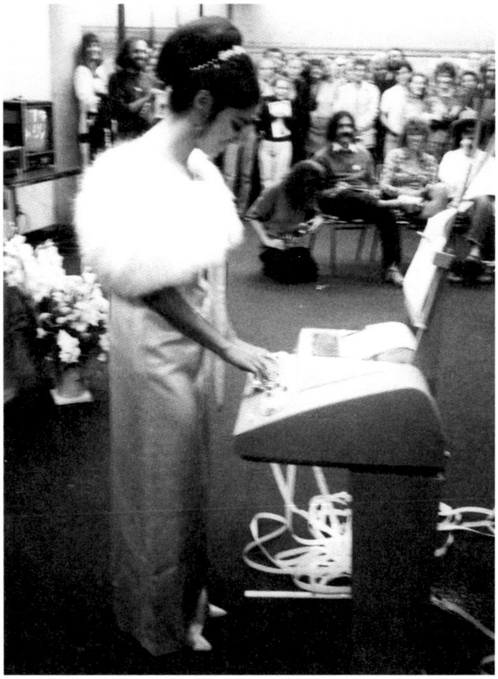

Miss Honey, Miss General Idea 1970, 1970

painting contest with a blank canvas, far from the gestural, paint-splashing antics of the other contestants.

Toronto, August 1970: *The 1970 Miss General Idea Pageant* is held at the St Lawrence Centre for the Arts as part of the Festival of Underground Theater. Whereas all the beauty contestants, male and female (gender having absolutely no significance here) wear bear costumes and perform various numbers in an attempt to win over audience and jury, the latter is enthralled by the delicious Miss Honey, who is dressed all in white. She astonishes the crowd and ultimately wins the pageant given her great skill at a telex machine!

This first truly collective performance by General Idea provided the opportunity to introduce the "Miss" who bears their name, simultaneously a muse and an object, an image and a concept. "Our search for the spirit of Miss General Idea is the search for inspiration," asserted Jorge Zontal in the *Pilot* TV program (1977). The following year the pageant was held at the Art Gallery of Ontario in Toronto, a more complex and lavish event, but still based on a set of clichés in a format typical of television in North America—it was thus a spectacular show. *The 1971 Miss General Idea Pageant* crowned Marcel Idea[4] the winner for his ability to "capture Glamour without falling into it."[5] The title was to remain valid until 1984—that mythical date, around which the trio's oeuvre would henceforth be geared—when the 1984 Miss General Idea Pageant was scheduled to be held in a pavilion erected for that purpose—*The 1984*

The 1971 Miss General Idea Pageant

Dear Mrs. Campbell,

General Idea is now prepared to offer you the chance of a lifetime. This is no trick offer. There are no fake prizes, no money-spending hoaxes, no elaborate advertising gimmicks. General Idea is now offering you the chance to become Miss General Idea 1971.

Yes, you have been hand-picked by the General's personal staff as a finalist in the pageant, and we hope you are as excited by the prospects as we are. The selection took many months of intensive research and secret gossip-mongering and we are pleased to announce your position as one of the 16 beauties from across the country chosen to represent General Idea.

The Miss General Idea Beauty Pageant is an annual affair of unusual prestige and glamour. Enclosed you will find a brochure describing last year's fabulous pageant in Toronto's luxurious St. Lawrence Centre of the Arts. Included is a PERSONAL message from Miss General Idea herself.

Also enclosed you will find your personalized set of rules and regulations, your secret pageant documents, and of course your very own Miss General Idea Gown for judging purposes.

Please read the rules carefully and return your acceptance form immediately. You then have until the indicated deadline to mail us your finalized General Idea Entry including snapshots in your lovely General Idea Gown. The contest will be judged by an unequalled panel of judges and your own personal records of the results will be mailed to you promptly. The pageant will be covered by international magazines and displays will be exhibited in prestige locations across the country.

Imagine, all this can be yours: fame, fun, and fortune; the reassuring slam of a limousine door; those jealous stolen glances in the most exclusive hotels. All this and much, much more will be yours in the 1971 MISS GENERAL IDEA BEAUTY PAGEANT.

Yours sincerely,

(Miss) Granada Gazelle
(Miss General Idea 1969)

Granada Gazelle

General Idea, 87 Yonge Street, Toronto.

The 1971 Miss General Idea Pageant Entry Kit, 1971

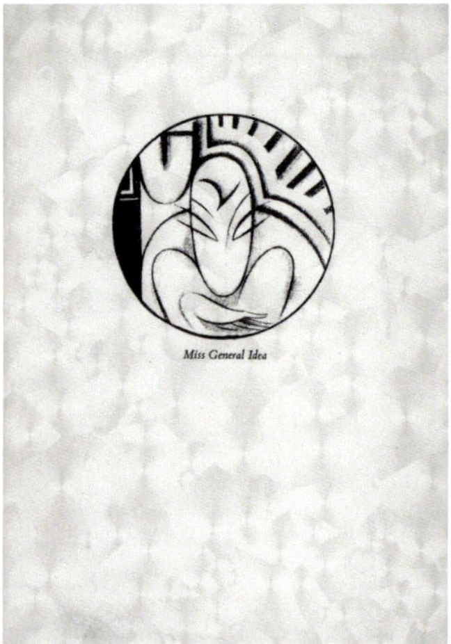

General Idea presents

THE 1971 MISS GENERAL IDEA PAGEANT GRAND AWARDS CEREMONY

Art Gallery of Ontario

Friday, October 1

"On August 25, 1932, the General appeared in Paris at the Hotel Behy Lafeyette. He had last been seen in Bournemouth, England, on April 16th of the same year at a skating match. On August 28th, after returning from a day's excursion to Deauville, the General attended the Folies Bergeres at 8 Rue Saulnier. There seated at a ringside table and puffing quietly on his De Reszke cigarette, the General viewed with pleasure a variety of entertainments, including the memorable 'Le Sexe-Appel'. Five acts, stylized in the Egyptian manner, culminated in 'Le Triomphe des Vamps', starring Mlle. Gina Palmieri as la Vamp-femme and the unforgettable Mlle. Troutowska as la Vamp-ire. The General, in his usual manner, incorporated the programme into his notebooks with only slight alteration."

COPYRIGHT GENERAL IDEA. 1971

The 1971 Miss General Idea Pageant Programme, 1971

General Idea is basically this: a framing device within which we inhabit the role of the artist as we see the living legend.

Showcard 1-001, General Idea, 1975

Degraded and humiliated,
the glamorous image
is brilliant in its vacancy,
glorious in its degradation.
The image retains
signs of a former purity.
The face of reality is
still evident beneath
the thin skin of Glamour.

Showcard 1-007, Brilliant in its Vacancy, 1975

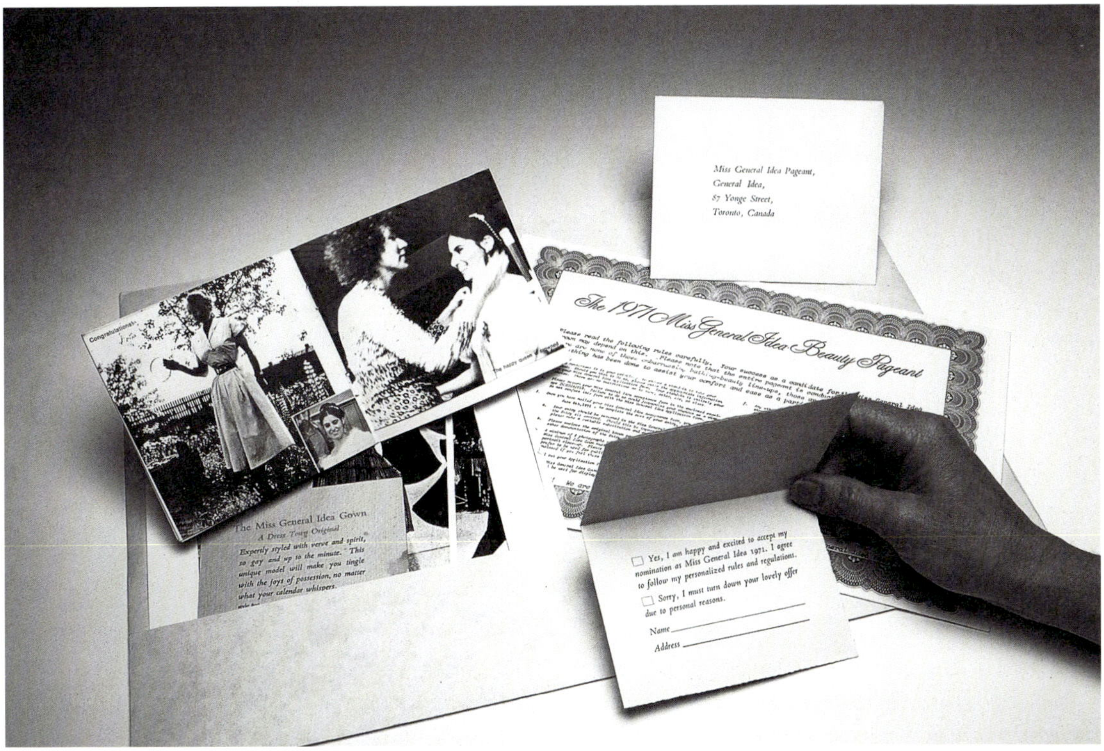

The 1971 Miss General Idea Pageant Entry Kit, 1971

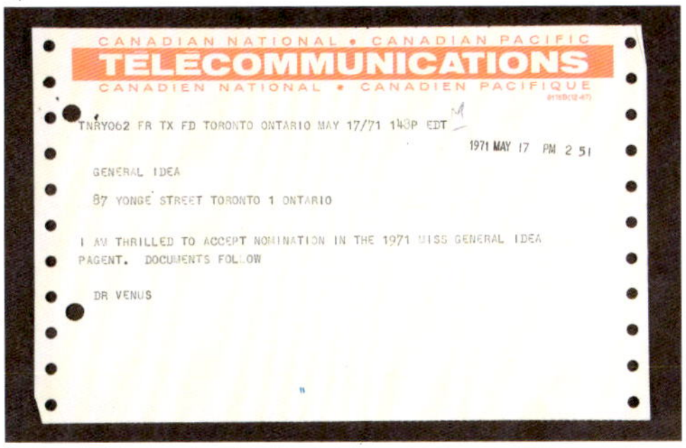

CANADIAN NATIONAL • CANADIAN PACIFIC
TELECOMMUNICATIONS
CANADIEN NATIONAL • CANADIEN PACIFIQUE

TNRY062 FR TX FD TORONTO ONTARIO MAY 17/71 148P EDT
1971 MAY 17 PM 2 51

GENERAL IDEA
87 YONGE STREET TORONTO 1 ONTARIO

I AM THRILLED TO ACCEPT NOMINATION IN THE 1971 MISS GENERAL IDEA PAGENT. DOCUMENTS FOLLOW

DR VENUS

The 1971 Miss General Idea Pageant, 1971
Dr. Venus announces her participation to the competition

The Miss General Idea Gown, 1971

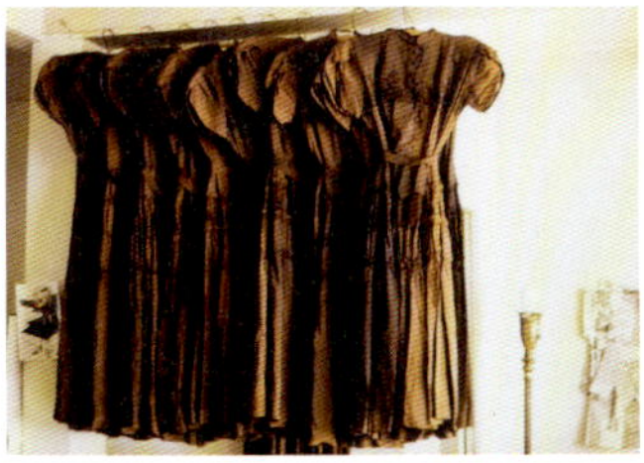

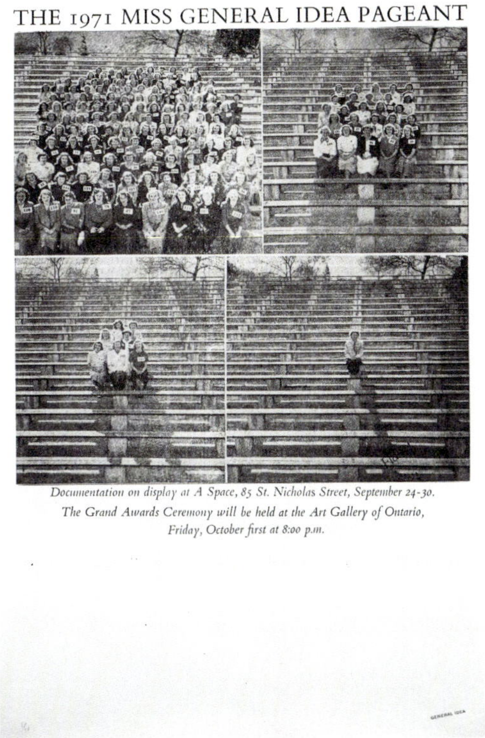

The 1971 Miss General Idea Pageant Poster, 1971

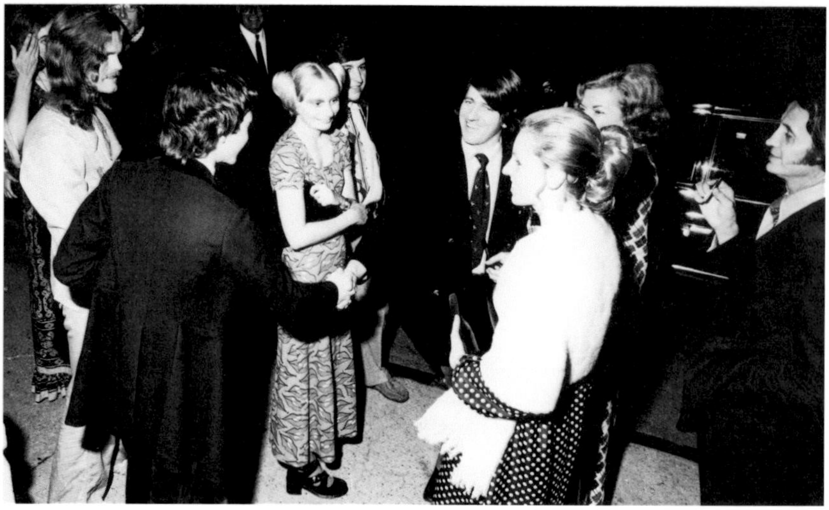

The 1971 Miss General Idea Pageant, 1971
Arrival of the judges

Miss General Idea Pavillion. In addition to the fact that they laid the foundations of a vast, reality-defying fiction that the collective exploited throughout its career, these beauty contests were presented right from the start as metaphors for the overall artistic process; they inaugurated a kind of "mythologizing" of culture and cultural icons that subsequently became ever more resonant not only in General Idea's oeuvre but in the art world in general.

These three sets of work, although highly varied in terms of appearance, theme, and expression, nevertheless all shared an intense connection to artificiality and ultimately to the notion of travesty. By shamelessly appropriating cultural and popular clichés, they all exploited concrete forms of reality via a mimetic technique that eliminates everything but the varnish, which itself soon cracks due to the effect, notably, of manipulations of the channels of communication on which they depend, manipulations that spurred these Canadian artists to take liberties—at all times and in all places—with well-known or habitual customs and forms.

The generalized use of fiction as a constituent feature was not of course innocuous, and in order to be effective and acquire a measure of credibility it obviously had to borrow its vocabulary from reality. The shock slogan, "Form follows Fiction," launched in 1973 as an ironic mockery of modernist architecture's doctrine of "Form follows Function," says as much.[6] The slogan furthermore asserts the primacy of the fictional apparatus within the creative process, especially since the form in question rarely fails to involve some mode of theater or other, as demonstrated by the group's numerous performances and ongoing play on the idea of image.

From this angle the art of General Idea was nevertheless unique in that it could often be compared to a kind of stage set, without however maintaining or claiming artifice as its goal. That was because the way the trio viewed and employed fiction allowed it to reach another a kind of "stage" beyond which there lies an alternative reality free from the deviations that afflict and constrain "true" reality.

AA Bronson expressed himself clearly when he stated that, "the current reality wasn't sufficient for us, or we didn't feel we belonged, so we had to create our own world, which was a kind of parody, an imperfect simulacrum of a perfect world."[7] The link between a staged world and the real one was explicitly made here and, even while adopting a measure of ambiguity, it evoked a presumed antinomy in order to assert, conversely, total complementarity.

The reconfigured, transgressive *LOVE* logo; poodles-as-paint-brushes in a simulacrum of painting; and beauty contests envisaged as an allegory of artistic creativity: "there is a reality shortage," assured an off-screen voice in the 1979 video piece *Test Tube*, and "General Idea is doing something about it."

Glamour Forever

"This is the story of General Idea and the story of what we wanted.

"We wanted to be famous, glamorous, and rich. That is to say we wanted to be artists and we knew that if we were famous and glamorous we could say we were artists and we would be. We never felt we had to produce great art to be great artists. We knew great art did not bring glamour and fame … We knew that if we were famous and glamorous we could say we were artists and we would be. We did and we are. We are famous, glamorous artists.

"This is the story of Glamour and the part it has played in our art."[8]

General Idea consistently and extensively expressed its vision of art and practice, notably with the convenient help of the magazine it founded in 1972, *FILE*. In 1975 *FILE* published a special issue on "Glamour," which included an article with that title. This text functioned like a basic manifesto even as it took a critical and humorous look at the condition of the artist. With a fine, lucid irony that with hindsight reads like a visionary prediction of the future development of much behavior and posturing in the realm of contemporary art, the group directly posited, with a hint of provocation, the preeminence of artists and of an artistic attitude.

Thus appearance was everything, and glamour became a factor of recognition; an artist's biggest asset was his or her image.

In fact, the "Glamour" manifesto opened with an appealing photograph of the three protagonists contemplating the plans for their *1984 Miss General Idea Pavillion*,[9] and included many examples of the staging of (and play on) their own image, stressing the iconic—and henceforth absolutely crucial—power of the artist.

General Idea's undeniable ability to steal the show was obvious in their occasionally experimental video pieces such as *Test Tube* (1979), *Loco* (1982), and *Shut the Fuck Up* (1985). Thus *Open Line* (1978) used innovative "slow-scan video" technology—which did not survive—involving the transmission of video images along telephone lines. Their uninhibited talent for telling their own story also scored a hit on the boob tube on April 1, 1977, when they broadcast their program *Pilot*, specially made in a televisual format for the TV Ontario channel.

General Idea literally "inhabited" the image of the artist, which was just asking to be occupied,[10] as demonstrated by the group's many photographic depictions and poses—serious characters when surrounded by symbolic objects of their work (*Self-Portrait with Objects*, 1981–1982), or shady graduates of the academy founded by Miss General Idea (*Nightschool*, 1989), or friends at a party displaying a Velvet Underground album for a Polaroid snap (*Self-Portrait [Velvet Underground]*, ca. 1969), to mention just a few.

Even *Playing Doctor* (1992), a solemn portrait from a troubled period that logically stemmed from their AIDS project, is extremely sophisticated: their slick faces hover against a white background marked by the three colors of their stethoscopes—red, green, and blue, obviously. Terribly present yet paradoxically kept at a distance, the artists—aware of their role—maintain a lucid aloofness from their object. "Playing" doctor means not really being one: back to reality!

Another character in this slick staging of "the artist" was the poodle, which became the group's alter ego and hence a recurring presence in its visual pantheon. In addition to the cultural context of the period, mentioned above, the poodle appealed to General Idea for its banal yet sophisticated, civilized image, which can furthermore be viewed not only as a critique of the bohemian artistic life but also as a decorative device related once again to ornamental concerns.[11]

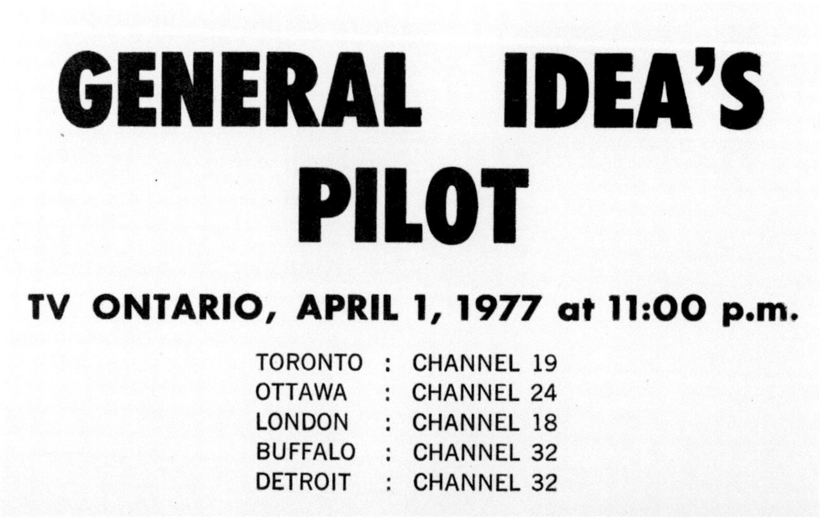

Flyer for the broadcast of Pilot, April 1, 1977

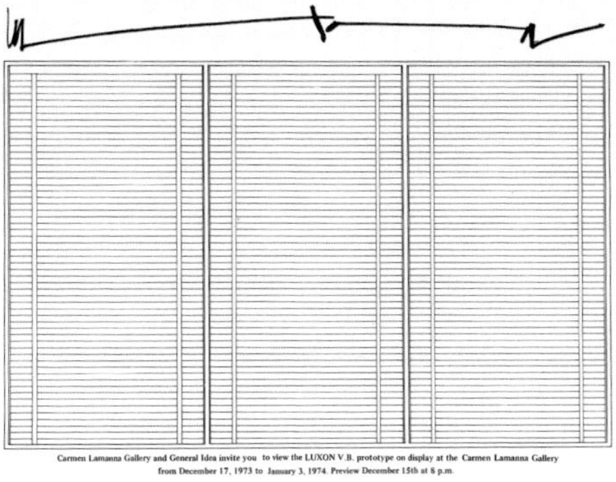

Invitation card for the exhibition Luxon V.B., Carmen Lamanna Gallery, Toronto, 1973–1974

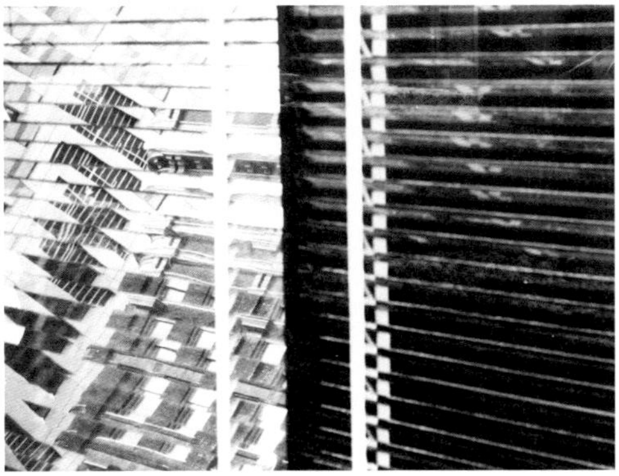

Luxon V.B., 1973

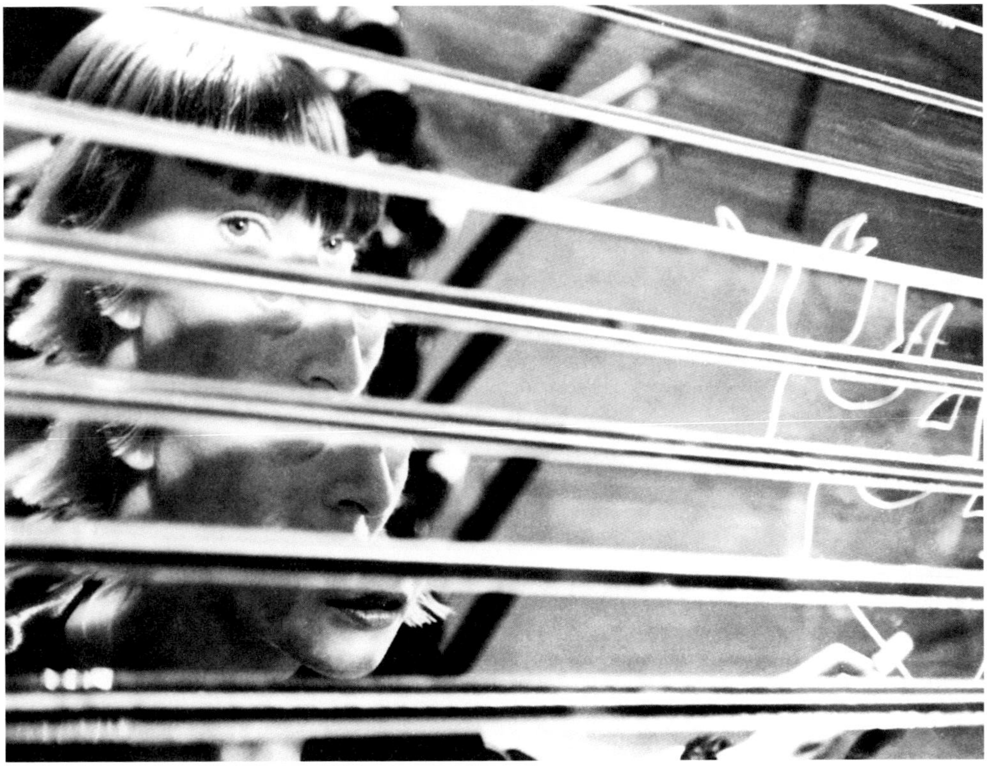

Sandy Stagg and The Hand of the Spirit behind Luxon V.B., 1973–1974

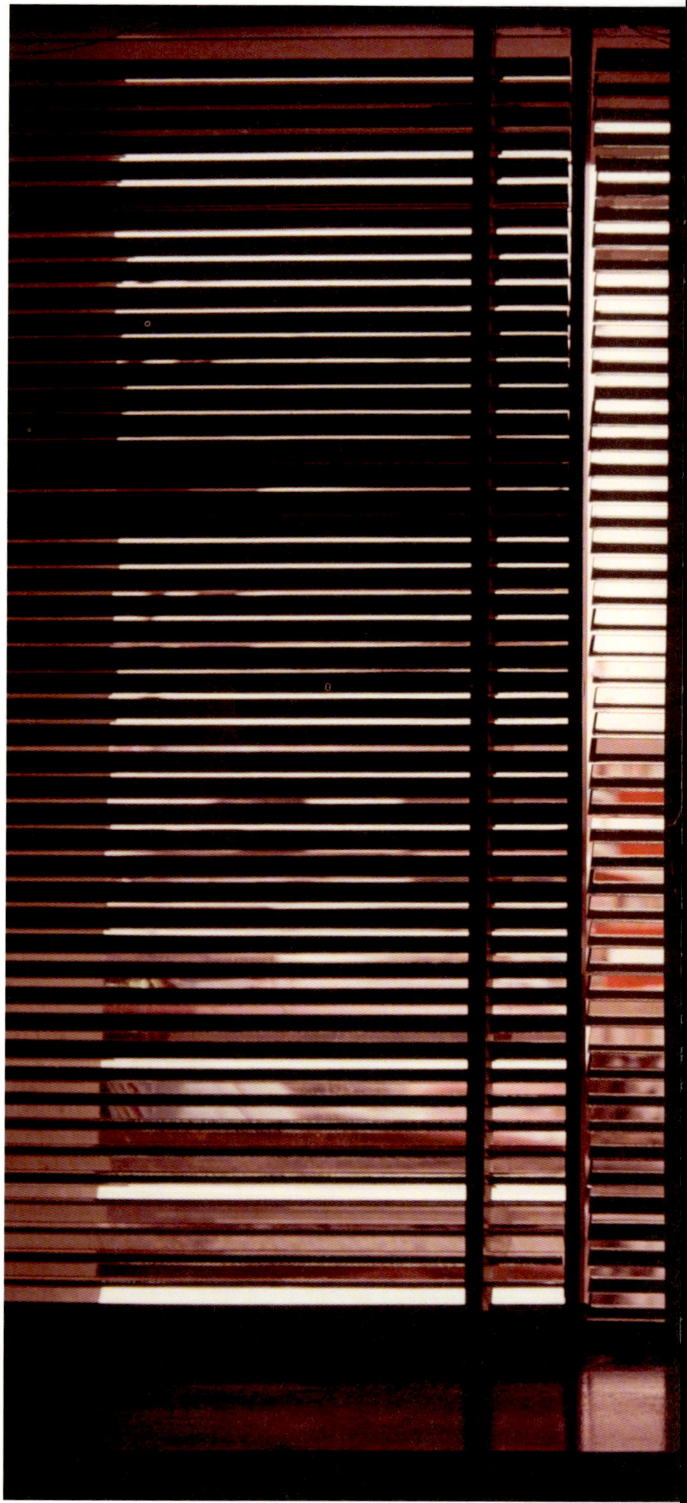

Lux-on, 1974

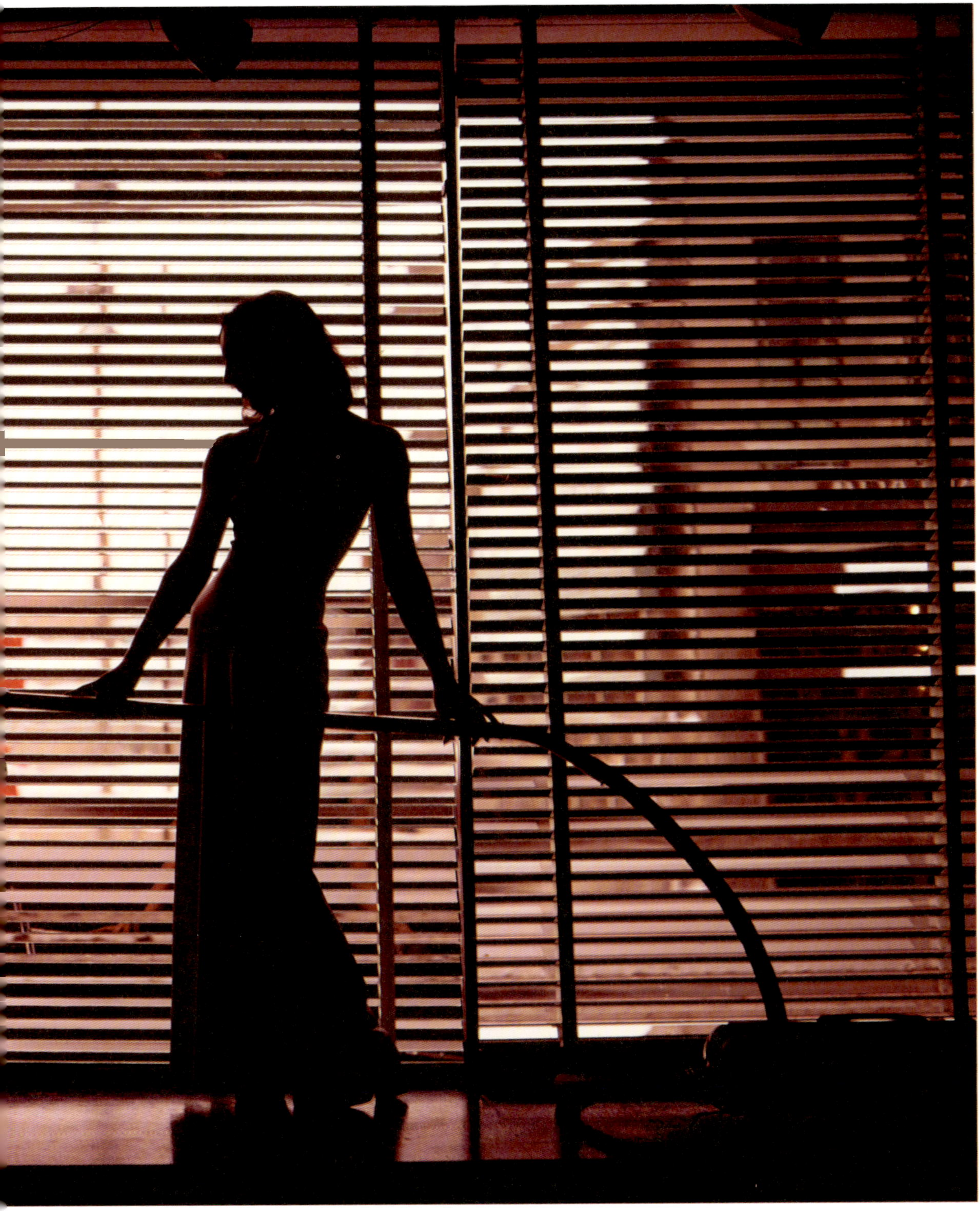

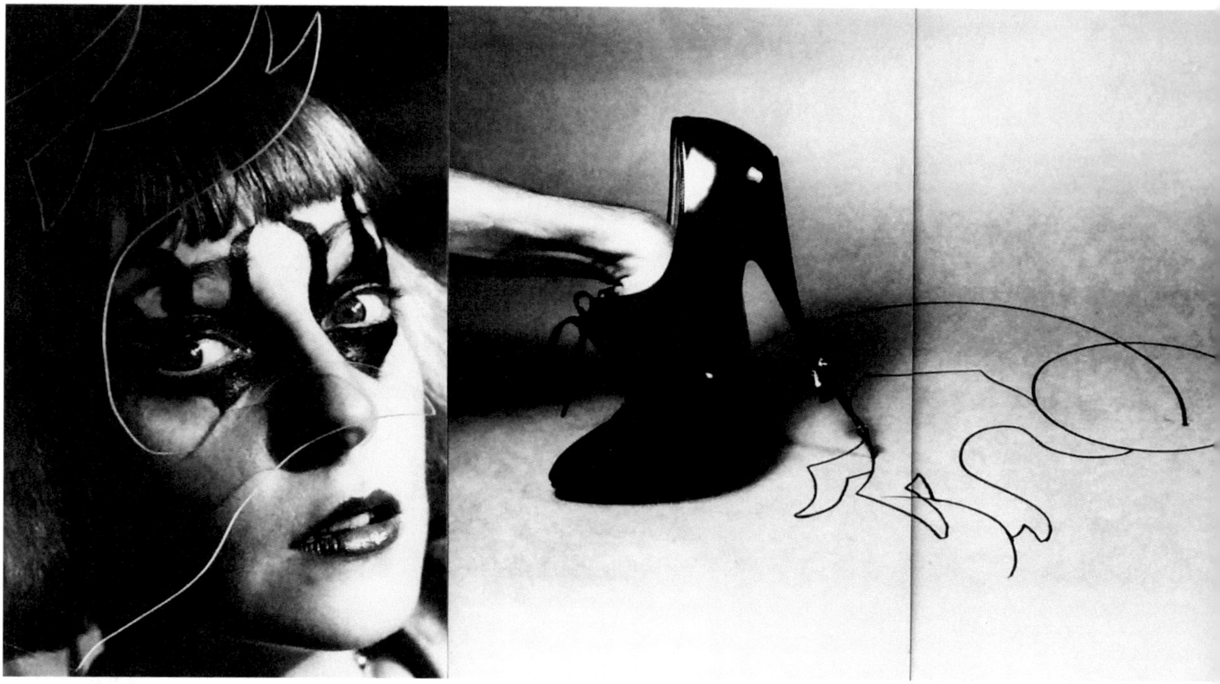

Thus *Reverie* (1985), a large photographic triptych that projects a melancholy, almost timeless mood, featured a dog photographed in the salon and gardens of a chateau. Meanwhile, the terribly ironic and grotesque *P Is For Poodle* (1983) shows the members of General Idea themselves sporting poodle wigs and silly expressions. More enigmatic and numerous were the pictorial works that showed the trio with the stylized features of these same canines: *Process of Elimination* (1991), *Three Graces: Mural Fragment from the 1984 Miss General Idea Pavillion* (1982), *Three Leashed Poodles with Cornucopia (Mural Fragment from the 1984 Miss General Idea Pavillion)* (1982), *Three Poodles with Cocktails (Mural Fragment from the 1984 Miss General Idea Pavillion)* (1982), and so on.

These allegorical portraits are often endowed with attributes such as a cocktail glass (symbolizing concoctions of cultures and ideologies that should sometimes be poured out), a lunar crescent (the artist's mooning intuition), or a cornucopia (from which flows an inspirational elixir)—all "glamorous" emblems of the artistic process.

In fact, General Idea's notion of glamour was a long way from being limited to the personification of artworks; their manifesto went far beyond the sole problematic of "posing." Indeed, the text laid down the principle of treating existing images as empty shells just awaiting an artist to fill them with new layers of meaning.[12] This principle, which the beauty contests had already established, would dominate their entire oeuvre. There thus began a pas-de-deux between nature and culture, in which each would pervert the other in ways that spurred the emergence of new forms and uses in terms of both appearance and meaning, always via the appropriation of reality through

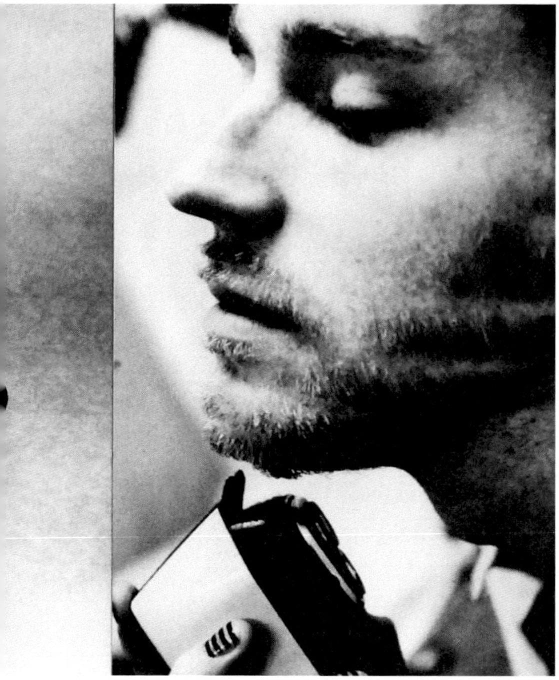

Painting Drawing Sculpture, 1978

existing imagery, objects, and systems.

Luxon V.B., the first part of the *1984 Miss General Idea Pavillion* to be built, was exemplary from this standpoint. In 1973 a window of the Carmen Lamanna Gallery in Toronto was covered with special venetian blinds (hence *V.B.*) whose blades were completely covered in a mirrored substance. Thus the blinds reflected everything happening outside into the interior, while everything happening inside could be seen outside. The reflected image was nevertheless partial and fragmentary, becoming an altered state of reality. It sustained a pluralist vision that entertained uncertainties and contradictions even as it played on the question of borderline, notably since the artists sought to explore the narrow, blank space between blinds and window, the borderline between inside and outside worlds. They claimed it should be explored precisely because it was invisible, an "infra-thin" zone whose inaccessibility embodied the world's ambivalence along with a balanced awareness of it. "In this show, which concerns the prototype for *Luxon V.B.*, we address ourselves to that exact and exacting space marked by glamour: the interface between content and context, nature and culture, inside and out," they stated.[13] Venetian blinds, thanks to their ability to shift gaze and reality, subsequently became a tool with multiple applications, one of the more striking being *V.B. Gowns* (1975), namely the venetian-blind dresses that appeared in a number of situations: at a fashion show in a performance titled *Going Thru The Motions* (1975), or else set in almost excessively real fashion in the built-up environment of downtown Toronto, or at the pool, or even going skiing.

Another equally essential glamour accessory was the "Miss General Idea Shoe." Found in the street sometime around 1973, this heady piece of footwear with fetishistic appeal was of a size that suggested it belonged to a transvestite. It appeared in many photographs, including *Luxon V.B.* In particular, in two black-and-white photographs the shoe was transformed into a creative tool once a compass was added to the heel and a man's hand "wore" it in order to make drawings (*No Mean Feet*, 1973–1974; *Painting Drawing Sculpture*, 1978). "We knew in order to be artists and to be glamorous artists we had to be artificial and we were."[14] That was how they set the stage.

Myth and Transgression: Mingled Meanings

According to AA Bronson, "the environment in North America is dominated by the mass media, so … there is no sense of reality … So our retaliation is to create our own construct which twists, stretches, and deconstructs the media reality around us."[15] Starting from the observation of a reality altered by the way it is constantly staged and represented in the media, General Idea aestheticized consumerism and consistently established a direct, frontal relationship between issues of "reality" and "image." Invading the visual scene and the broadcast media consequently became a priority, as did occupying the field via the grandiose project of the *1984 Miss General Idea Pavillion*.

The spectacle of unbridled, everyday consumerism became a favored locus of investigation, particularly with the "Pasta Paintings." Concocted from pigmented noodles, these paintings mimicked immediately recognizable logos; there was no need to mention the brand names which, through that very vacantness, displayed a certain weakness, as seen in *Untitled (Marlboro; Mastercard; Visa; Vantage*, 1985–1986).

Right from 1980 this problematic had been broached in *The Boutique from the 1984 Miss General Idea Pavillion;* from its

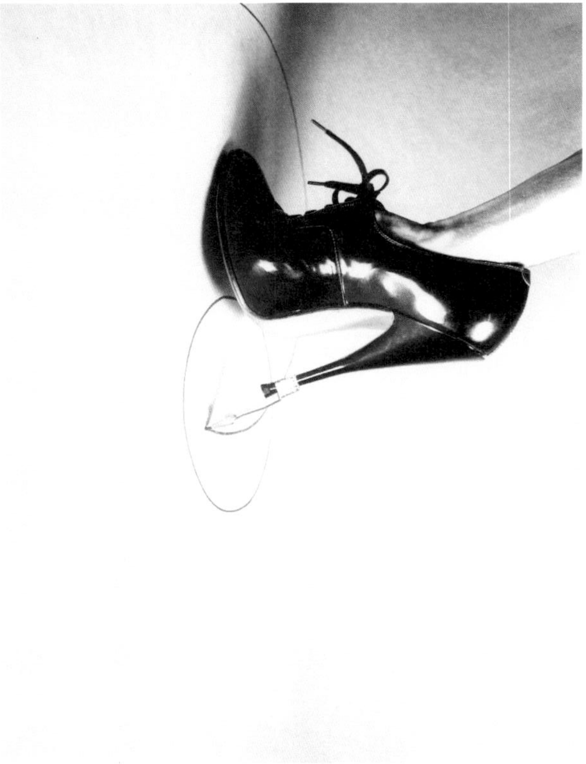

No Mean Feet, 1973–1974

Untitled (Sandy Stagg Models the Miss General Idea Shoe and the Hand of the Spirit Against the Backdrop of Luxon V.B.), 1973–1974

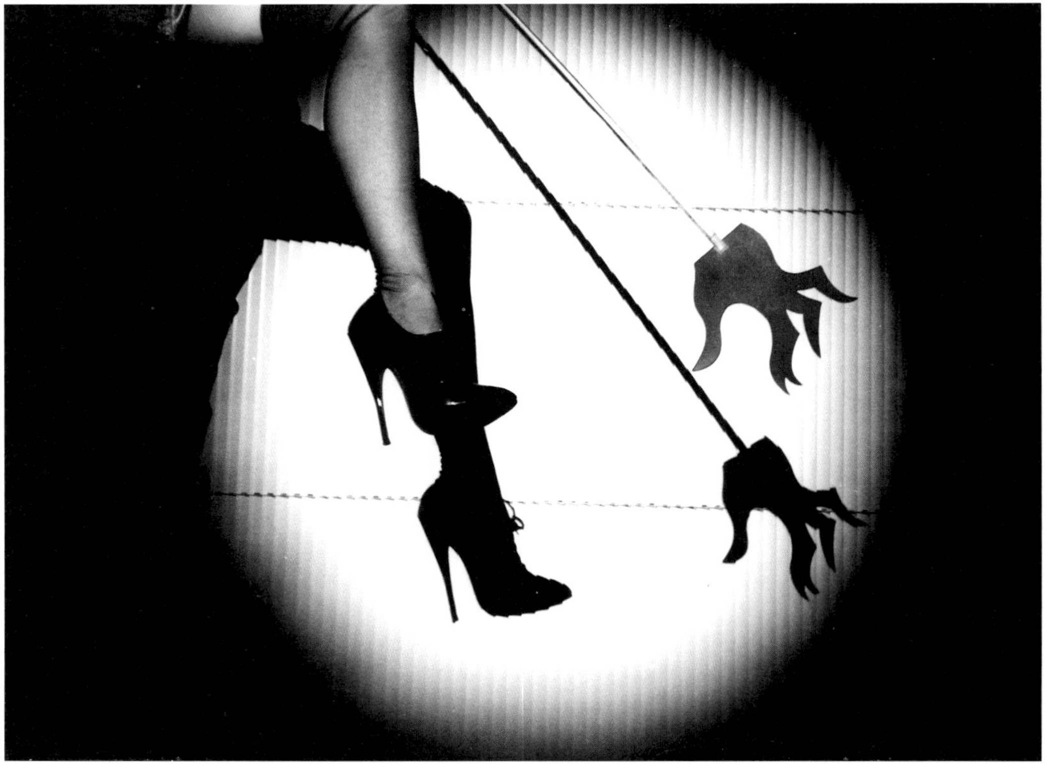

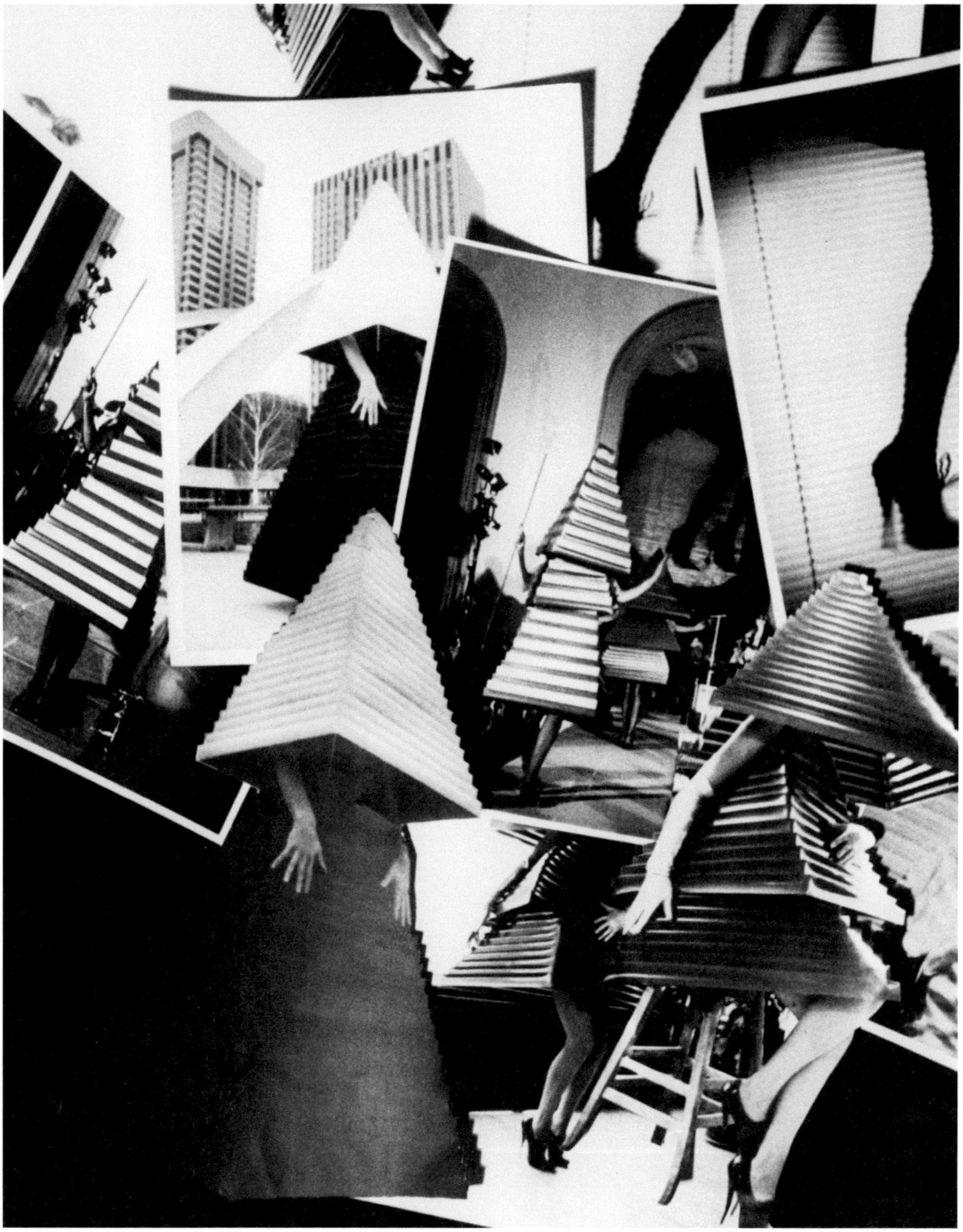

Collage from photographs of V.B. Gowns, ca. 1977

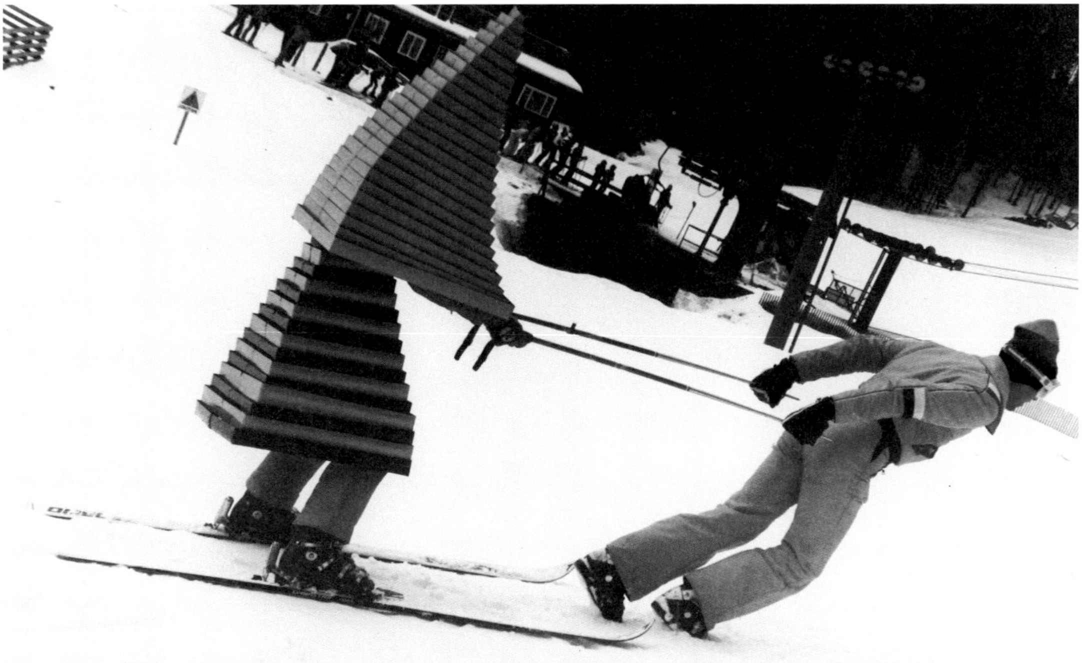

Production shot during filming of Pilot,
"V.B. Gowns take to the ski slope," Lake Louise, Banff, 1977

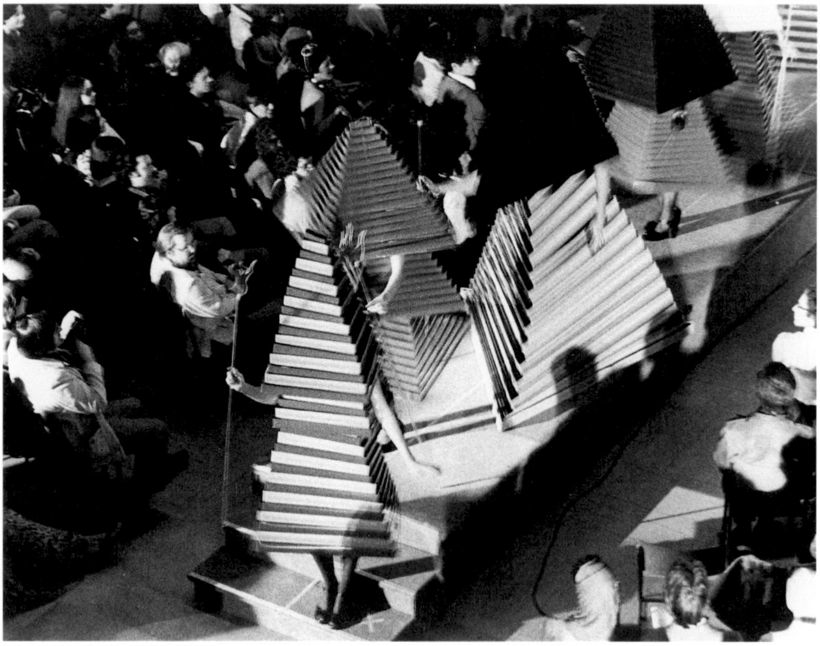

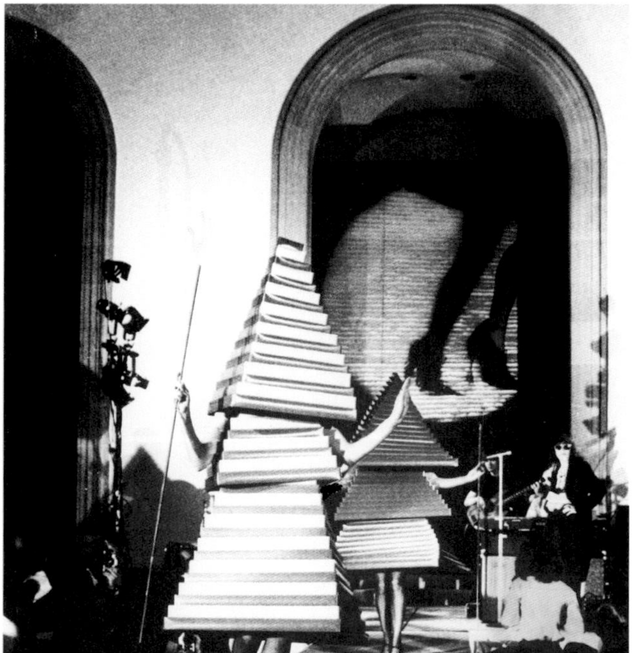

Going Thru The Motions, Walker Court, Art Gallery of Ontario, Toronto, 1975

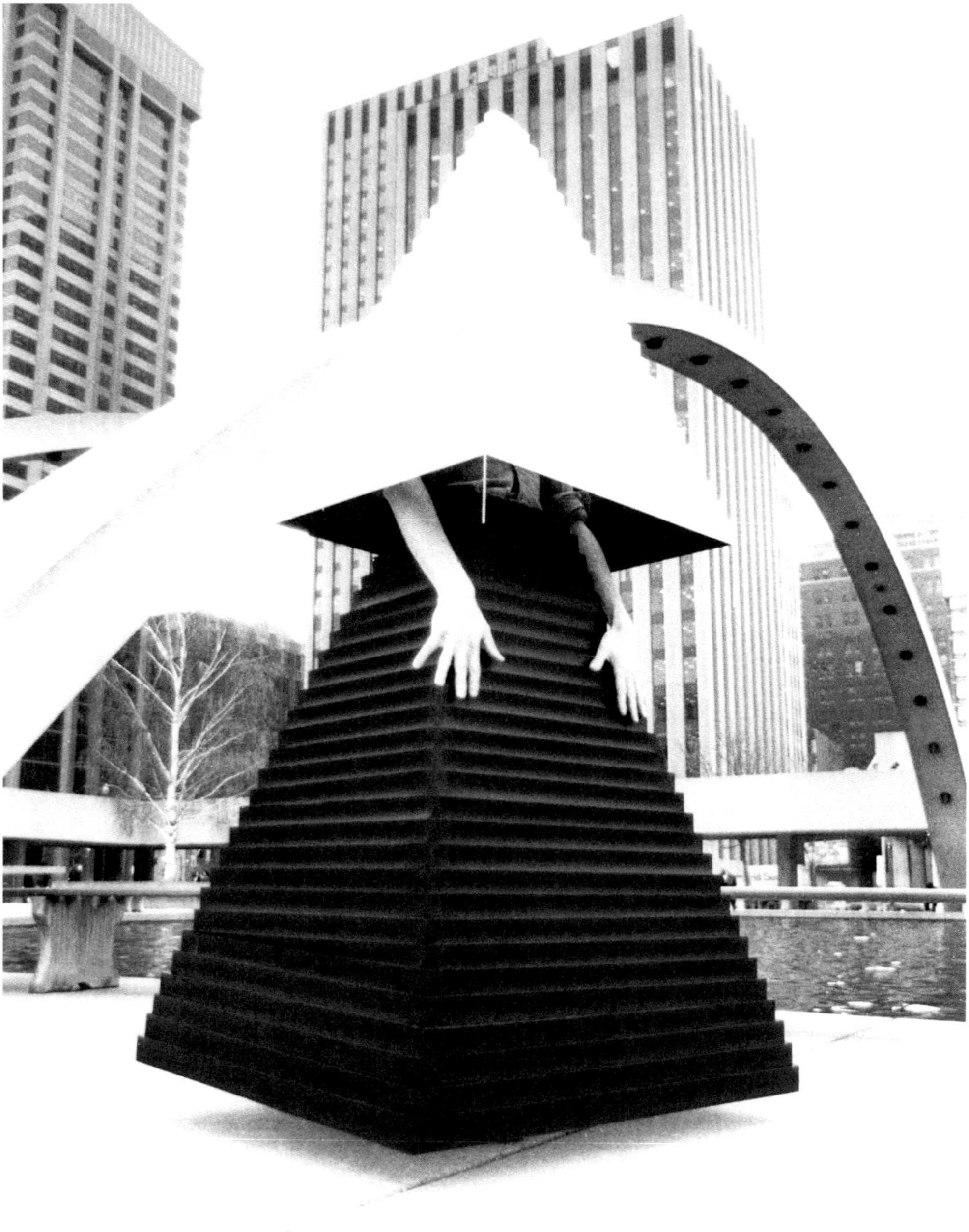

Felix Partz models V.B. Gown #3 at City Hall, Toronto, ca. 1975–1977

counter in the shape of a dollar sign ($), the boutique sold multiples and limited editions produced by the group. This work takes on additional significance in so far as it clearly marked a major turning point in General Idea's art, which in a matter of years evolved from conceptual work (largely based on mail art and on experiences related to the body) toward a steady, deliberate reintroduction of objects as such. This watershed was the subject of a highly telling editorial in *FILE*: "The Re-Materialization of the Art Object."[16]

When it comes to the quality of, and access to, images, a key work was the installation titled *Test Pattern: TV Dinner Plates from the Miss General Idea Pavillion* (1988), which invited visitors to sit on a bench and watch television. Instead of cathode ray tubes, however, visitors were faced with three gigantic screens, each composed of 144 ceramic plates arranged in the form of the colored stripes used as a TV test pattern. In a veritable critique of the media's excessive aestheticizing of "image"—beyond its mere deviation—the artists pursued a recomposition they had begun with *The Colour Bar Lounge* and its accompanying *Test Tube* video piece (1979), notably by associating test-pattern colors with an artist's palette. With this wall of authentically artificial TV sets, the "boob tube" became an artifice that did not ape reality but rather allowed everyone to project their own reality onto it, giving free rein to their impressions.

Logically enough, the critical gaze brought to bear on the way the public is manipulated by imagery led General Idea to manipulate such imagery itself, notably through performance art. In *Blocking* (1974) and *Going Thru The Motions* (1975), the audience was induced to applaud, laugh, or give a standing ovation on command, whereas in *Hot Property* (1978) it was instructed to prepare for an emergency evacuation in the event of a fire in the pavilion. Incorporating people into the performance this way meant erasing the barrier separating audience from stage; in other words, everyone got in on the act.

The 1984 Miss General Idea Pavillion, a key aspect of the extensive fictional development of their oeuvre, was itself like a huge stage set, which was converted—via fragmentation—into a continuously evolving, narrative superstructure. Its numerous incarnations from exhibition to exhibition, whether built or simply depicted, became so many chapters that transformed, here and there, the museums where they were installed as a new wing of the building, once again pursuing an appropriationist approach to image and object. Behind a fence supposedly shielding the construction site, *The Hoarding of the 1984 Miss General Idea Pavillion* (1975) offered glimpses of plans and/or sketches of several features of the pavilion, from revolving doors that led to the future (*Bottle-Neck Entrance for the Pavillion: Rotating Doors of the Future*, 1984) to the fantastical *Dr. Brute Colonnade (Dominant Imagery)* (1975) via a labyrinth (*Ziggurat Maze Project*, 1984–1985) and an arrangement of 1984 seats (*Proposed Seating Arrangement [Form Follows Fiction]*, 1975). Recurrent and emblematic throughout the entire grammar of this project was the Mesopotamian shape of the ziggurat, which was adopted for the plan of the pavilion and many of its decorative features, and had also appeared in early paintings conjugated in a variety of bright colors on large canvases (*Carmen, Granada*, etc., 1968–1969).

Glamour, like myth,
miniaturizes reality,
making it visible
in a single glance.
All major characteristics
are retained.
Any “real-life” context
may be simulated.
Glamour is the perfect
simulation technique
for on-going battles,
the perfect tool
for re-shaping history:
adding, subtracting,
indeed MAKING history.

Showcard 1-009, Battle Plans, 1975

Like all artists, s/he is intent on the definition of unoccupied territory. S/he wants to describe the background by simplifying the foreground. S/he wants to occupy a central position in the general state of affairs.

Showcard 1-071, The Artist Constructs a Model, 1977

Yet the history of the pavilion pitted construction against deconstruction, legend asserting that the pavilion was ravaged by fire in 1977 (as staged in a performance given in Kingston, Ontario). With the temporal confusion that arises from the coexistence of past and future, these architects mutated into archaeologists whose rich finds, ranging from shards of pottery to wall paintings inspired by the Villa dei Misteri in Pompeii, brought to light an entire iconography dense with countless poodles and cornucopias. The most spectacular item was a 40-foot-long piece intriguingly titled *The Unveiling of the Cornucopia: A Mural Fragment from the Room of the Unknown Function in the Villa dei Misteri of the 1984 Miss General Idea Pavillion* (1982), conveying the idea not of discovery but of unveiling—which here again assumes a certain theatricality.

Furthermore, this theme of unveiling "the cornucopia" (an object symbolizing a fertile artistic imagination) was underscored in an installation in which, on a ziggurat-shaped base, were displayed seven ceramic sculptures representing variations on the horn of plenty (*Cornucopia: Fragments from the Room of the Unknown Function from the 1984 Miss General Idea Pavillion*, 1982–1983). The installation was accompanied by a video piece that employed a narrative, documentary tone to reveal the ruins of this room with "unknown function" by itemizing its elements. Adopting the straightforward style of an anthropological study, it unearthed an ancient history whose emblems mingled with those of the present (poodles, cocktails, and so on), efficiently confusing things that stem from the science of archaeology (hence have historical validity) with things that stem from an interpretation of a mythified past.

Everything in the *Miss General Idea Pavillion* was staged, yet every element had a clearly announced and assumed function/fiction—because form follows fiction. This form's polysemic narrativity and skillful crossing of boundaries sustained doubt and thereby transformed a cleverly cultivated myth into reality.

In one of his notebooks, Felix Partz recorded in 1968—hence at an early

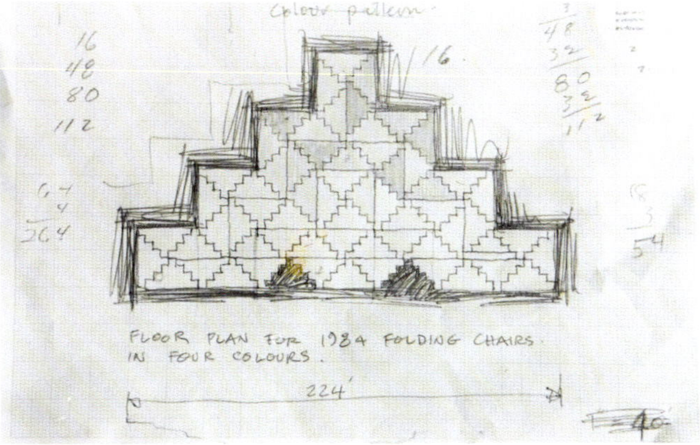

Floor Plan for 1984 Folding Chairs for the Pavillion, 1974

date—a comment that can be read with hindsight as a foreshadowing of what the art of General Idea would build in the gap between reality and artifice, with its typical ambiguity and terrific subversive quality: "Art may allow complete concentration but it should always be in the form of Super Reality. It should not be an escape but an actual experience in your life."[17]

Setting the stage: back to reality!

V.B. Gown against the skyline of Calgary, 1977

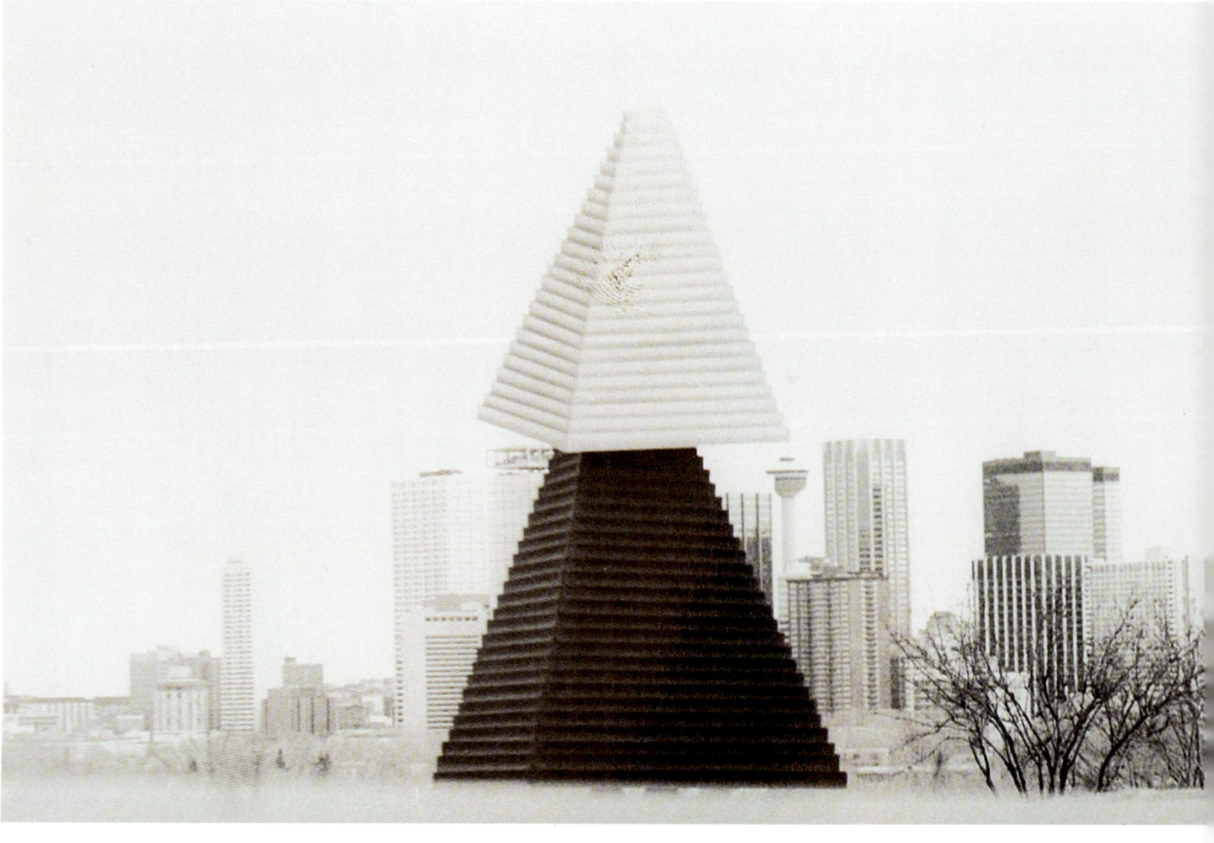

Translated from the French by Deke Dusinberre.

1 Art Against AIDS, a project designed to raise funds for the American Foundation for AIDS Research.
2 AIDS: The Public and Private Domains of the Miss General Idea Pavillion, Artspace, San Francisco, 1988.
3 The title of the performance in Geneva was General Idea XXX (bleu): Une activité de l'atelier 1984 Miss General Idea Pavillion.
4 A.k.a. Vancouver artist Michael Morris, who founded the Image Bank visual archive there.
5 General Idea, "'How our mascots love to humiliate us … ,' Revelations from the doghouse," General Idea, 1968–1984, exh. cat,. Kunsthalle Basel, 1984, p. 28.
6 See General Idea, Luxon V.B. The 1984 Miss General Idea Pavillion No. 101, artist's book, Toronto 1973, n. p.
7 AA Bronson, "General Idea," interview with Hans Ulrich Obrist, Uovo, Turin, April–June 2008, p. 205.
8 General Idea, "Glamour," FILE Megazine, vol. 3, no. 1, special Glamour issue (Fall 1975), p. 21.
9 Rodney Werden, Portrait of General Idea, 1974.
10 "The image of the artist is easiest to inhabit. Because of its historic richness, its ready but empty mythology (berets, paint brushes, palettes, in a word FORM without content), the shell which was art was simple to invade … Thus we became glamorous, made art, made ourselves over in the image of art." General Idea, "Glamour," p. 32.
11 "Note the poodle, banal and effete; its relished role as watchdog, retriever, and gay companion; its wit, pampered presence, and ornamental physique; its eagerness for affection and affectation; a delicious desire to be groomed and preened for public appearances; in a word, its desire to please." General Idea, "Mondo Cane Kama Sutra," File Megazine, vol. 5, no. 4, special General Idea issue, Toronto, 1983, n. p. It is interesting to note that this text was reprinted the following year in an exhibition catalogue, with a direct comparison of artist to poodle, the neutral pronoun designating the animal in its initial appearance having shifted into the first person plural: "We are the poodle, banal and effete; note our relished role as watchdog … " General Idea, "'How our mascots love to humiliate us … ' Revelations from the doghouse," General Idea, 1968–1984, p. 23.
12 "We moved in on history and occupied images, emptying them of meaning, reducing them to shells. We filled these shells then with Glamour … " General Idea, "Glamour," p. 22.
13 General Idea, Luxon V.B., n. p.
14 General Idea, "Glamour," p. 32.
15 Philippe Parreno, "Interview with General Idea," Documents sur l'art contemporain, no. 4 (October 1993), p. 26.
16 General Idea, "Editorial: The Re-Materialization of the Art Object," File Megazine, vol. 5, no. 2 (Fall 1981), p. 17.
17 Felix Partz, "Blue cardboard book," 1968, General Idea archives, Library and Archives of the National Gallery of Canada, Ottawa.

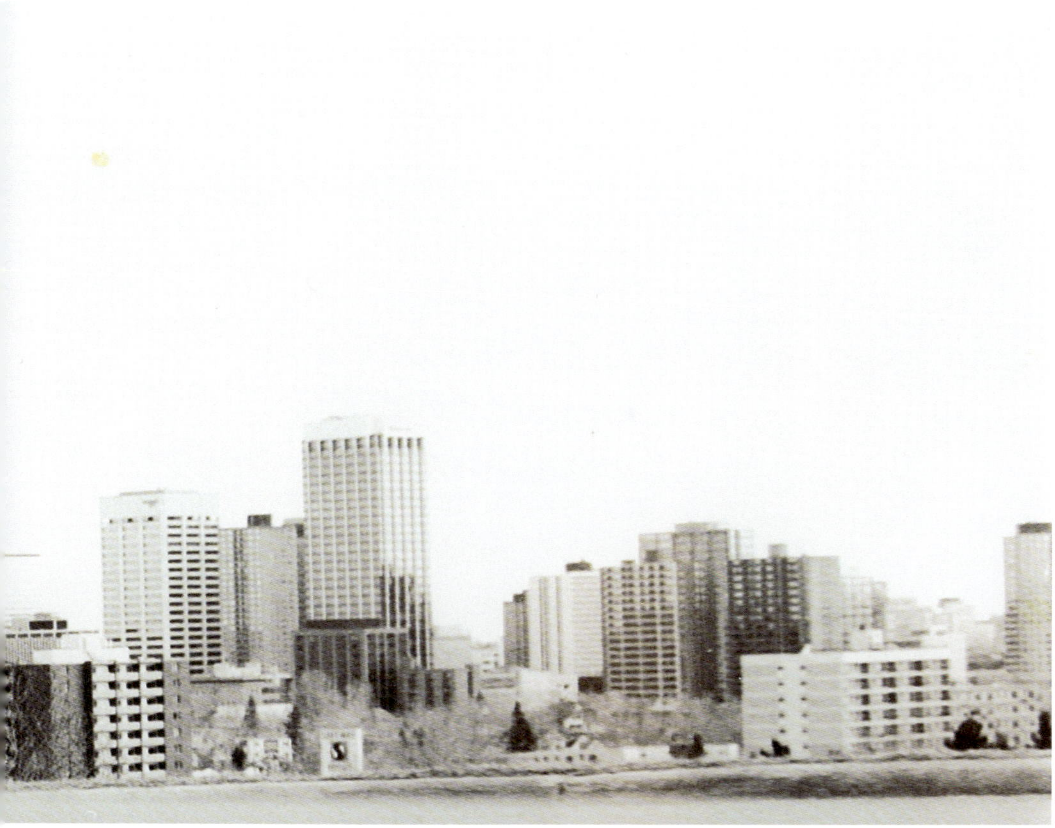

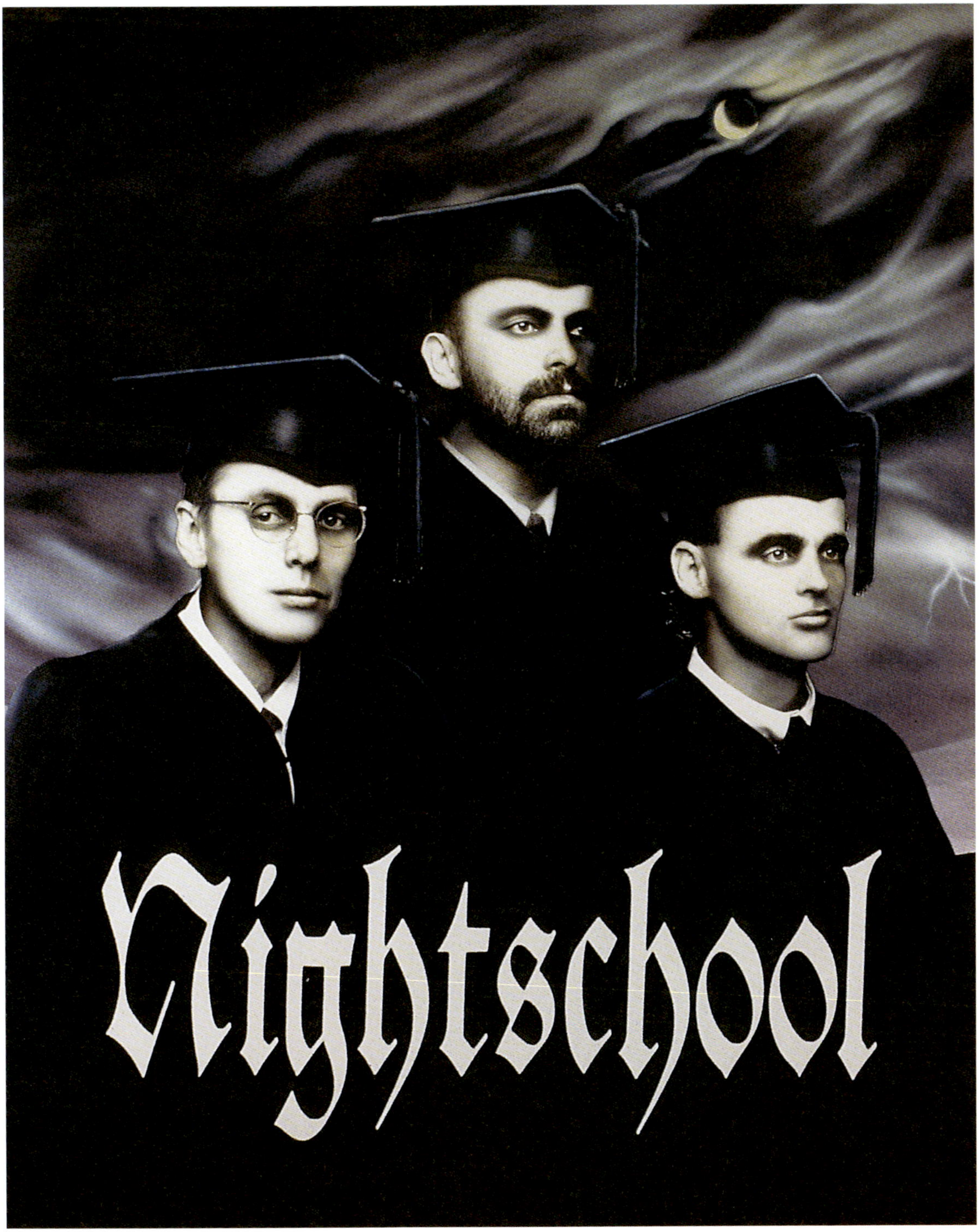

Nightschool, 1989

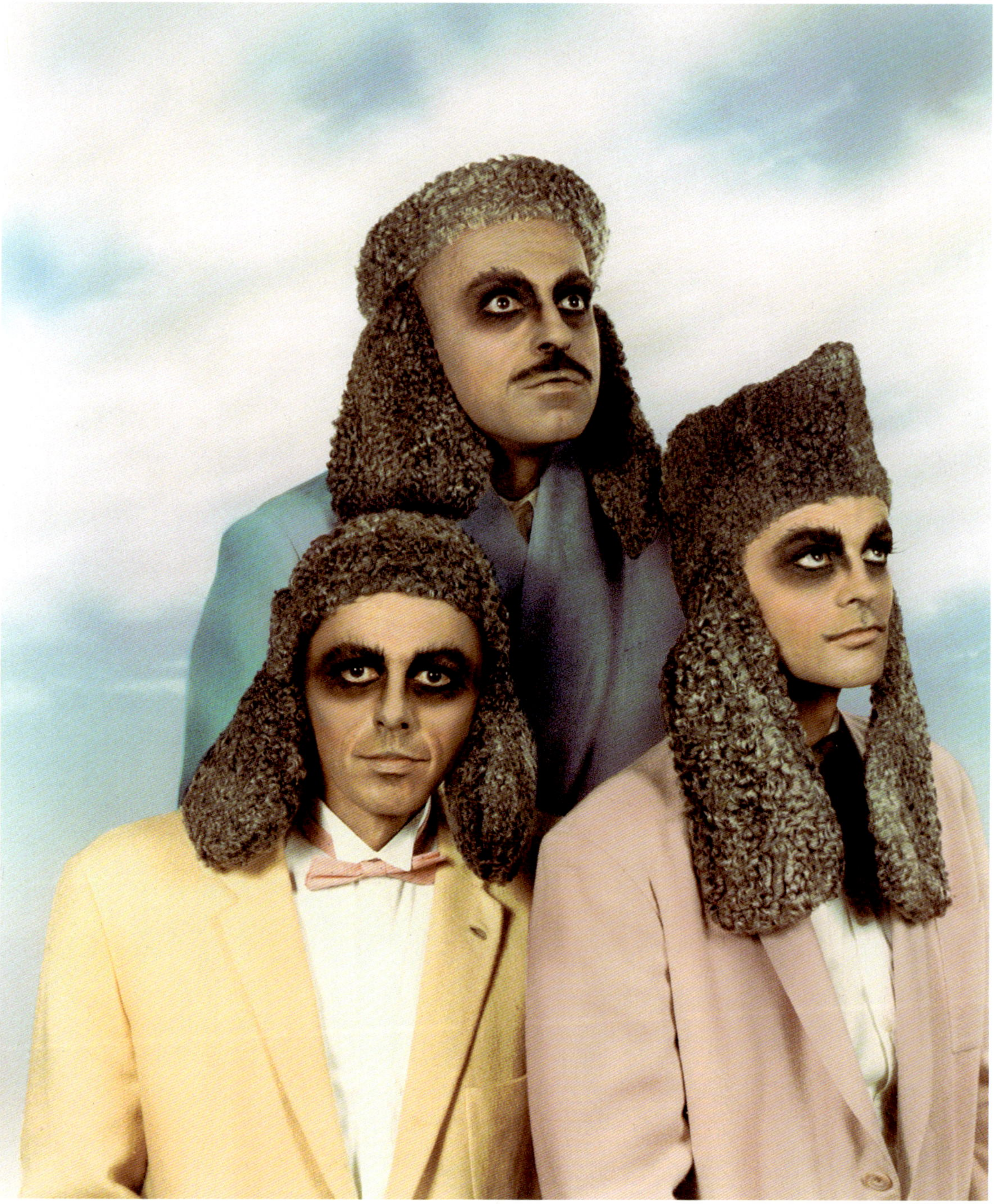

P Is For Poodle, 1983–1989

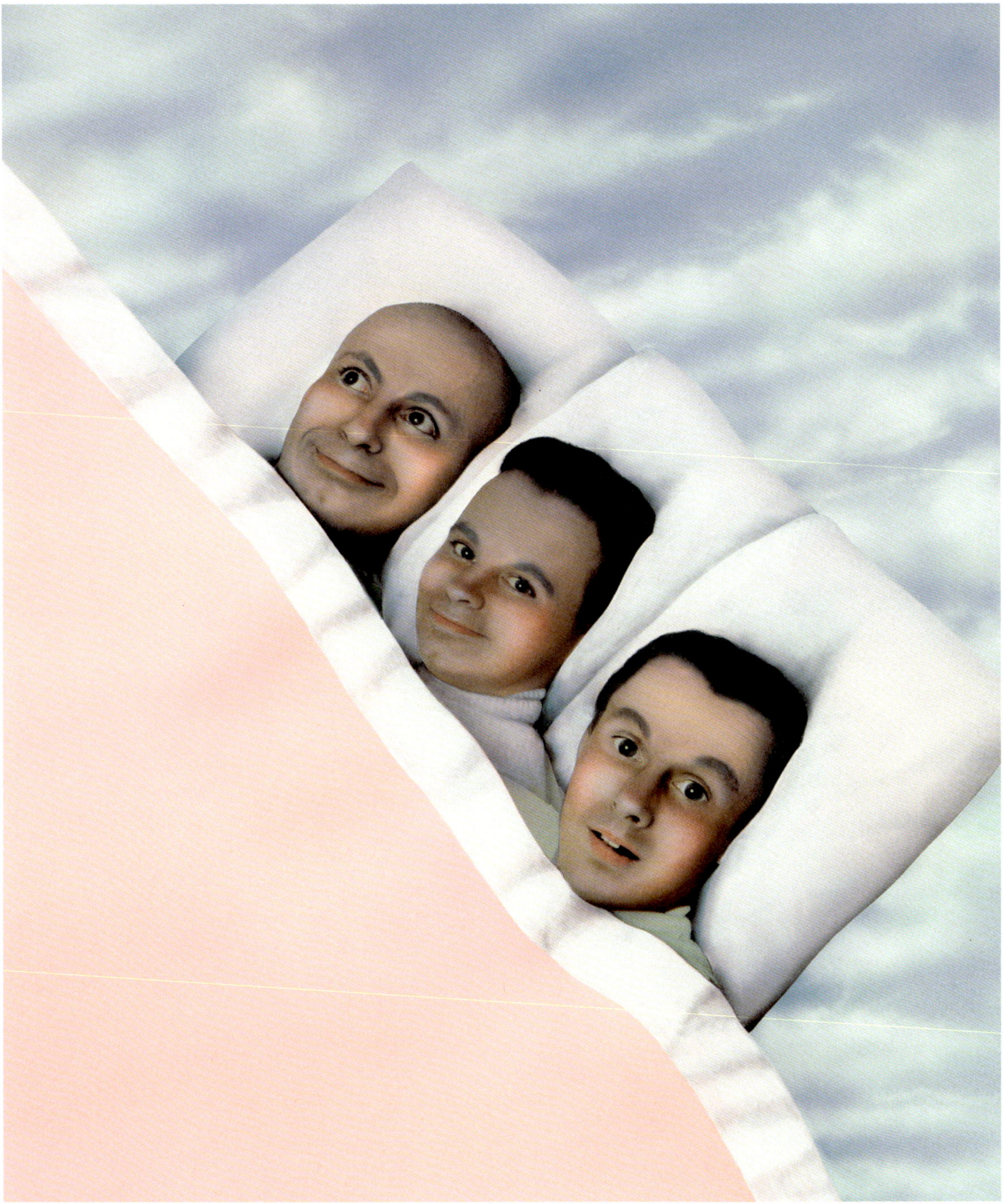

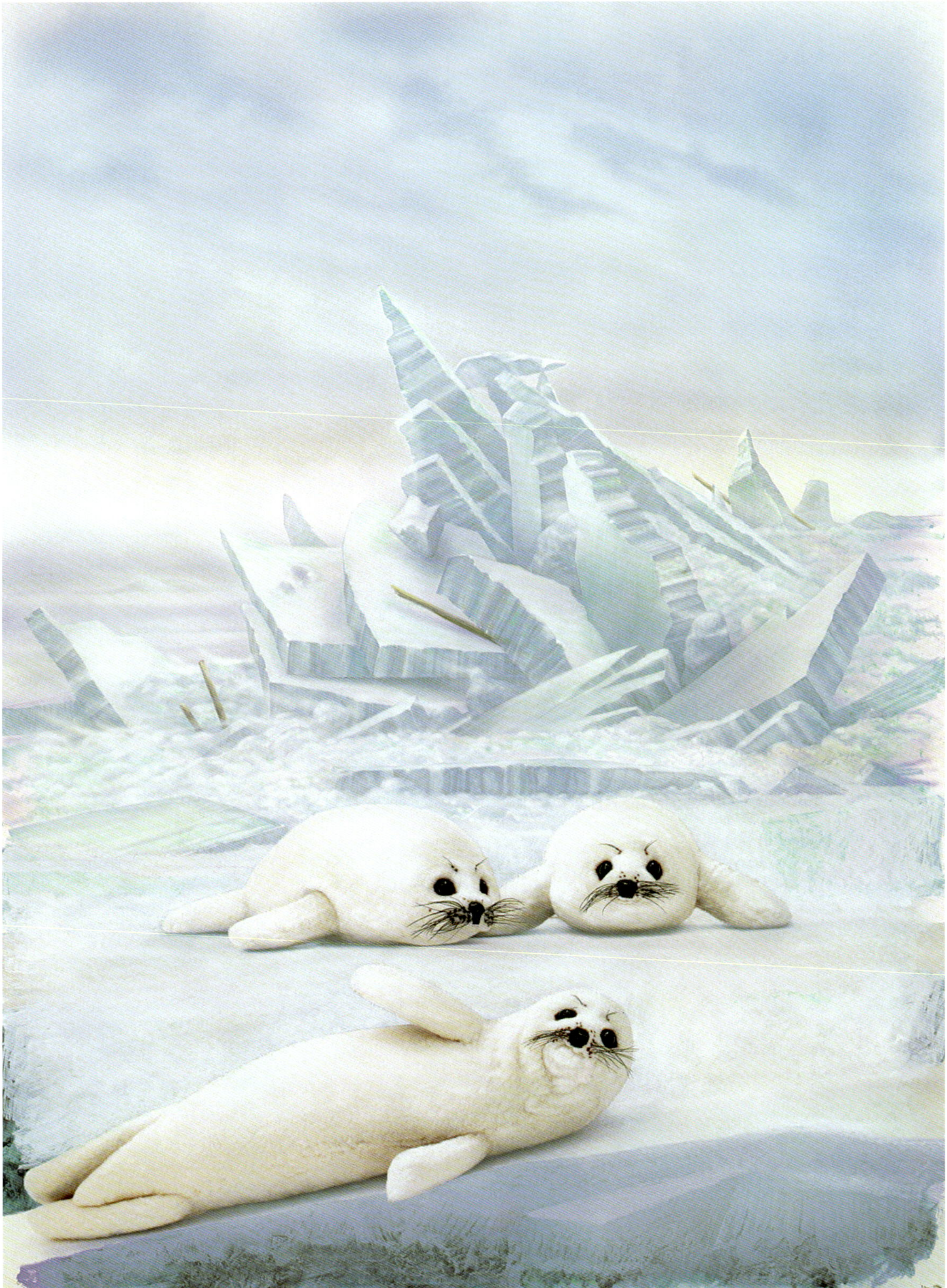

Fin de siècle, 1994

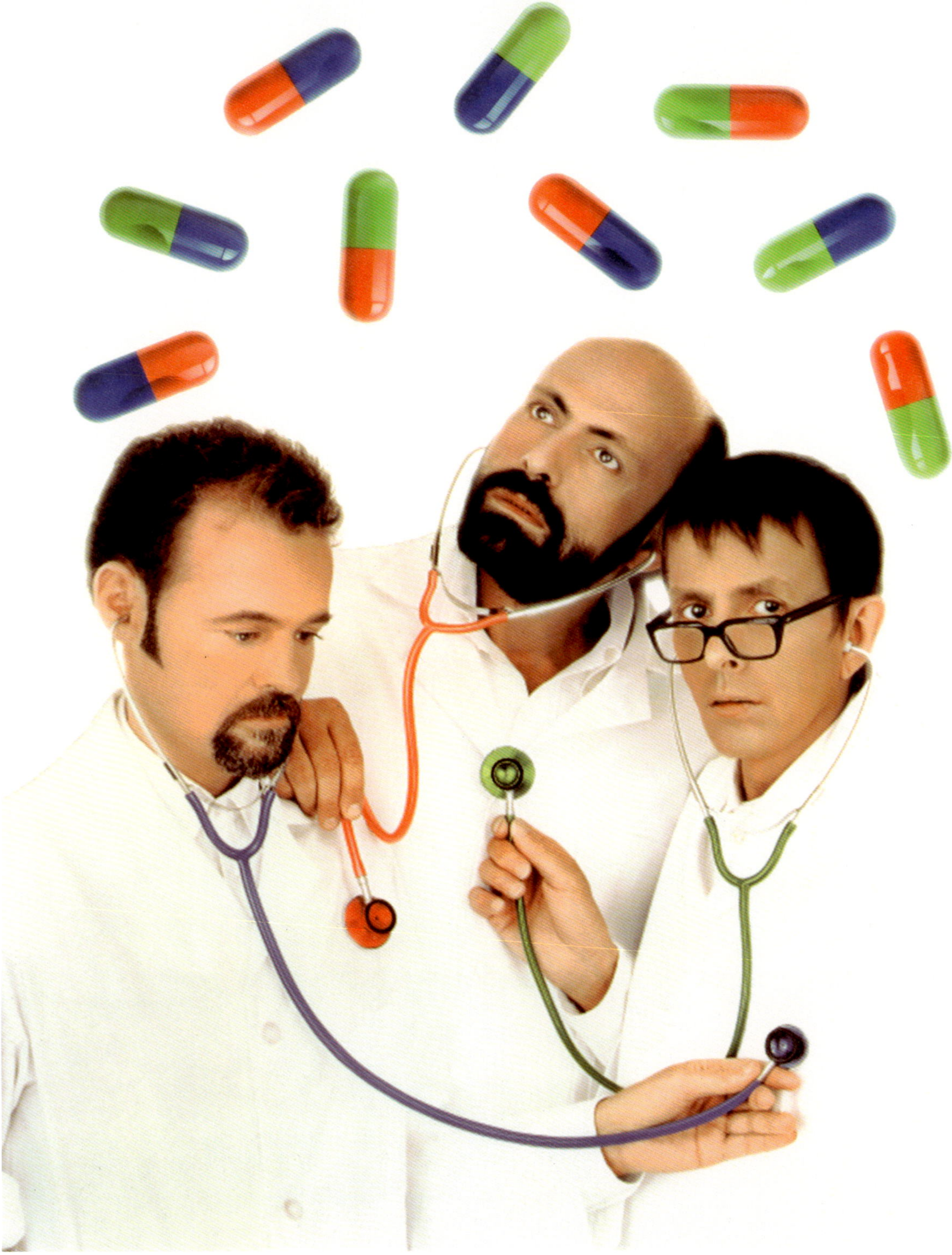

Playing Doctor, 1992

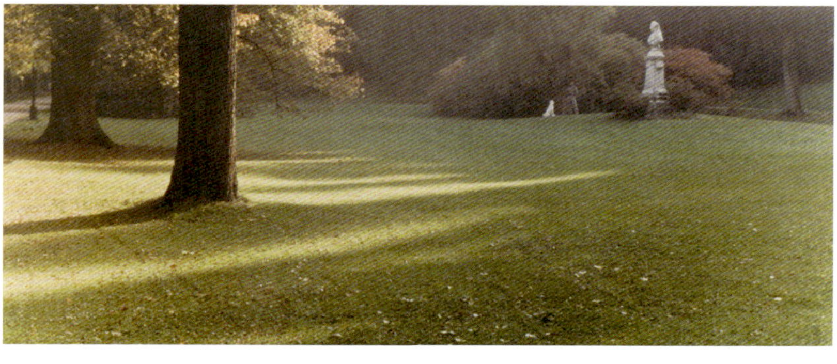

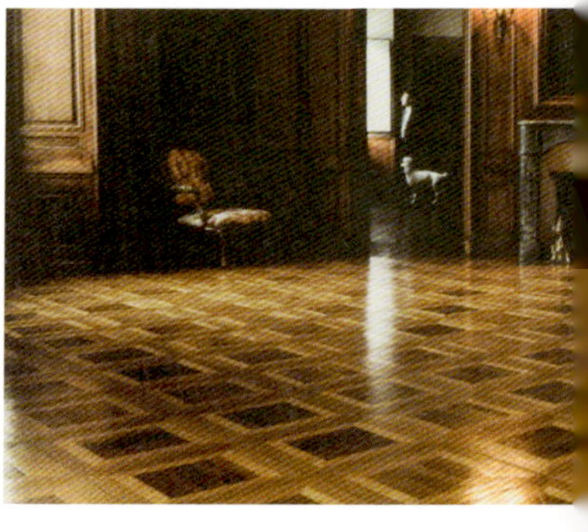

Reverie, 1985

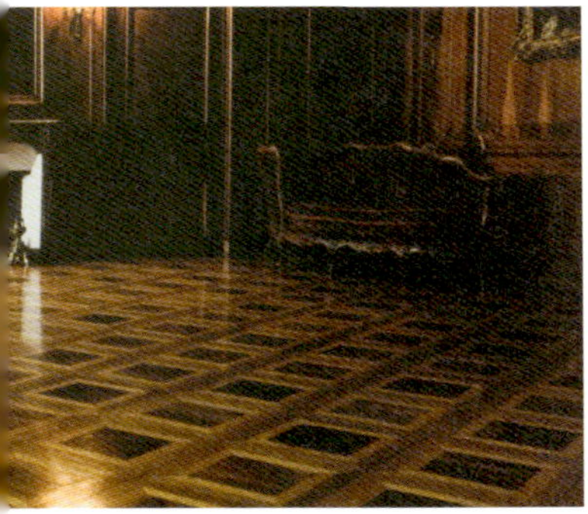

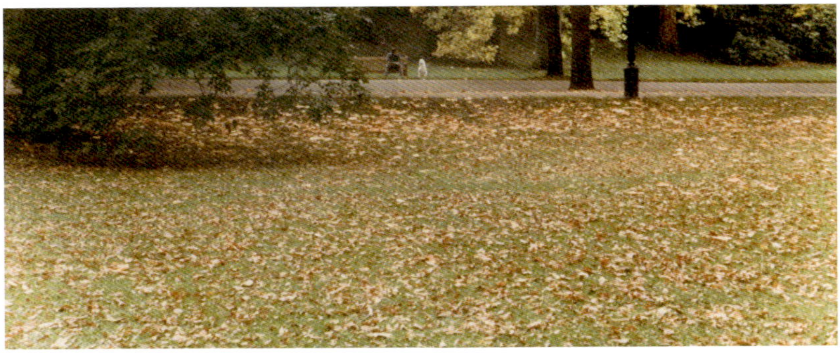

The Colonnade: Staging the Museum in the Work of General Idea

David Moos

"We never felt we had to produce great art to be great artists."
General Idea, FILE Megazine, 1975

The invitation card for The 1984 Miss General Idea Pavillion exhibition at the Art Gallery of Ontario displayed a quote describing the artists' intention: "We wanted to be famous; we wanted to be glamorous; we wanted to be rich. That is to say, we wanted to be artists … We knew that if we were famous, if we were glamorous, we could say we were artists, and we would be. We did and we are. We are famous, glamorous artists." Summarizing their arc of accomplishment, the statement, first published in their own instrument of image dissemination, *FILE Megazine*, in 1975, reads like a self-fulfilling prophecy. If in 1975 General Idea had merely existed for six years and had created sundry works that were difficult to categorize, by April 1985, when the exhibition opened at Toronto's Art Gallery of Ontario, the terse self-actualizing phrase "we did and we are," originally intended as an ironic critique of celebrity, was becoming dangerously close to reality.

The Toronto opening of the *The 1984 Miss General Idea Pavillion* (1985) was the third in an international tour that had begun the previous year at the Kunsthalle Basel, and then traveled to the Stedelijk Van Abbemuseum in Holland. Unlike openings at the European museums, the AGO event had a special resonance for the artists, serving as a homecoming. Throughout the early evolution of GI, the Art Gallery of Ontario functioned as a venue for seminal events, including the performances *The 1971 Miss General Idea Pageant* (1971) and *Going Thru The Motions* (1975). Although the 1985 opening was not a choreographed spectacle in the manner of the earlier events, it was nevertheless scripted. An internal memo detailing how events should unfold has the artists arriving promptly at 5:15 pm in the museum Director's office.

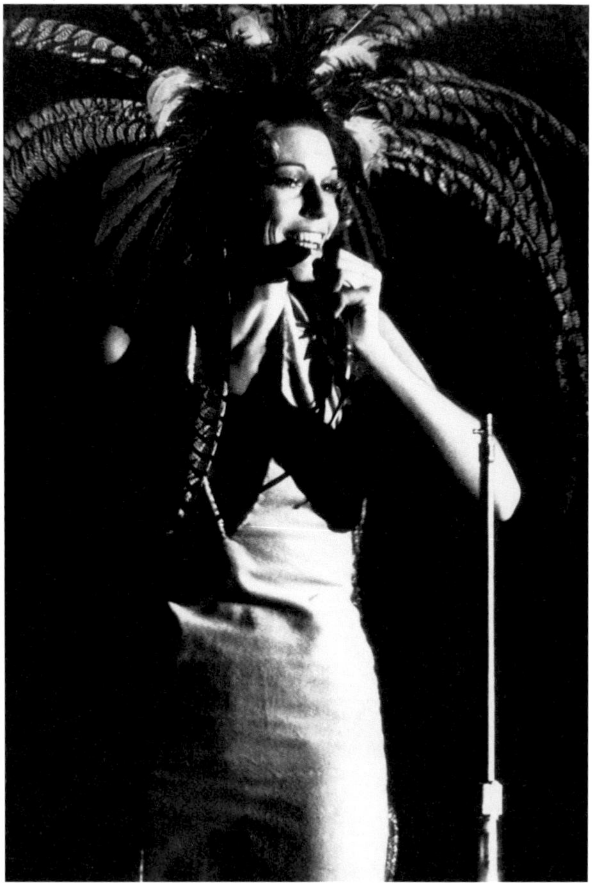

Pascal, "chanteuse extraordinaire," performs at the 1971 Miss General Idea Pageant, 1971

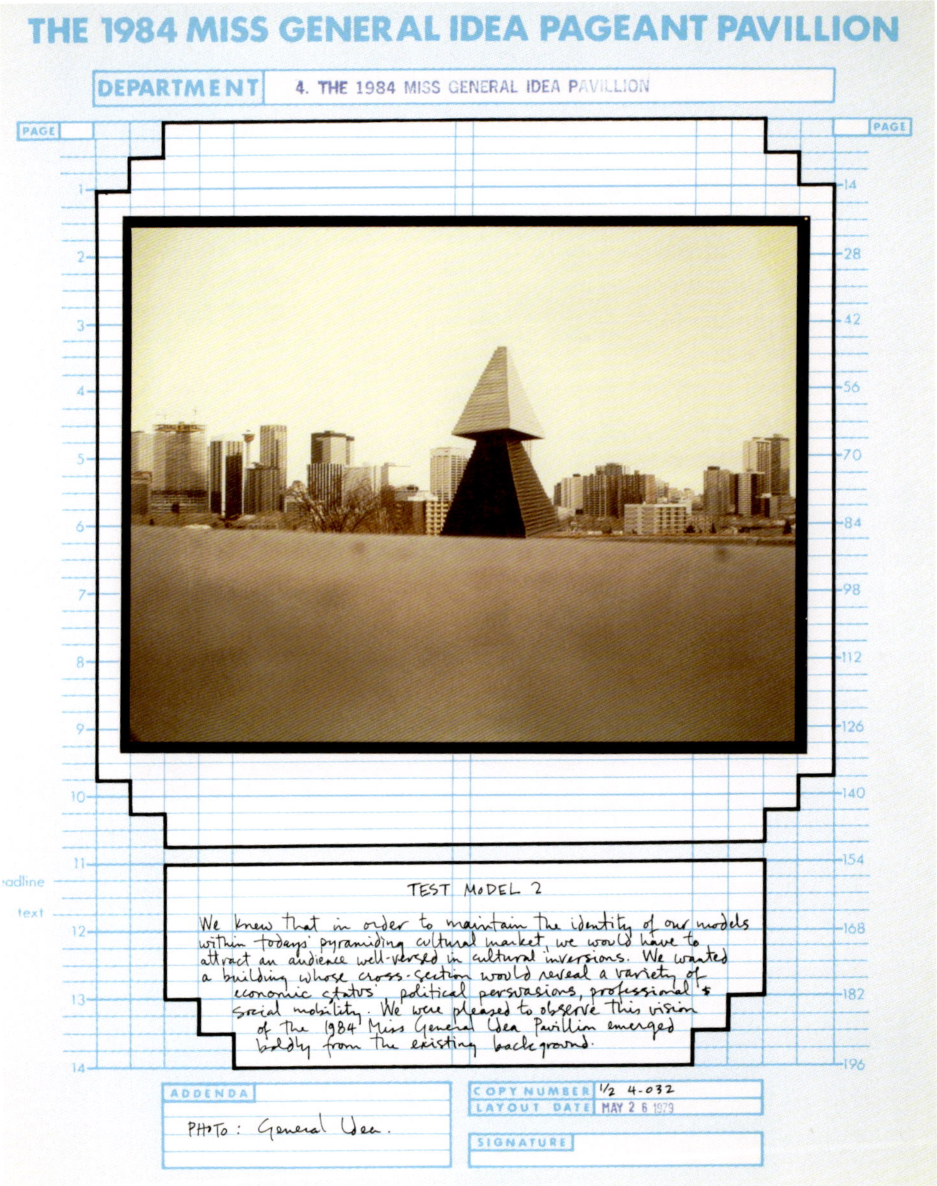
THE 1984 MISS GENERAL IDEA PAGEANT PAVILLION

DEPARTMENT 4. THE 1984 MISS GENERAL IDEA PAVILLION

PAGE PAGE

TEST MODEL 2

We knew that in order to maintain the identity of our models within todays' pyramiding cultural market, we would have to attract an audience well-versed in cultural inversions. We wanted a building whose cross-section would reveal a variety of economic status', political persuasions, professional & social mobility. We were pleased to observe this vision of the 1984 Miss General Idea Pavillion emerged boldly from the existing background.

ADDENDA
PHOTO: General Idea.

COPY NUMBER 1/2 4-032
LAYOUT DATE MAY 2 6 1979
SIGNATURE

__Showcard 4-032, Test Model 2__, 1977

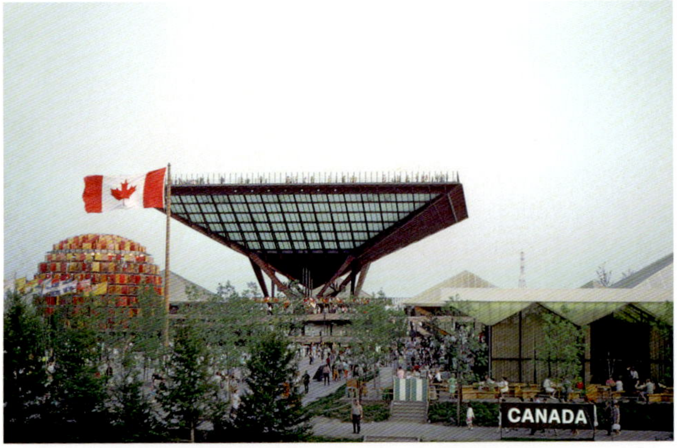

The Katimavik, a giant inverted pyramid, towers above the other structures that composed the Canada Pavilion at Montreal's Expo '67

This three-way relationship is easy to set your sights on. Let's call it a Freudian slip. The patriarchal family is the basic training unit for teaching Oedipal hang-ups.

Showcard 1-104, Oedipal Triangle, 1979

This modified family group is trying to keep in balance. It takes daily exercise to avoid a relapse into all-too-familial roles.

Showcard 1-105, Menage A Trois, 1979

The Chairman of the AGO Board, retail magnate Fredrik Eaton, with AGO curator Philip Monk and Director William Withrow constituted, along with the artists, the so-called Platform Party that, at the appointed hour of 6:00 pm, ascended a stage set up in Walker Court, the Beaux Arts central atrium of the museum, to make formal remarks and preside over the official opening of the exhibition.

In a letter written earlier that year on AGO letterhead, Mr Eaton wrote to Prime Minister Pierre Elliot Trudeau: "We would be very honoured if you would officially open the exhibition to our Members. General Idea have expressed their keen desire to invite you as our guest of honour for this evening, as the creation of *The 1984 Miss General Idea Pavillion* coincides exactly with the timeframe of your term as Prime Minister." The notion of having Canada's political and diplomatic eminence preside at the opening ceremony would have been a crowning asset for the Toronto artists. Yet Trudeau promptly replied, expressing regret along with a measure of intrigue around the exhibition. The fact that Trudeau did not materialize is nevertheless entirely in keeping with General Idea's fabrication of unfulfilled expectations.

The subversive essence of their enterprise comes into sharp focus when one simply considers the scope of their activities at the AGO—the art museum that may be regarded as *the* museum par excellence in their oeuvre. The AGO became the metonym for the institution, allowing GI to transform their local museum into a pliable stage set for their ever-evolving conceptual enterprise. Indeed, the 1985 opening of the *1984 Pavillion* was the culmination of a project that had been envisioned some 14 years earlier, and the 1985 exhibition afforded an occasion to bring together a panoply of their diverse, trans-media works. The material scope of their production included the following components presented as an overall encompassing presentation: painting, sculpture, video, installation, photography, drawing, printmaking, publishing, posters, objects, costumes, ephemera. The list of artworks and artifacts is overwhelming because each is somehow related to, if not dependent upon, other objects for resonance and meaning—so none should properly be considered in isolation.

Beyond this elaborately detailed and meticulous array of contingent objects (a strategy fundamentally opposed to the assertion of the discrete so-called masterpiece), GI embodied the prospect of audience participation and through a communal experience, the prospect of shared transcendence, or at least the illusion of shared transcendence. This elusive construct—that mimics traditional art's effect upon the viewer (or might one better consider it affect)—is central to GI's ambitions. Indeed, the captivating allure of a communal meta-spectacle quickly took root in their imaginations, becoming an ideal to which much of their work would constantly refer.

Early in their thinking the museum emerged as seminal site for the staging of this ambition, supplanting previous theatre-based incarnations of their event-oriented approach. At the museum glamour, art, influential people, and money were cathected—materialized in the imaginations of the artists and audience alike. In 1971, when the three artists had been working collaboratively for only two years, they managed to orchestrate *The 1971 Miss General Idea*

Pageant, a one-night extravaganza mounted on October 1, 1971. The elaborate staging of a faux event that is experienced as real is a powerful, emblematic declaration of their creative enterprise. The evening was at once a simulation, and an actual spectacle imbued with theatrical elements that conjured the aura of a pageant or awards ceremony, choreographing a self-consciously ebullient, elegant sense of wonder.

Much of the effectiveness of the project resided in its ambiguous use of hard-core glamour imagery: arc lamps, limousines, past queens, and poignant invitations … On one level the pageant recreated all the working structures of any layer of the art hierarchy: the Canada Council or the Art Gallery of Ontario itself. The pageant included art critics, art products, judges, and aesthetics within a competitive process that eliminated the individual artist from the actual art proposition.[1]

The event transpired in Walker Court, the architectural and symbolic heart of the AGO—transmuting the museum into sheer backdrop, a stage-set and transitory venue for the embodiment of an imaginary experience. The night de-emphasized the museum as a container of artworks and valuable objects, re-coding it as … call it the "Pavillion," a theatrical, special-purpose structure.[2] The high, curving arches of Walker Court were ideally suited to such a fabulation, connoting a by-gone classicism that GI would embrace and variously exploit throughout their work.

The giddy pomp and ceremony of the Pageant triggered fertile possibilities for the artists, who quickly realized that it would take another decade or more to realize a spectacle of commensurate impact and importance. The artists came to construct their project within the context of this far-sighted view—unfolding forward and backward in time, fraught with anticipation of yet-to-be-realized aspects, constantly blending fact and fiction in an effort to create not a "mythology," but a meta-mythology that they called "Glamour."[3]

In an effort to perpetuate their inventive enterprise, in 1973 the artists first made public *The 1984 Miss General Idea Pavillion*, an encompassing construct that would serve as a "metaphor" (to use GI's word) for the museum, an arbiter of taste and value with creative tendrils that stretched in innumerable directions.[4] Resonant with utopian expectations, the concept of the pavilion perfectly served associative needs of GI—a triumvirate whose lapidary working methods accommodated so many impulses, expressions, and assertions that a suitably nefarious and difficult-to-define container needed to be devised.

With its eschatological date redolent with Orwellean overtones, the *1984 Pavillion* allowed GI to work toward the erection of the grand structure in a manner similar to the way that nations labored to construct and present pavilions at world expositions. The deco era remnants of the 1939 New York's World's Fair, and the recently abandoned

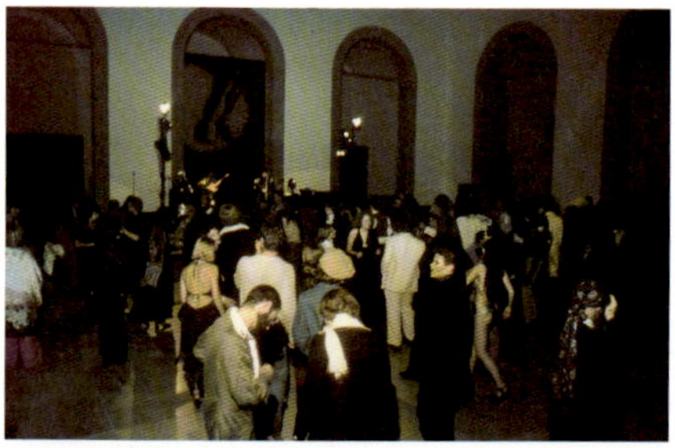

Going Thru The Motions,
Walker Court, AGO, Toronto, 1975

pavilions of Expo ’67 in Montreal both fertilize how one might think of GI’s great conduit (what they referred to as a “framing device”). The many pavilions that defined world fairs, like the expansive Canada pavilion in Montreal, became sites for intensive communal experience—destination architecture where people joined in a ceremonial viewing of highly scripted cultural information.

The self-contained nature of the pavilion as a purpose-built entity for a highly specified function was amplified and explored in 1970 at the Osaka World’s Fair in the American pavilion. Inside a faceted geodesic dome, artists were invited to present performances and to experiment with the acoustic and creative potential of various technological devices provided by a group of engineers and scientists. This pavilion represented the culmination of a dialogue begun by artists Robert Rauschenberg and Robert Whitman several years earlier with engineer Billy Klüver, who collaborated in setting up the group EAT (Experiments in Art and Technology). After Osaka, the very notion of a pavilion—an intensive site of human creative potential and experiential enterprise—assumed a truly utopian, almost otherworldly allure. When GI launched *The 1984 Miss General Idea Pavillion*, these pavilions may have served as points of reference. But GI’s vision was highly customized, distinct to their needs. On September 18, 1975, they mounted another large event, titled

General Idea with Light On Mirror, 1971

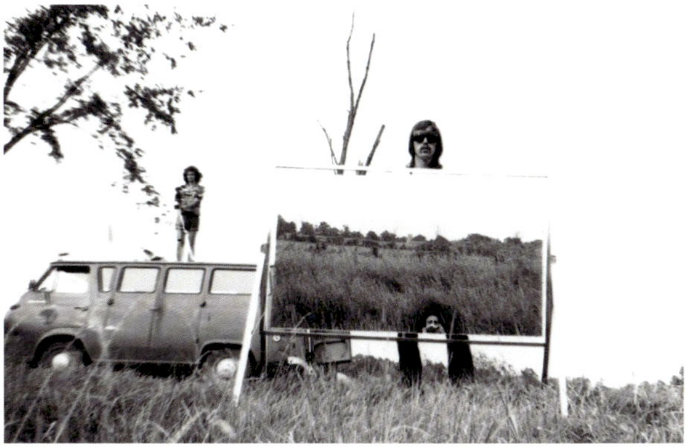

Light On (Double Mirror), 1971

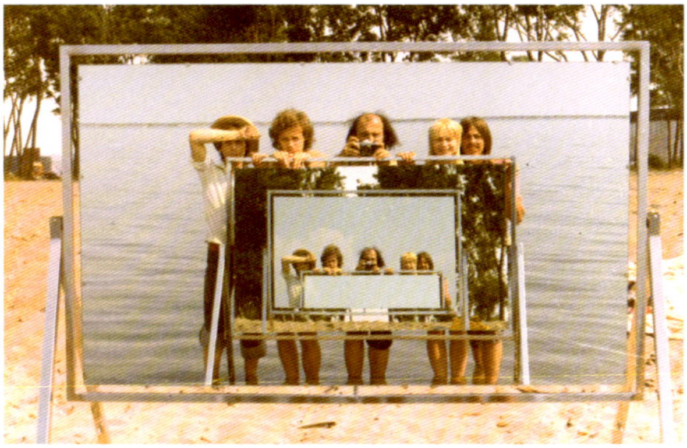

General Idea’s Headquarters, Toronto (Light On), 1971

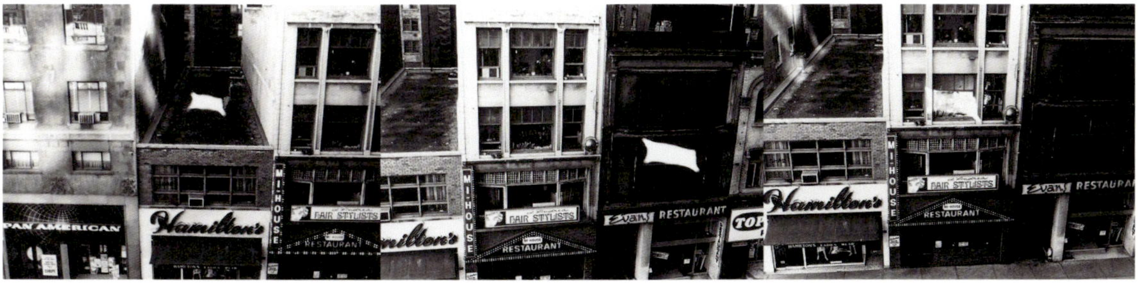

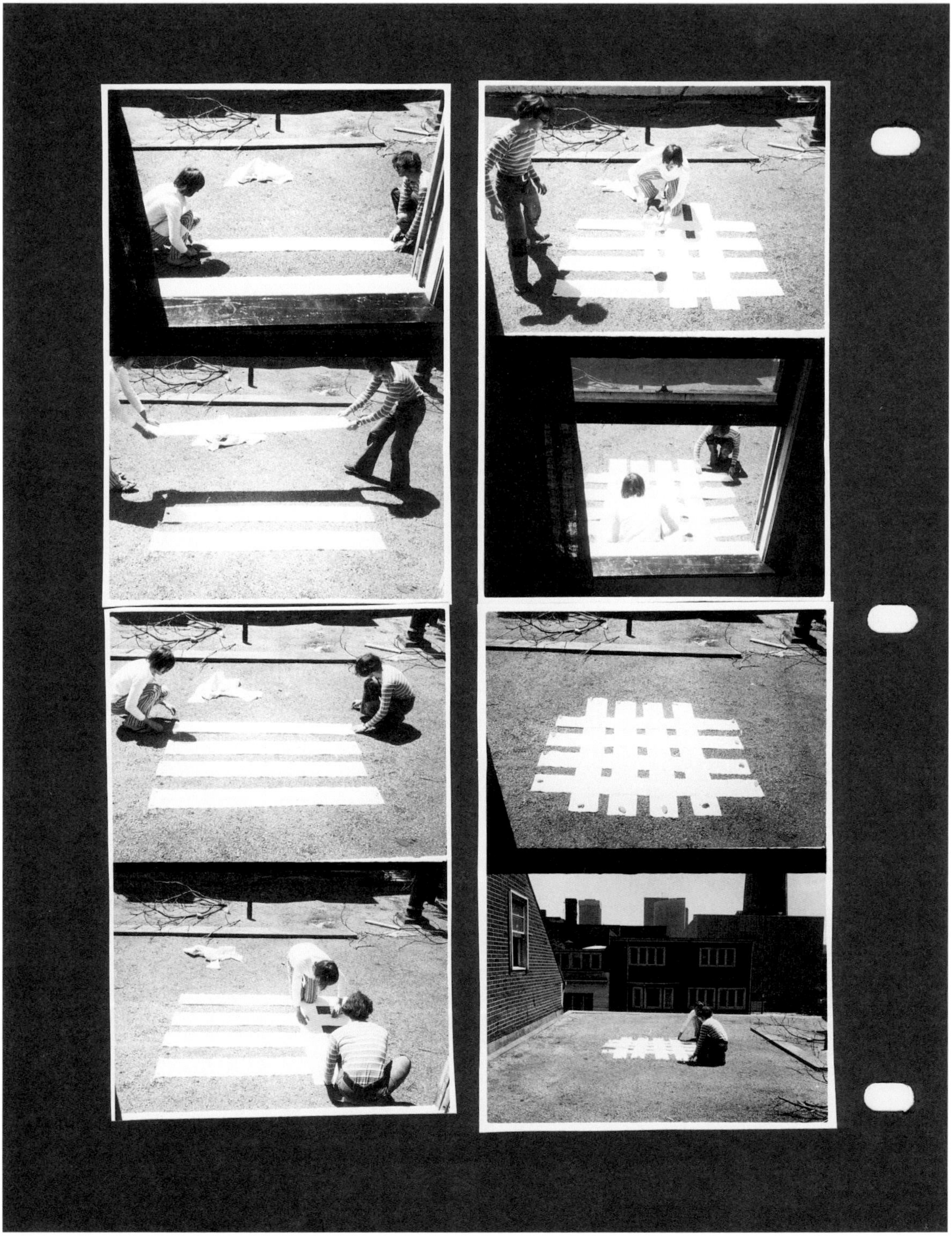

Canvas Weaving, 1970

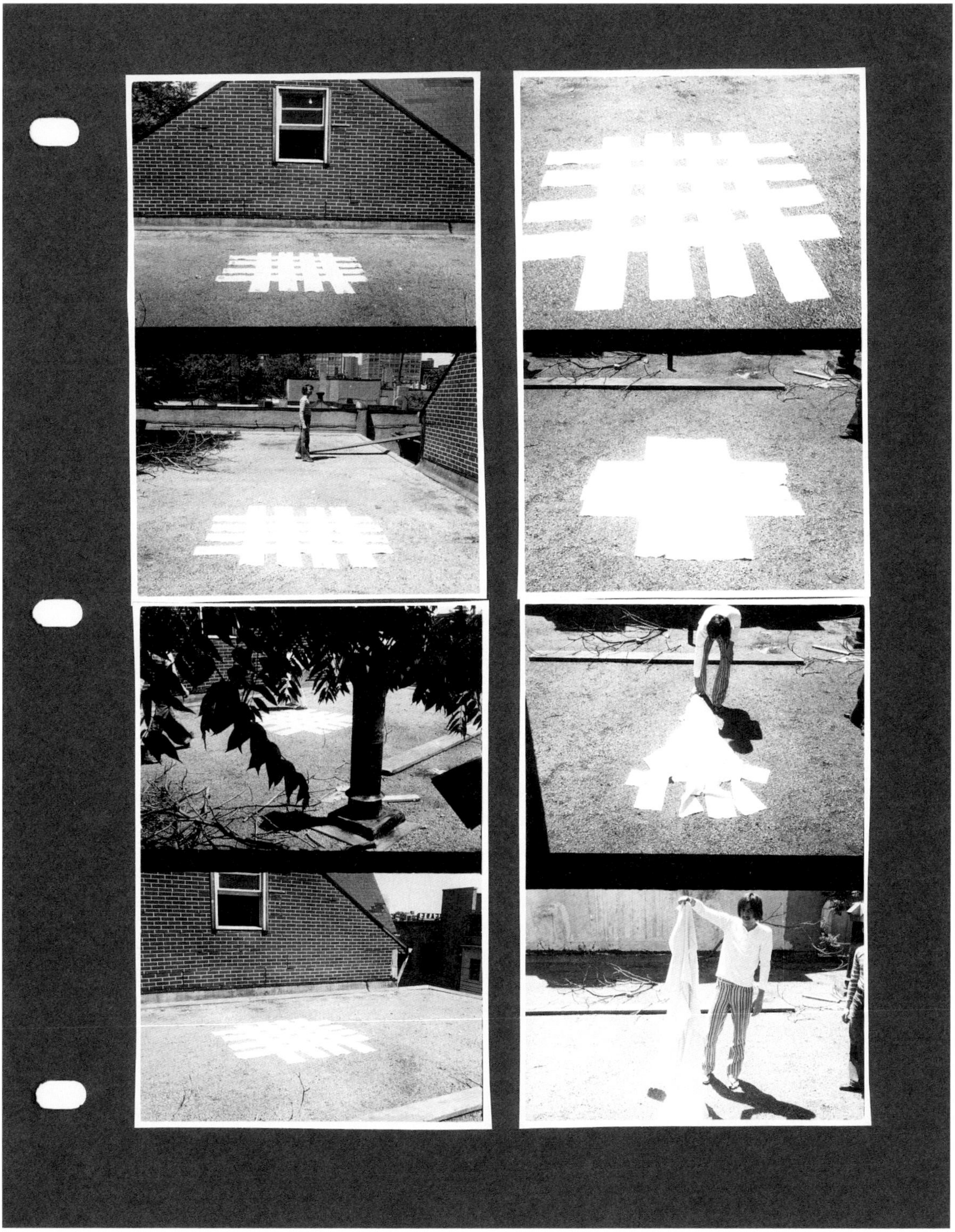

Going Thru The Motions, which was also staged in Walker Court. If some aspects seemed to recall the earlier pageant, now there was a deeper emphasis on audience engagement and development. *Going Thru The Motions* introduced the *V.B. Gowns*, which appeared as costumes and couture, as well as wearable architectural mock-ups for the *1984 Pavillion*. Their form rhymed well with the Canada pavilion at Expo '67 with its heraldic inverted pyramid. Yet beyond this affinity, GI revised definitions of the pavilion to subsume the essence of the museum, pitting notions of fleeting temporality against the putative ideals of permanence and of added value that the museum connotes.

Walker Court became such a frequent site of engagement because its architecture—an atrium framed by a colonnade—conveyed classicism, the mythic order of the ancients. Beneath the porticoed walkways beyond the court itself, the artists operated backstage, orchestrating the events in the imaginations of the audience that, for a transitory instant, became the work itself. Such may be the terms that best describe the aspirations of GI, artists who contended from the outset that their work need not be object based: "We never felt we had to produce great art to be great artists." For them, the effect of great art was a specter that could materialize through the intensive group energy of events.

Although difficult to define, this approach has been influential. It is, for instance, impossible not to think of GI when one views a recent work by Pierre Huyghe, *The Host and The Cloud* (2009–2010). If the visible product Huyghe delivers assumes the form of a film, the essence of the work is rather a sequence of arranged events, discrete nights that coincide with festivals such as Hallowe'en, Valentine's Day, and May Day. Like GI, Huyghe uses the museum as the ideal site within which to frame a scripted yet not controllable series of episodes. Within the sequenced events which took place in the eerily evacuated Musée des Arts et Traditions Populaires in Paris, one cannot but recall Miss General Idea, for in Huyghe's film one watches how a door is flung open to reveal the striding French supermodel Audrey Marnay attired in angel's wings, vintage chiffon, and a mini slicker, among other costumes. She alights in the museum lobby only to retreat, a lingering beauty that calls to mind the earliest appearances of Miss General Idea.

If the logic of Huyghe's sequencing is not immediately apparent, one realizes that such ambiguity (or simply the lack of a need to specify the meaning of objects, actions, or ideas) is also a hallmark of GI. By the time that the members of GI constitute one half of the platform party at the opening ceremonies of the *1984 Miss General Idea Pavillion* exhibition, they were already operating in the future they had envisioned for themselves, initially intuited in 1969 when as interlopers they strode into the museum and set onto the floor of Walker Court a series of circular mirrors. Performed as an intervention to the perplexed stares of passersby, early actions such as *Mirror Sequence* (1969) inscribe the central space of the museum as a vital locus and place of departure.

As self-appointed outsiders, GI realized that the museum was the ultimate insider space. Their project is aimed at the museum, but only to exploit it as a trope, a transitory container of meaning and potential. The proscenium of Walker Court was ideally suited for their deconstruction of the delirious uncontrollability of spectacle, a task that GI thrived on. Many of their objects and works refer to events and fictions, demanding that viewers become immersed in the requisite "mythology" in order to access the narratives at play. This process of familiarizing oneself with the work of GI is analogous to becoming an insider, entering an elite and privileged realm. By using the museum as their stage set and pavilion, GI dissolved boundaries, inviting audiences inside, even if only fleetingly.

1 General Idea, The 1971 Miss General Idea Pageant (Artscanada), 1971, 3 pages, photostat on paper, each 253 x 189 mm. Prototype for an edition never completed. Designed as a faux article for the December 1971 issue of Artscanada magazine, reviewing The 1971 Miss General Idea Pageant held at Art Gallery of Ontario, Toronto. It is in the layout style of Artscanada itself, but with all three pages numbered "84." The project was refused by the editor at the last moment and was never published.

2 The program for the evening was a slim booklet, based on an old playbill from the Folies Bergères.

3 General Idea, "Glamour," FILE Megazine, vol. 3 no. 1, Autumn 1975. General Idea's "Glamour" article in FILE takes Roland Barthes' essay "What is a myth today?" (from Mythologies, first published in English in 1972) and proposes that as mythology is in relation to everyday life (the subject of Barthes' essay), so General Idea's "Glamour" is in relation to mythology.

4 Of the many evolving definitions offered by the artists, the following, which first appeared in the videotape Pilot (1977), relays the specificity and ambiguity of their pavilion: "The 1984 Miss General Idea Pavillion is basically this: a framing device for accommodation. A terminal in which to rest the case of open and closed frameworks. A superstructure of containment formats like walls framing the theatre of operations. Architecture playing the part of the Master of Ceremonies directing all eyes to this stage to perform the single point of view." General Idea, 1968–1984, exh. cat., Stedelijk Van Abbemuseum, Eindhoven, 1984, p. 33–34.

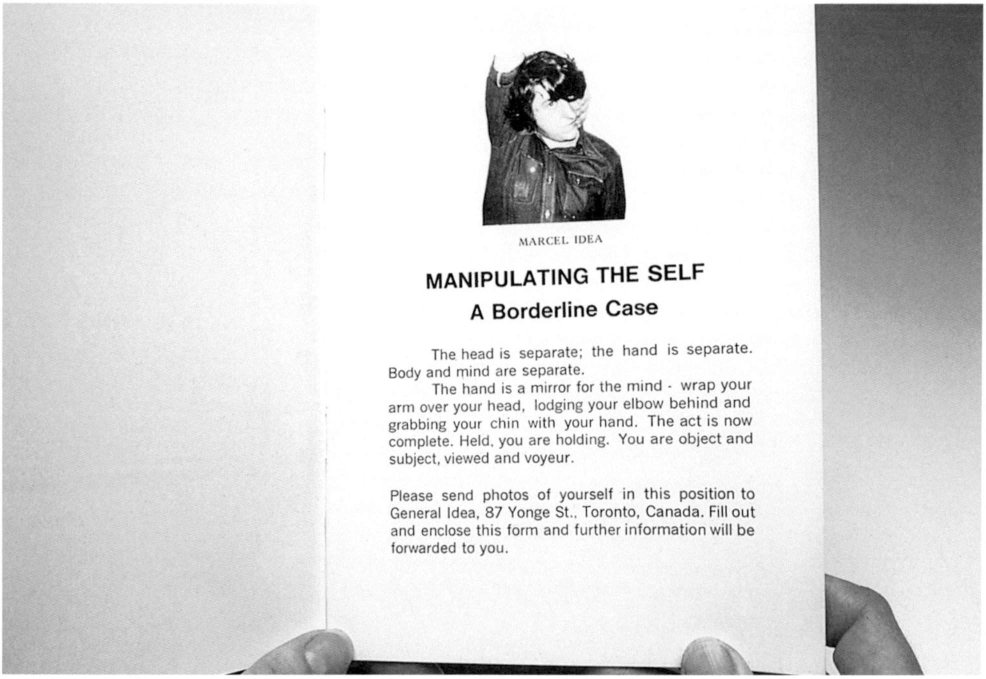

Manipulating the Self, 1971

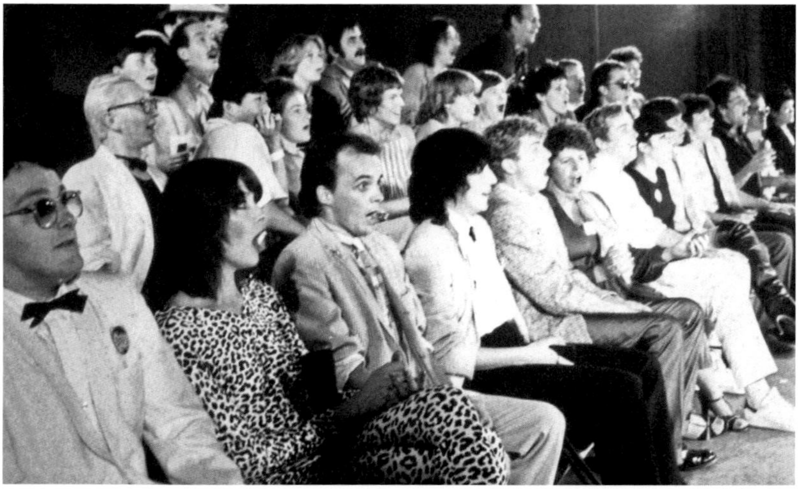

Towards an Audience Vocabulary, 1978

Club Canasta, FILE's Filathon Telephone Canasta Party, 1972

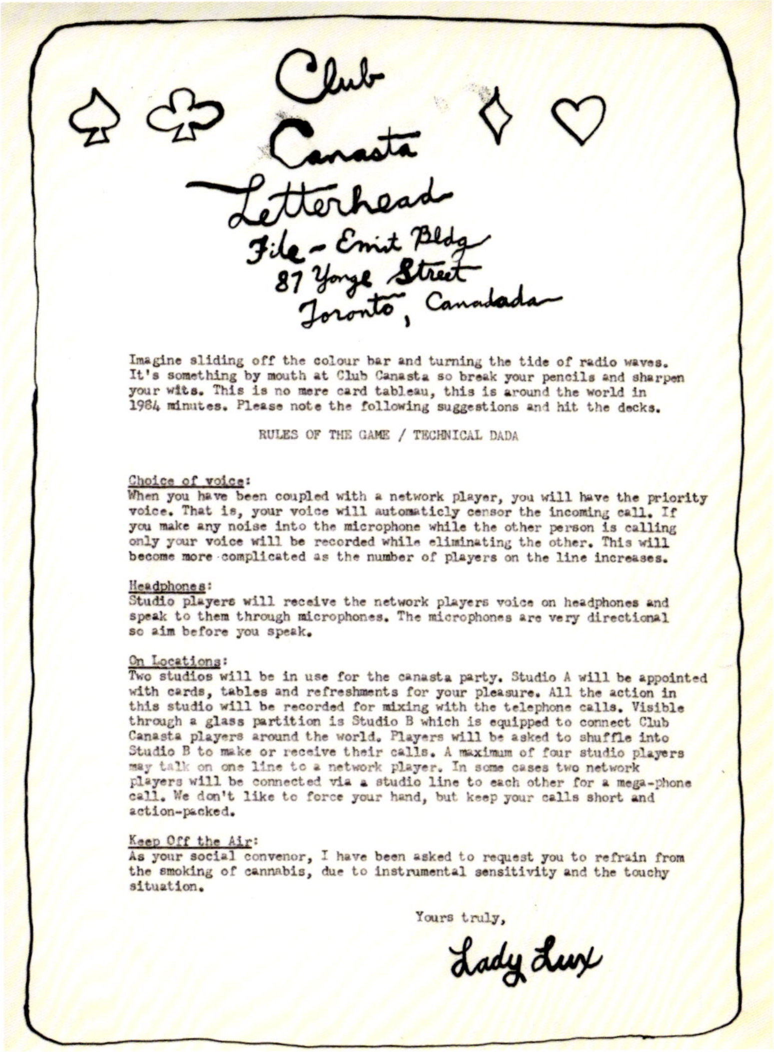

Club Canasta Letterhead
File - Emit Bldg
87 Yonge Street
Toronto, Canadada

Imagine sliding off the colour bar and turning the tide of radio waves. It's something by mouth at Club Canasta so break your pencils and sharpen your wits. This is no mere card tableau, this is around the world in 1984 minutes. Please note the following suggestions and hit the decks.

RULES OF THE GAME / TECHNICAL DADA

Choice of voice:
When you have been coupled with a network player, you will have the priority voice. That is, your voice will automaticly censor the incoming call. If you make any noise into the microphone while the other person is calling only your voice will be recorded while eliminating the other. This will become more complicated as the number of players on the line increases.

Headphones:
Studio players will receive the network players voice on headphones and speak to them through microphones. The microphones are very directional so aim before you speak.

On Locations:
Two studios will be in use for the canasta party. Studio A will be appointed with cards, tables and refreshments for your pleasure. All the action in this studio will be recorded for mixing with the telephone calls. Visible through a glass partition is Studio B which is equipped to connect Club Canasta players around the world. Players will be asked to shuffle into Studio B to make or receive their calls. A maximum of four studio players may talk on one line to a network player. In some cases two network players will be connected via a studio line to each other for a mega-phone call. We don't like to force your hand, but keep your calls short and action-packed.

Keep Off the Air:
As your social convenor, I have been asked to request you to refrain from the smoking of cannabis, due to instrumental sensitivity and the touchy situation.

Yours truly,

Lady Lux

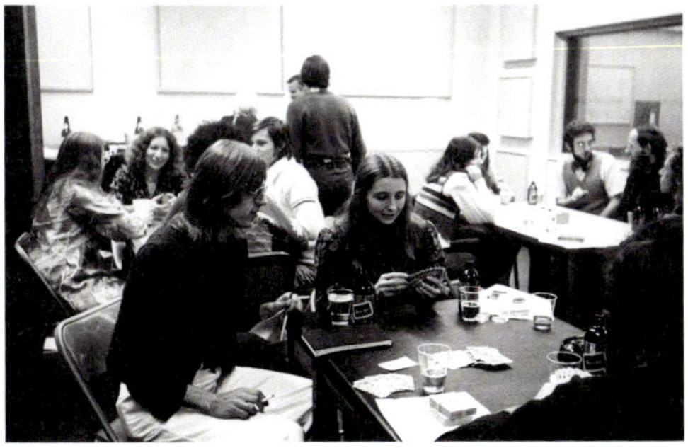

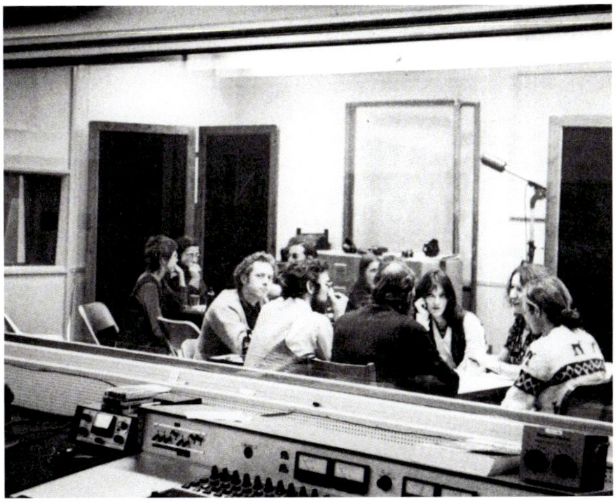

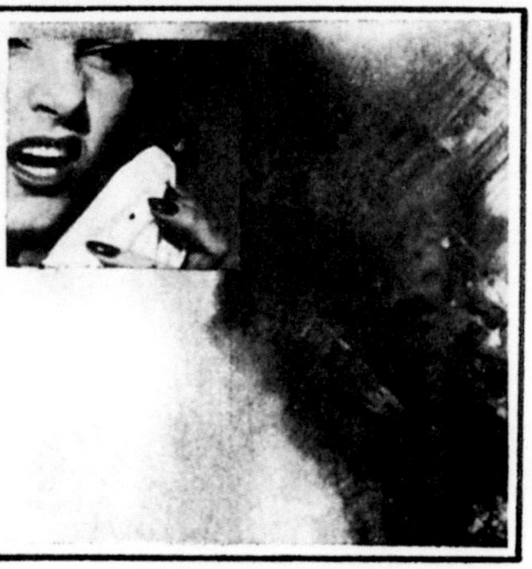

air
becoming it.

copy this card 5
times. send it
to 5 friends.

please
burn this card

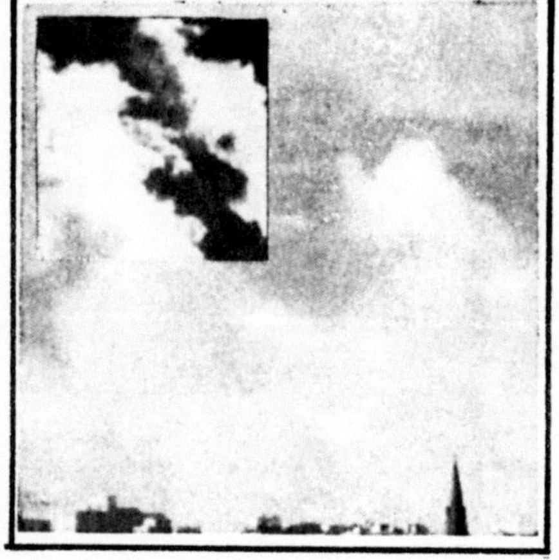

cloud
being one.

copy this card 5
times. send it
to 5 friends.

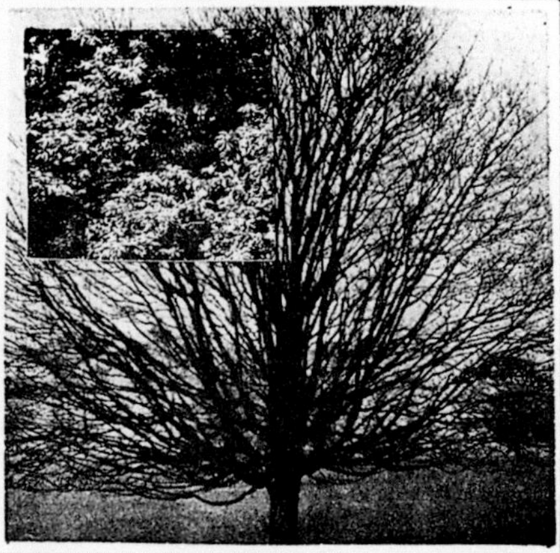

tree
getting to know one.

copy this card 5
times. send it
to 5 friends.

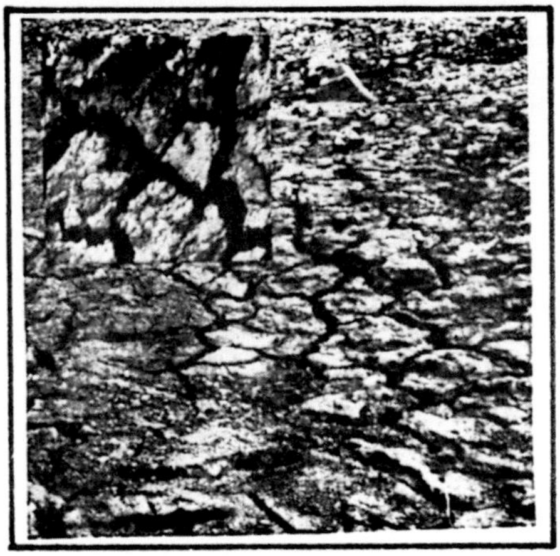

earth
digging it.

copy this card 5
times. send it
to 5 friends.

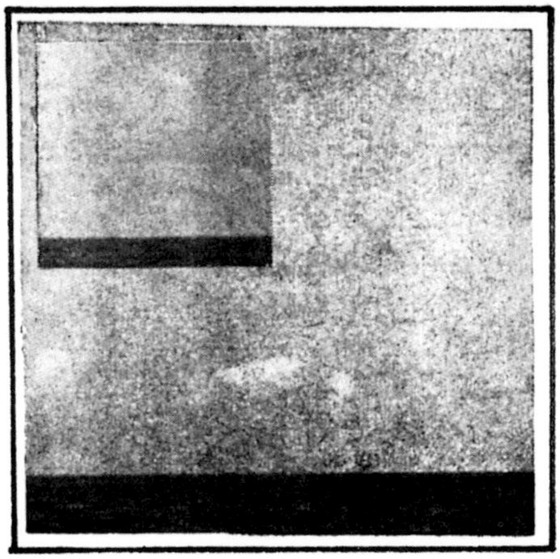

sky

copy this card 5
times. send it
to 5 friends.

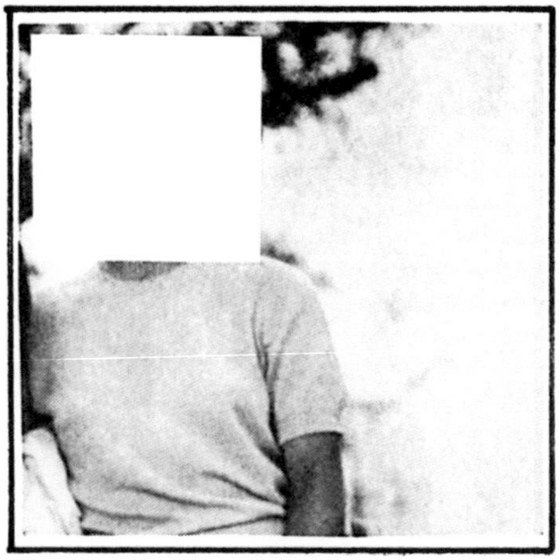

dissolve your portrait
in a glass of water.
drink it.

copy this card 5
times. send it
to 5 friends.

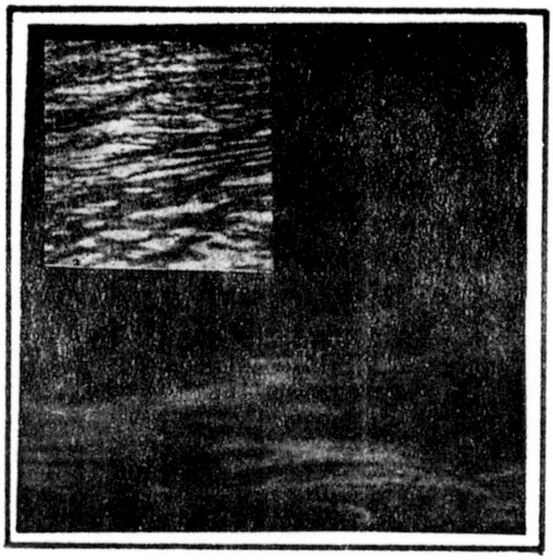

water
tasting it.

copy this card 5
times. send it
to 5 friends.

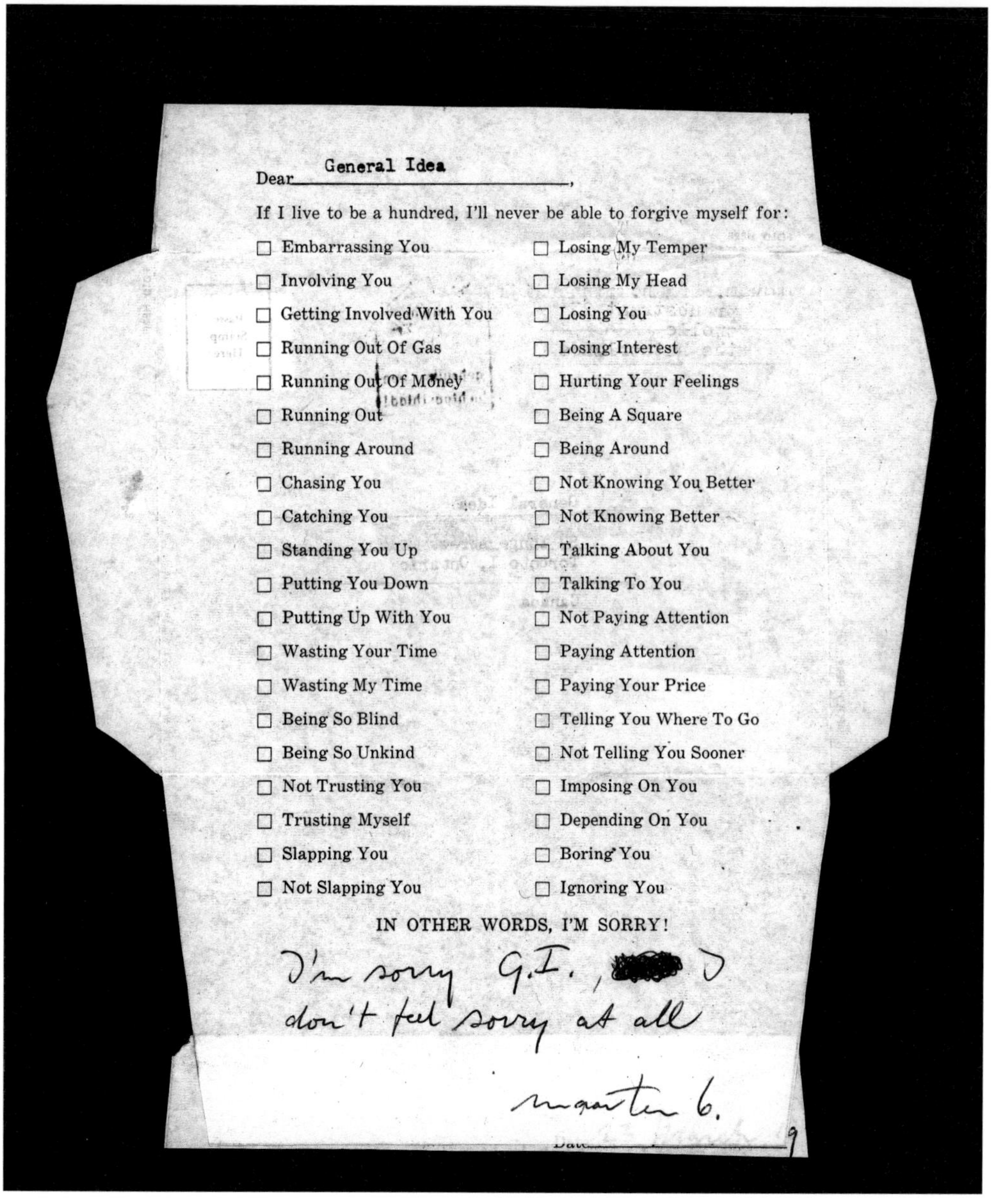

Dear General Idea,

If I live to be a hundred, I'll never be able to forgive myself for:

- ☐ Embarrassing You
- ☐ Involving You
- ☐ Getting Involved With You
- ☐ Running Out Of Gas
- ☐ Running Out Of Money
- ☐ Running Out
- ☐ Running Around
- ☐ Chasing You
- ☐ Catching You
- ☐ Standing You Up
- ☐ Putting You Down
- ☐ Putting Up With You
- ☐ Wasting Your Time
- ☐ Wasting My Time
- ☐ Being So Blind
- ☐ Being So Unkind
- ☐ Not Trusting You
- ☐ Trusting Myself
- ☐ Slapping You
- ☐ Not Slapping You
- ☐ Losing My Temper
- ☐ Losing My Head
- ☐ Losing You
- ☐ Losing Interest
- ☐ Hurting Your Feelings
- ☐ Being A Square
- ☐ Being Around
- ☐ Not Knowing You Better
- ☐ Not Knowing Better
- ☐ Talking About You
- ☐ Talking To You
- ☐ Not Paying Attention
- ☐ Paying Attention
- ☐ Paying Your Price
- ☐ Telling You Where To Go
- ☐ Not Telling You Sooner
- ☐ Imposing On You
- ☐ Depending On You
- ☐ Boring You
- ☐ Ignoring You

IN OTHER WORDS, I'M SORRY!

I'm sorry G.I., [redacted] I don't feel sorry at all

Dear General Idea, if I live to be a hundred I'll never forgive myself for ..., 1972

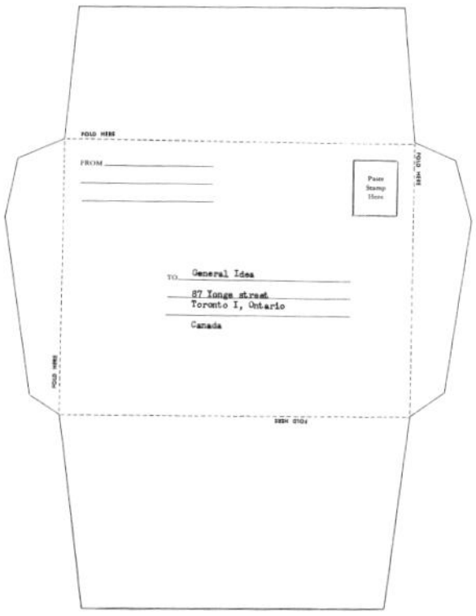

CHAIN LETTER

Paste a photo of yourself onto a picture of sky. Send it to the name at the top of the list below. Deleting this name, add your own name to the bottom of the list. If there are no names, supply them. Copy this letter 5 times; send it to 5 friends. Within a few weeks you may receive as many as 3125 sky portraits.

list: name address

1. ....

2. ....

3. ....

4. ....

5. ....

Skyportraits Chain Letter Project, 1969

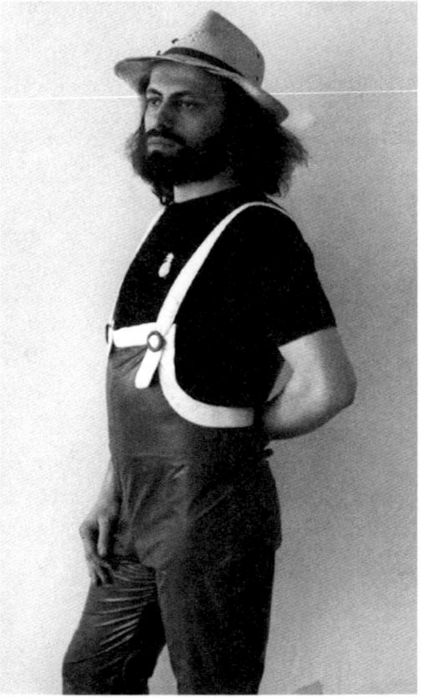

Jorge sans Girdle–Evidence of Body Binding, 1970

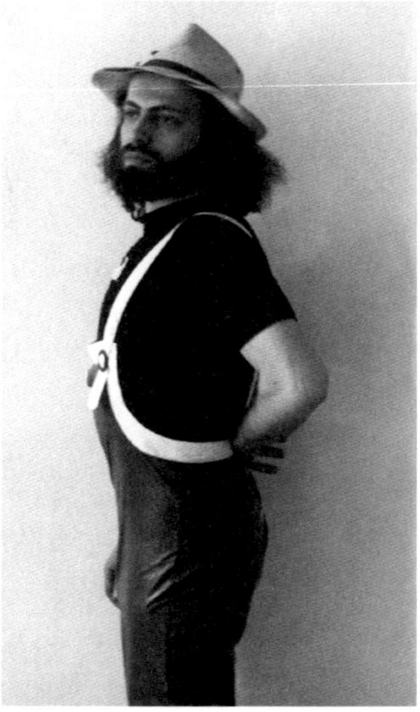

Jorge avec Girdle–Evidence of Body Binding, 1970

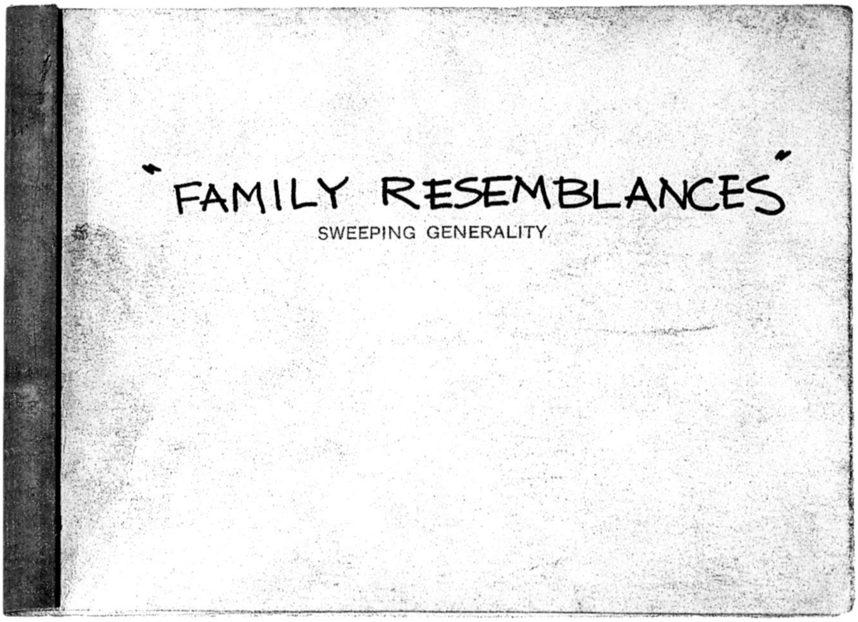

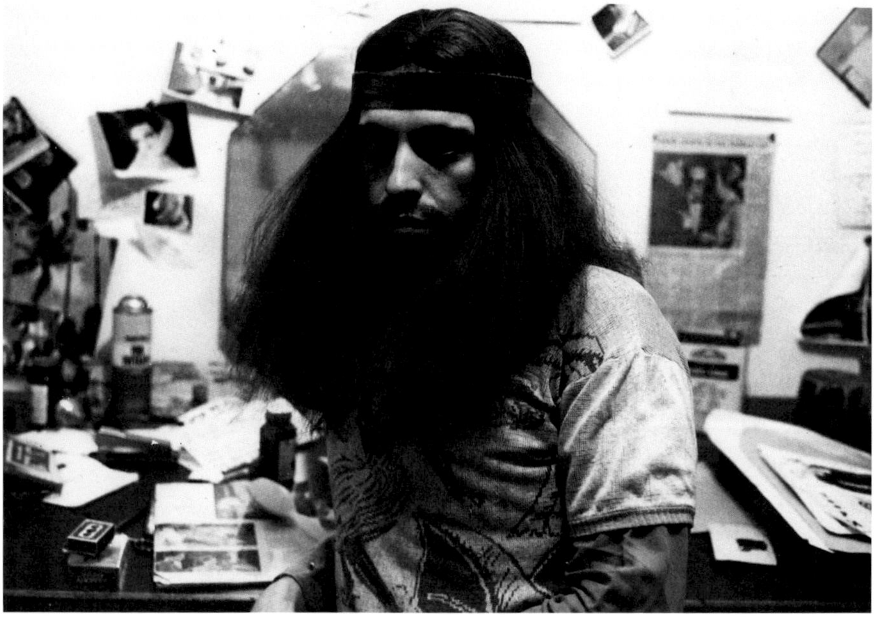

Jorge Zontal

Family Resemblances, 1972

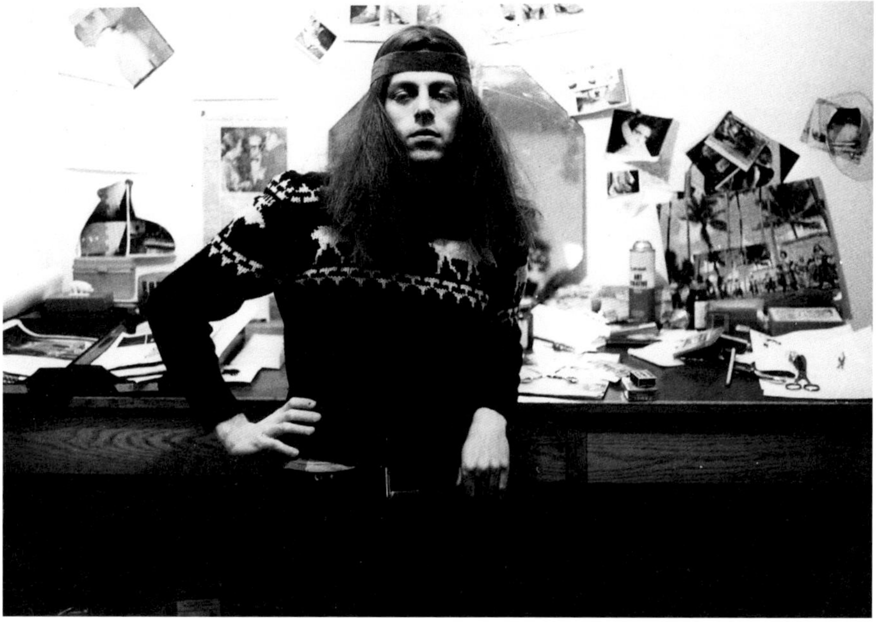

Felix Partz

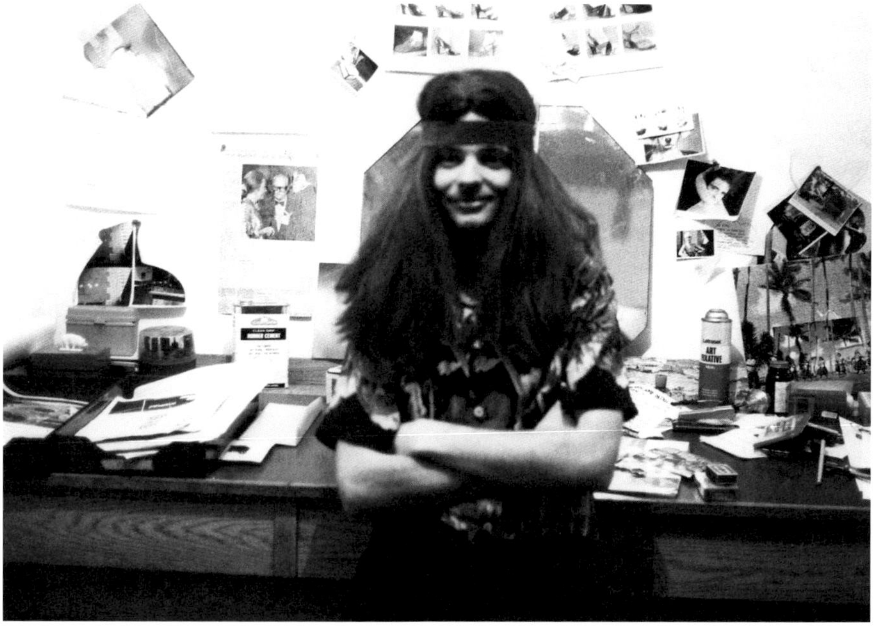

AA Bronson

EXPOSÉ

A VIDEO DEVICE
BY GENERAL IDEA
AT A SPACE
JULY 1 - 6

WAITING FOR THE PRESENT? THE MEMORY
OF WHAT IS NOT IS BETTER THAN THE
AMNESIA OF WHAT IS. A NO MAN'S
LAND, OF BETTER SAID, A NO SIGNALS
REGION, EXTENDS BETWEEN PAST AND FUTURE.

(JOHN BRECKMAN, 1970
ROBERT SMITHSON, 1969
LEON BRILLOUIN, 1964)

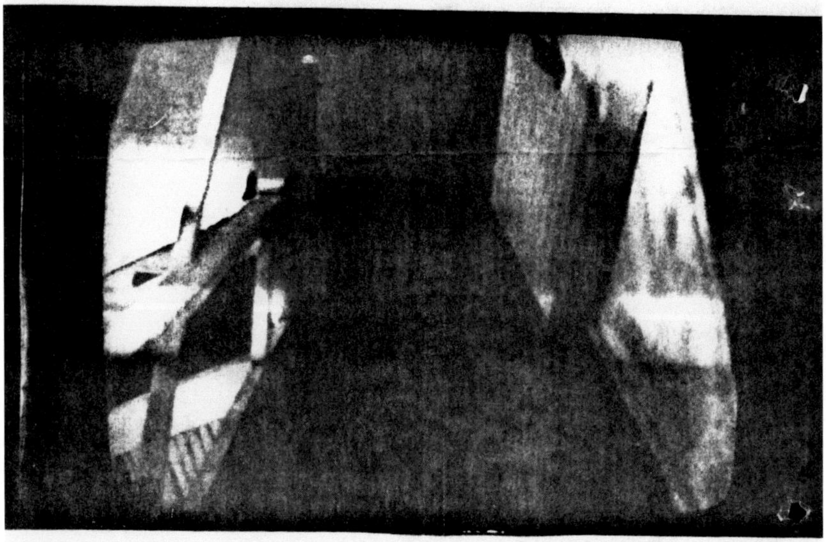

Invitation card for Exposé, A Space, Toronto, 1971

Three men working create the basic collaborative unit for avoiding hierarchical ossification.

Showcard 1-106, An Animated Trio, 1979

The 1984 Miss General Idea Pageant is basically this: a framing device we have framed for our own devices to contain our frame-ups. The Search for the Spirit of Miss General Idea is the ritualized pageant of creation, production, selection, presentation, competition, manipulation, and revelation of that which is suitable for framing.

Showcard 2-001, The 1984 Miss General Idea Pageant, 1975

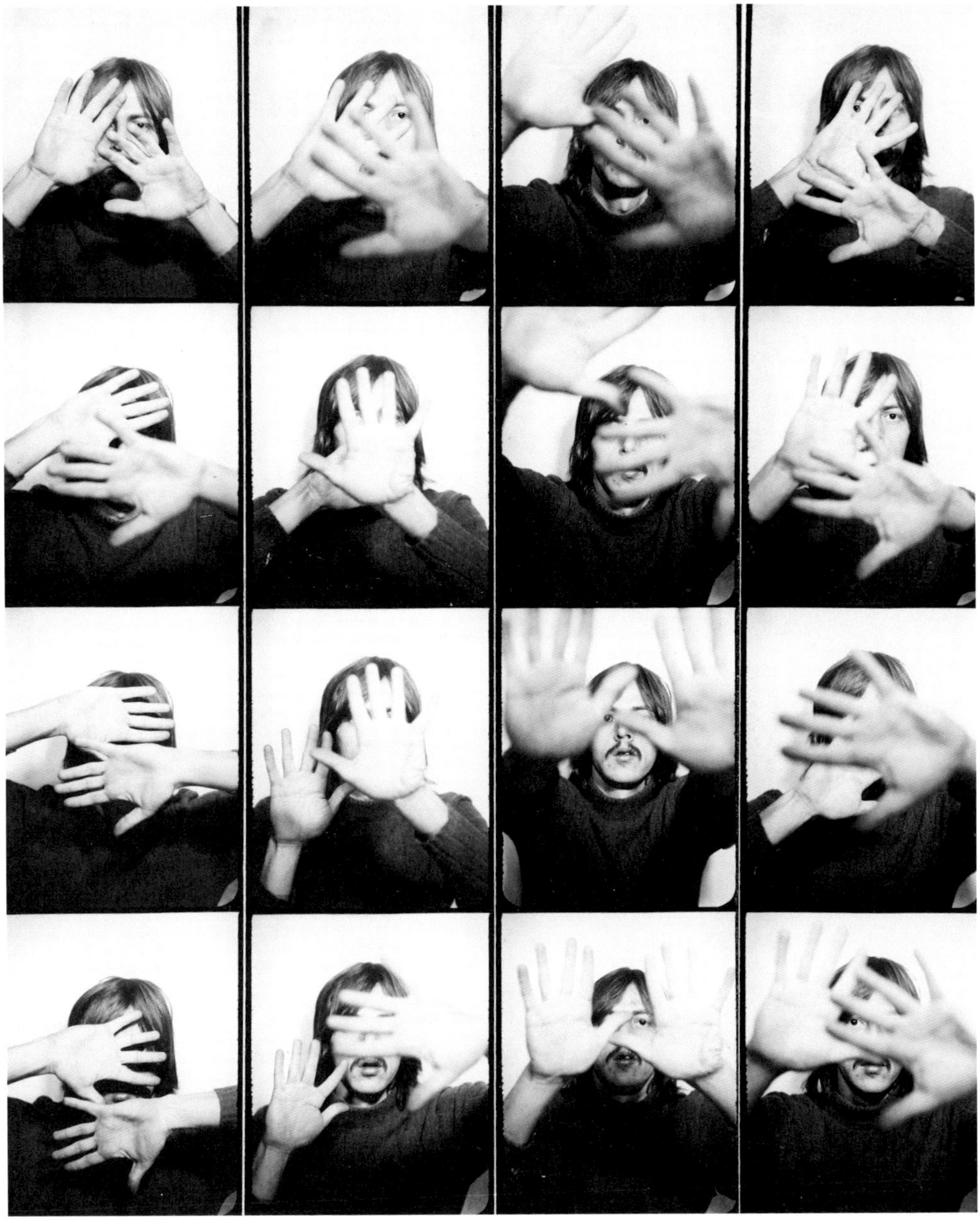

Off Hand Photo-Booth Hands, 1969–1970

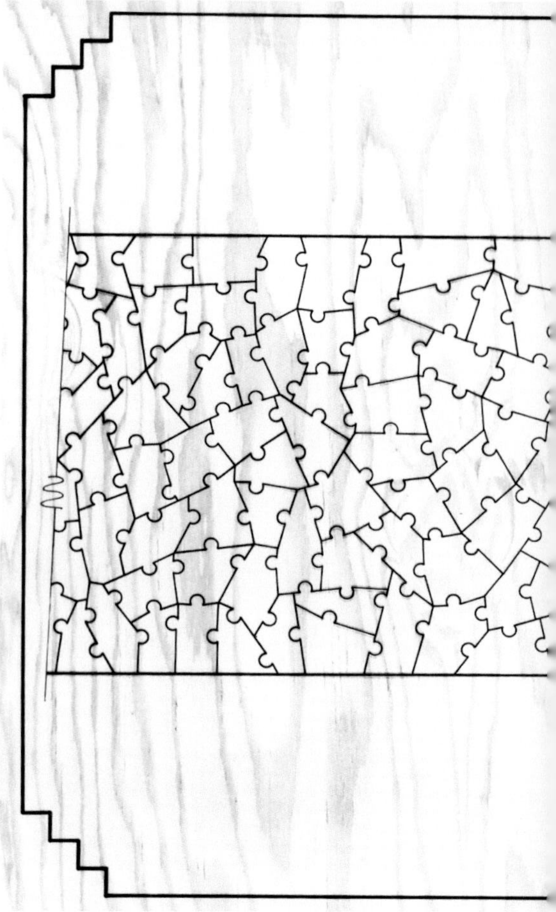

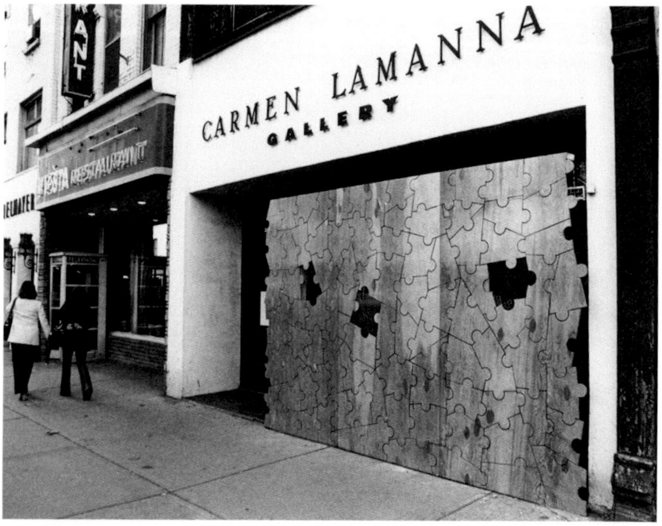

The Hoarding of the 1984 Miss General Idea Pavillion, 1975

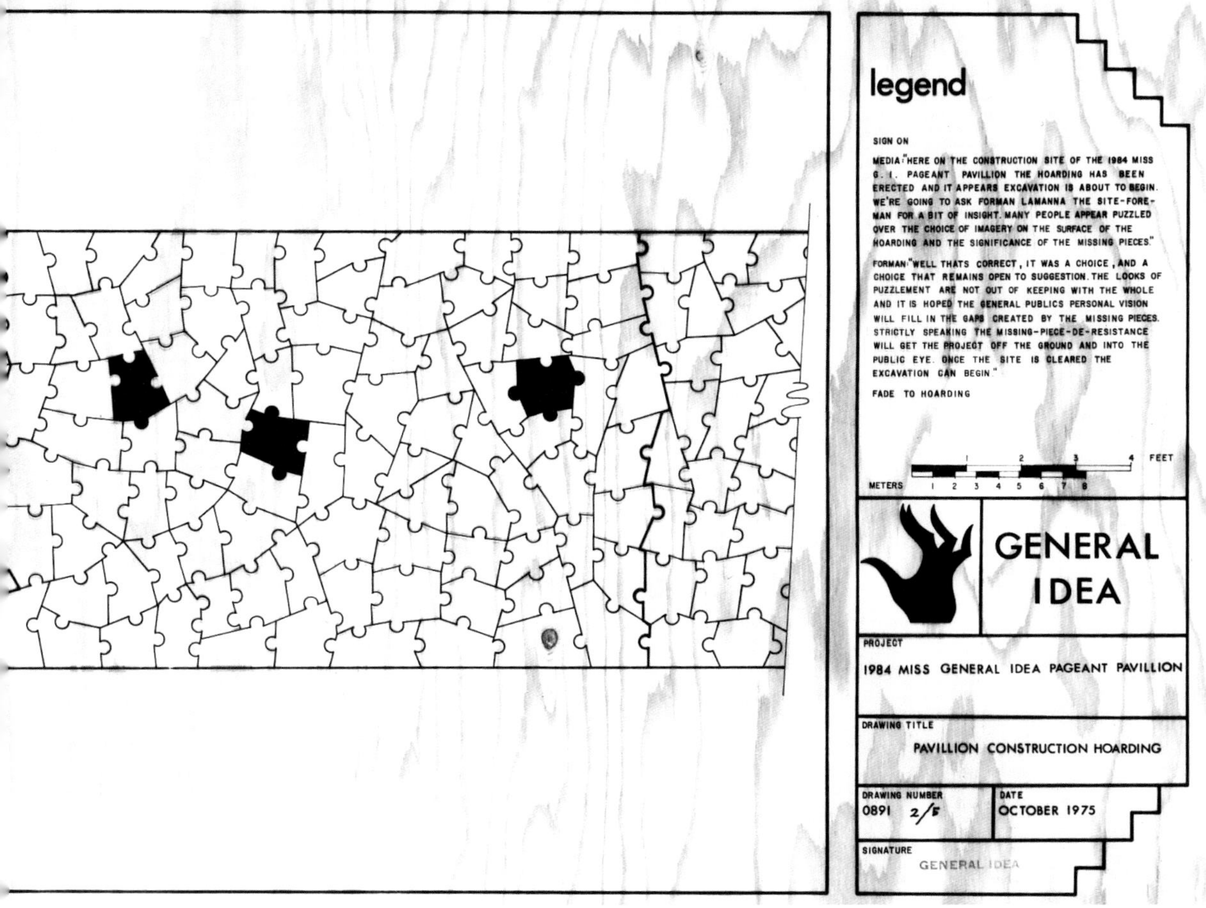

Pavillion Construction Hoarding, 1975

The Life and Work of Miss General Idea

Jean-Christophe Ammann

Theoretically, the birth of Miss General Idea should coincide with her creation in the minds of her makers. That happen-ed in 1968, which would now make her 14 years old. Lolita? I'm not so sure. I think she must have been about 20 when she was born. Mythological years are different from ordinary ones anyway, and Miss General Idea's makers are not exactly garrulous about her. I think that's her own doing. Their silence was her idea. In any case, she's been keeping artists on the run; it had always been planned to devote a pavilion to Miss General Idea in Orwell's 1984—which does not mean any old space but rather an entire complex of buildings that were half-finished in 1977 when they went up in flames just before the three makers of Miss General Idea were to take part in a group show at the Kunsthalle Basel. The exhibition included photographs to show visitors the disastrous consequences of the blaze. The fire was, of course, a major setback for Miss General Idea; she had already invested considerable amounts of energy in the project. The most important step at the time was to breathe new life and courage into her makers. This problem was solved by setting up a bar with refreshments for them. The *Cocktail Book* of 1980 not only shows how broad-minded Miss General Idea was in catering to every conceivable wish from milk to nectar, but also reveals her diabolic delight in the way her makers enjoyed their drinks.

While the artists were working on the reconstruction of the building, Miss General Idea had ample time to think about how she was going to design her boudoir. She was forever done with sleeping bags, cots, and nights spent outside on the beach or in the open field. Not to speak of all the adventures she had already been through. She hinted as much to her makers and her stories encouraged them to become increasingly audacious about transforming attributes, one and all, into generalizations.

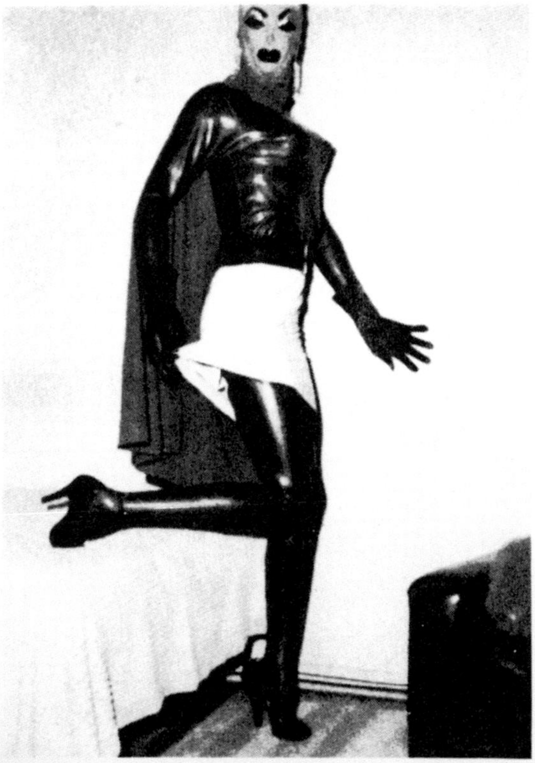

Artist's Conception; Miss General Idea 1971.

Artist's Conception: Miss General Idea 1971, 1971

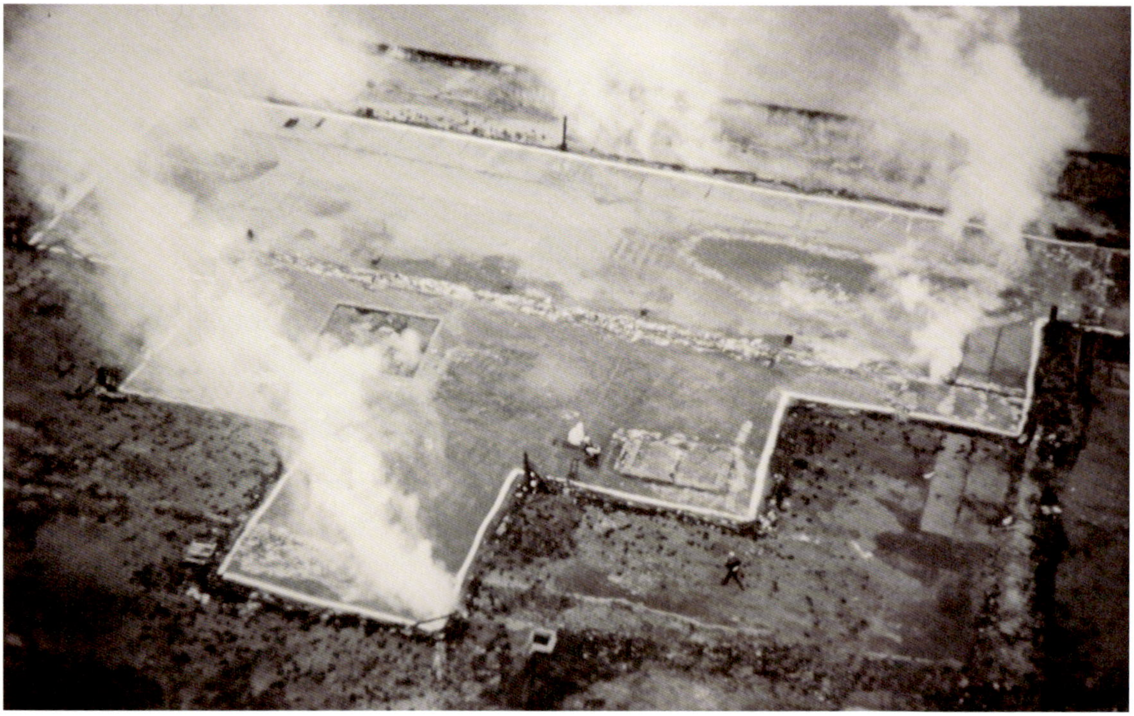

Ruins of the 1984 Miss General Idea Pavillion, 1977

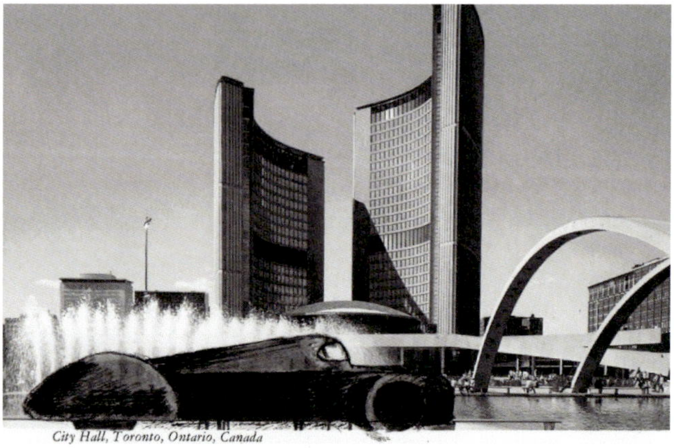

The 1984 Spirit of Miss General Idea Vehicle, 1973

The better they got at doing this, the more they would be able to master their guilty feelings. This was the enlightened side of Miss General Idea, who considered herself amoral, not immoral. She had often thought about the connection between generalizations and guilty feelings. Guilt is the consequence of an action, of something we do. She had noticed that people who don't work or have sex regularly feel guilty. Over the years Miss General Idea had kept reminding her makers that generalizations must not turn into a new king of code. The ubiquity of generalizations only makes sense if independence of thought and action are thus enhanced. Were everything really to become generalized, then the general would no longer determine the particular; instead the particular would be bundled into different forms of consensus, thus doing away with deviation (i.e. guilt). These theoretical discussions with her makers—"discussion" is hardly the right word because they understood each other so well—always ended up with figuring out ways and means of form and presentation.

The sophisticated irony of the early years, initially an adequate device, became increasingly less so as time went on; it was time for a change. It was no good for people to know more than the makers of Miss General Idea were trying to conceal. Thus the blaze in the pavilion also had its advantages; it provided the chance to make a new start. After Miss General Idea had given her makers the inspiration for the videotape *Cornucopia* (1982/1983), the boudoir began to take shape. She was particularly proud of the film. She vaguely remembered the film Walter de Maria shot in 1969, *Hard Core* it was called, although it did not contain what the title generally implies. All you see is a desert horizon that keeps revolving 360 degrees around a cowboy holding a rifle. In *Cornucopia*, however, a stick that changes color circles in front of a pretty girl's mouth with the ecstatic complacency of a lollipop. The time had come to make people's mouths water and then to parch them before they get a chance to swallow.

As a lady of leisure, Miss General Idea had developed a liking for pampered poodles. These creatures are of course a status symbol. Lamborghinis are to pimps as dolled up poodles are to brassy tarts. Actually she didn't know where her preference for poodles had come from. While the pavilion was under construction, she had detected a distinctly masculine side to herself, but after the fire she felt more feminine. Maybe her desire to acquire some of those idiotically over-groomed creatures was actually a half-conscious, half-unconscious desire to provoke. It could well be that people would think she was a transvestite. The poodles inspired fantasies connected with her

Luxon Louvre (Ambiguity Without Contradiction), 1975

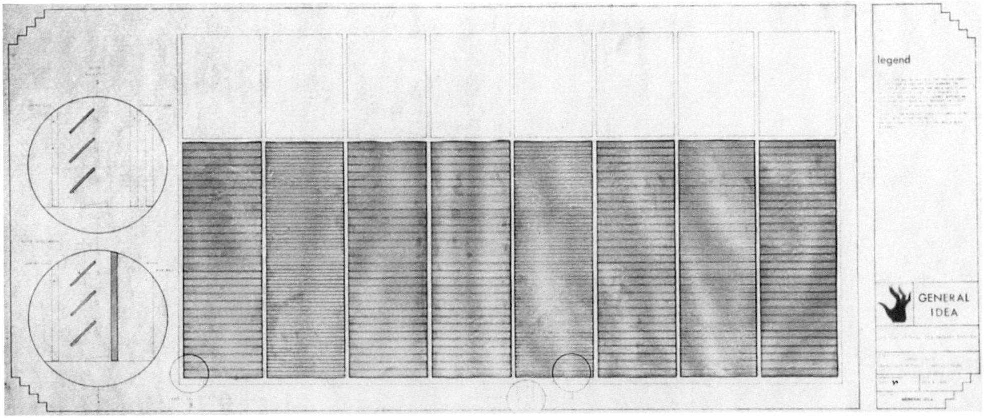

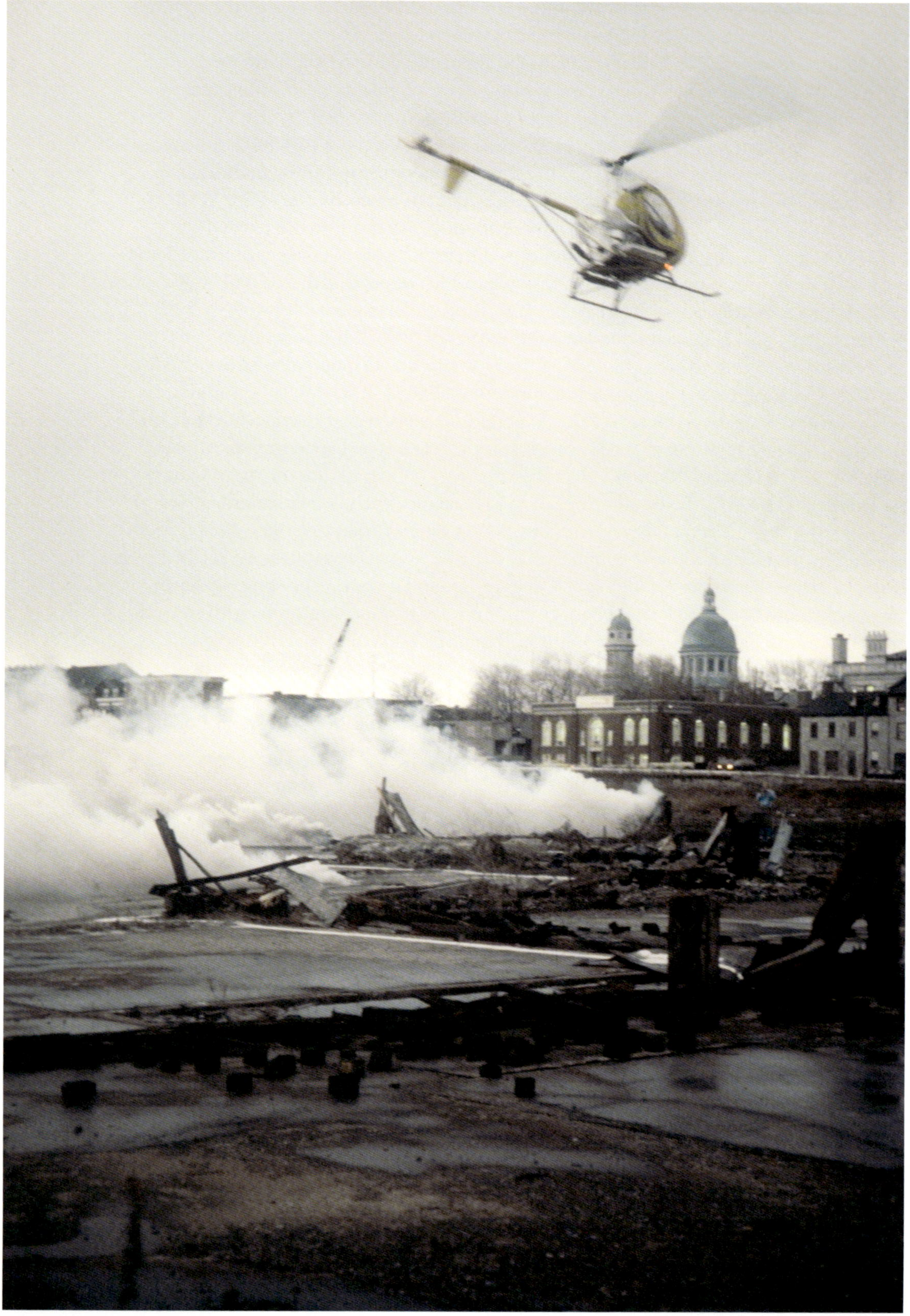

Ruins of the 1984 Miss General Idea Pavillion (Helicopter Landing at the Site), 1977

boudoir, which she immediately passed on to her makers. Her mind was particularly productive after she had read the Marquis de Sade while reclining on a Madame Récamier sofa. People must have been in awfully good shape to withstand all those gyrations. In her opinion, poodles were far better suited for such activities. She wanted them to be like puppets or little machines that would obey the whims of human lust like clockwork, in images that never jade because they are powerful in every position. The result was amazing, the more so since she had urged her makers to present these subjects not only as monumental murals but also as notebooks or travelogues. The three artists were so thoughtful that they even created a scene on her Madame Récamier sofa; though for a fleeting moment she wasn't sure whether they were being insolent or charming.

Miss General Idea became so involved in her boudoir that her makers began to wonder if she wanted to have a baby. The idea wasn't all that farfetched. Having sprung from the heads of her makers, she had impregnated them again and again with her ideas without having been impregnated herself, which was only natural: being the largest common denominator, she could not very well produce a larger one. But she became so obsessed with the idea of a baby that she decided one day to have the copulating poodles replaced by chubby little copulating babies. After all, Baroque putti had often been witness to scenes of a delicate nature. Since man is imitative from birth, it is quite conceivable that after such a long time, babies now know how to imitate grown-up games.

In Miss General Idea's dreams the poodle murals showed mechanical sequences, whereas the babies balled up in rolypoly confusion. The poodles fucked in goose step; the babies as if they were romping in mid-air. Miss General Idea loved these changes of rhythm and abandoned herself to them in an ecstasy of surrender.

Having a critical mind, she wondered whether the pictures for her boudoir really did qualify as generalizations. There were no hitches as far as art history was

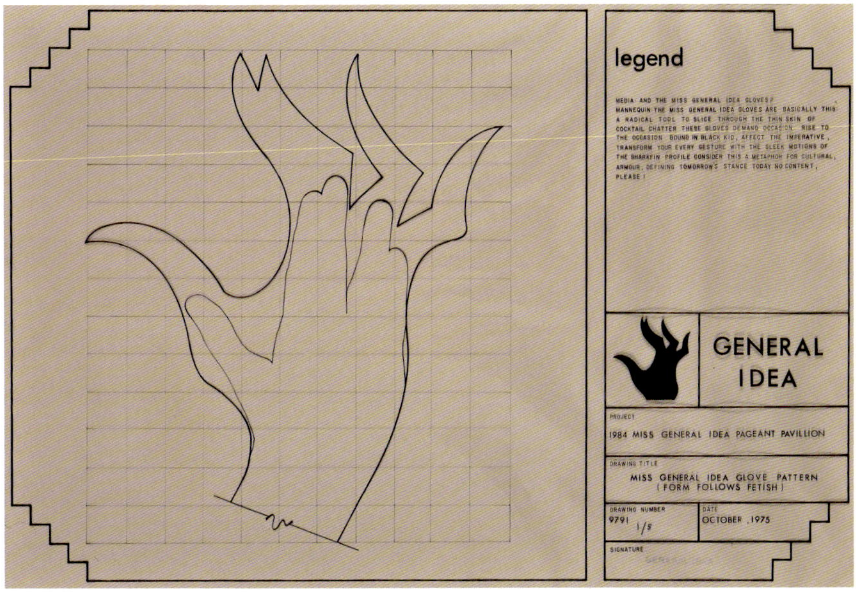

Miss General Idea Glove Pattern (Form Follows Fetish), 1975

concerned. She was reminded for instance Jean-Honoré Fragonard's (1723–1806) *Girl with Dog* in the Bavarian State Collection at the Alte Pinakothek in Munich. The girl is lying on a rumpled, canopied bed. It is probably morning. The covers are thrown back. The dog has jumped onto the bed where the girl is playing with him. Evidently a clever animal, he knows how to give the girl a special thrill. She is lying on her back, her legs bare, her knees in the air, her hands holding her parted thighs. Her feet are crossed so that the dog can sit on them and move his tail unhindered. He seems to be doing so with such devotion that the girl has raised her head from the pillow to smile at him.

It also occurred to Miss General Idea that these works might yield a generalization for her boudoir, which would turn all the ineffable fantasies that move people day in and day out into a cool and cooling metaphor—with that touch of irony that lends an element of surprise, making the incredible seem credible.

Since 1984 was not getting any younger and reconstruction of the pavilion was slow, Miss General Idea's makers appealed to some museums. Perhaps they would be able to put up *The 1984 Miss General Idea Pavillion* for a while. As she had anticipated, the response was most encouraging. How could anyone reject such an attractive, active, imaginative young lady? Museum people were naturally eager for new insights into the erotic dimensions of generalizations, and interior decorators can't wait to see what conclusions they might draw from Miss General Idea's boudoir. The rooms are ready. We are looking forward to the coming of Miss General Idea with great excitement.

Reprinted from General Idea, 1968–1984, exh. cat., Kunsthalle Basel, Stedelijk Van Abbemuseum, Eindhoven, Art Gallery of Ontario, Toronto, Musée d'Art Contemporain de Montréal, 1984–1985

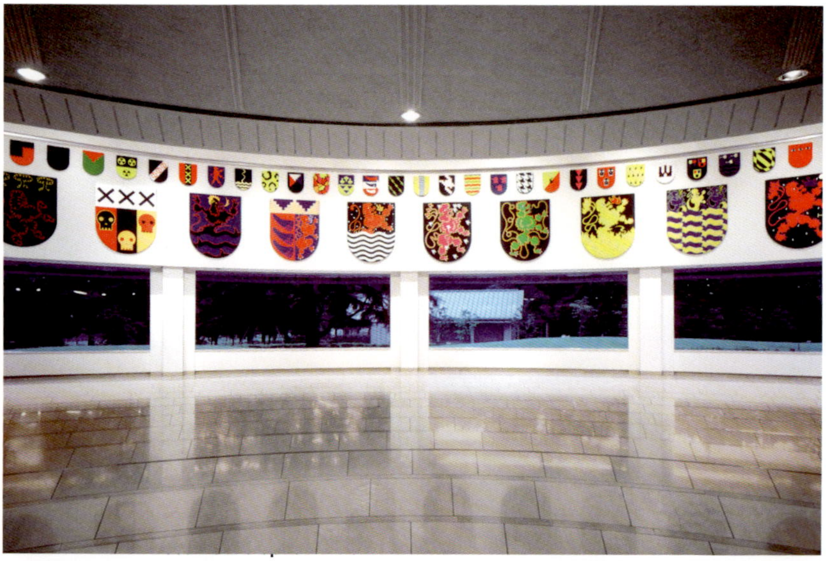

The Armoury of the 1984 Miss General Idea Pavillion, 1985–1990

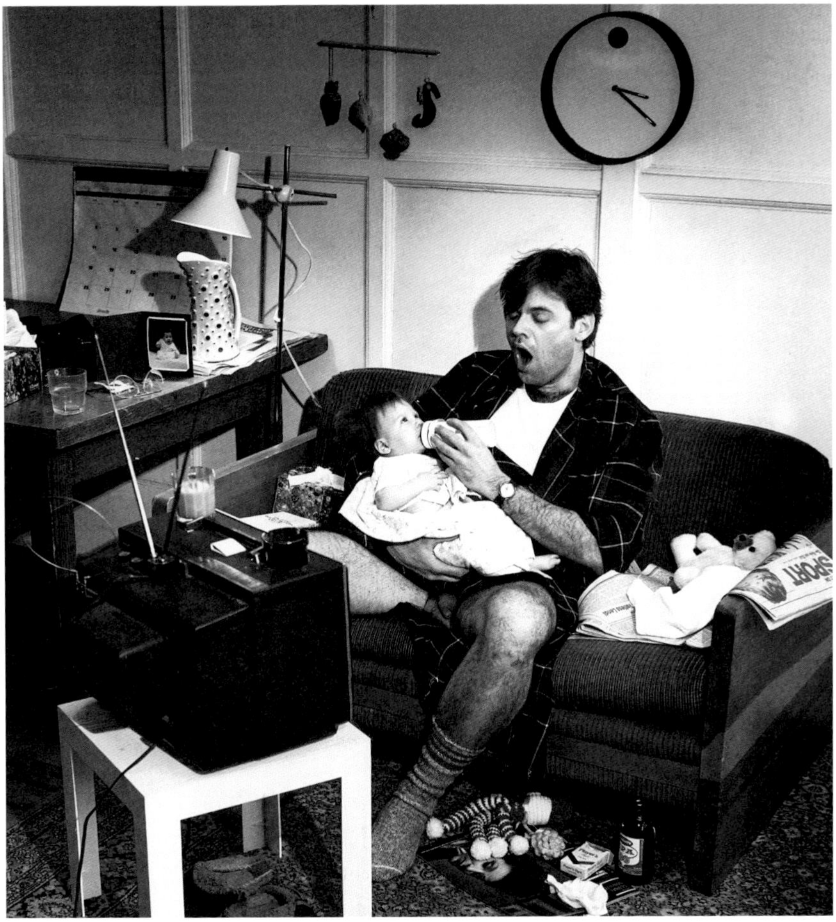

Rude Awakening, 1982

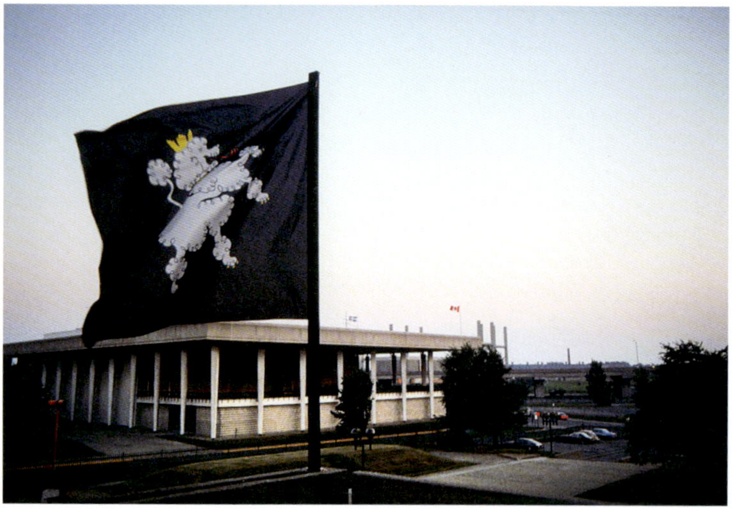

<u>Ghent Flag</u>, 1984

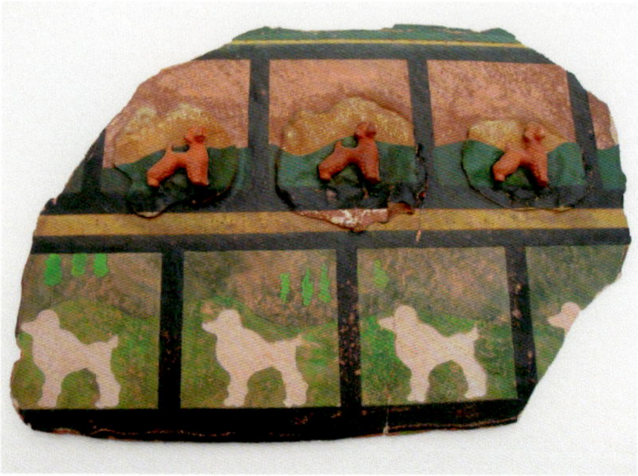

<u>Tuscany Poodles–Fragment With Trees</u>, 1984

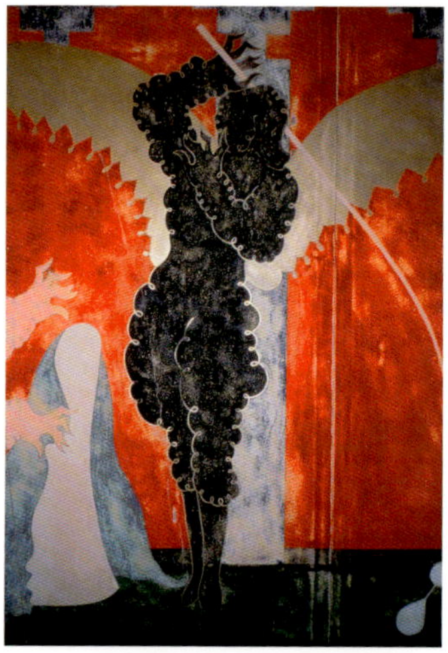

<u>The Unveiling of the Cornucopia: A Mural Fragment from the Room of the Unknown Function in the Villa dei Misteri of the 1984 Miss General Idea Pavillion</u>, 1982 (detail)

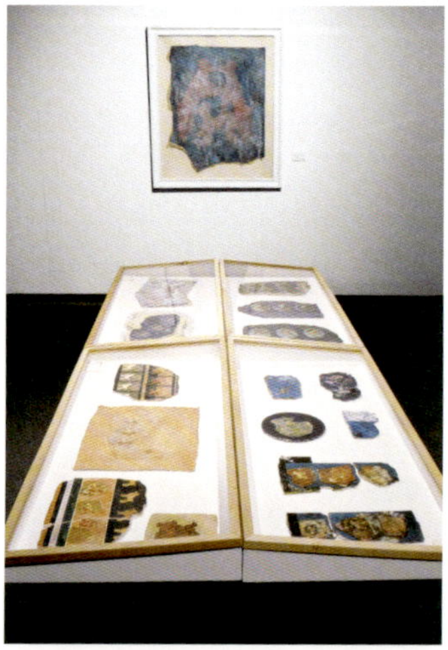

<u>Pavillion Poodle Fragments</u>, 1983–1984

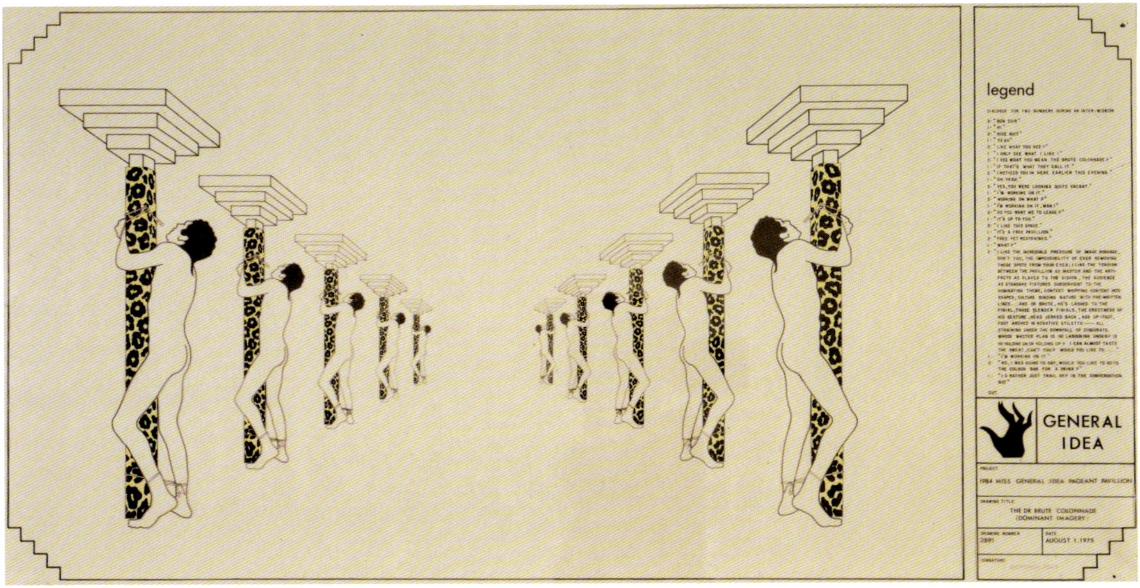

The Dr. Brute Colonnade (Dominant Imagery), 1975

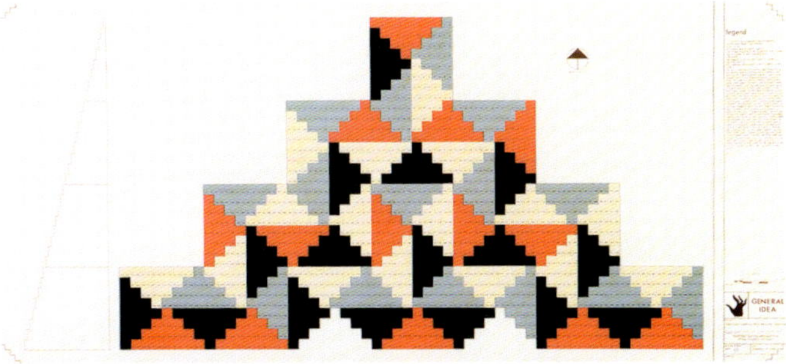

Proposed Seating Arrangement (Form Follows Fiction), 1975

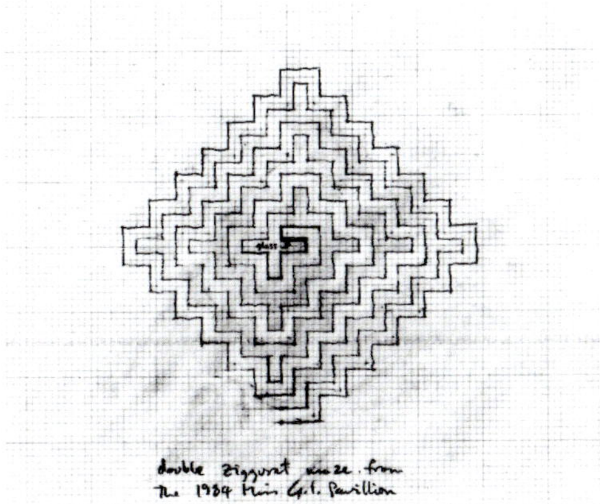

Double Ziggurat Maze from the 1984 Miss General Idea Pavillion, 1984–1985

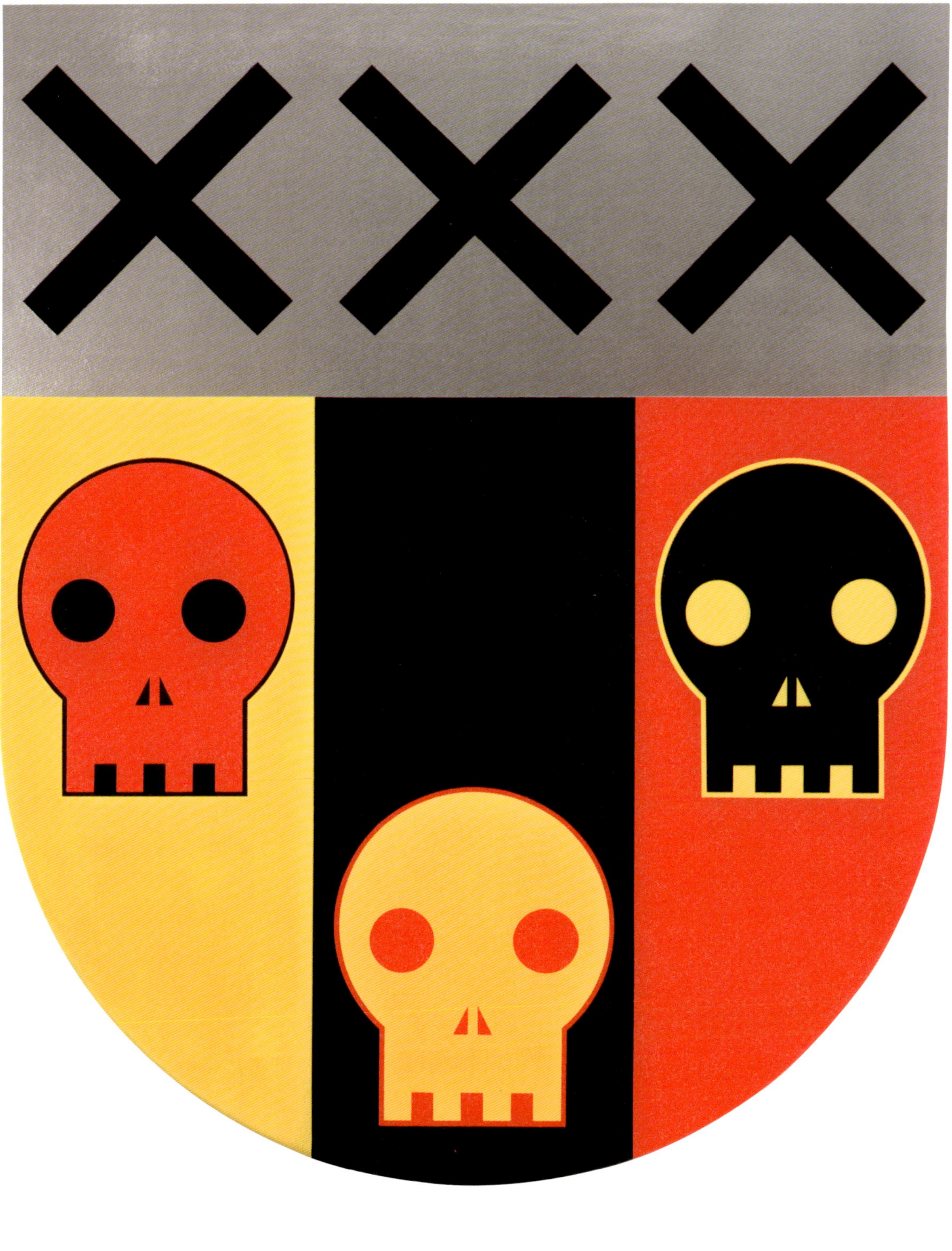

Post Mortem, 1985

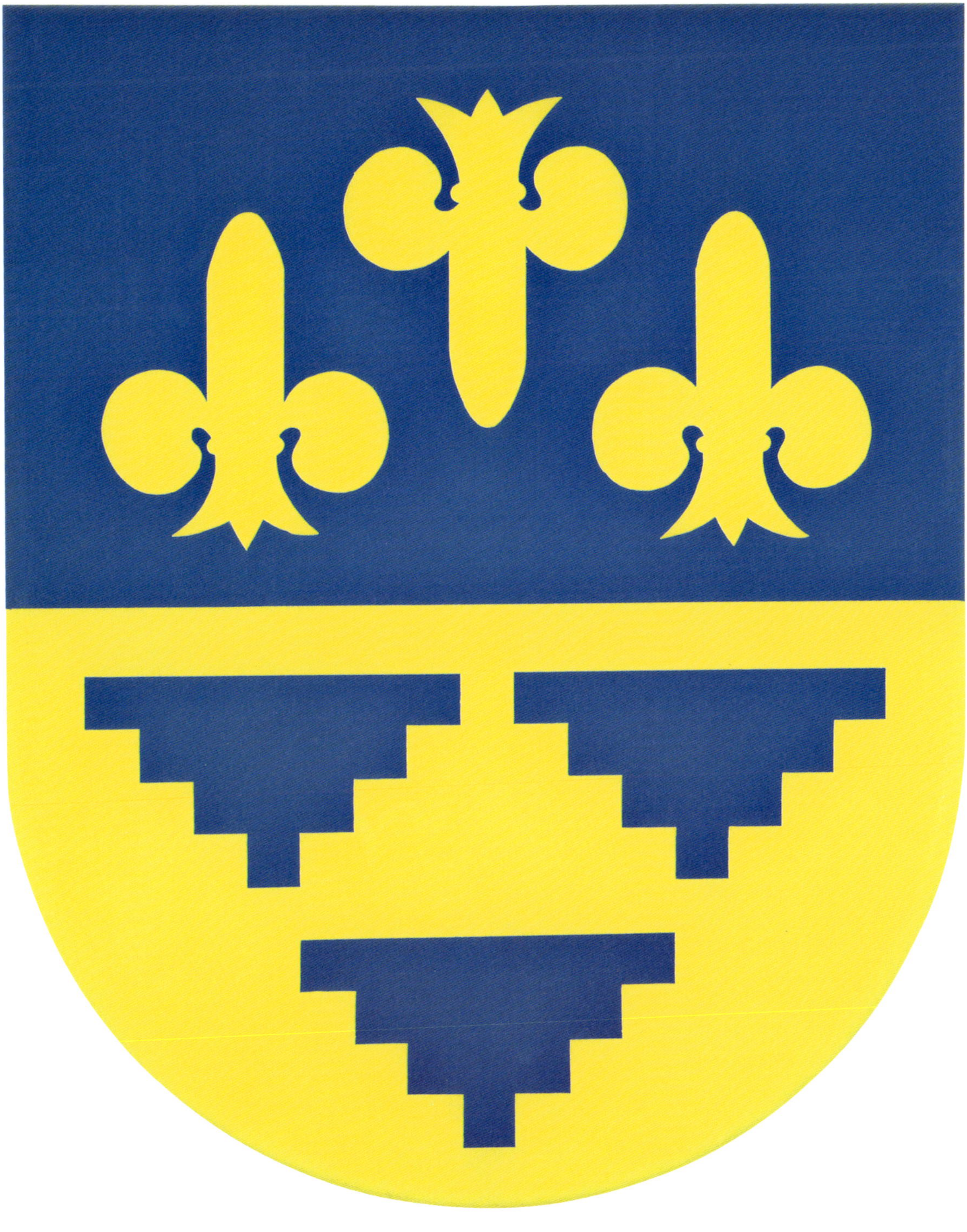

Passion Over Reason, 1986

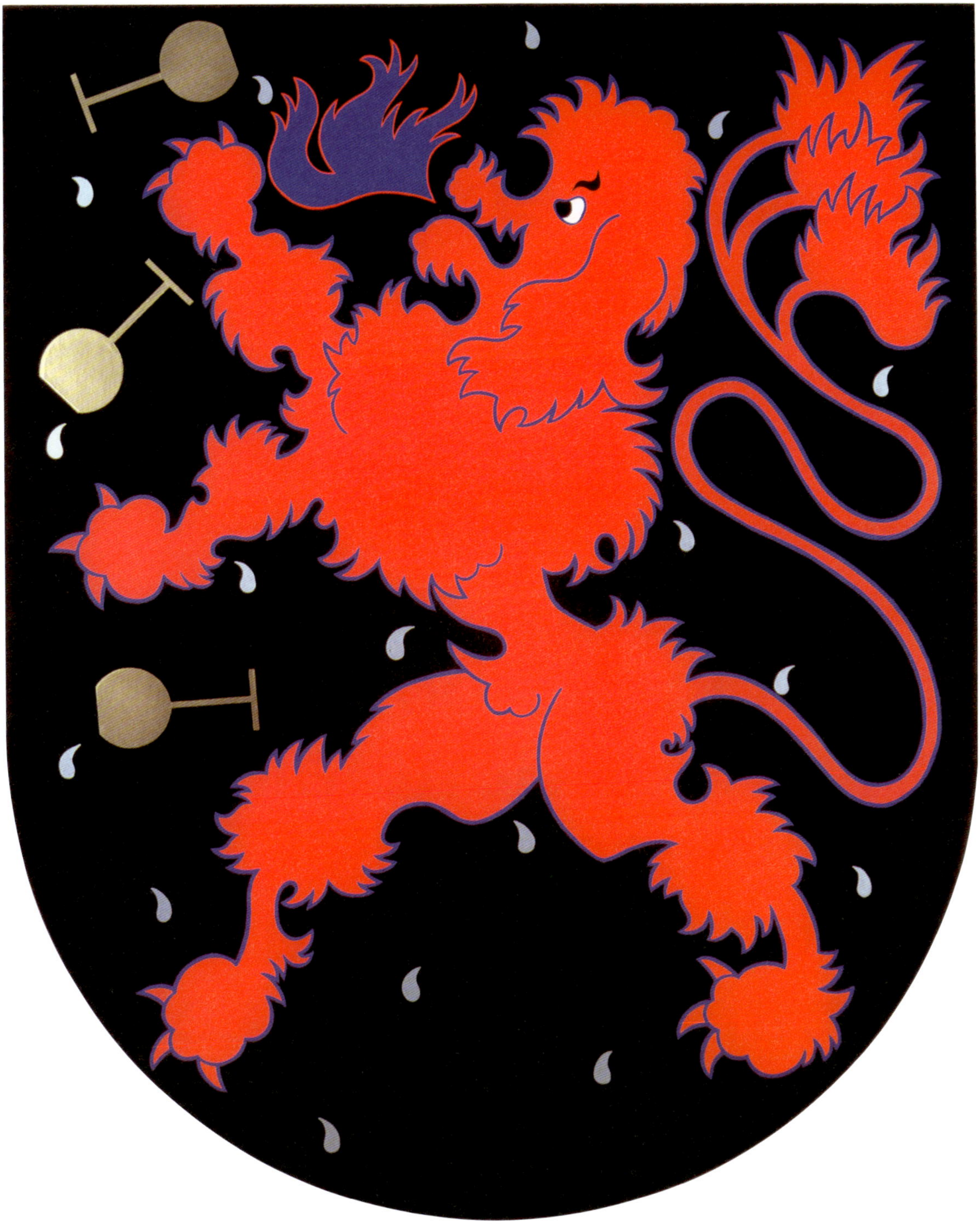

<u>The Juggler</u>, 1985

Gender "Trouple"[1]

Elisabeth Lebovici

Too obvious? Not general enough? Or maybe both? The theme of sex at work, that is in the body of work of General Idea, presents us indeed with such a dilemma: you can feel it everywhere without being able to pin it down anywhere. Even the spring of 1982 issue of *FILE Megazine*, entitled *X Ray Sex*—a tribute, were it not for the missing "p," to the punk group X Ray Spex?—is not particularly more sexual than the other issues despite the fact it includes a long mention of Pierre Molinier and nudes by Les Krims in addition to photographs by Cindy Sherman and a short story of erotic musing by Salvador Dalí; in the same vein, the *Special Transgressions* issue of the *Megazine*, published in the autumn of 1979, is somewhat more sexual. However, there is no actual fucking going on in the images. The only series of explicit fornication is *Mondo Cane Kama Sutra* (1984), but sexuality could never amount to mechanic and canine combinations. For isn't that obsession—which surely stems from a "dirty mind" inclined to dig up sex even where there seems to be none—the willful product of the general idea behind General Idea? The sexual figure of the triangle, the threesome, the couple of three men, or rather, as I would prefer to call it from here on, the "trouple," produces an instant rupture with the geometry of patriarchal representations. The trouple as a war machine against the heterosexual couple, the nuclear family, and the Oedipal configuration. It is written on one of the *Showcards*, the conceptual tools—files, index cards—of GI's propositions: "Felix: 'The triangle is an Oedipal reference: the equilateral stability of General Idea replaces the structural rigidity of the family triangle.'"[2]

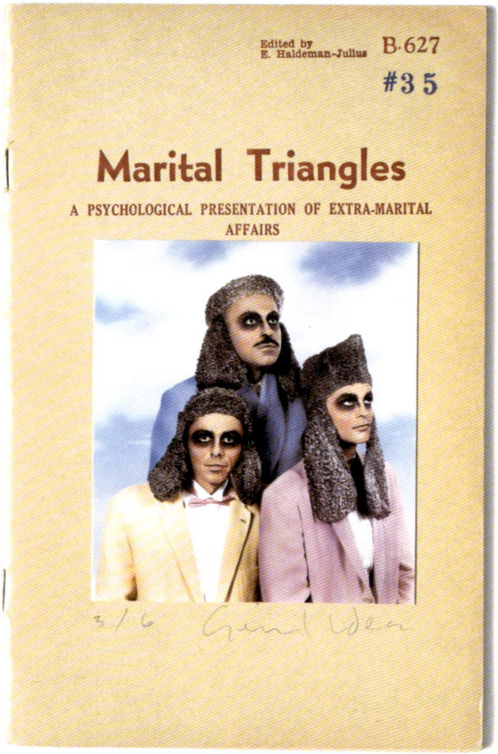

Marital Triangles: A Psychological Presentation of Extra-Marital Affairs, 1984

General Idea is basically this: the oblique course of a *Menage A Trois*, as evoked in their pamphlet-edition (for Lucio Amelio in 1978), leading to a critical and ironical look into the binarity of domestic sexual associations—all of them, up to and including homosexual couples. In short, an oblique course *is worth more than two in the bush*.

That was how General Idea was formed as a triangle, beckoning us to trouple it in its unity—hasn't GI often declared being a single body, a single product, a single trademark giving up all kinds of individual property?—and its fellow-feeling shape: "Three heads are better" than two, which are better than one, if you want to put domestic life in a state of flux. The equilateral triangle is certainly a complete figure, yet it requires a "fourth element"[3] to play with as GI immediately points out: the indication of a fourth player then also implies an empty space. So, the triangle is both closed and open.

A Transcanada Art Organ

FILE

87 Yonge Street, Toronto 1

"The Emit of our File"

JUN 5 1972

The Orgasm Renewal Project was performed for General Idea by A.A. Bronson, January 1, 1971 to January 31, 1972. Partial documentation is reproduced below. Further documentation may be found in the collection of General Idea, 87 Yonge Street, Toronto 1, Ont.

Orgasm occurred at 10:07 p.m., January 1st, 1971 and was repeated
at 10:25 p.m., January 1st, 1972.
Orgasm occurred at 12:15 p.m., January 2nd, 1971 and was repeated
at 12:20 p.m., January 2nd, 1972.
Orgasm occurred at 3:00 a.m., January 3rd, 1971 and was repeated
at 3:05 a.m., January 3rd, 1972.
Orgasm occurred at 1:30 a.m., January 4th, 1971 and was repeated
at 1:40 p.m., January 4th, 1972.
Orgasm occurred at 12:05 p.m., January 7th, 1971 and was repeated
at 1:47 p.m., January 7th, 1972.
Orgasm occurred at 4:30 a.m., January 9th, 1971 and was repeated
at 4:50 a.m., January 9th, 1972.
Orgasm occurred at 11:15 a.m., January 10th, 1971 and was repeated
at 11:10 a.m., January 10th, 1972.
Orgasm occurred at 4:00 p.m., January 15th, 1971 and was repeated
at 4:06 p.m., January 15th, 1972.
Orgasm occurred at 10:45 a.m., January 16th, 1971 and was repeated
at 10:57 a.m., January 16th, 1972.
Orgasm occurred at 12:05 p.m., January 18th, 1971 and was repeated
at 11:50 a.m., January 18th, 1972.
Orgasm occurred at 5:45 p.m,, January 18th, 1971 and was repeated
at 5:45 p.m., January 18th, 1972.
Orgasm occurred at 3:00 a.m., January 23rd, 1971 and was not repeated.
Orgasm occurred at 12:30 p.m., January 23rd, 1971 and was repeated
at 1:00 p.m., January 23rd, 1972.
Orgasm occurred at 4:30 p.m., January 26th, 1971 and was not repeated.
Orgasm occurred at 11:45 a.m., January 28th, 1971 and was repeated
at 11:35 a.m., January 28th, 1972.
Orgasm occurred at 12:00 noon, January 28th, 1971 and was repeated
at 11:50 a.m., January 28th, 1972.

PRESS RELEASE

Press Release–Orgasm Renewal Project, 1972

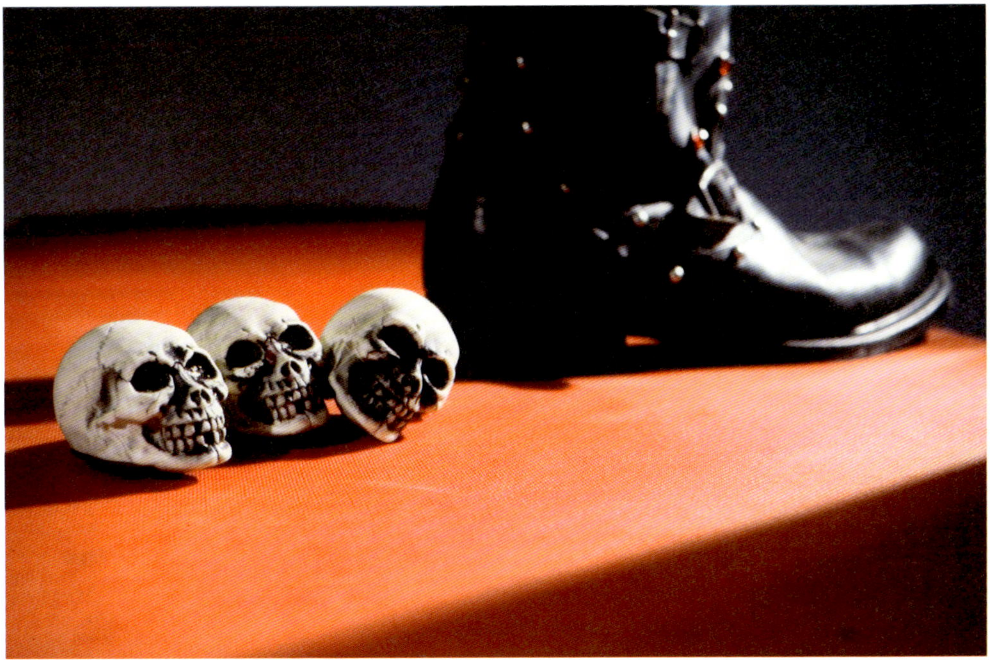

"Three Heads are Better," 1978

The notion of couple, or of trouple and plurality, as artist collectives, has become popular, notably thanks to Gilbert & George, Eva and Adèle, Claude Cahun and Marcel Moore, Jugnet-Clairet, Claire Fontaine, Reena Spauling, Chto Delat?, Société Réaliste, and many more society signs and acronyms. Their intimacy always seems a bit shady. Pierre Trividic and Patrick Mario Bernard, joint author of the films *Ceci est une pipe* (2000) and *Dancing* (2003), have never stopped stating that their cinematic intimacy—sexual or not—has naturally nothing to do with their private lives. The same was true of the three members of GI, whose oeuvre never specified the exact nature of their relationship to each other. Their name, General Idea, took into account both the theatralization implied by self-presentation in art and the deflating connotation carried by the term. As in all GI gestures, which claim responsibility both for doing and undoing, for constructing and destroying, the act of baptizing, that is to say the imposing of a name, simultaneously produced anonymity. In France, you have General Society

(Société Générale[4]). In Canada, you have General Idea (Idée Générale) and, as Jean-Jacques Rousseau would have put it: "General ideas are at the source of men's greatest mistakes."[5] GI under the sign of aberration.

Until the mid-1980s, General Idea's sexuality had not become apparent in a public way: neither in the artistic press, which "never referred to our sexuality, so we had to make it more and more explicit"[6]; nor in homosexual magazines, which perhaps did not consider them gay enough from an ideological point of view. In the interview presented in this book, General Idea emphasizes its indifference, rather than its distance or proximity, toward "gay art" and "homosexual artists" during the 1970s. We did not find it interesting at all, says GI: no more and no less interesting than defining yourself as a Canadian artist, "which was worse than being gay."[7] So renunciation seems to have been reciprocal. However, according to the posthumous version AA Bronson gives nowadays, the formation of the very triangle of GI in 1969 constituted a homosexual affirmation for all three members of the group. Felix, he points out, was not a homosexual yet, Jorge "knew it" at the age of 8, while AA himself made no secret of his multiple sexuality: "I slept with both men and women, then stopped sleeping with women. I have only done it with men ever since and I never hid it."[8]

To talk about sex was primarily to refer to life—GI's sexual life—not so much in terms of the innermost recesses of their bed and of who was sleeping with whom (in the singular and in the plural forms), but rather with a view to the formulation of a domestic machine that would go against binarities—and even against the—equally binary—logic of the motives of sexual liberation and gender regulation, notably active within protestant capitalism. It may be that life in the commune before GI's creation, its dynamic of existence, which introduced itself in the end of the 1960s in the United States and Canada (where numerous draft dodgers of the Vietnam War had found refuge), had left its alternative and libertarian trace. Militarization, homeland, liberal education, and the bourgeois family were all globally rejected by the political philosophy of those communities that, at the same time, nourished a keen interest in all alternative sexualities. Didn't the sexual radicalism of the "commune" have its roots just as much in the work of Walt Whitman as in that of Charles Fourier, even though the former had been accused of setting himself up as an enemy of free love in his editorials? (His poems rather state the contrary.) In any case, as far as Fourier is concerned, the notion that "association" participated in the foundation of all social formations included the idea of the body in a state of harmony where all sexual practices that take place by common consent have to be accepted and supported as expressions of human diversity. In its radical and anti-patriarchal vocation, the "idea" of General Idea stemmed both from a specifically homosexual affirmation and a free association of the "communes" as abolishing private property, including that of a private male or female partner. Moreover, according to AA Bronson,[9] the trouple initially experienced other patterns of life in common, for instance among seven or eight people, before the day that AA—or another one of them—cried out: "we should keep doing this for the rest of our lives,"[10] and before forming a triangle, which in 1969 assumed the name General Idea. They kept doing this for the rest of their lives indeed, yet they never let themselves settle down in a definitive way. It is of interest that GI had at first vowed to stay together at least until 1984. When you give birth to yourself, you also need to set a completion date; which was actually prolonged by ten years; General Idea eventually stopped existing when Jorge and Felix died of AIDS in 1994.

But let us go back to the "erotic year": 1969 is also the year of the Stonewall Revolt in New York, which supplies an origin myth to gay and lesbian movements all around the world and which numerous LGBT Prides celebrate each year, universalizing a debate "where white gays occupy all available space."[11]

The first Canadian Gay Pride took place in 1973, a time when the formation of numerous gay and lesbian organizations on the one hand and police raids in bars and saunas where homosexuals hung out on the other hand produced a polarity which shaped the history of homosexuality in the 1970s. Both in Montreal and Toronto, the police claimed there was a link between gay baths, organized crime, and—according to

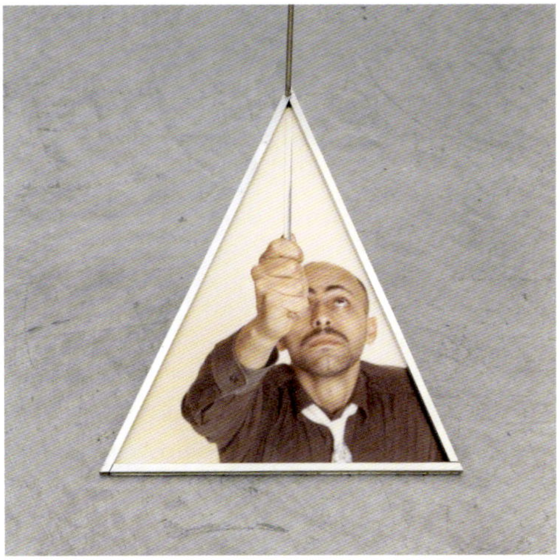

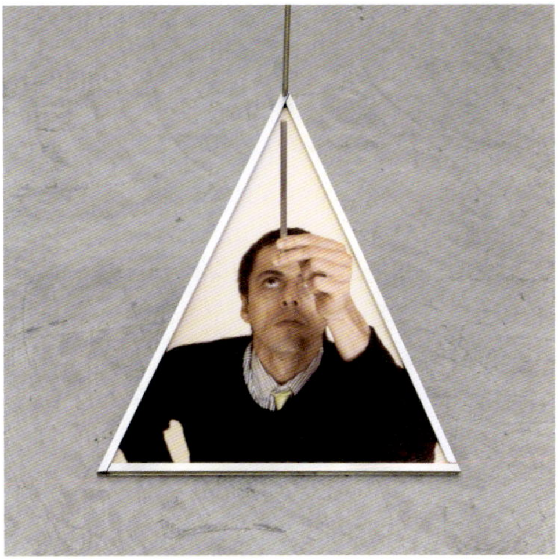

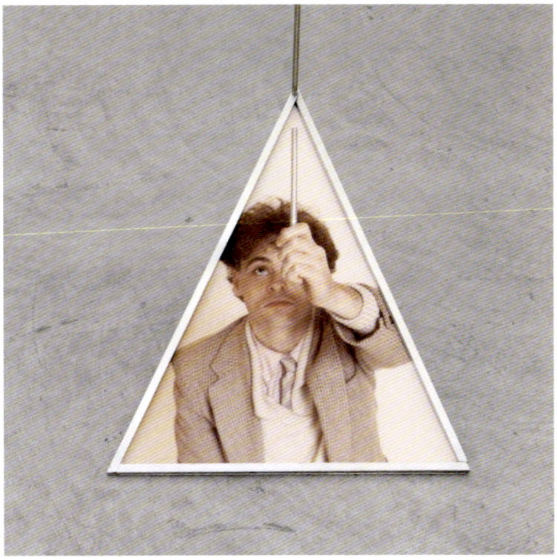

Playing the Triangle, 1979 (details)

General Idea's Dominant Dream, 1978 (detail)

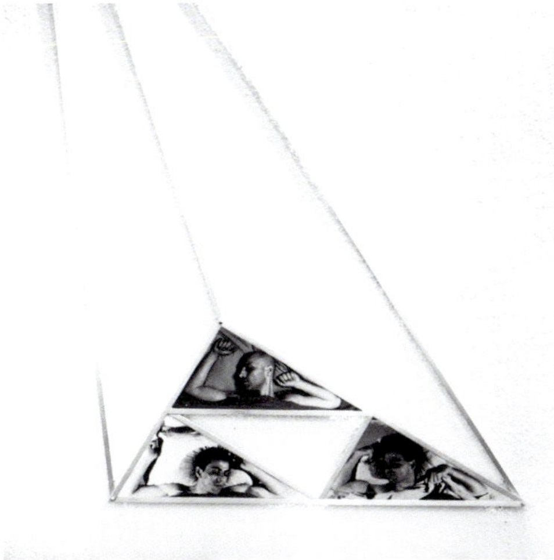

their allegations—trafficking in drugs and prostitution. They then publicly disclosed the names of all those who had been arrested. Not to mention that by the end of the 1970s claims concerning fundamental homosexual rights—which would be quite easily obtained once Canada was given its own Constitution in 1983—and the debate on pornography notably within feminist and/or lesbian movements were the target of religious fundamentalism and social conservatism. The arrival of activist homophobe Anita Bryant sparked off protests as she crusaded against lesbian and gay rights by highlighting the menace of homosexual recruitment among the youths to the eyes of Christian families.

It is at that time that General Idea got involved with the homosexual magazine *The Body Politic*, published from 1971 to 1987. The magazine never printed much on GI,[12] even though they knew the trouple and some of the journalists had been or were their lovers. The editorial team for instance turned down AA's text on William Burroughs, all the same, on the basis of it being "too personal."[13] But when in 1979, following the publication of issue 39 of *The Body Politic* containing Gerald Hannon's article "Men Loving Boys Loving Men"[14] the police searched Jorge Zontal's and many other subscribers' houses, and the threat of a costly trial, which eventually went on until 1983, was hanging over their heads, GI did a series of performance art events,[15] alongside other groups such as the Clichettes, numerous mentions of which are to be found in *FILE* and notably in the gossip pages of the *Megazine*, "BZZZZ BZZZZ BZZZZ." Their performance *An Anatomy of Censorship* showed images of buttocks, torsos, and cocks, inserted in squares, circles, or triangles accompanied by these words: "Watch the cock arise from the Oedipal triangle / See it as it mounts the pyramid / Listen to the little dictator / Put yourself in his hands and let your pleasure / be measured against the graduated cock."[16] Tumescent geometry and arithmetic.

In 1981, GI produced *Ruins of the Silver Bar*, a mountain of silver detritus in a waste collection site, with this comment: "We loved the idea that three faggots decorated a mass of litter in silver." In 1985, *The Body Politic* published "Getting the General Idea: Creation of Three Gay Artists." Though there had never been any doubt about the gay attitude of the three artists, that of the triangle, the imaginary place where art was produced and affected life, had just attained public life. "Our sensibility had always been very gay," adds GI, "but it is true that it took us a while to come out of the closet."[17]

In the meantime, it is the notion of camp that makes most sense for GI. AA Bronson retrospectively relates that the trouple read and commented Susan Sontag's *Notes on "Camp"* published in 1964. Incidentally, some subtle distinctions notwithstanding, the American essayist makes an explicit link between "Camp sensibility" (GI used the word sensibility a lot) and homosexuality: a point in her work that would later be fiercely criticized. But the permanent artificiality, derision, and pronounced favoring of aestheticism that Sontag connected to a kind of disengagement, or at least to an apolitical position, suggested stereotypes that GI would make the most of.

The same holds true for Rome, decadence, the Roman world, etc.: *Dr. Brute*

Colonnade (1975) puts forward the architectural drawing of a palace whose columns creates a mise-en-abyme perspective. All of them have reversed ziggurat-shaped capitals and leopard-patterned pillars with which, bound hand and foot as if in an embrace, naked young people mate—a vision repeated to satiety. It was indeed no accident that Derek Jarman's film *Sebastiane*, the erotic story of Saint Sebastian's martyrdom entirely acted in Latin and subtitled in English, was made in the same period (1976). The Roman Empire came to the fore as the site of a sexuality widely regarded as excluded: when 19th-century Western museums included archaeological findings in order to excite the historical imagination of the public, the erotic scenes were removed on the pretext that they could have shocked women and children, who had henceforth become part of the universalist calling of those establishments. Thus, in the conception of the museum we have inherited from the 19th century, sexual representations have been censored as pornographic, while, at the same time, pornography opposes the conservative, inclusive, and homogeneous mission that prevailed during the birth of the bourgeois museum. In GI's work, as in Keith Haring's for that matter, radiant babies irradiate sex (*Baby Makes 3*, 1984) reverting to the polymorphous perversity of their beginning.

Within the retroactive approach adopted by GI in all its operations ("FILE is Life in retrospect"), pornographic reference was inserted in archeological fragments. Toward 1982, GI designed the paneling of its Villa of Mysteries using the

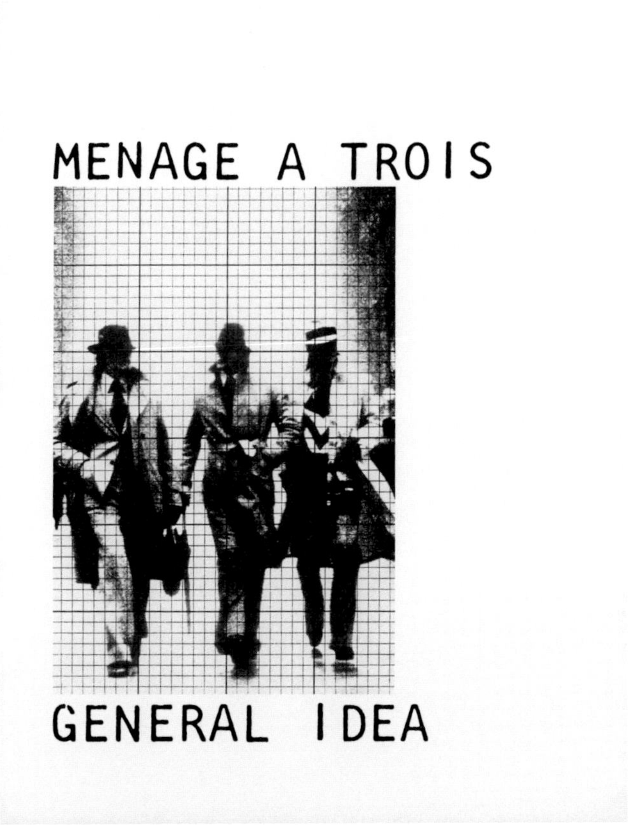

Menage A Trois, 1978

GENERAL IDEA,
87 YONGE ST.,
TORONTO,CANADA.

Please record your orgasms on the enclosed chart for one month and return to GENERAL IDEA. Master charts will be made, indicating distribution and frequency patterns and applying these to non-related maps, charts, graphs. New fields of unforeseen information are thus set up. If you wish further documentation of this project, please enclose your name and address with the chart.

Orgasm Energy Chart, 1970

commonplace Dionysian themes of traditional iconography. Except for the fact that all characters, major and minor, had become poodles. Thus, the supposed restitution of a wall fragment painted in watery blue depicted three poodles sodomizing each other (*Tableau Vivant, Natura Morta*, 1983) while *Eau d'Artifice* shows a combination of several "sandwiched" poodles fornicating. The title of the painting is a direct reference to Kenneth Anger's film of the same name (1953), shot in the gardens of the Villa d'Este in Tivoli. The camera follows the nocturnal promenade of a personage whose gender is unclear while the body of water never stops undergoing endless metamorphoses: a transformation of water into fire and of fire into cum[18] as an alternative to Marcel Duchamp's *Eau de Voilette (Belle Haleine)* (1923)?

In the sex issue of *FILE Megazine* labeled "X Ray Sex" (no. 3, vol. 3, 1982), the centerfold, as if in *Playboy* magazine, is dedicated to a drawing of the Three Graces: *Three Graces: Mural Fragment from the Room of the Unknown Function in the Villa dei Misteri of the 1984 Miss General Idea Pavillion*. On a Coca-Cola red ground placed between two friezes, the frizzy outlines of three canine personages with minuet dancers' legs perfectly imitate the group Canova immortalized in his sculpture, but slightly transformed, as the leg of one of the poodles is half up in the air (a trademark position in GI's work); one of them is holding a cornucopia, pouring white energy, while the other is holding the moon. The painting *Three Graces* (1982) takes up the same figure, this time on a panel made of wood planks painted in violet—the cornucopia held by the paw of one of the three poodles looking, in this case, much more like a penis gushing out large quantities of fluid. Another drawing followed in the same *FILE* issue: a working drawing in which one of the canine personages holds a long rod, the second one points at a veiled shape and the remaining visible part of the third carries a tray of cocktail glasses while several skulls serve as a frieze. This is *The Unveiling of the Cornucopia*: an unveiling which is not unveiled, which strips bare the desire rather than the interpretation typically at work in every research and thus makes us reconsider the way we understand artistic practices.

Allusions, rather than the illusion of a unique truth, swarm in GI's work: from the liquid moustache of *Nazi Milk* (1979) to the *Test Tube*(s) (from 1979 onward) and even the photographs that both decorate and compose the *Colour Bar Lounge* (1979);

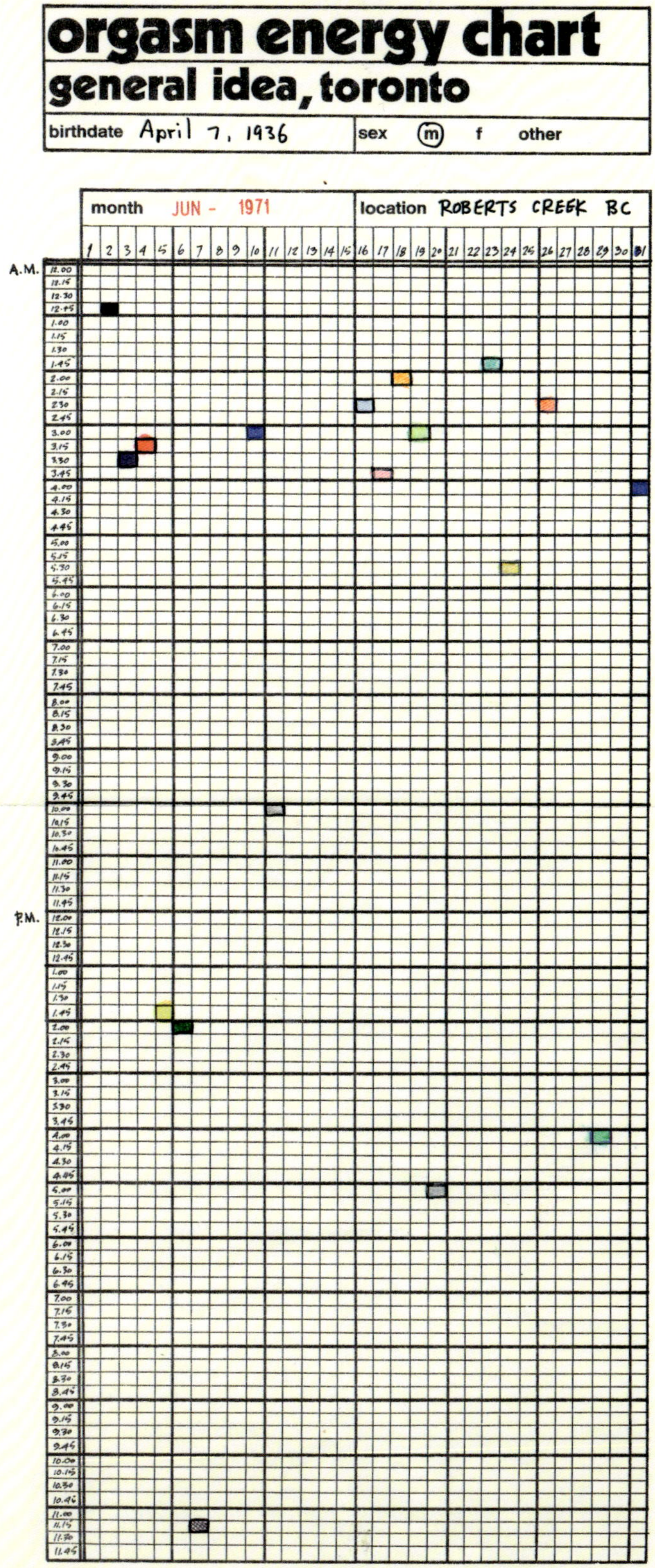

Orgasm Energy Chart, 1970–1971

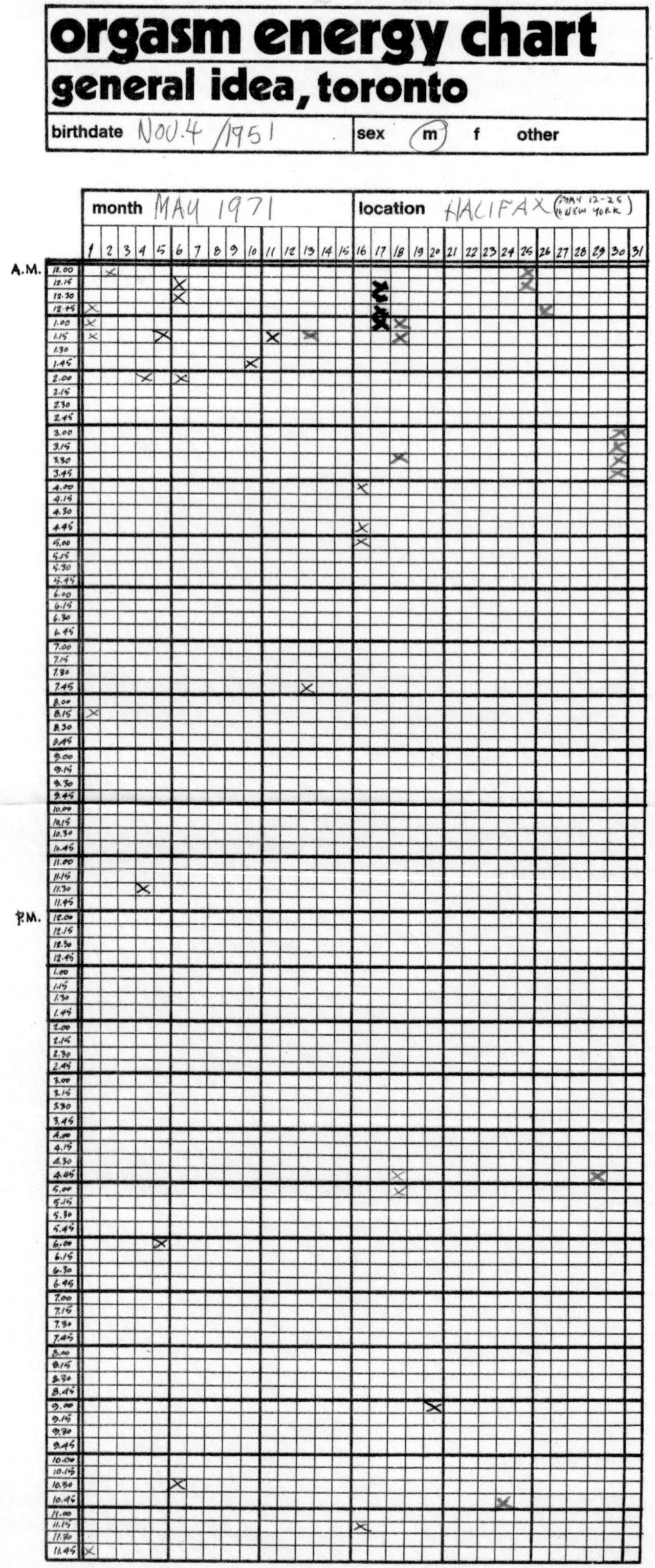

Orgasm Energy Chart, 1970–1971

from the shape of the stiletto heel to the green-red-blue of the *Infe©ted* (1990–1994), a code of recognition was being developed—similar to the color-coded bandannas which, worn in the right or left back pocket, participated in gay seduction hinting at such or such practice. "So, it became a game to create artworks which *would make* the Press speak of us as gay."[19] The ten paintings of *Mondo Cane Kama Sutra* could be considered a canine version of "mondo," a kind of amateur movie of little horrors, which made its first appearance with *Mondo Cane* in 1962. That Italian film combined diverse, short, fictional or documentary sequences that were depersonalized, disconnected, and sensationalist, and accompanied by a pontificating voice-over. But, in the paintings, the horror probably lies in the ever so present in the 1980s anxiety of the displacement of the body as biological unity that this *Kama Sutra* assents to. At the dawn of a new millennium, bodies as science objects are neither exterior to nor separable from the techno-scientific discourse that transcodes and modifies them. Donna Haraway drove that point home when she published *A Cyborg Manifesto* in 1985: she considered interspecies relations to re-conceptualize scientific and epistemological models.

In GI's work, there are transvestite as well as transgender elements, transpositions from one species to another, from canine to human and reciprocally: the line of demarcation is reduced to a trace. That is quite reminiscent of what Haraway accomplishes[20] when she looks into domestic interaction and the kind of mutual curiosity which makes dogs, cats, birds, dolphins, and even landscapes and technology become our pets.

Some dogs seem to have been produced for the single purpose of serving as pets and are endowed with a kind of artificiality which has very little to do with the wildness of certain other dogs—just like with humans, actually. "There is no assured happy or unhappy ending—socially, ecologically, or scientifically. There is only the chance for getting on together with some grace,"[21]

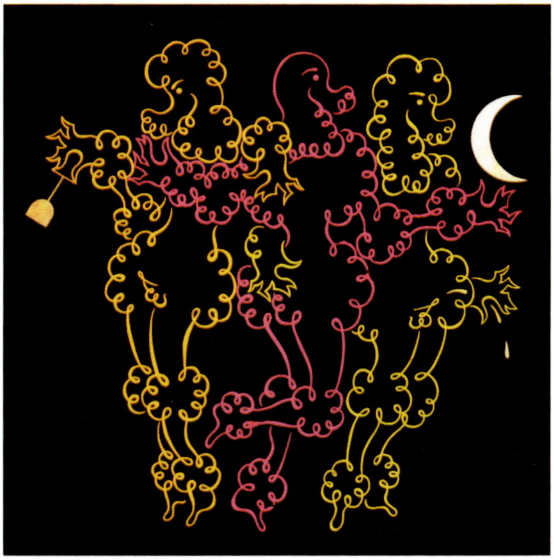
Process of Elimination, 1988–1991

writes Haraway. Thus, the figurations of the poodles—suggestive of the stereotype of the sophisticated grooming of exhibition poodles and their likeness to the gay hairdresser—and the representations of GI *as* poodles interrelate. *P Is For Poodle* (1983) is one of the self-portraits in which GI makes "a trinity of glamorous guys, guys mucho garrulous, gallantly groovy and très gay, an artistic ménage à trois"[22] for the future. Dressed up in blue, yellow, and pink dinner jackets respectively, they all have extravagant smoky eyes and long-eared, frizzy fur hats.

After the emergence of the AIDS epidemic, gay discourse became a necessity. Especially in the United States, where, as it's often been said, General Idea used the acronym AIDS and spread it like a virus long before the American President ever mentioned the word. Ever since Rock Hudson, it has frequently been noted that the revelation process of one's seropositivity is often tightly linked to the process of "coming out"; of an affirmation of one's sexual orientation.

But I would never allow myself to finish the present essay without alluding to—even though it might be seen as anachronistic—"another moment in which the countercultural map was perhaps a bit queerer, which is to say more expansive and including of various structures of feeling and habits of being that the relatively restrictive categories of gay and lesbian identities are incapable of catching"[23]: the moment of never-ending, unfinished, romantic, and pre-identity projects; of the queer archives that theoreticians such as Gavin Butt[24] and José Esteban Muñoz have described. Ray Johnson's work belongs there. He was the president of the very enigmatic New York Correspondence School—Johnson used both "correspondence" and "correspondance" to signify "pregnant similarities that dance."[25] Though he only traveled outside the United States twice, he still had numerous contacts with Canadian artist groups such as Image

<u>Evidence of Body Binding</u>, 1971–1972

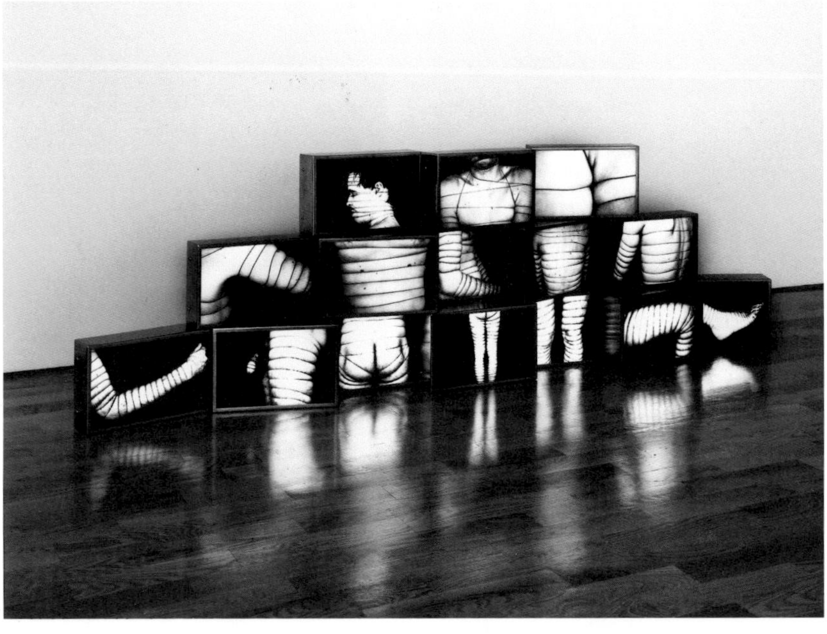

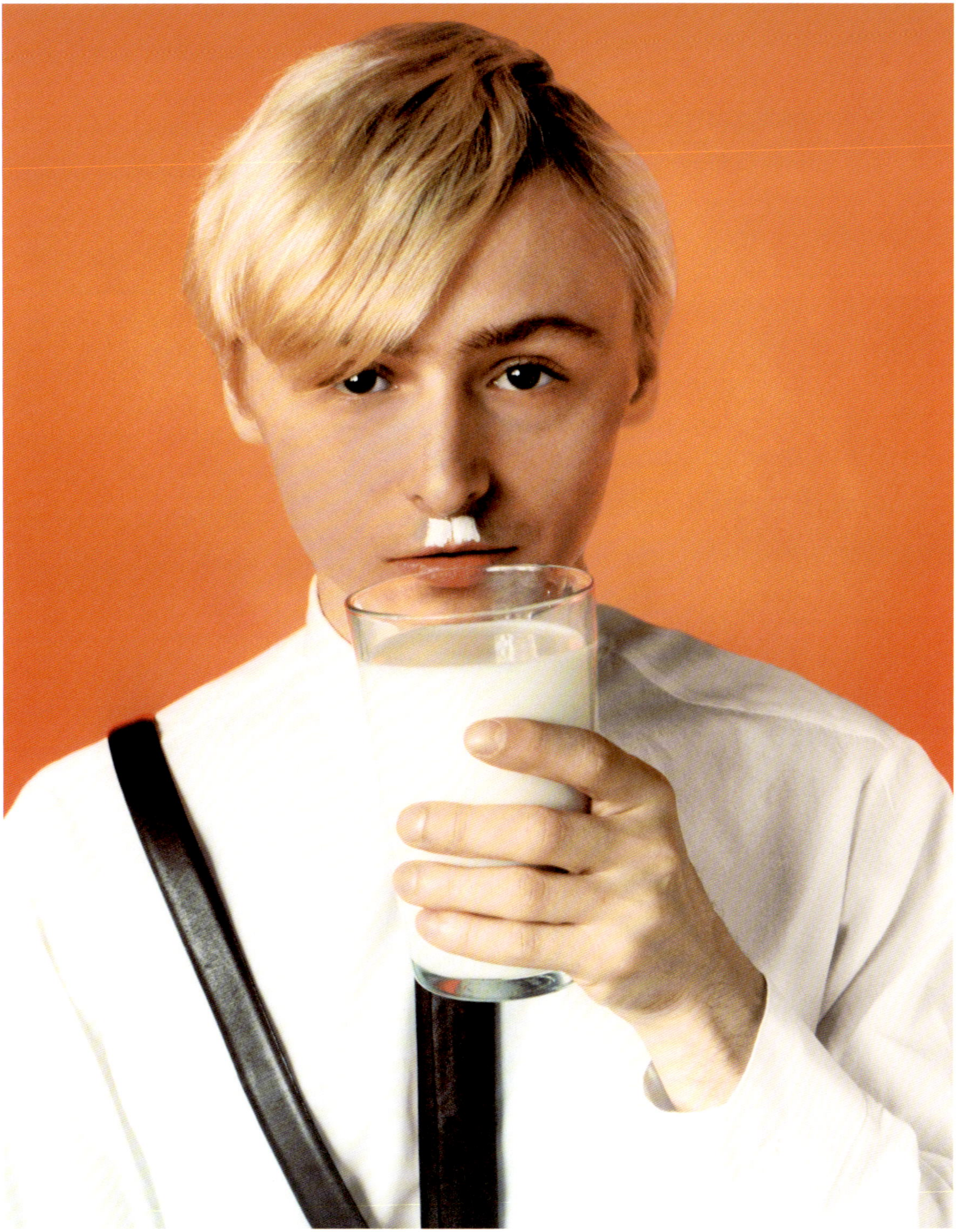

Nazi Milk, 1979–1990

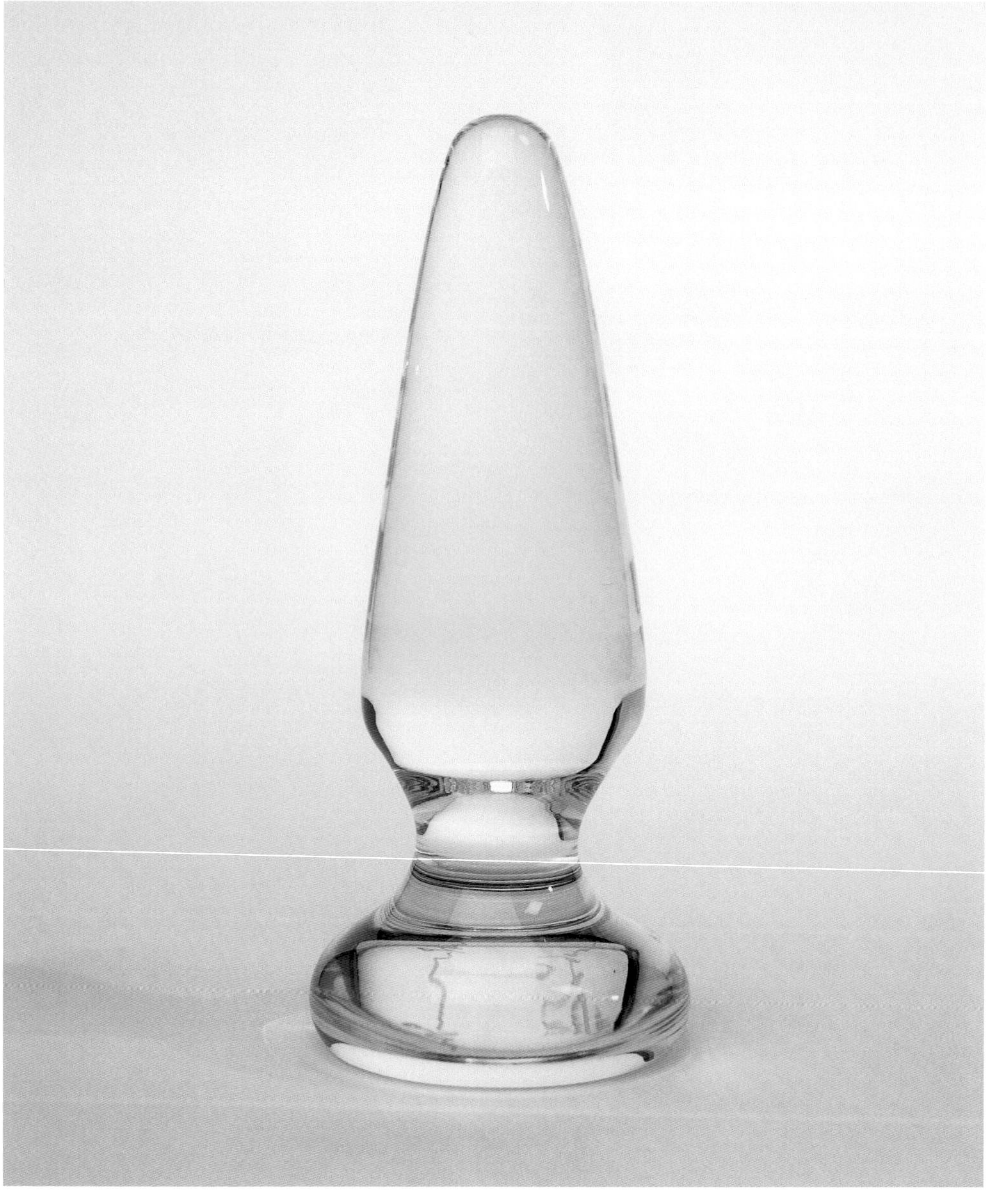

Dick All, 1993–2001

Elisabeth Lebovici

Bank (Michael Morris, Vincent Trasov), the New York Cores Sponge Dance School of Vancouver, Dr. and Lady Brute (Eric Metcalfe, Kate Craig), Anna Banana, and General Idea whom Ray Johnson met in Toronto. Their meeting was the start of an enduring relationship as GI would regularly meet up with Ray Johnson in New York and would become his correspondent, bringing him into contact with a lot of artists such as Luke Dowd, also a friend of Muñoz who serves as inspiration to the present essay ("name dropping" becomes important as far as seduction and networking go). AA Bronson has recently related how in 1973 Ray Johnson offered him his first visit to the Piers, the disused docks of Manhattan's west coast, a highly sexualized meeting place. "Frankly the tour from Ray was better than anything and any big jumbo of public sex," comments AA, who came back as many times as possible, since "many times always makes better sex."[26]

And of course, GI and Ray Johnson were connected by postal sendings: since its first issue, *FILE* included Ray Johnson's letters ("dear VILE," starts the first of them) and each *Megazine* received his invitations (for instance, to the Paloma Picasso Club) and projects which implicated the exchange of bodily evacuations: shit, nail clippings, and spit (*New York Correspondence School Spit for Dadaland*, including their answer: *General Idea Split for Ray Johnson*).

Ray Johnson (1927–1995) was the elegant maker of an art (anti)system of fine resemblances, the system of an art known as mail art or postal art, but which actually celebrated the end of the postal era, opening up, on the contrary, to a thinking of communication. As art historian Ina Blom subtly indicated, there was a passage from postal art to "post" art.[27] Posting letter fragments, collages, names that can be added to a person's image; sending out fan club mailing to a community based on affinities among known and unknown recipients, created a social space that belonged to art. That social space was modeled on the interplay between affinities, names, buzz, nasty remarks, and dissonance. Real or fictional, the reunions of the New York

Bondage, 1987

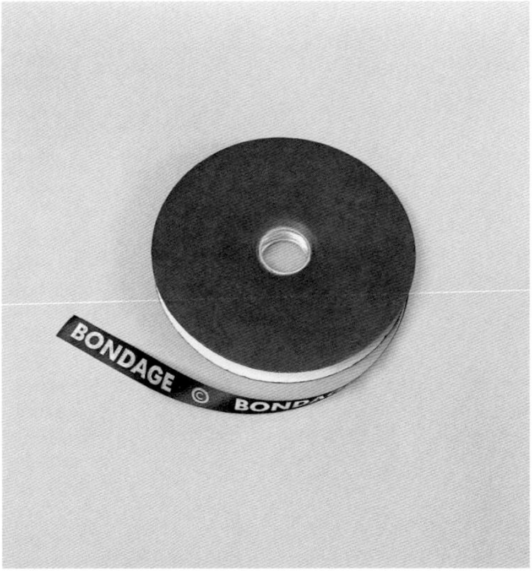

Correspondence School—a "private, secret society without rules" rereading the history of art ("the New York School") through mail-order methods—showed shady motives such as, for instance, the reunion of a network of proper nouns, meticulously arranged by Johnson, which were an occasion for a vertigo of permutations, invitations, and erotic openings. Johnson opened up the world to coded "postal connections" which fed, as Muñoz suggests, not only on sexual experimentation but equally or, better yet, mostly on an experimentation of the world. It is not a trivial matter that this queer sociality drive was also to be found in *FILE*, which was not only LIFE "in retrospect"—a confusion of dates that contemporary theory would perceive as "a queering of temporality"—but also the site of the archive. That is the very meaning of the English word "file": registration, filing, documentation.

We could thus suggest that General Idea's conceptual art is impregnated with sexual politics. Not only in the representation of the connection, calculated by the *Orgasm Energy Chart* (1970): a graph resulting from answers to a questionnaire aiming at listing your orgasms during a month according to your birth date, place of orgasmic activity and gender (incidentally, all retrieved documents indicated "masculine" with the exception of one "polymorph" and two "other"). But, equally, in the making of resemblances,

<u>An Evening with the Maids</u>, 1969

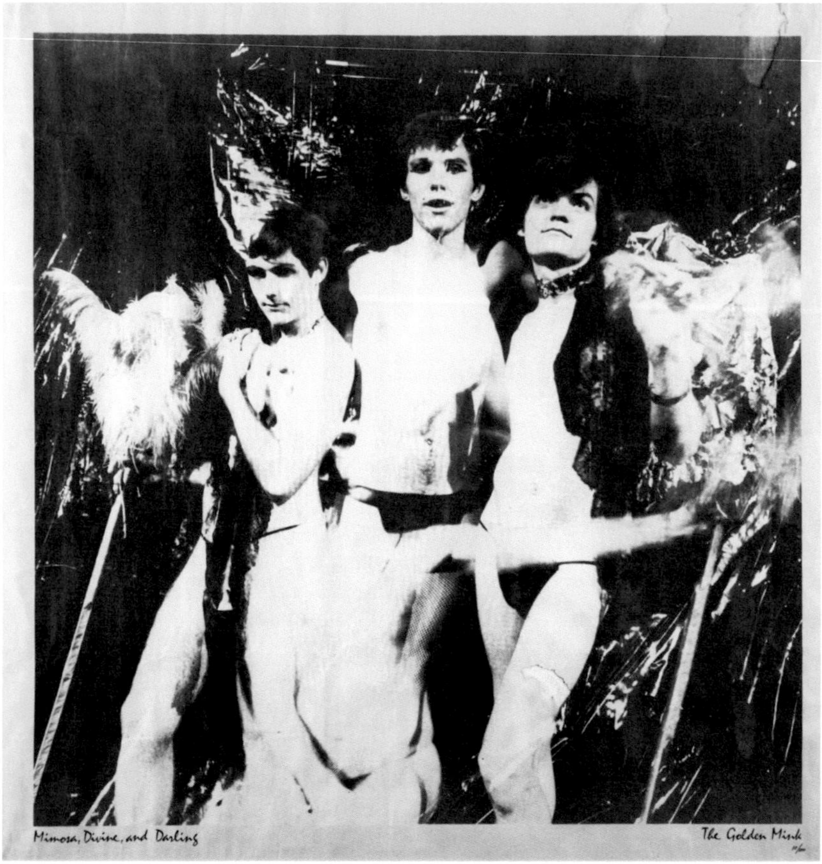

correspondences, tests and graphics, files and beauty pageants, fictitious names and unknown names: GI developed the erotic geography of a "vibrant collage,"[28] where no less than three men of many parts were bidding higher and higher.

It is along those lines that for 25 years General Idea—together in sickness and in health and in infidelity—led a homosexual way of life, if by this term we are to understand, as Michel Foucault formulated it, the act of sharing "among individuals of different ages, status, and social activity (able to) develop intense relationships not resembling those that are institutionalized"[29]; a way of life that would yield "a culture and an ethic."

Translated from the French by Madeleine Aktypi.

1 Association of three, troupe and couple: a troupe or a couple made up of three people.
2 Showcard 2-080, Playing The Triangle, 1979.
3 See Showcard 2-078, 2-079, 2-080, Playing The Triangle, 1979.
4 A major French bank, involved in one of the biggest trading frauds in history and other financial scandals.
5 Jean-Jacques Rousseau, "Profession de foi d'un vicaire savoyard," in Émile ou De l'Éducation, Book IV, 1762, p. 986.
6 AA Bronson, interview with the author, Paris, February 2010.
7 Jorge Zontal in the interview with Louise Dompierre.
8 AA Bronson, "Was General Idea Gay Enough?" Monstre, no. 1, Paris 2009, p. 38f.
9 AA Bronson, interview with the author, Paris, February 2010.
10 Ibid.
11 Martin Manalasan IV, "In the Shadows of Stonewall: Examining Gay Transnational Politics and the Diasporic Dilemma," The Politics of Culture in the Shadows of Capital, Lowe and Lloyd, Duke University Press, Durham 1997, p. 486.
12 Two references to the magazine can be found in General Idea's official bibliography: "General Ideas," The Body Politic, Toronto, May 1972, p. 20; and Douglas Durand, "GI Image and Enforcement," The Body Politic, Toronto, June/July 1980.
13 AA Bronson, interview with the author, Paris, February 2010.
14 The Body Politic, December 1977/January1978. The article "Men Loving Boys Loving Men" incited the ire of the mainstream press. See Claire Hoy's editorial in the Toronto Sun Column: "Our taxes help promote abuse of children."
15 GI's performance: An Anatomy of Censorship, Body Politic Rally, Toronto, 1979.
16 Showcard 2-069, Δ The Graduated Cock, 1979.
17 AA Bronson, "Was General Idea Gay Enough?"
18 Erik Bullot: www.lecinemadeerikbullot.com/la-foudre-a--b.
19 AA Bronson, interview with the author, Paris, February 2010.
20 Donna Haraway, The Companion Species Manifesto (2003), and When Species Meet (2007), both University of Minnesota Press, Minneapolis.
21 in When Species Meet, p. 15.
22 The quote dates from 1986.
23 José Esteban Muñoz, Cruising Utopia, The Then and There of Queer Futurity, New York University Press, New York and London 2009, p. 115.
24 Gavin Butt, Between You and Me: Queer Disclosures in the New York Art World 1948–1963, Duke University Press, Durham 2005.
25 According to artist May Wilson, a friend and correspondent of Ray Johnson. See http://muse.jhu.edu.gate3.inist.fr/journals/postmodern_culture/v007/7.3saper.html#foot8.
26 AA Bronson in Randal Wilcox's video-documentary on photographer Alvin Baltrop and life on the piers of New York: http://www.randalwilcox.com/randalwilcox.com/documentary.html.
27 Ina Blom, The Name of the Game: Ray Johnson's postal performance, National Museum of Contemporary Art, Oslo, 2003.
28 Muñoz, op. cit., p. 127.
29 "Michel Foucault, an Interview: Sex, Power and Politics of Identity," published in The Advocate, no. 400, August 7, 1984. The interview was conducted in 1982 in Toronto for The Body Politic.

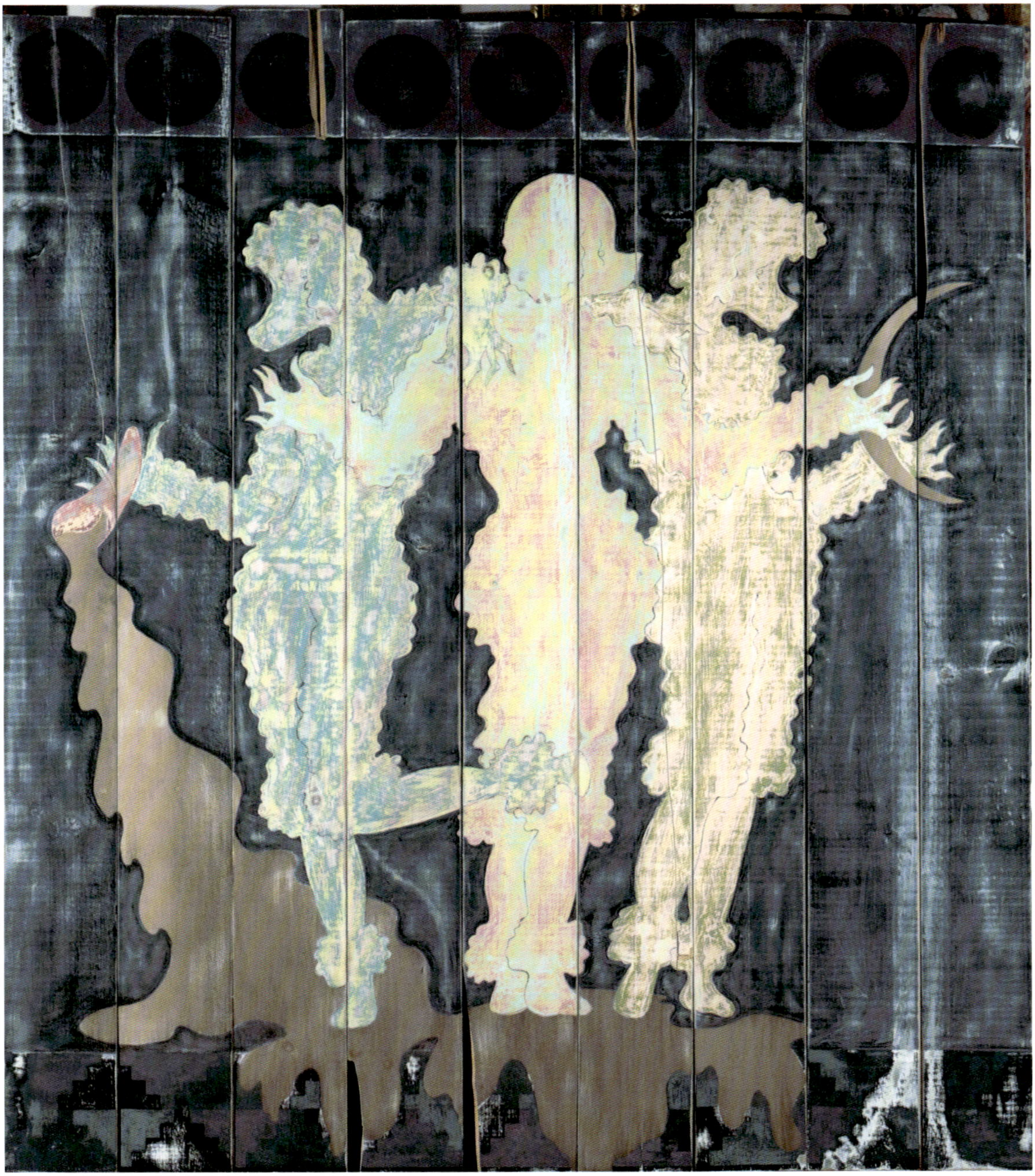

Three Graces: Mural Fragment from the 1984 Miss General Idea Pavillion, 1982

Lunatic Poodle Panels (Partial Reconstruction) (from the Room of the Unknown Function in the Villa dei Misteri of the 1984 Miss General Idea Pavillion), 1982

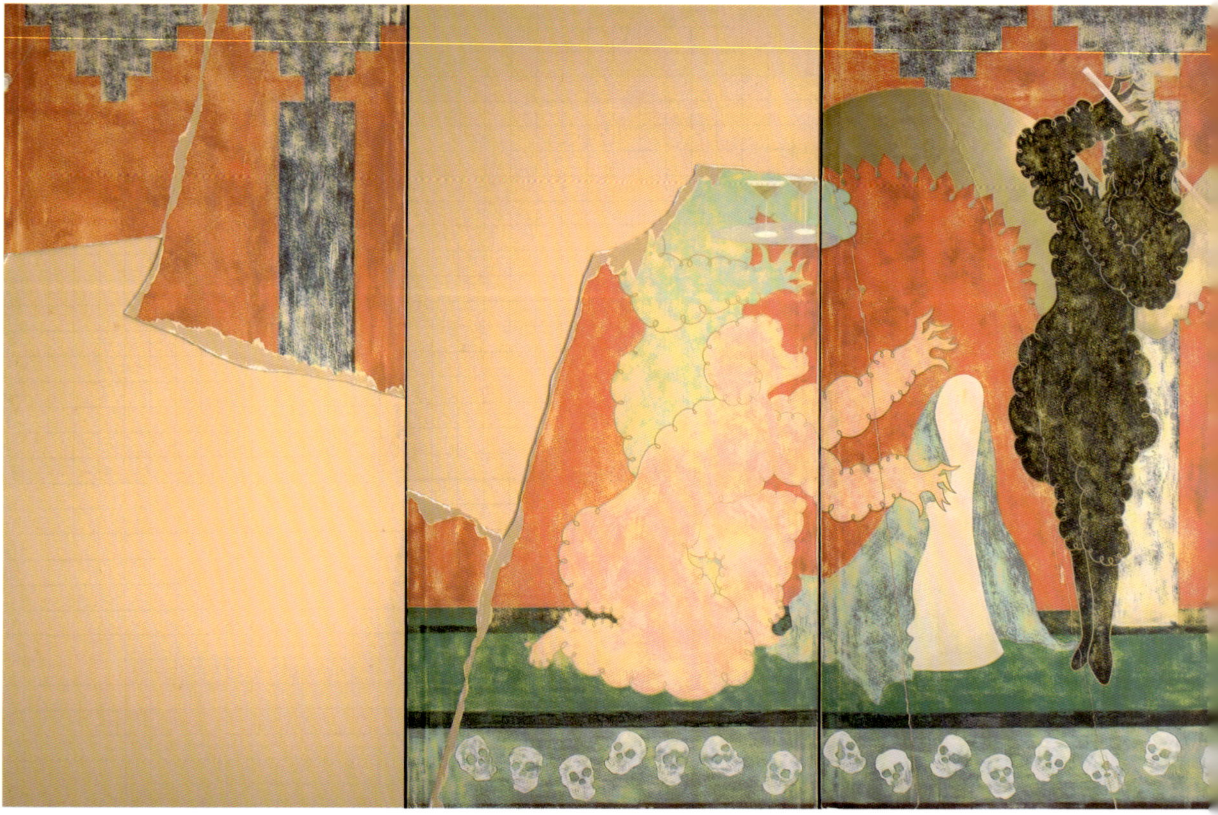

The Unveiling of the Cornucopia: A Mural Fragment from the Room of the Unknown Function in the Villa dei Misteri of the 1984 Miss General Idea Pavillion, 1982

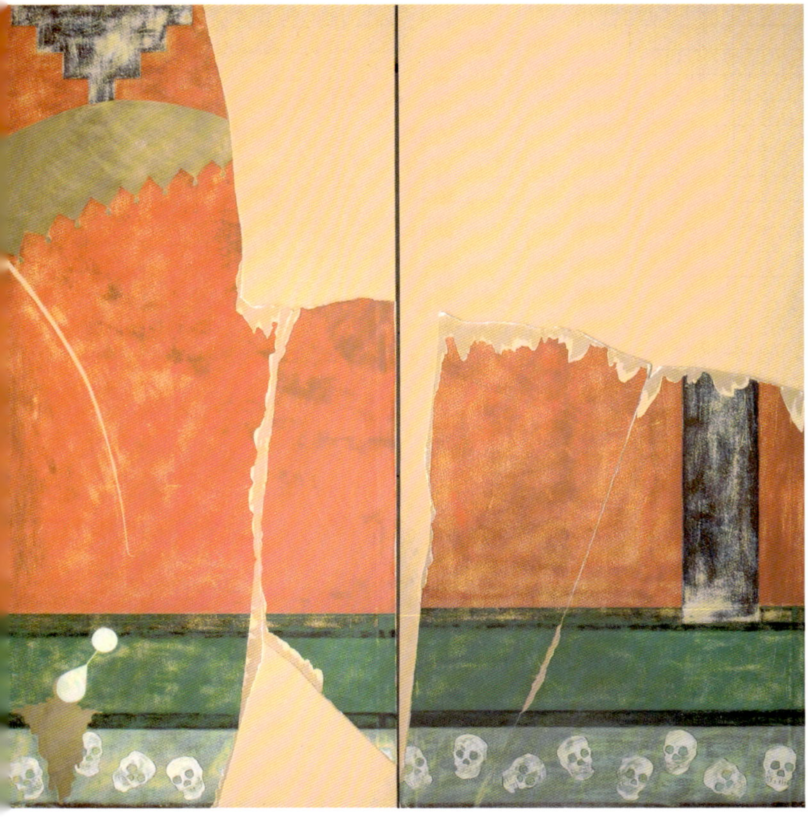

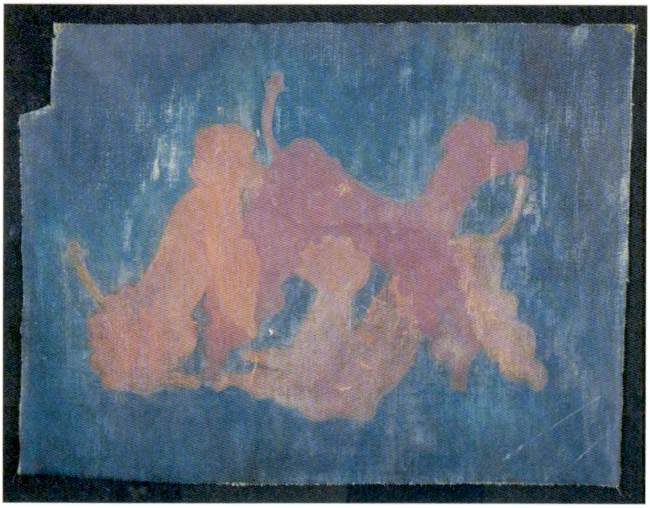

Mondo Cane, 1982

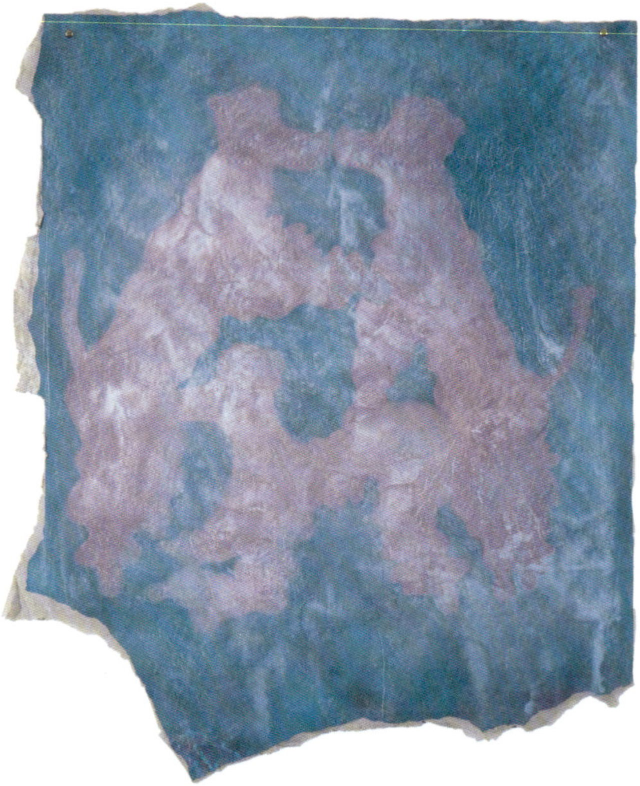

Eau d'Artifice, 1983

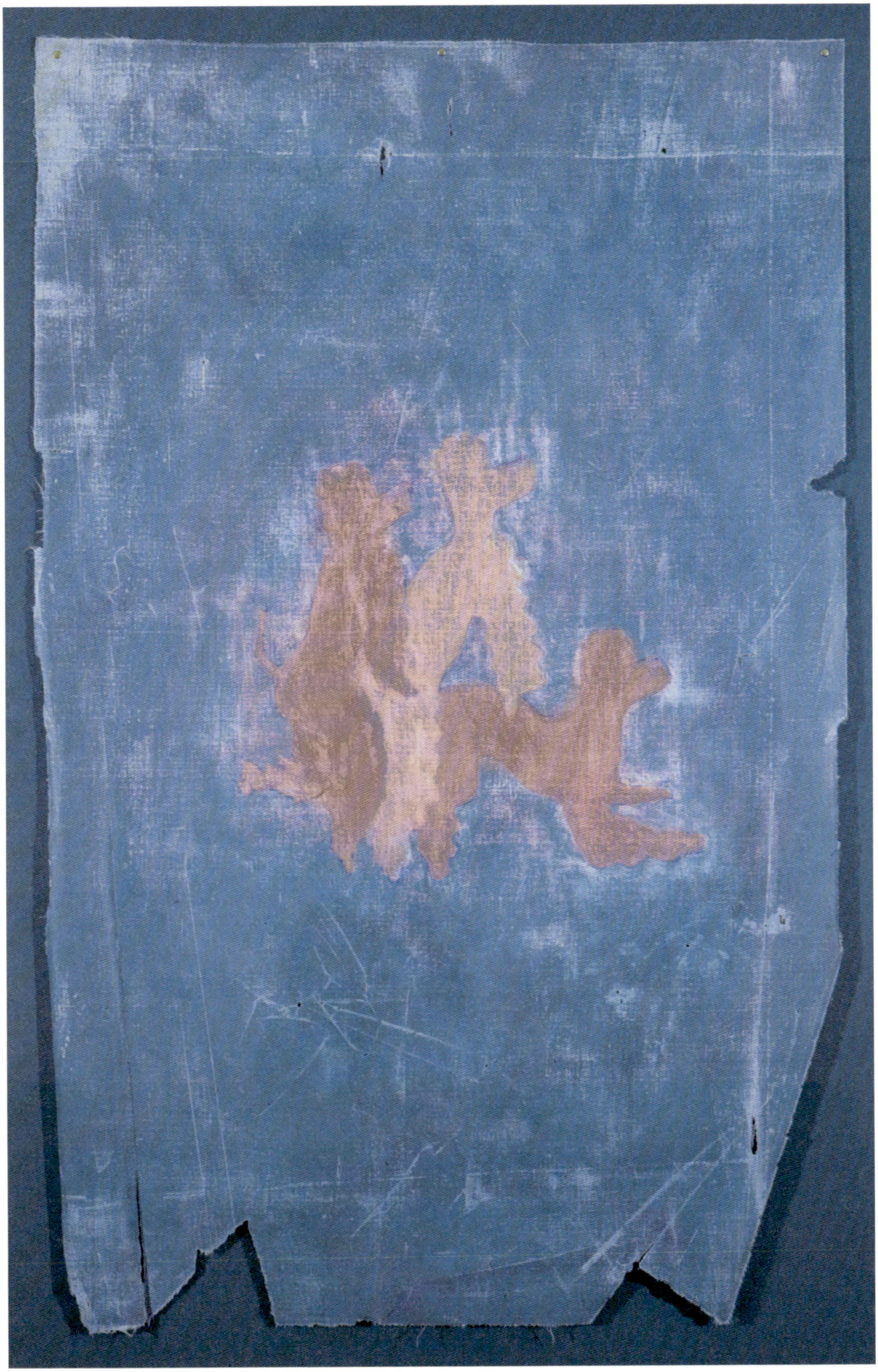

Tableau Vivant, Natura Morta, 1983

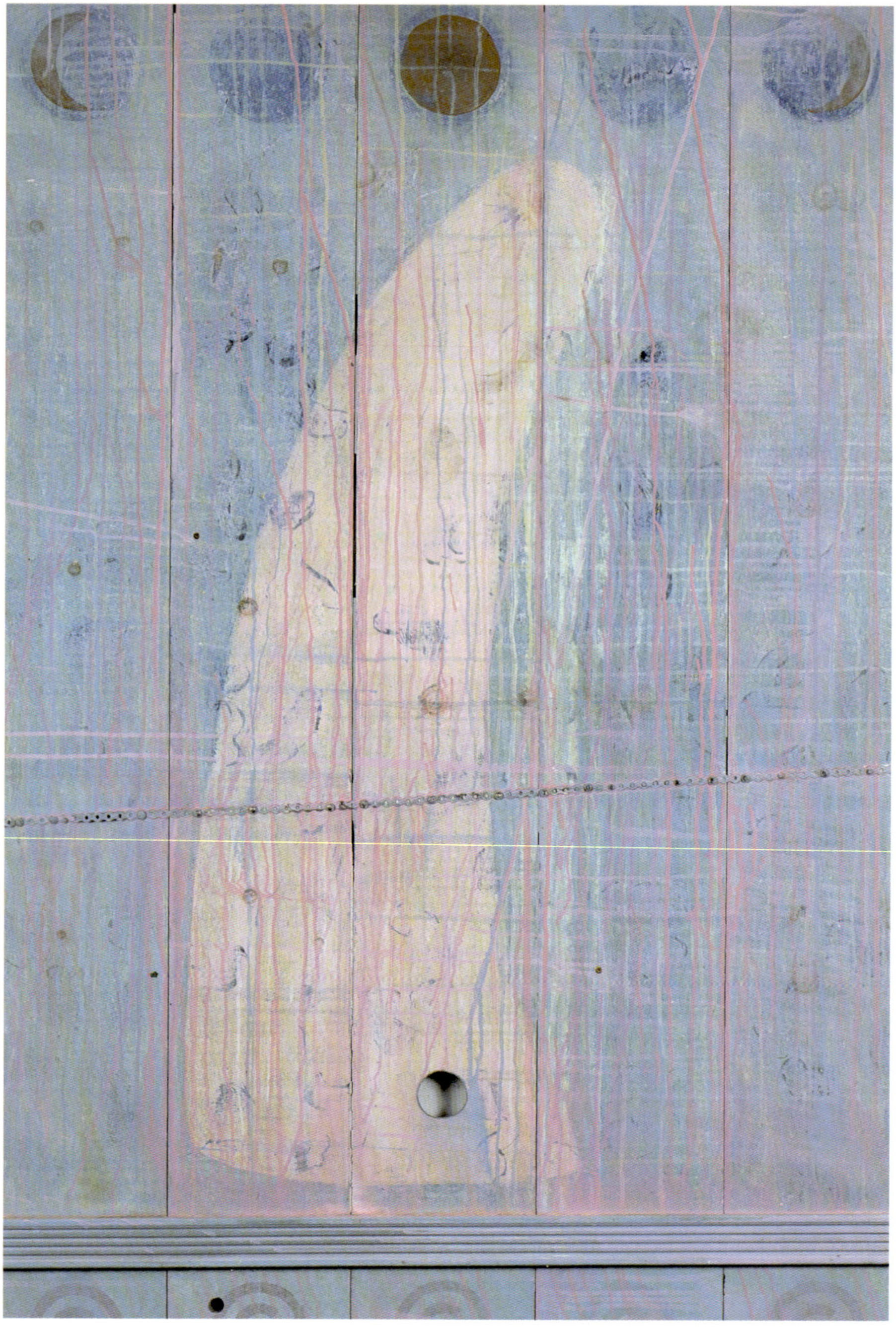

Représentation Confusé, 1981–1994 (recto/verso)

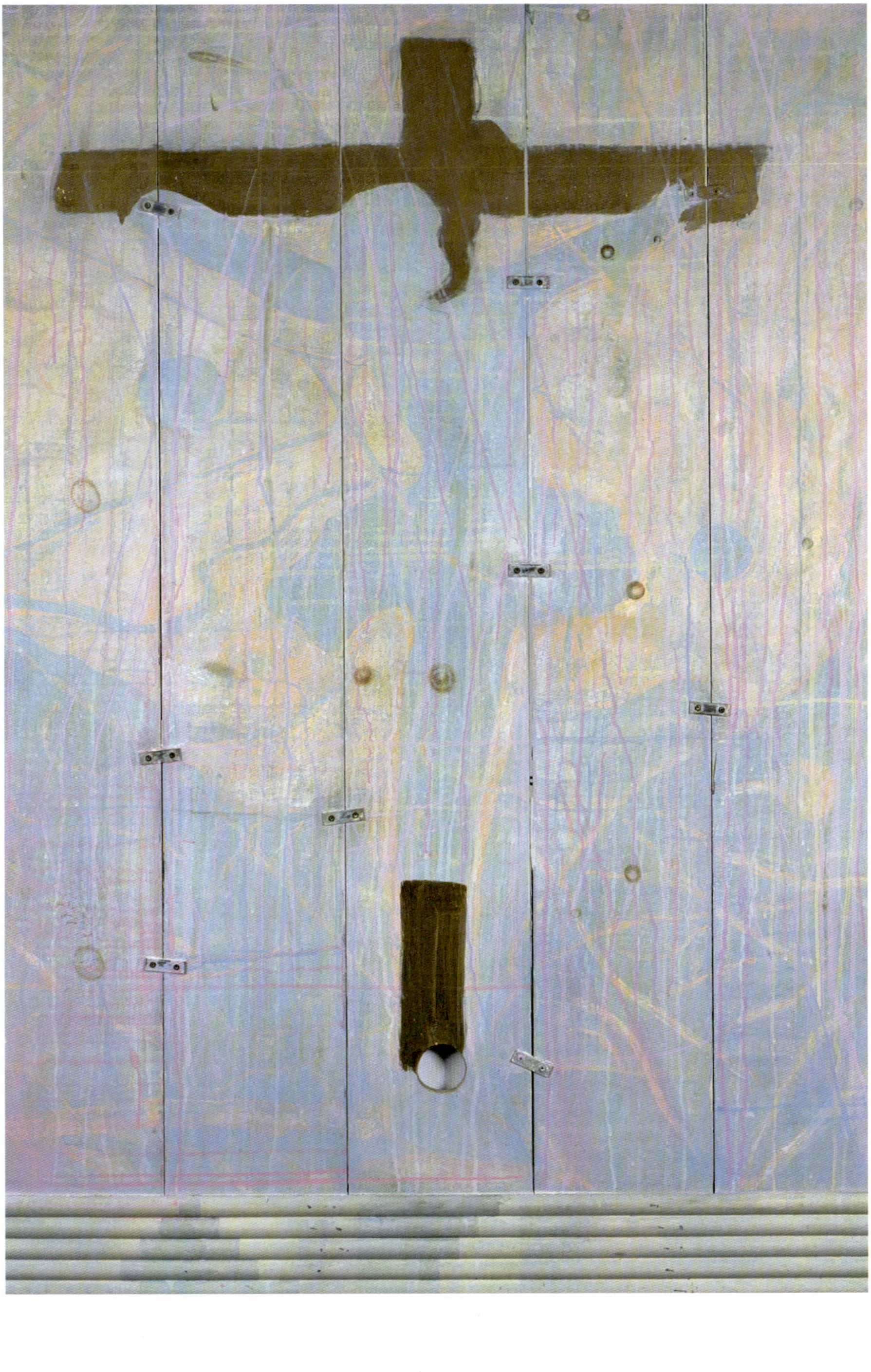

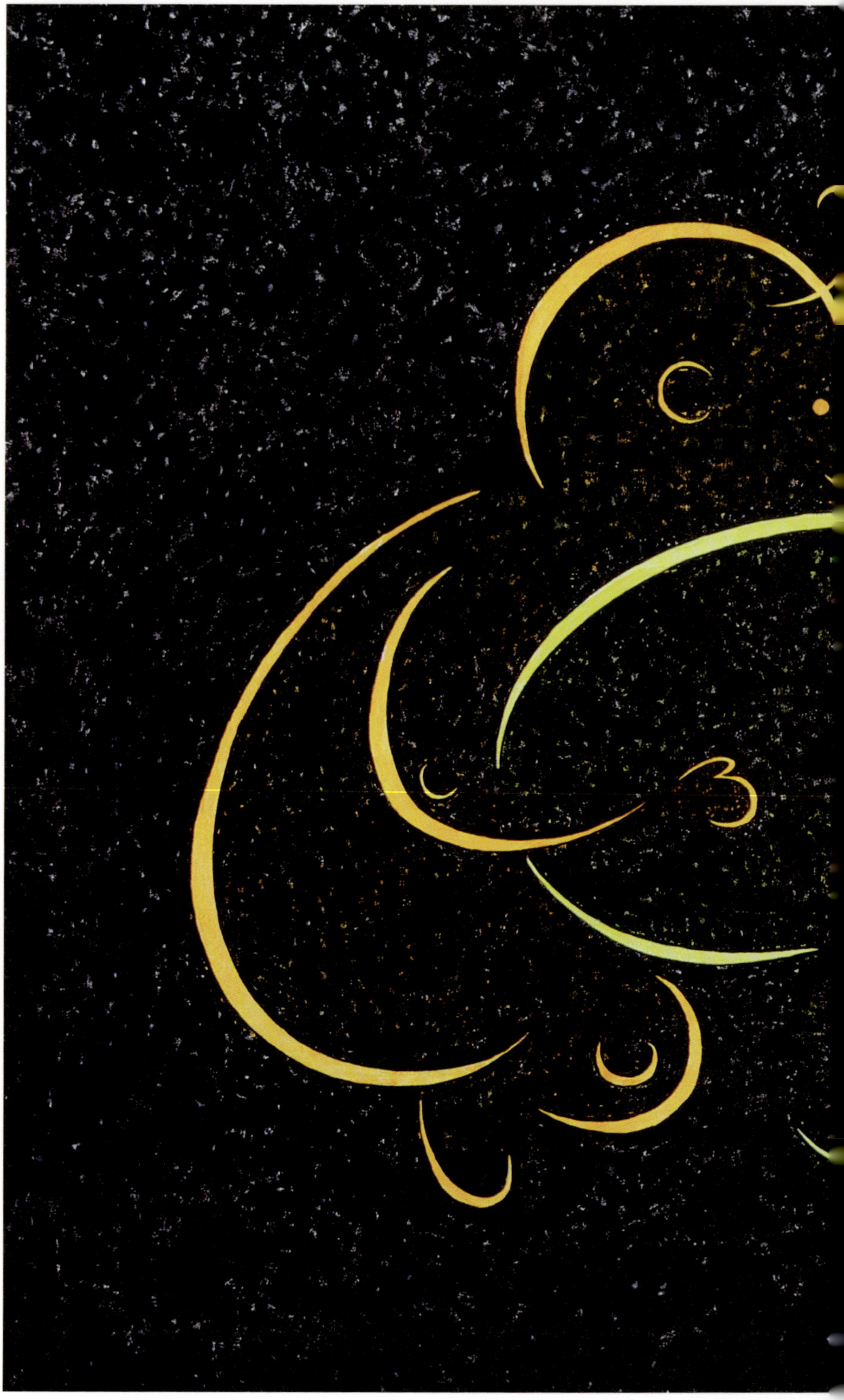

Baby Makes 3, 1984

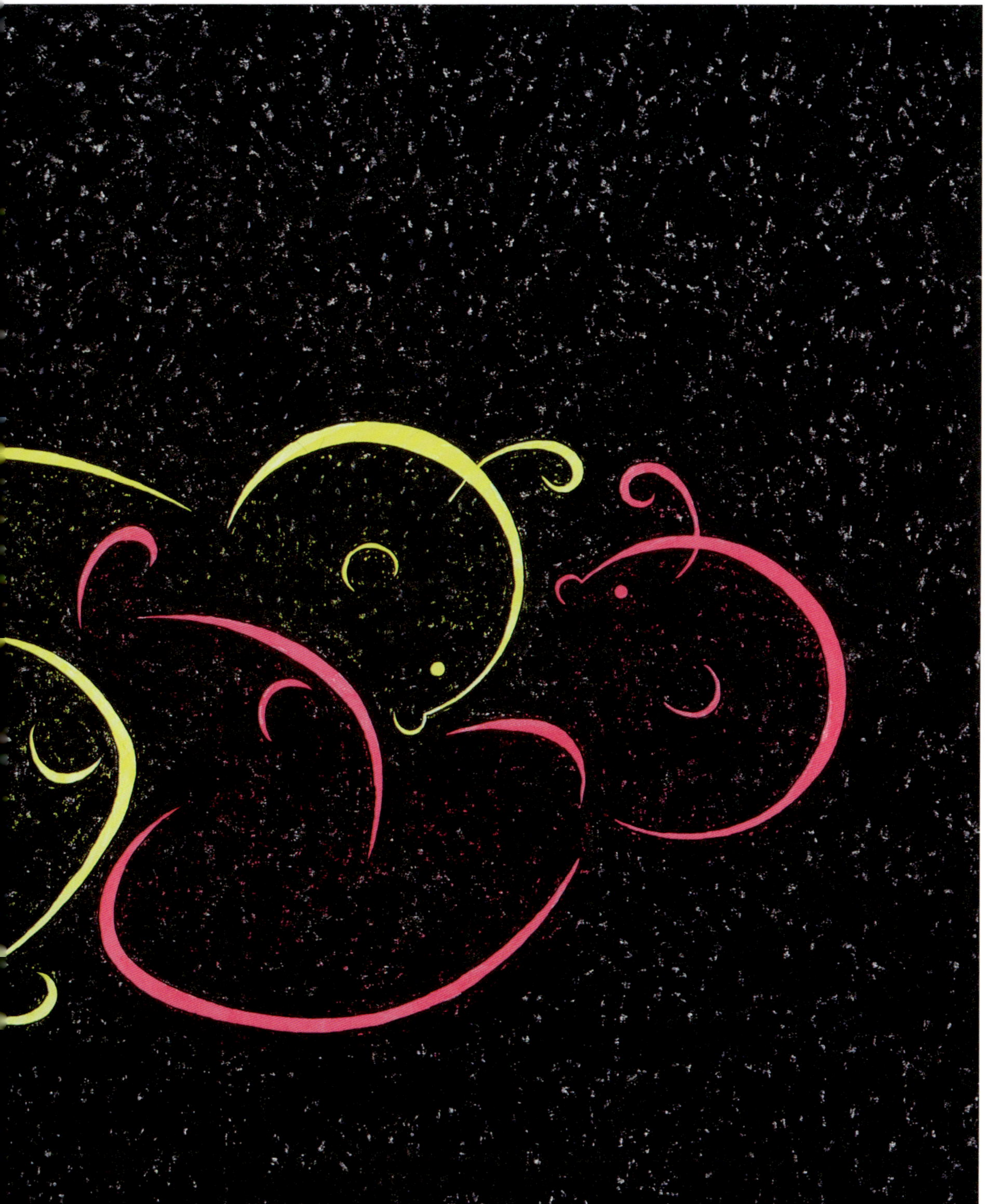

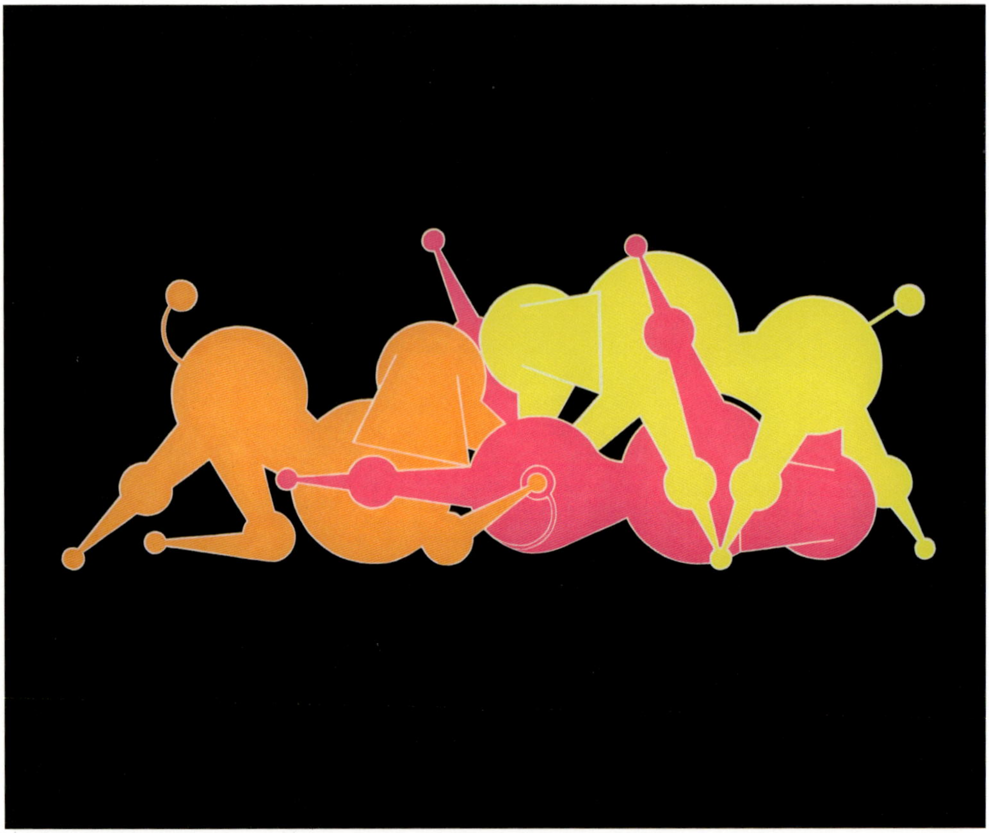

Mondo Cane Kama Sutra, 1984

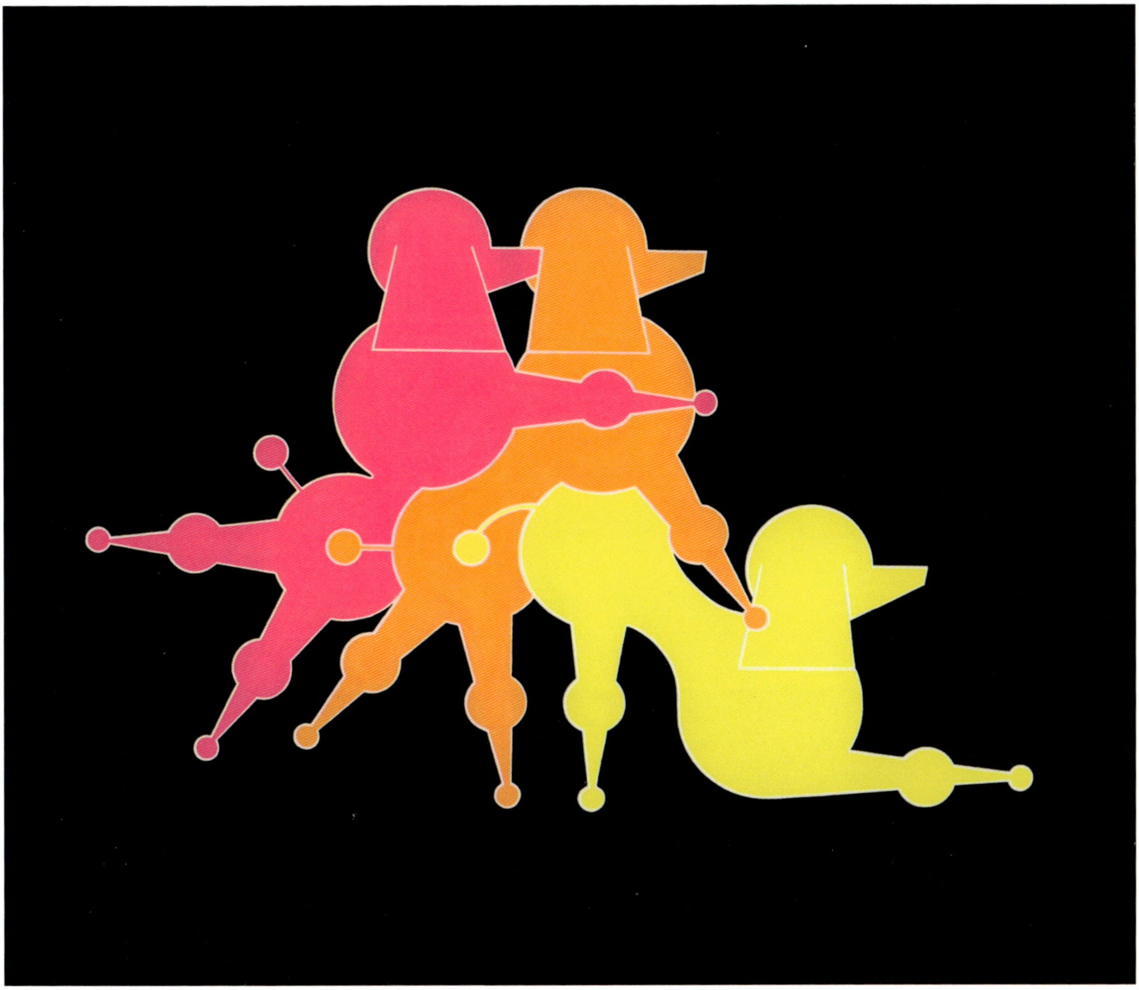

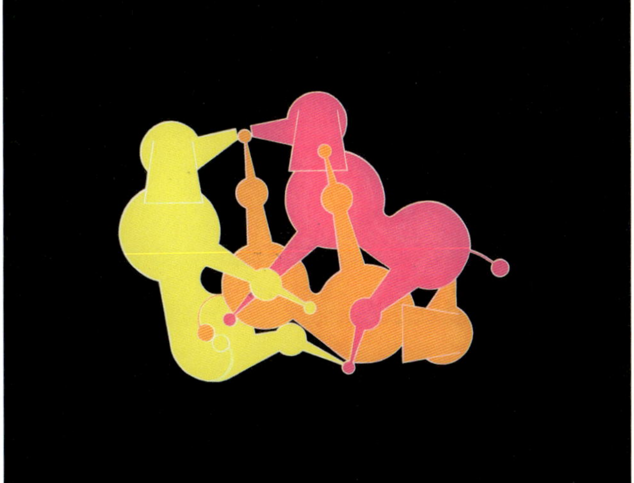

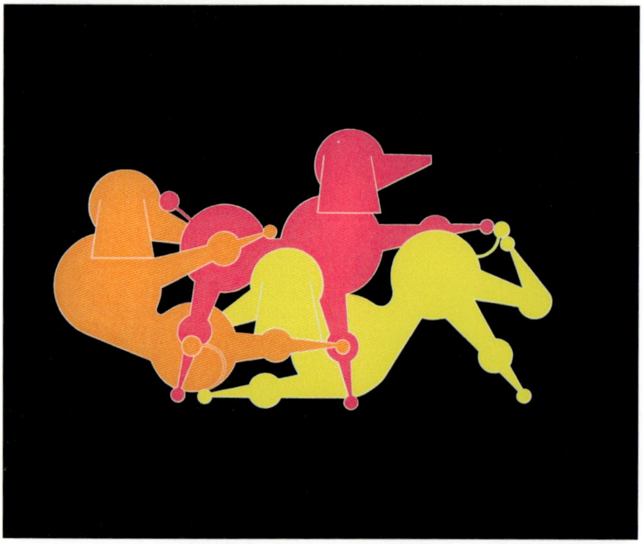

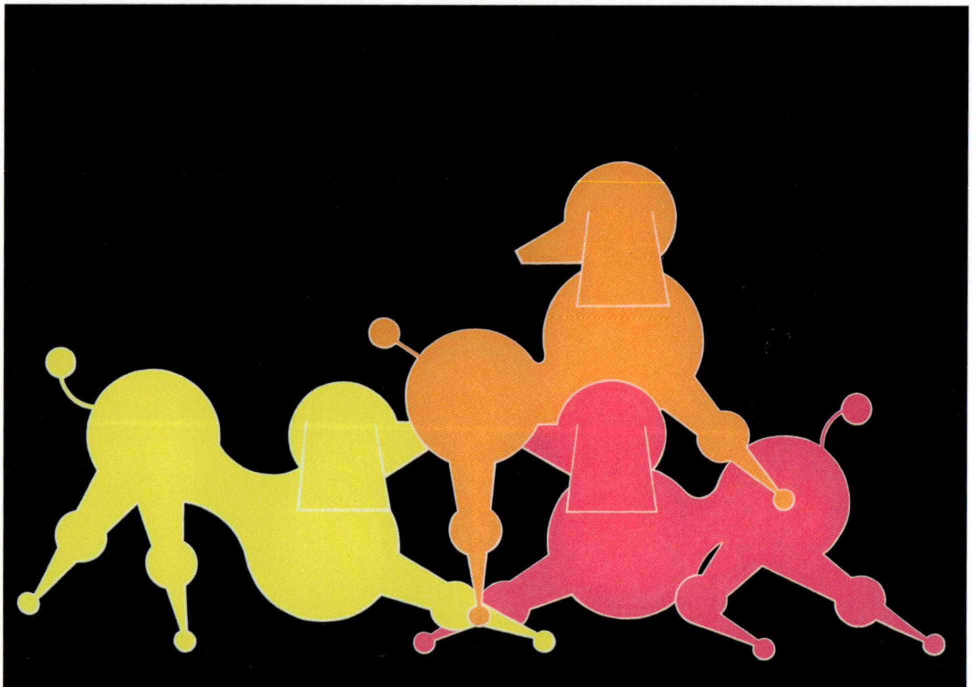

Mondo Cane Kama Sutra, 1984

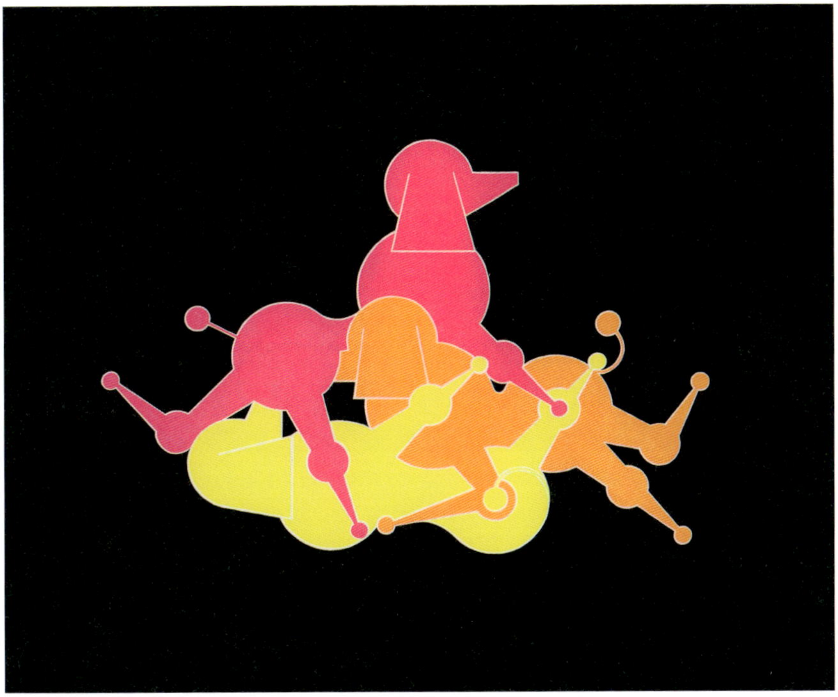

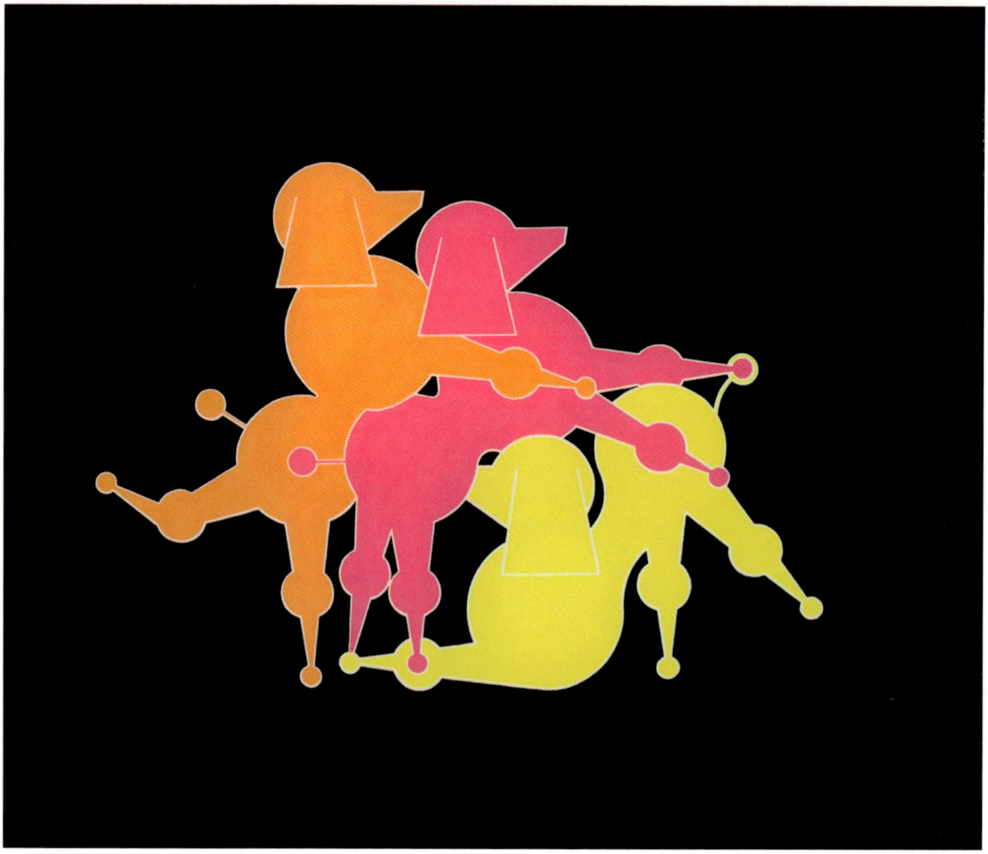

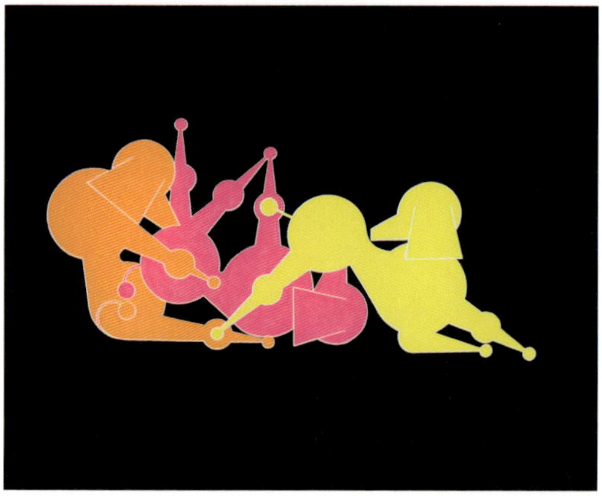

Mondo Cane Kama Sutra, 1984

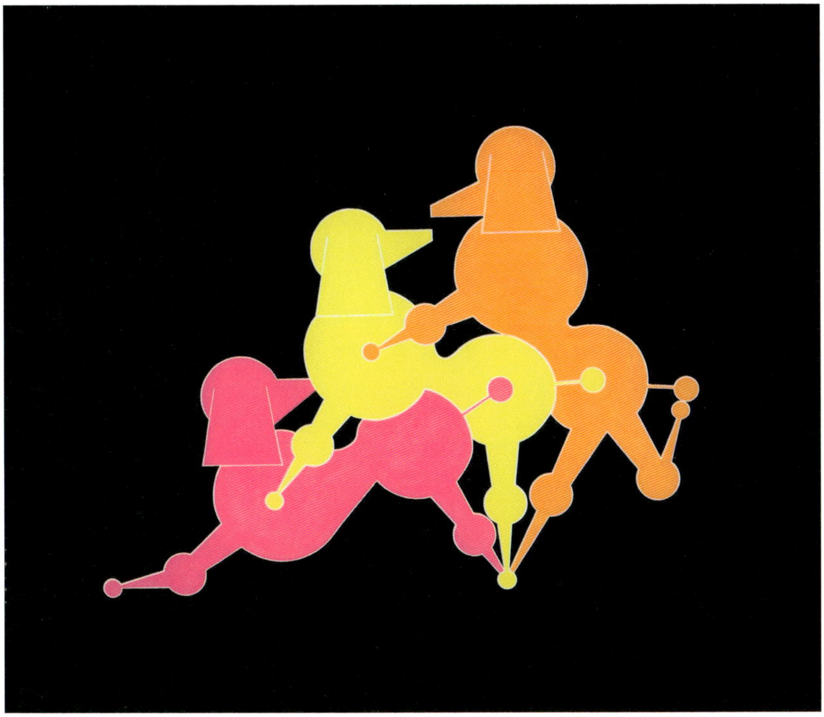

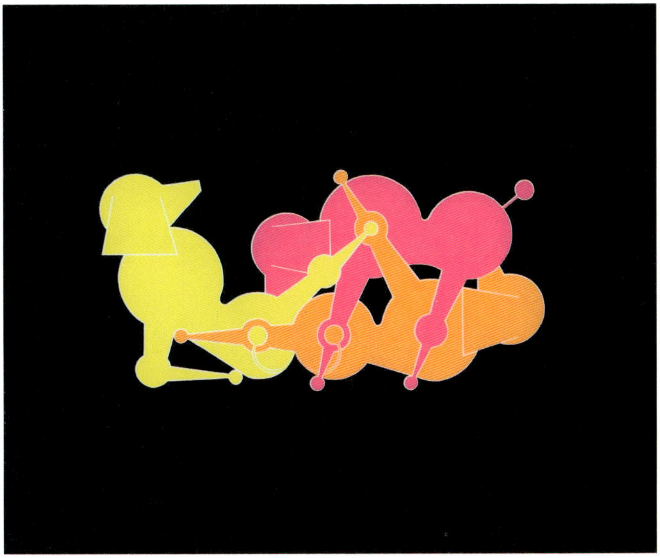

Copyright, Cash, and Crowd Control: Art and Economy in the Work of General Idea

AA Bronson

General Idea emerged in the aftermath of the Paris riots, from the detritus of hippie communes, underground newspapers, radical education, Happenings, love-ins, Marshall McLuhan,

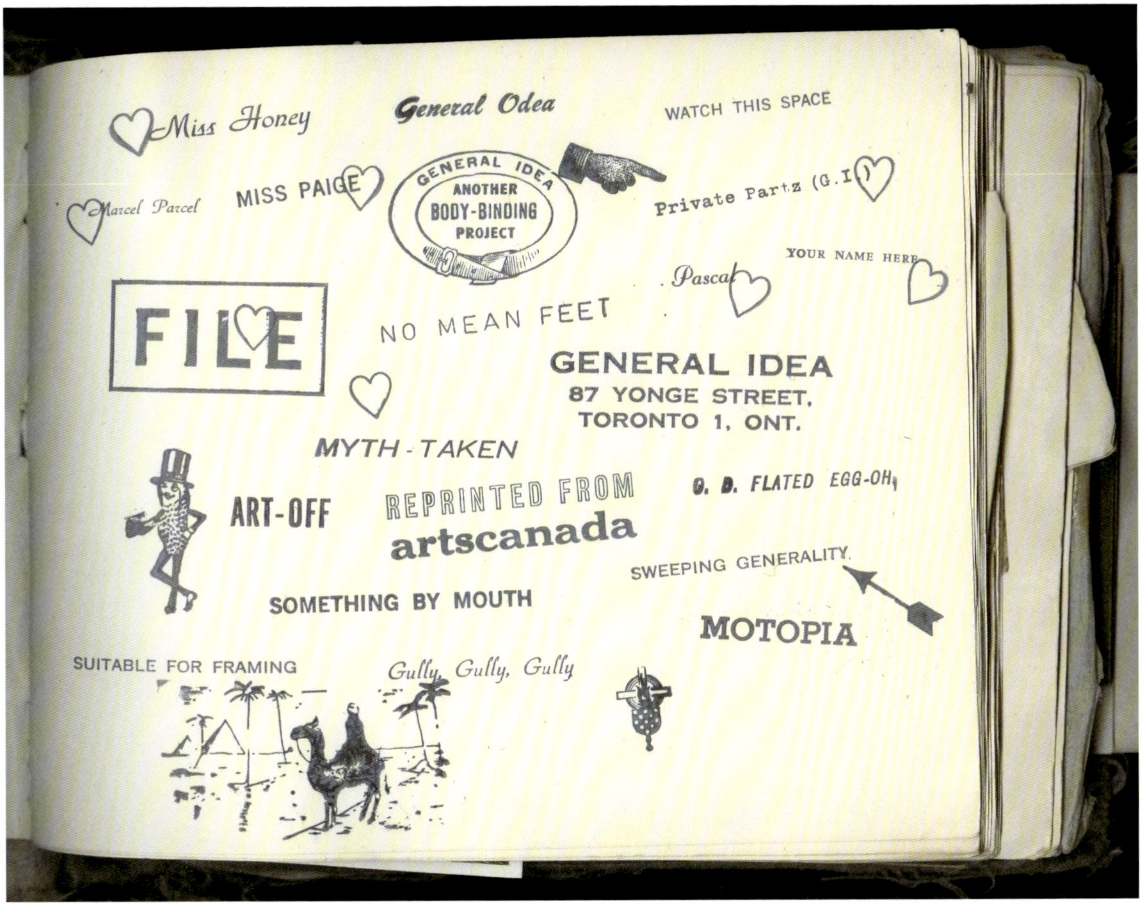

Antic Across the Atlantic Scrapbook, 1972

and the International Situationists. We believed in a free economy, in the abolition of copyright, and in a grassroots horizontal structure that prefigured the Internet. I want to briefly describe here the strategy by which General Idea defined the territory between art and commerce, and challenged the battle lines of copyright that define culture today.

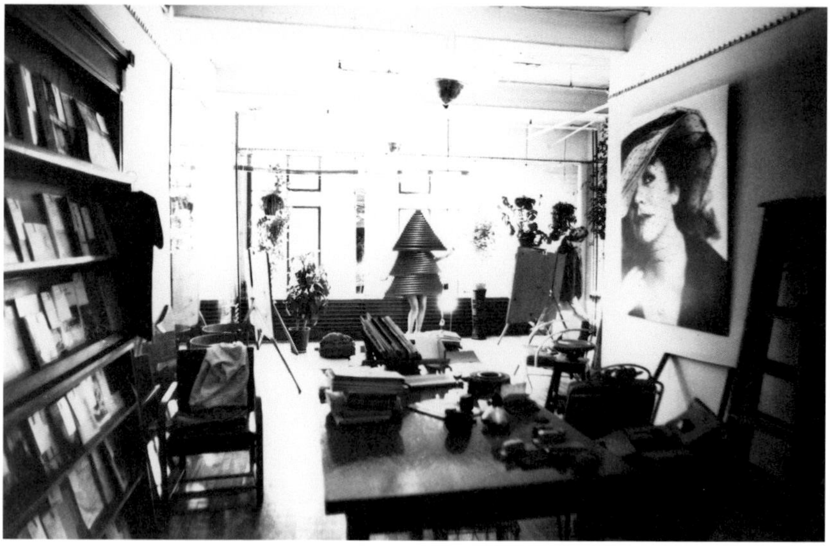

General Idea Studio/Art Metropole,
241 Yonge Street, Toronto, 1974

Boutique Culture

When Jorge, Felix, and I began living and working together as General Idea in 1969, we were already aware of two opposing forces in our communal life: the desire to produce art, and the desire to survive. And in a sort of natural inflection of the Conceptual and Process art which immediately preceded us, we turned to the idea of incorporating the commerce of art and the economy of the art world into the art itself:

"We wanted to be famous, glamorous, and rich. That is to say, we wanted to be artists and we knew that if we were famous and glamorous we could say we were artists and we would be … We did and we are. We are famous glamorous artists."[1]

In our earliest works, such as *The Belly Store* (1969) or *Betty's* (1970),[2] we opened our storefront living space to the public as a series of "shops," projects in the format of commerce. Our earliest multiples were the products we offered for sale there, sometimes found objects, sometimes

AA Bronson

fabricated of cheap or scavenged materials (see *George Saia's Belly Food*, 1969). Some of the shops were in fact never open: the viewer could look into the display window and see the contents, but a little sign on the door perpetually proclaimed "back in 5 minutes." Like the work of the Fluxus artists, whom we soon met, our low-cost multiples were intended to bypass the gallery system, that economy of added value, and to travel through the more alternative audience of students, artists, writers, rock' n'roll fans, new music types, trendoids, and media addicts.

In 1980, we first exhibited *The Boutique from the 1984 Miss General Idea Pavillion* at the Carmen Lamanna Gallery in Toronto. Built in the form of a three-dimensional dollar sign, the boutique structure transformed the street-level gallery into a retail outlet, with General Idea's multiples and publications for sale, for example *Liquid Assets* (1980), and *Nazi Milk* (1979). A full-time shop girl sat within the tiny compartment we provided, and her presence, as well as the exchange of cash, product, and information across the counter were integral aspects of the work.

The true problematic of the *Boutique* was revealed when it began to be exhibited in museums. Some museums were unable to sell from the *Boutique* because of conflicts with their museum shops; most were unwilling to sell from the *Boutique* because of the heresy of commerce infecting the pure white cube. Although times have changed, and museums are now more public about their all-consuming need for money, none of the General Idea *Boutique* have been allowed to function as working installations participating in the financial economy of the museum.

In the exhibition *The Museum as Muse*, The Museum of Modern Art in New York exhibited the *Boutique* with the multiples under Plexiglas, so they could not be touched, in a sort of castrated and purely archival state. I think of this as the ultimate revenge on the artwork that dared to expose the hypocrisy of the museum.[3]

General Idea's *Yen Boutique* (1989) went through a similar series of humiliations at the Centre Pompidou, when a large group of *Test Pattern: T.V. Dinner Plates* (1988) was stolen during the first 45 minutes of the opening, causing the curator to strip the boutique of its wares for the duration of the exhibition.[4]

Boutique Cœurs volants (1994–2001), a free-standing sales exhibit in a three-dimensional replica of a Duchamp graphic, is the most recent of these works, and is designed for easier control in today's high-traffic museums. It exhibits only one General Idea multiple: the posthumously produced *Dick All* (1993–2001), based on Duchamp's *Wedge of Chastity* (1954).

AIDS (Lottery Ticket), 1989

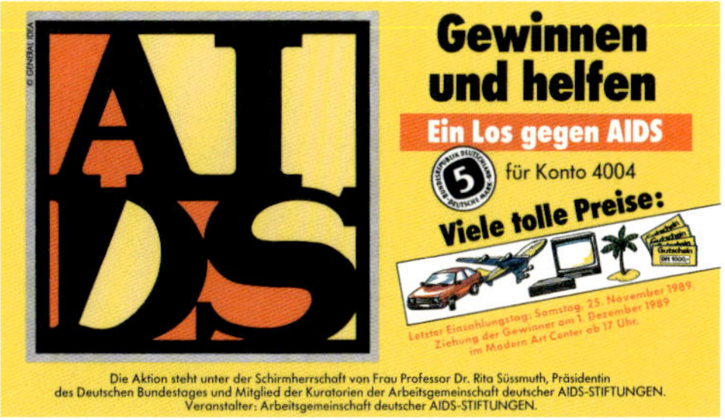

Copyright

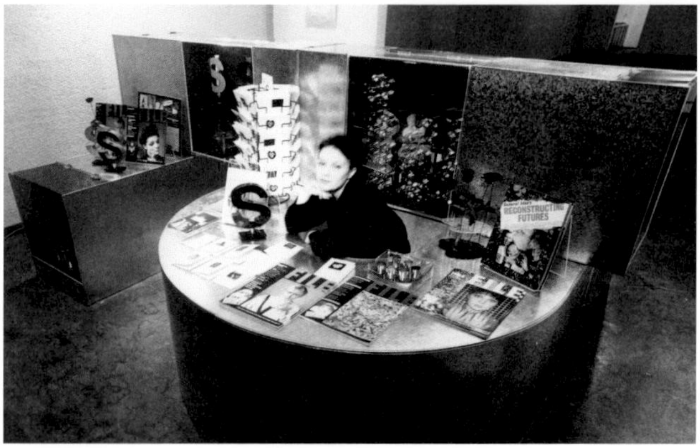

The Boutique from the 1984 Miss General Idea Pavillion, 1980

The key to contemporary consumer culture is the copyright: without the copyright and the sanctity of (individual and/or corporate) authorship, today's mega-economics would collapse—imagine Microsoft, for example, without copyright. Museums act as symbolic keepers of the virtue of copyright, and an art expert's opinion on the authenticity of a work can send values soaring or crashing by vast amounts of money.

General Idea has always believed in the public realm, and much of our production was carried out there. For many years we used commercial fabrication of works to avoid the fetishism of the artist's hand, of the mark of the individual genius. Similarly, our corporate name belied individual authorship. For the entire 25 years of our collaboration, we questioned and played with various aspects of authorship and copyright.

FILE Megazine (1972–1989), General Idea's work in magazine format, was sued by the Time-Life Corporation for its simulation of *LIFE magazine* in 1976. We had always been interested in William Burroughs' ideas about images and viruses, and especially the copyright of specific forms and colors. Corporate culture used copyright-protected logos (and even colors, such as Kodak yellow) as a virus to be injected into the mainstream of our society, infecting the population, and creating a sympathetic cash flow. Time-Life holds copyright on "white block lettering on a red parallelogram." It was only when Robert Hughes, *TIME* magazine's current art critic, ridiculed his employers in the pages of *The Village Voice* that the corporation dropped its suit against us.

Robert Indiana's *LOVE* painting of 1964 is an example of an artist's work that escaped copyright and entered the public realm, appearing as cocktail napkins, keychains, and other commercial paraphernalia. We might think of this as an image virus gone awry, a sort of image cancer. Similarly, General Idea's AIDS logo (1987), a plagiarism or simulacrum of Indiana's *LOVE*, was intended to escape copyright and travel freely through the mainstream of our culture's advertising and communications systems. And so it has, as a series of posters, billboards, and electronic signs, on the street, on television, on the Internet, and in periodicals:

The Journal of the American Medical Association carried it on its cover in 1992; *Newsweek* used it on every page of a special issue; and the Swiss art journal *Parkett* published sheets of AIDS Stamps (1988) which the reader could inject into the postal system on envelopes and parcels—a sort of visual anthrax.

In our final days, General Idea attacked and celebrated the bastion of art history itself. We produced a series of works challenging the copyright of Mondrian, Rietveld, Reinhardt, and Duchamp, with altered simulacra of frankly fake materials: Mondrian paintings on Styrofoam panels, for example, or an altered photographic print of a catalogue reproduction of a work by Duchamp which was itself an alteration to a found print by another artist (*Infe©ted Pharmacie*, 1994).[5]

Living in Contradiction

General Idea was at once complicit in and critical of the mechanisms and strategies that join art and commerce, a sort of mole in the art world. Our ability to live and act in contradiction defined our work: we were simultaneously fascinated and repulsed by the mechanisms of today's cultural economy. We injected ourselves into the mainstream of this infectious culture, and lived, as parasites, off our monstrous host.

This text is reprinted from General Idea Editions, 1967–1995, Blackwood Gallery, Mississauga, 2003, p. 24–27.

1 General Idea, "Glamour," FILE Megazine, vol. 3, no. 1 (Fall 1975).

2 The Belly Store, a collaboration between General Idea and the artist John Neon, opened on December 11, 1969, in the living room of 78 Gerrard Street, the house rented by General Idea in 1969–1970. Jorge Zontal had a stand where he sold George Saia's Belly Food, plastic bottles filled with cotton, with labels designed by AA Bronson. Betty's was inaugurated on January 1, 1970, at 78 Gerrard Street. A shop of women's clothes, and a collaboration between Jorge Zontal, Ken Coupland, and Ron Terrill, it was the subject of an article in the fashion pages of the Toronto Globe and Mail. Certain dresses were used for the Miss General Idea events (note from the editor).

3 The Museum as Muse, The Museum of Modern Art, New York, March 14–June 1, 1999.

4 Let's Entertain (touring exhibition), Walker Art Center, Minneapolis/Centre Pompidou, Paris, 2000–2001.

5 Many of these were "infected" with the green from red/green/blue of the AIDS/LOVE logo.

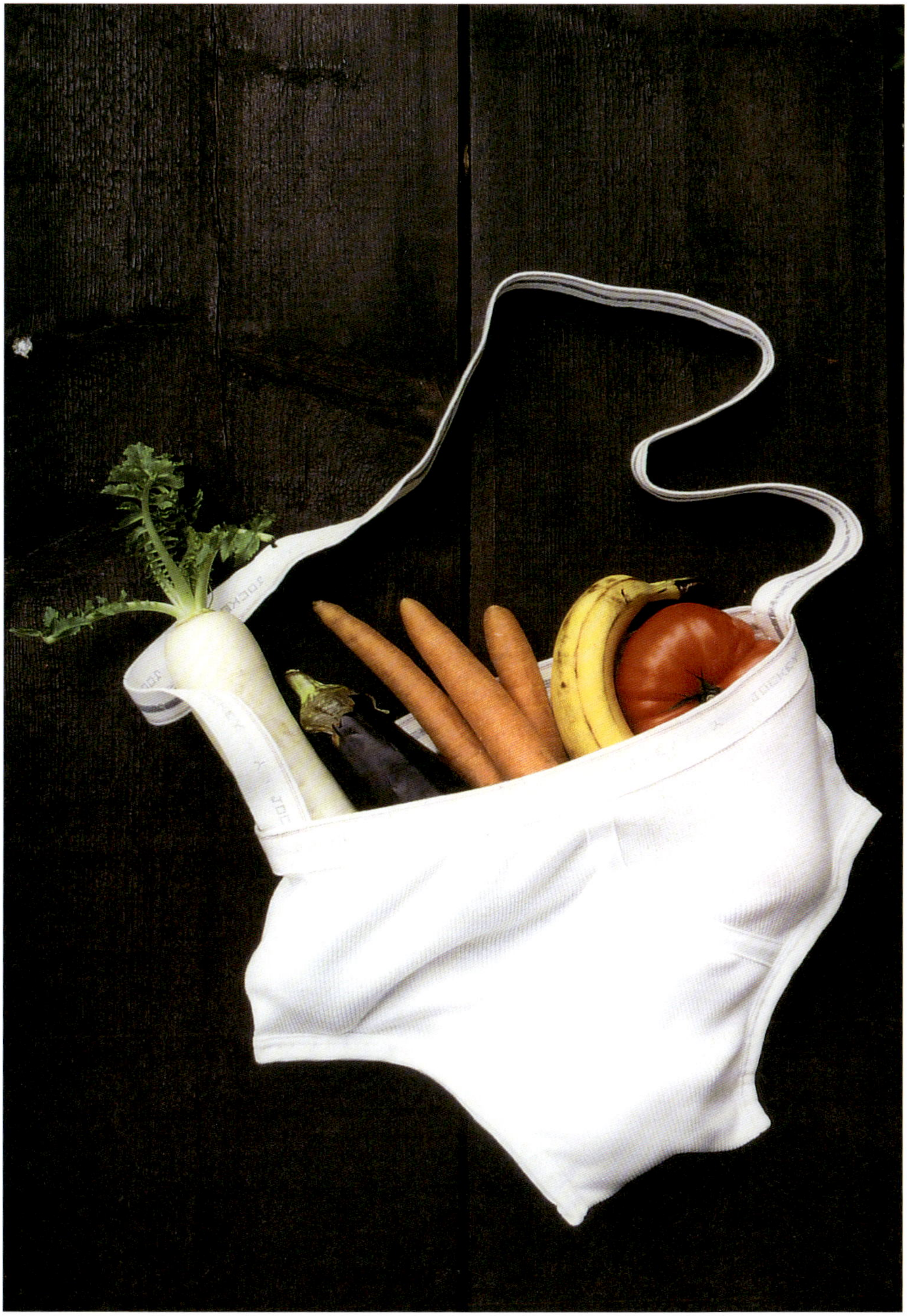

Jockey Short Shopping Bag, 1991–1998

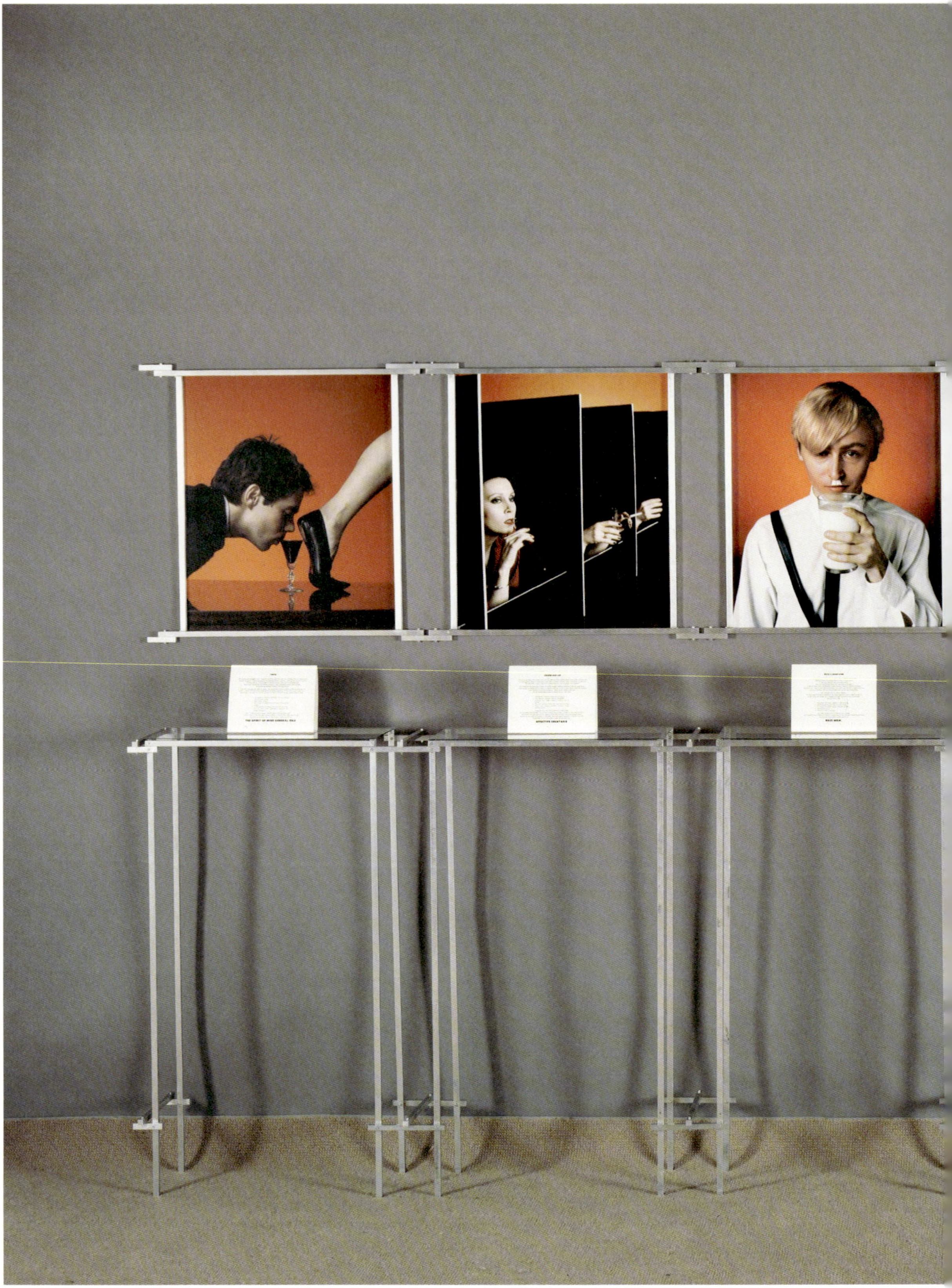

Colour Bar Lounge, 1979

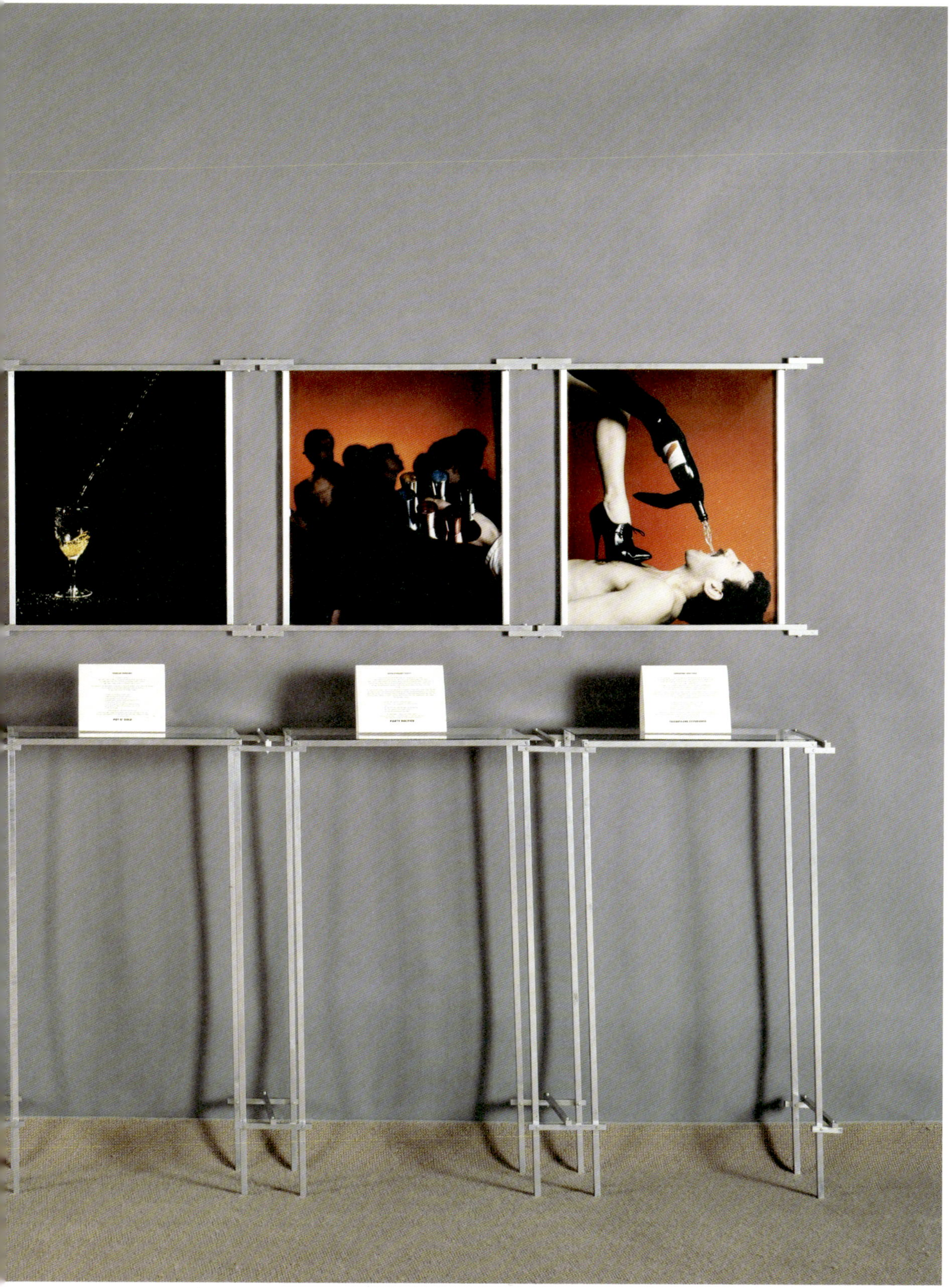

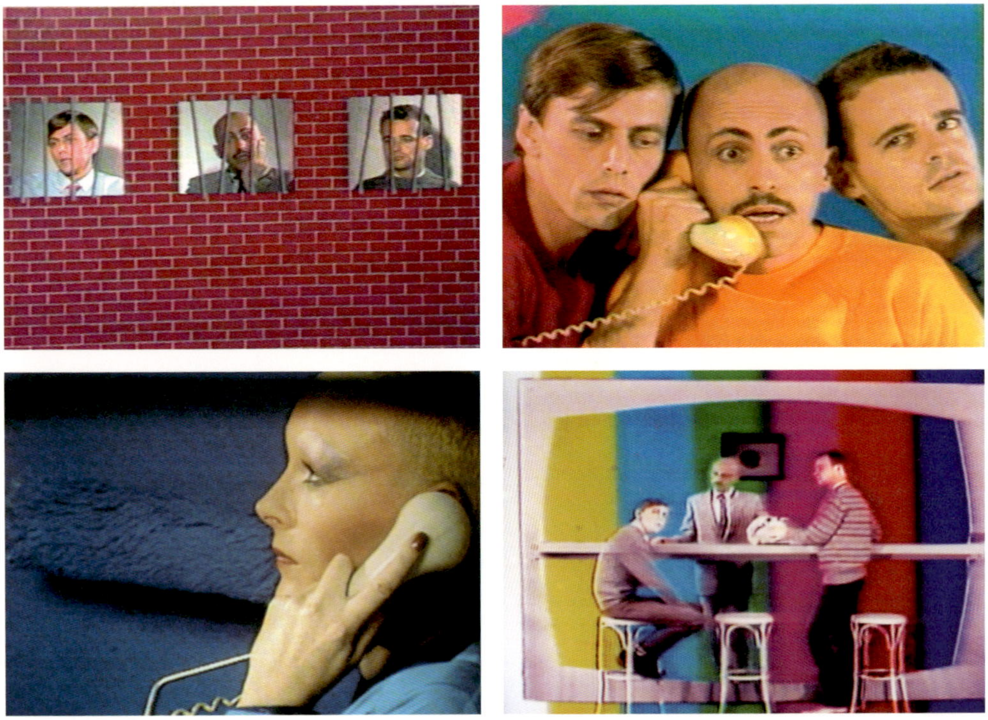

Test Tube, 1979

Test Pattern: T.V. Dinner Plate, 1988

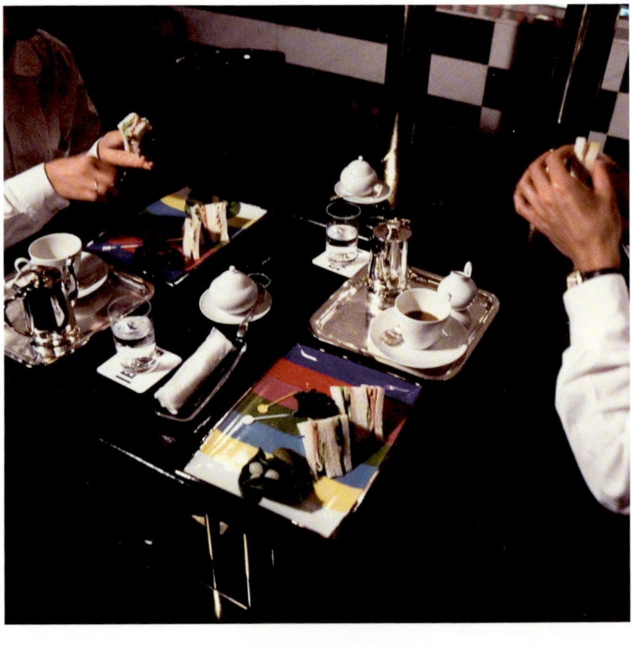

Miss General Idea
played the part
of the art object
playing the part
of the artist.
We fitted her cutout
into the picture
and called it collage.

Showcard 2-006, At Home, 1975

That soon turned out to be
a breakthrough for us …
to realize that our Pavillion,
like some sort of cultural
parasite could be built
in other people's architecture.

Showcard 2-050, Some Sort of Cultural Parasite, 1977

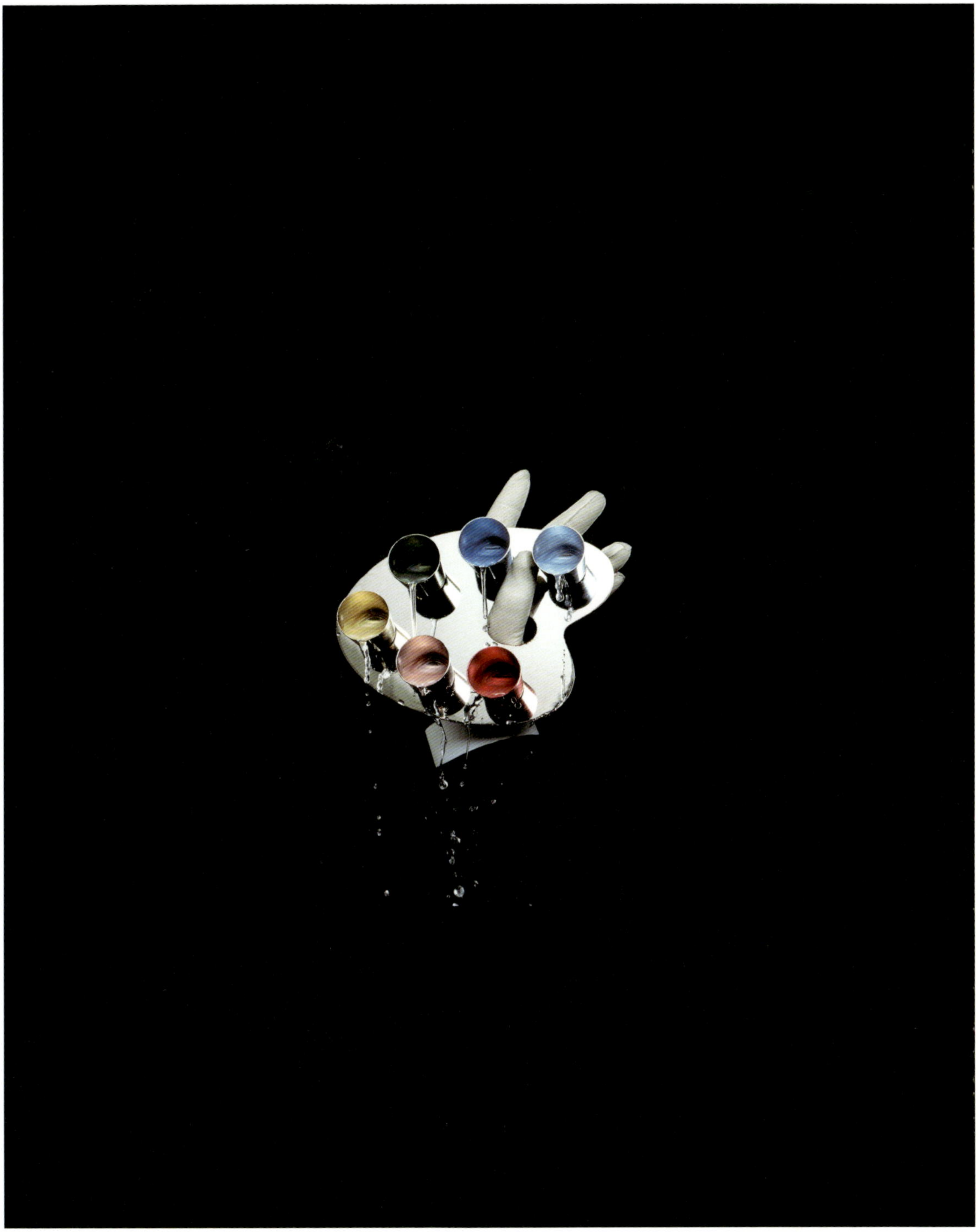

Magic Palette, 1980

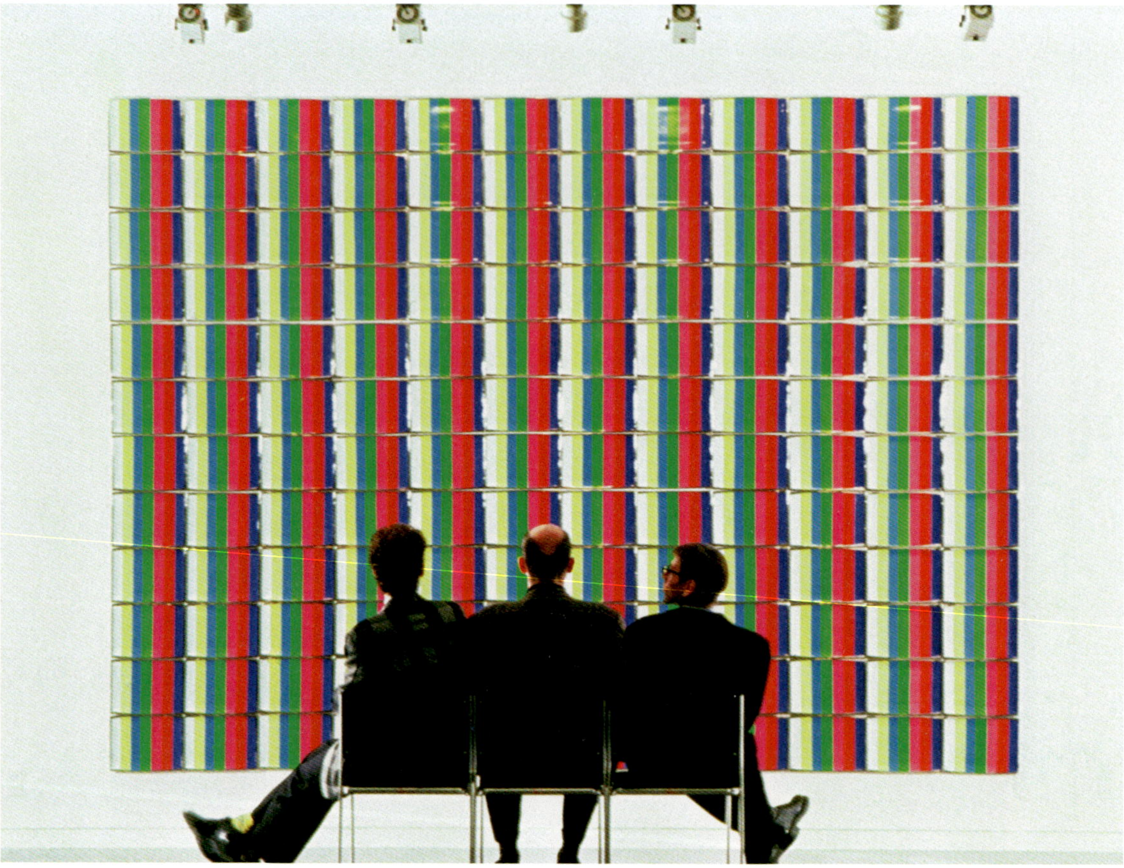

General Idea in front of Test Pattern: T.V. Dinner Plates from the Miss General Idea Pavillion, 1988

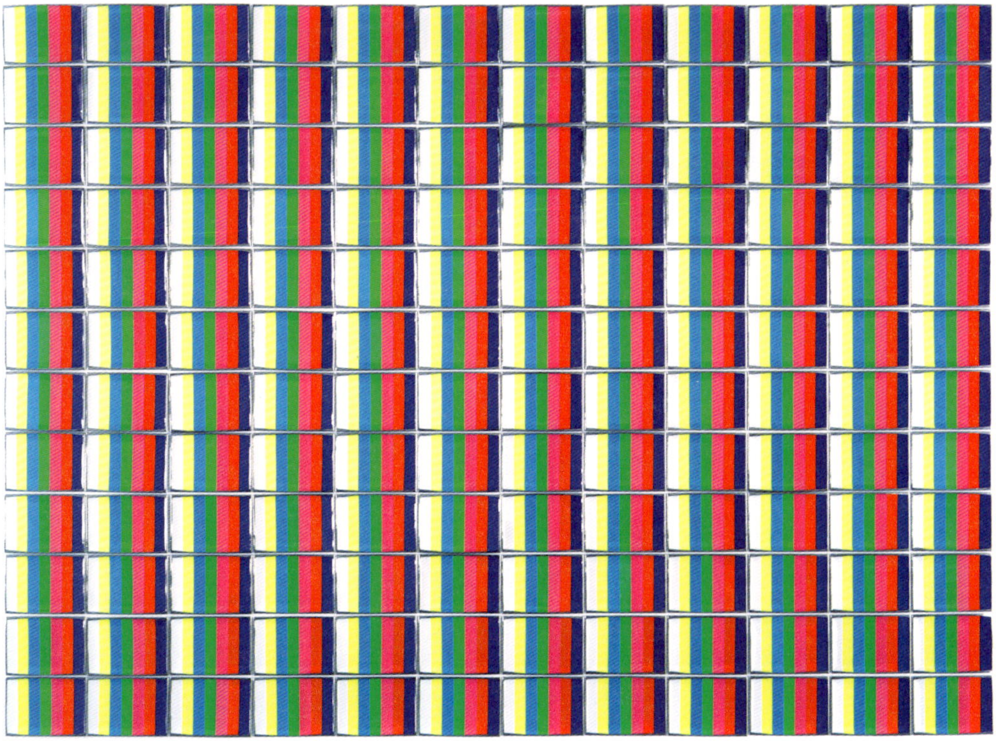

Test Pattern: T.V. Dinner Plates from the Miss General Idea Pavillion, 1988

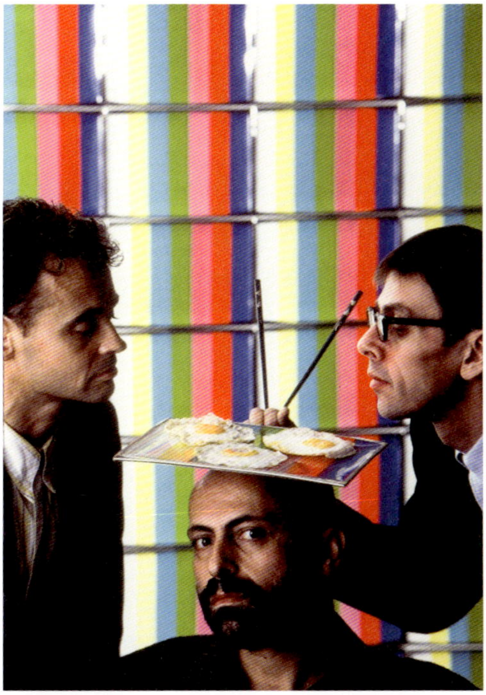

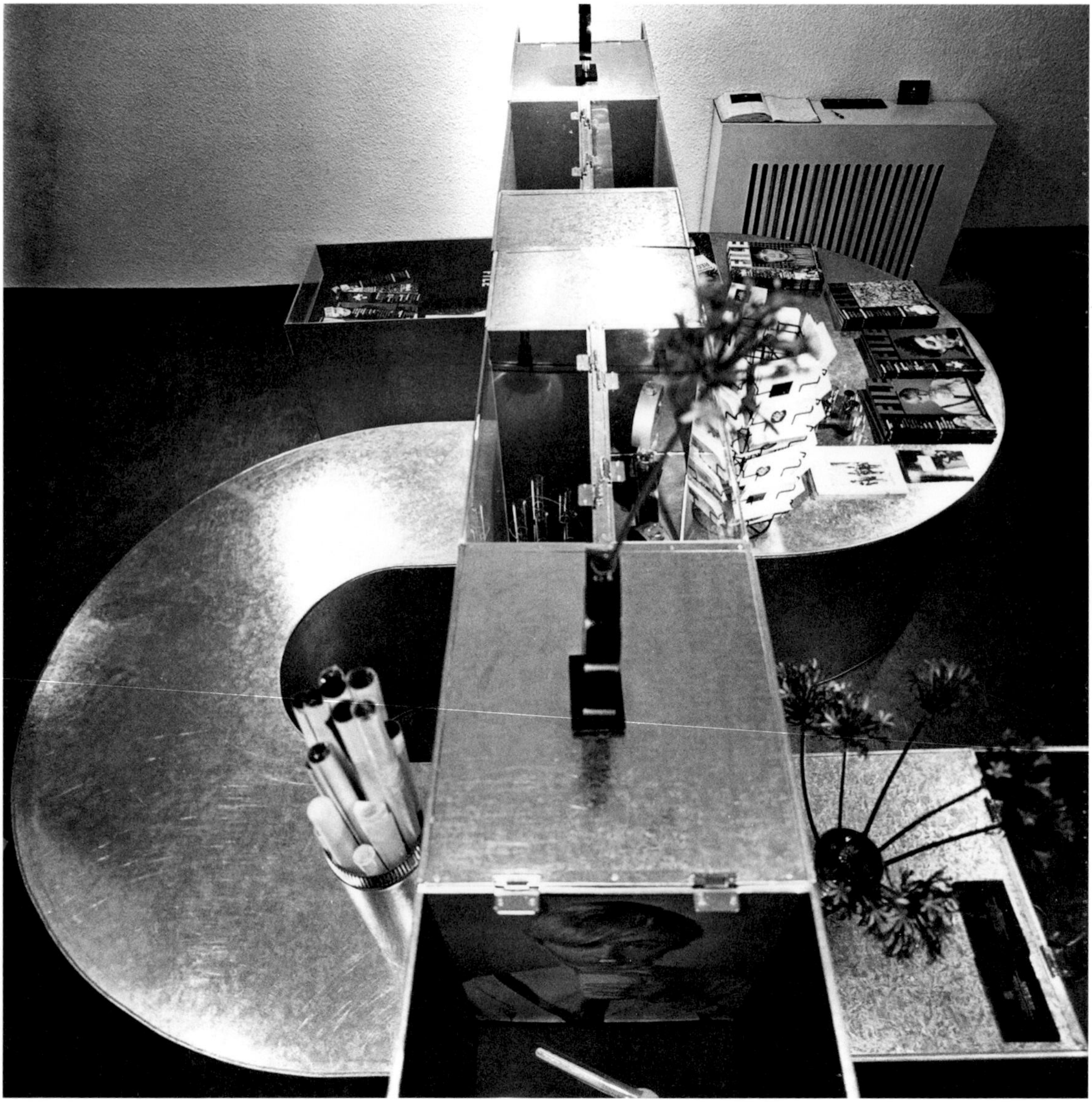

The Boutique from the 1984 Miss General Idea Pavillion, 1980

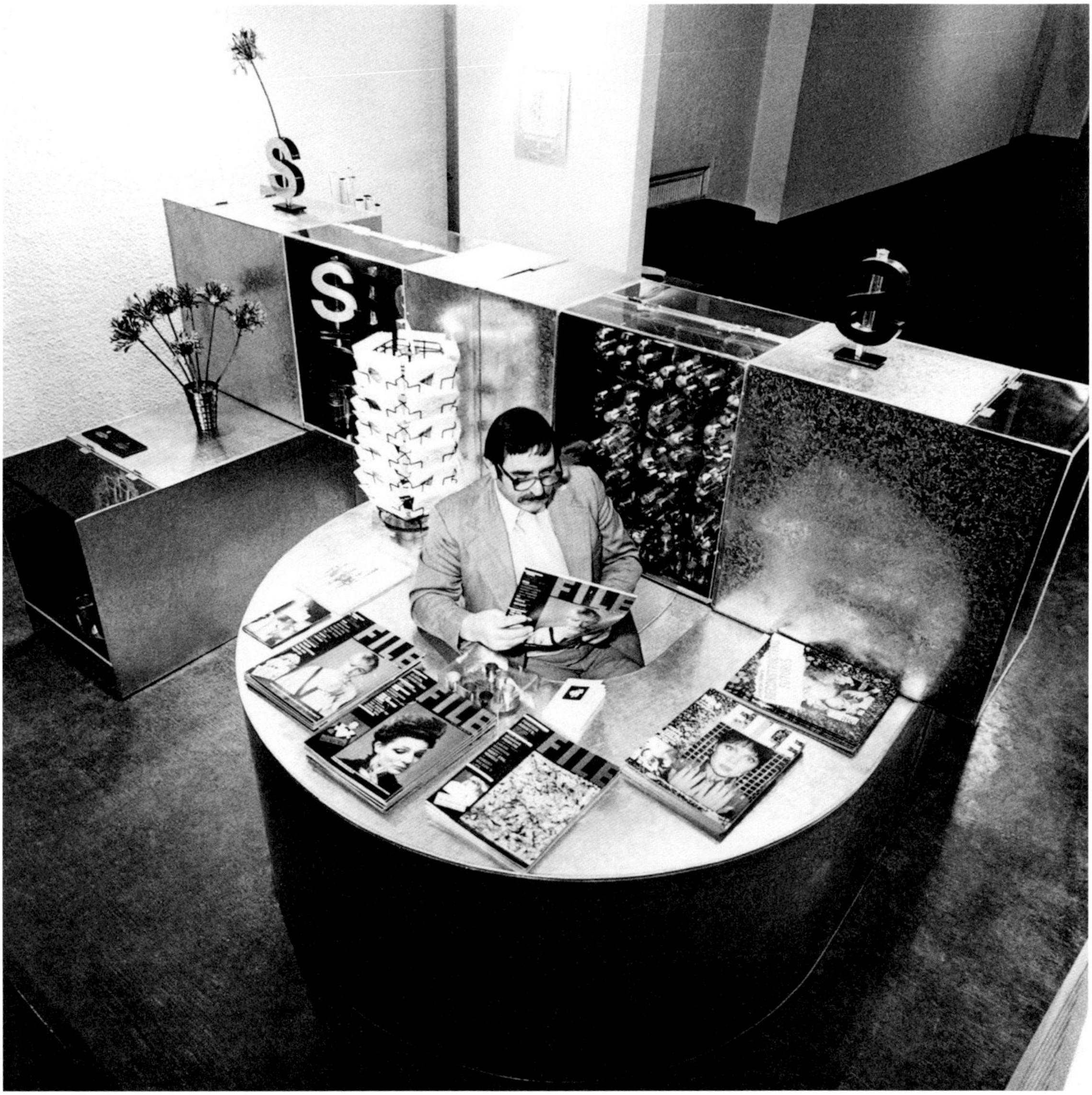

132–133

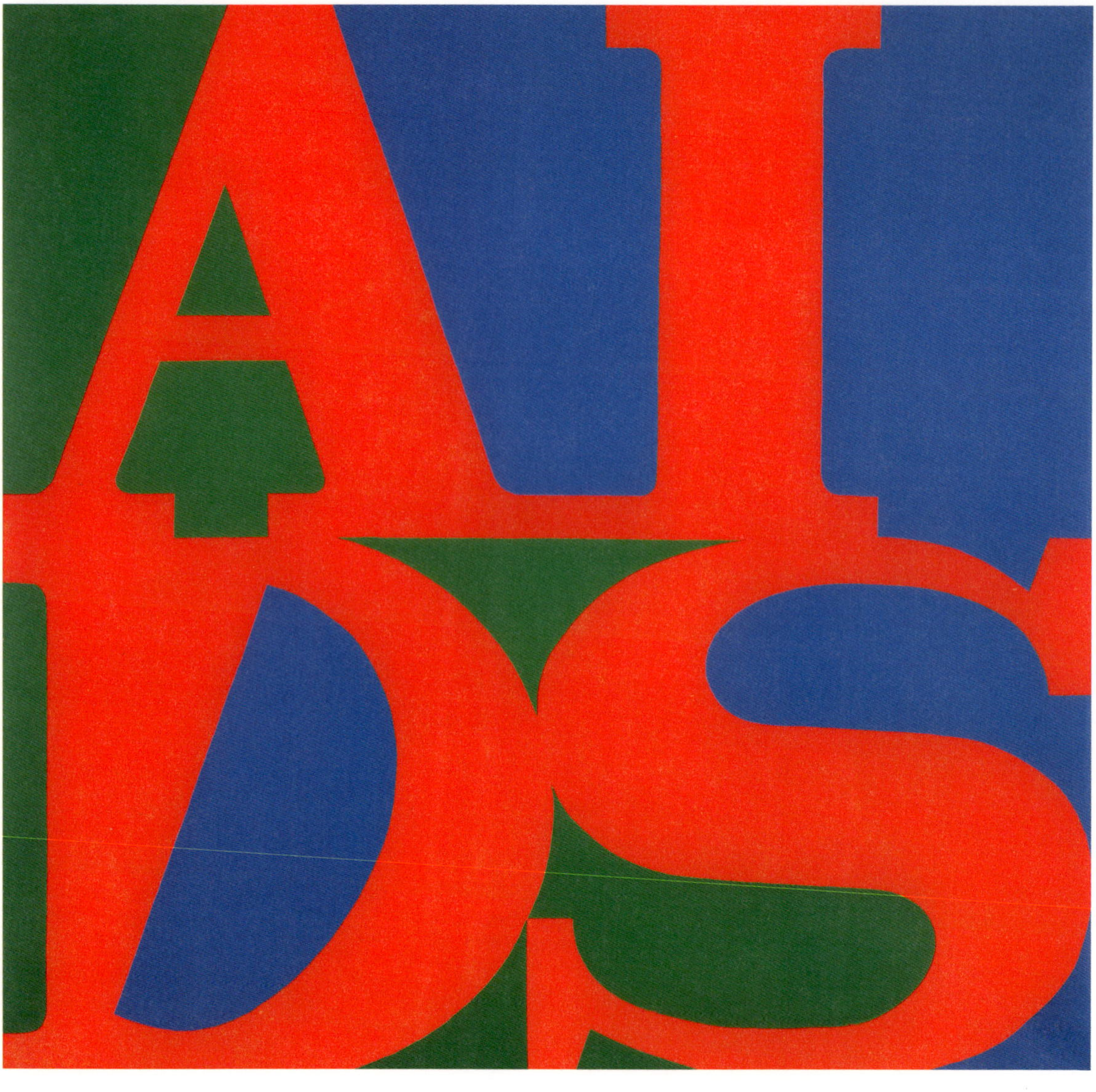

AIDS, 1987

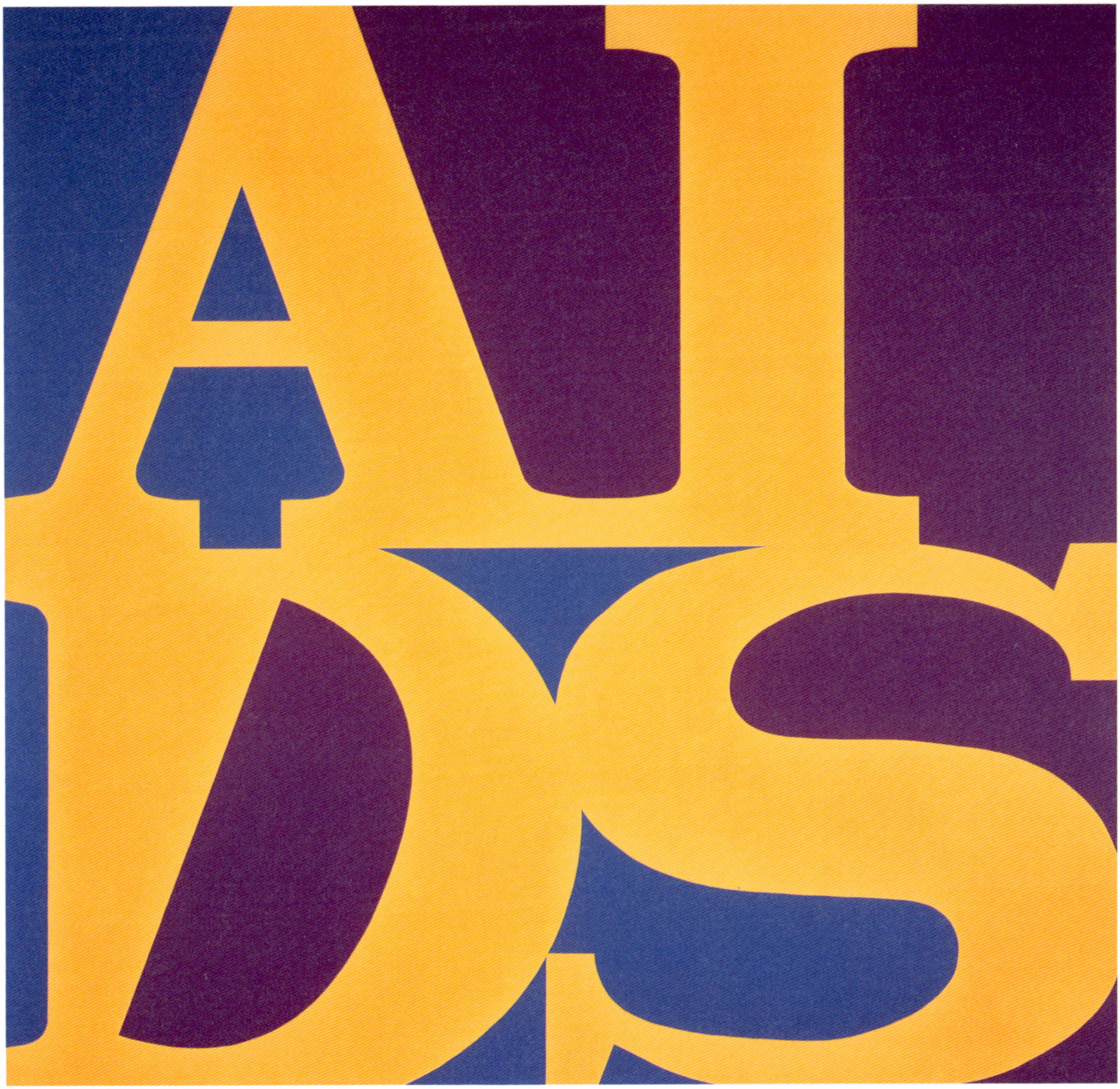

AIDS (Cadmium Orange Light), 1988

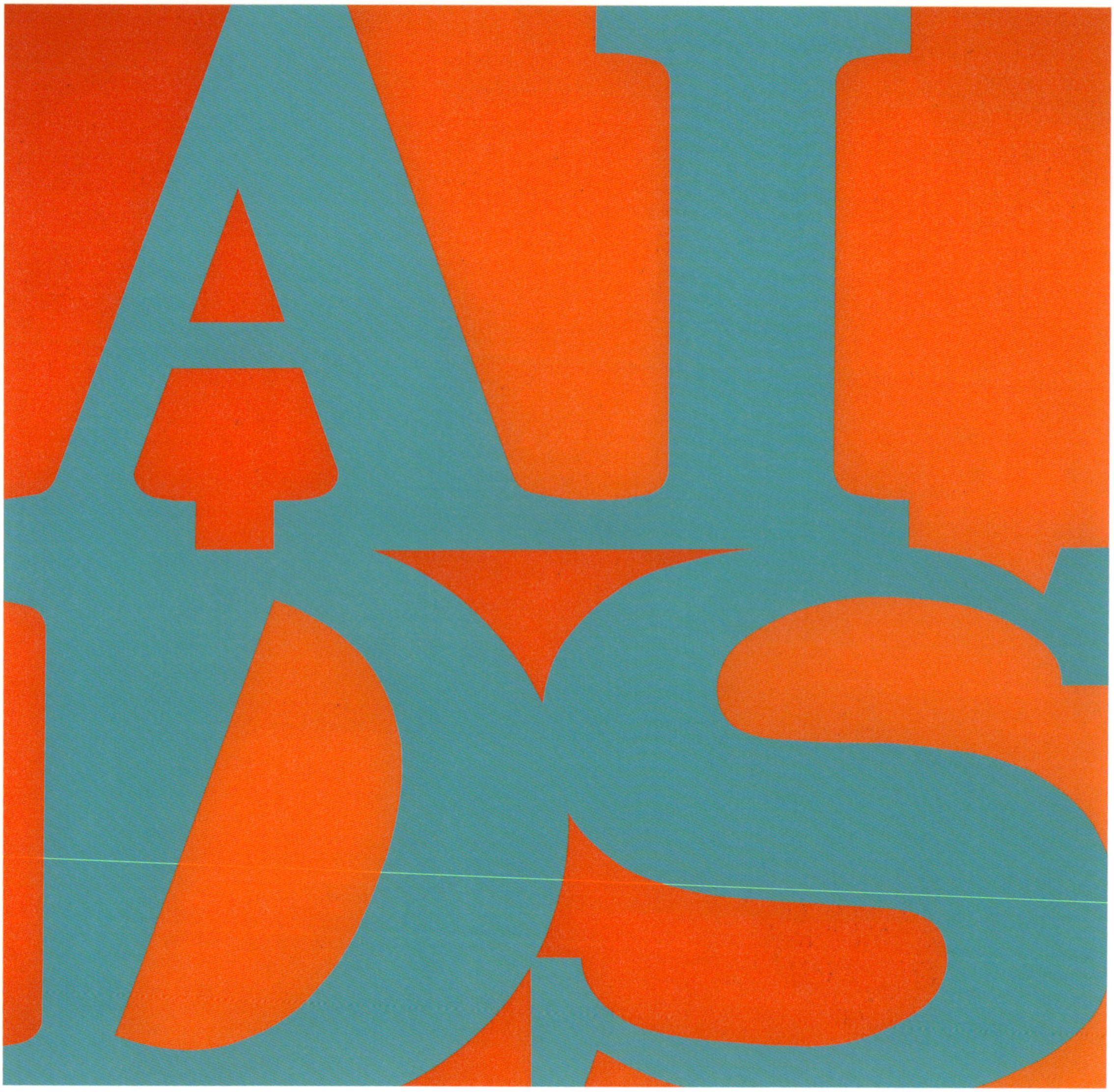

AIDS (Lascaux Green Light), 1988

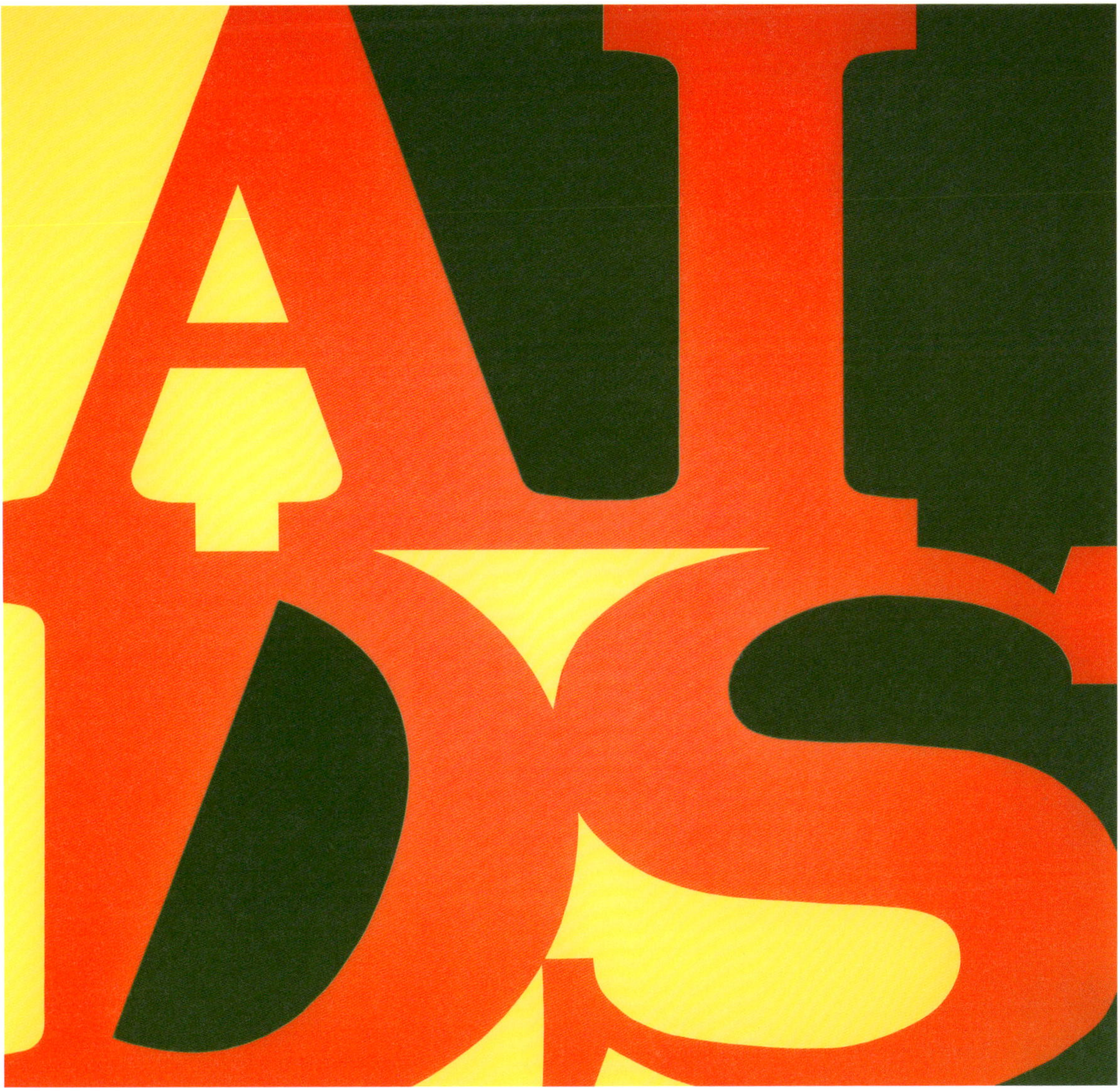

AIDS (Permanent Rose Deep), 1988

White AIDS #6, 1993

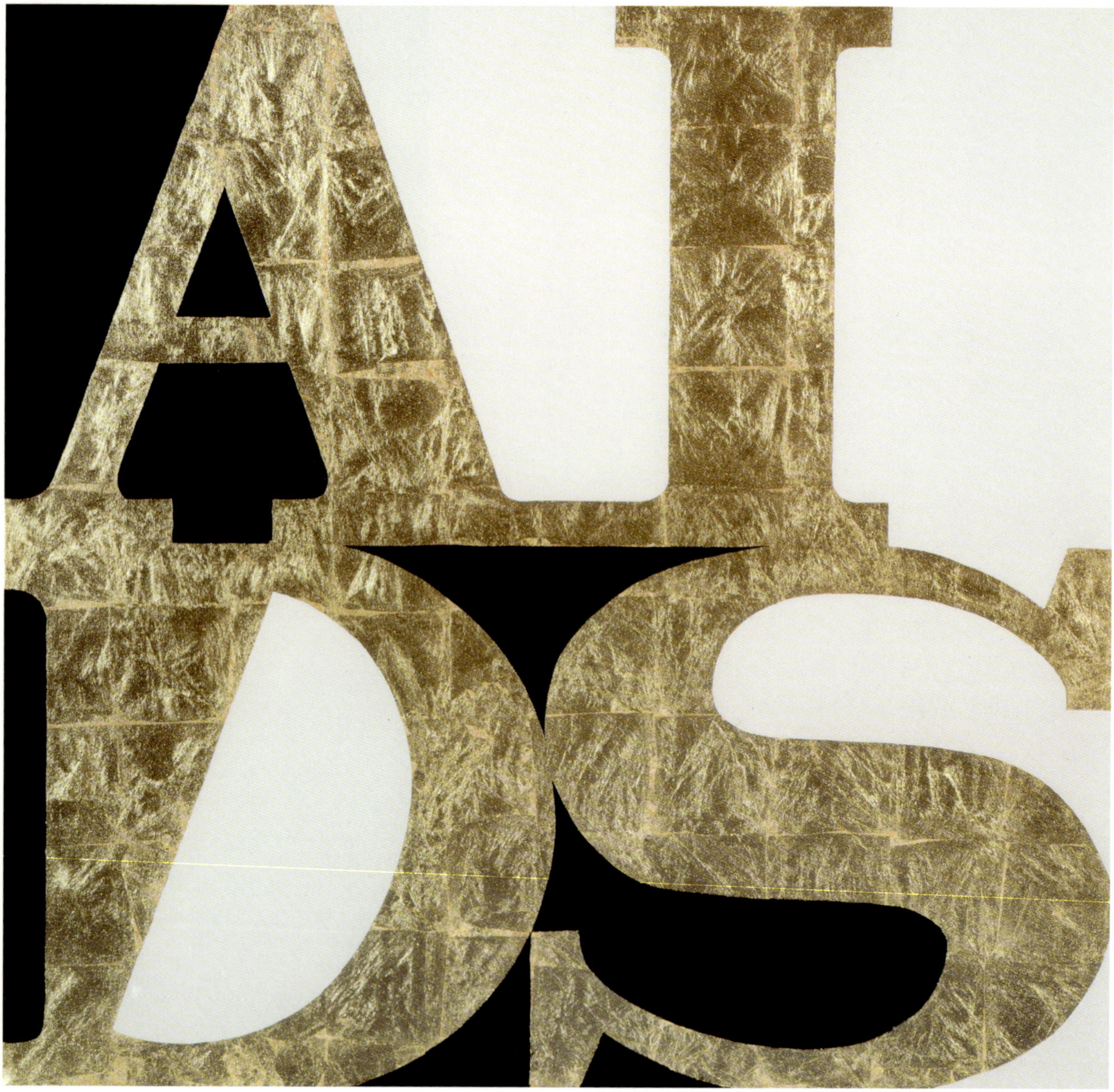

AIDS (Gold) [a.k.a. AIDS (Black and Gold)], 1987

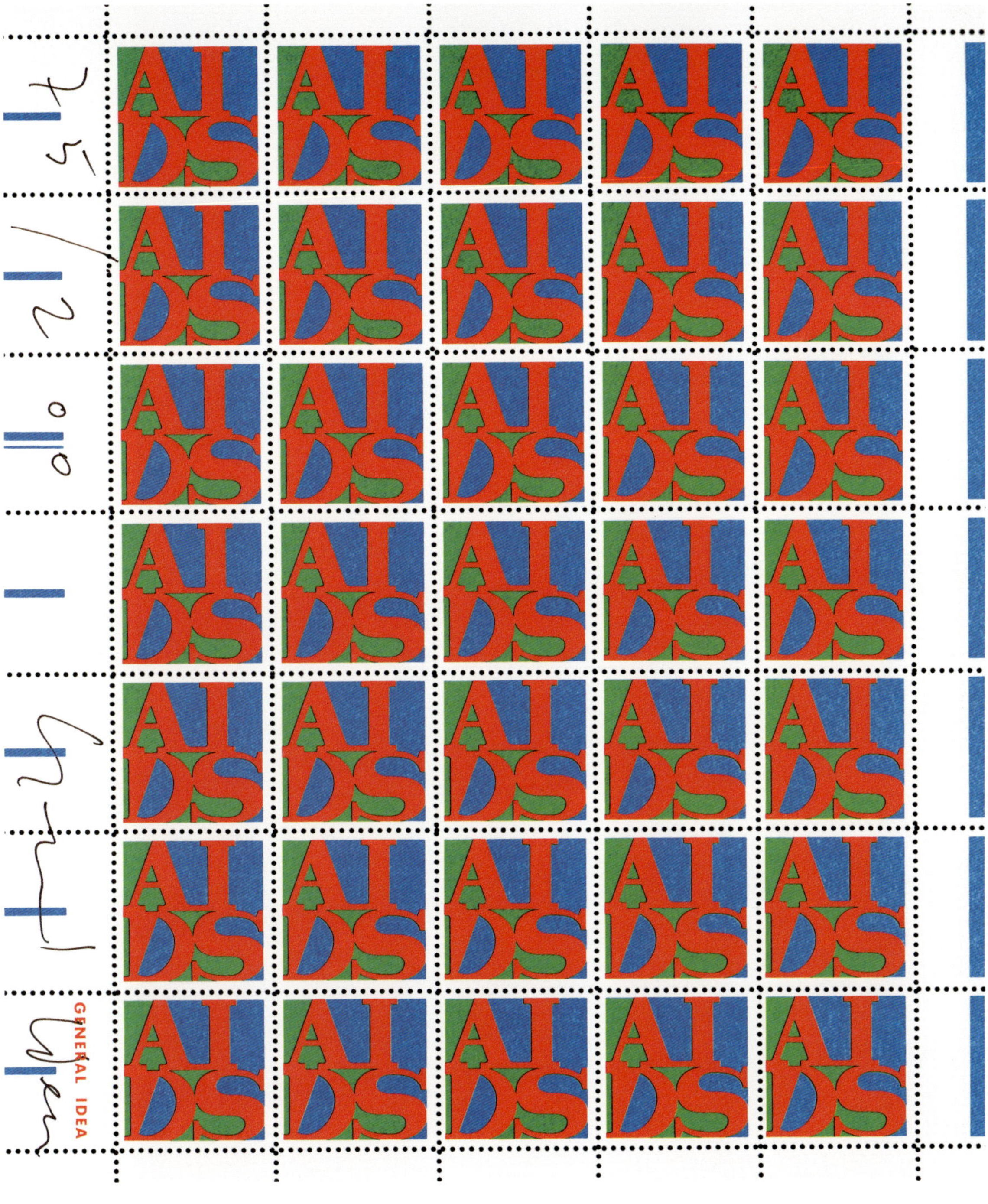

AIDS Stamps, 1988

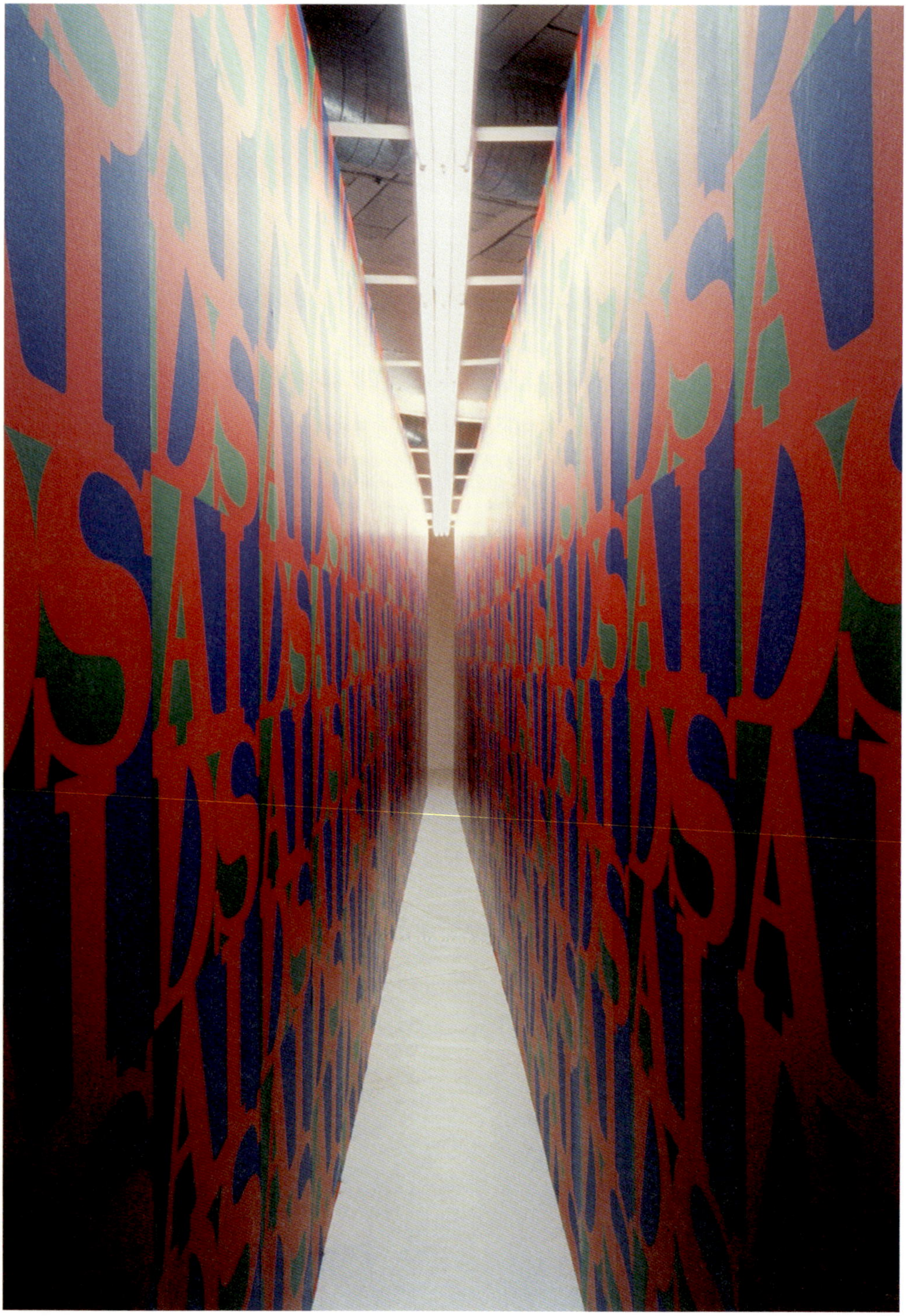

AIDS (Nauman), 1991

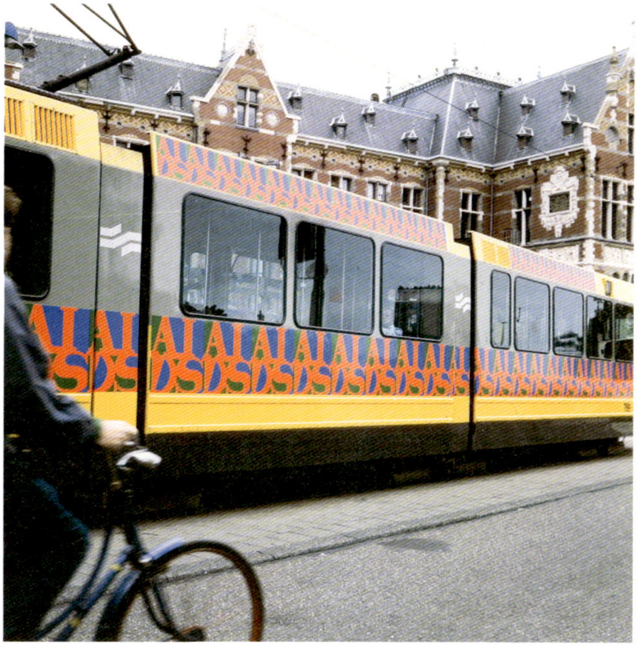

AIDS (Amsterdam Trams), 1990

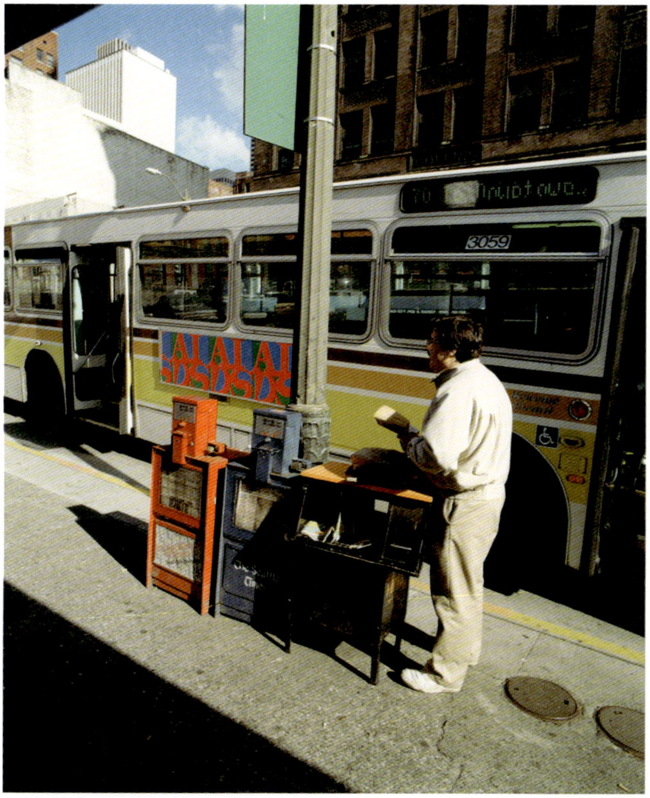

AIDS (Seattle Arts Commission), 1991

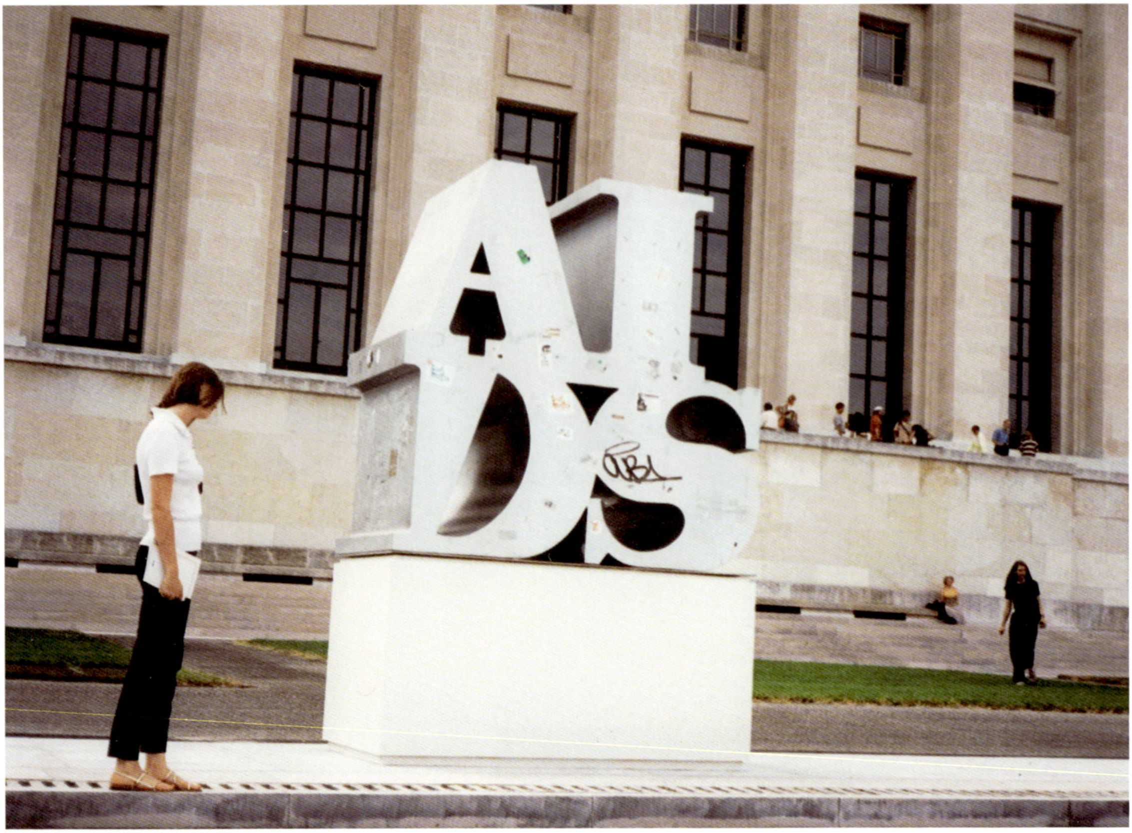

AIDS, 1989, in front of the Palais des Nations, Geneva, 1995

Being a trio freed us from the tyranny of the myth of the individual genius. It left us free to assimilate, synthesize and contextualize influences from our own immediate cultural environment.

Showcard 2-052, The Tyranny of the Myth of the Individual Genius, 1977

Miss General Idea
is basically this:
an idea framing device for
arresting attention without
throwing away the key …
We are surfacing on the
surface of our desires
defined by the intersection
of differing points of view.
Elevated she reigns;
idealized she contains;
artfully she maintains;
dominantly she sustains
our interest.

Showcard 3-001, Miss General Idea 1984, 1975

AIDS, 1989

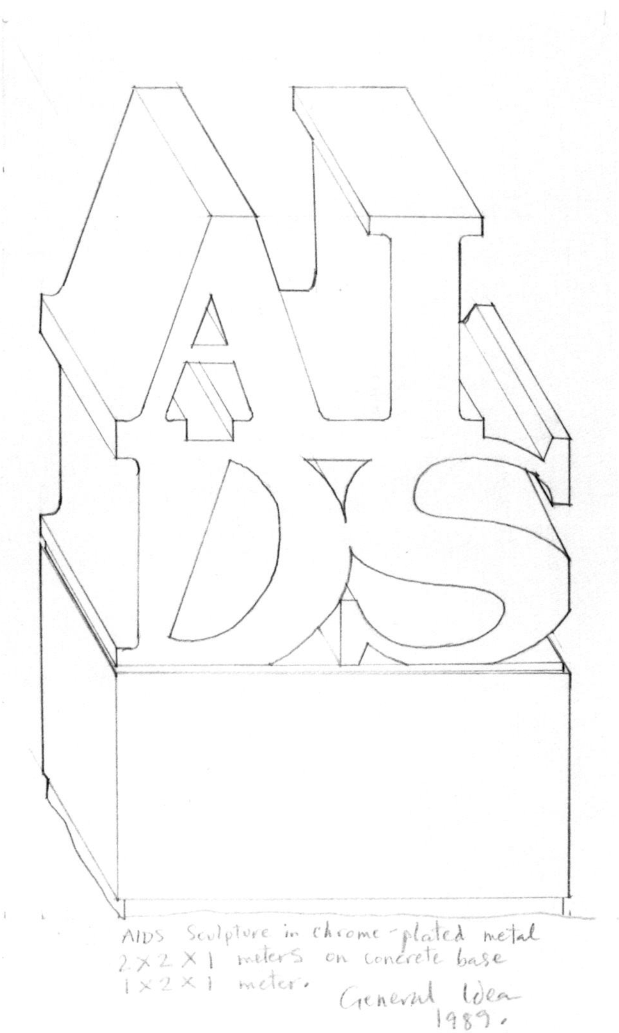
AIDS Sculpture in chrome-plated metal
2 X 2 X 1 meters on concrete base
1 X 2 X 1 meter.
General Idea
1989.

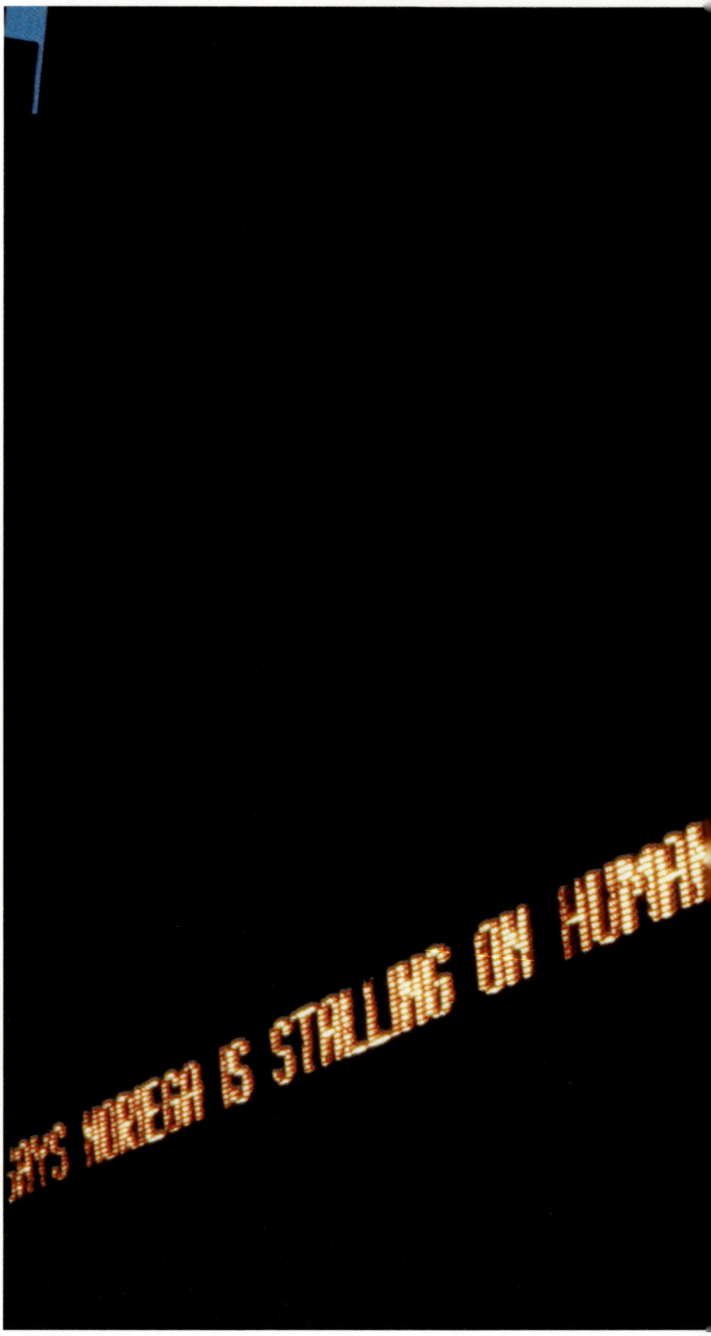

AIDS, Times Square, New York, 1989

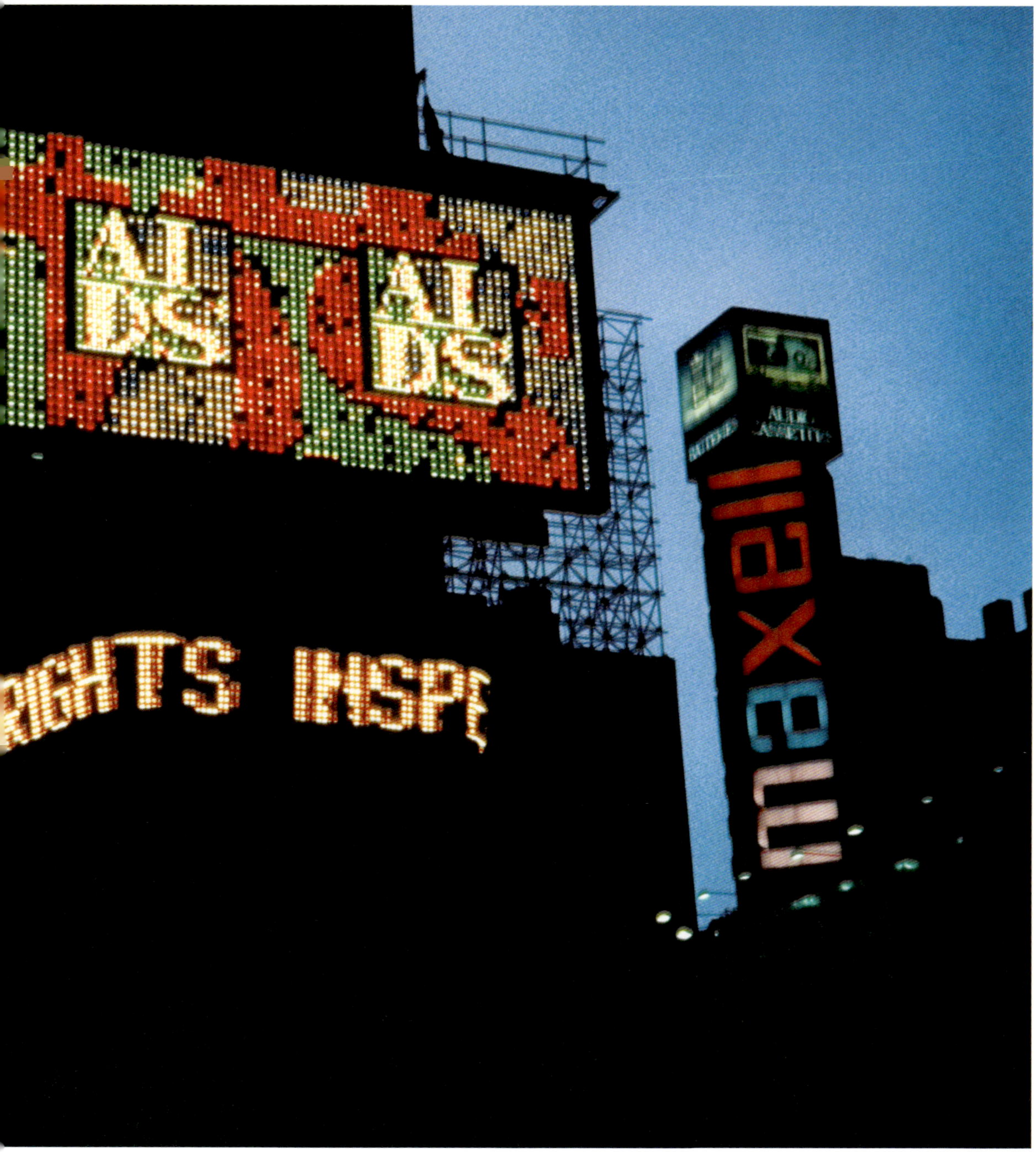
AI
DS
AI
DS
maxell

Interview with AA Bronson, Felix Partz, and Jorge Zontal by Louise Dompierre (New York City, Friday July 26, 1991)[1]

Louise

It seems to me that the first work that you did was to create an identity for your-selves. Individually, you took what could be described as a pseudonym or a stage

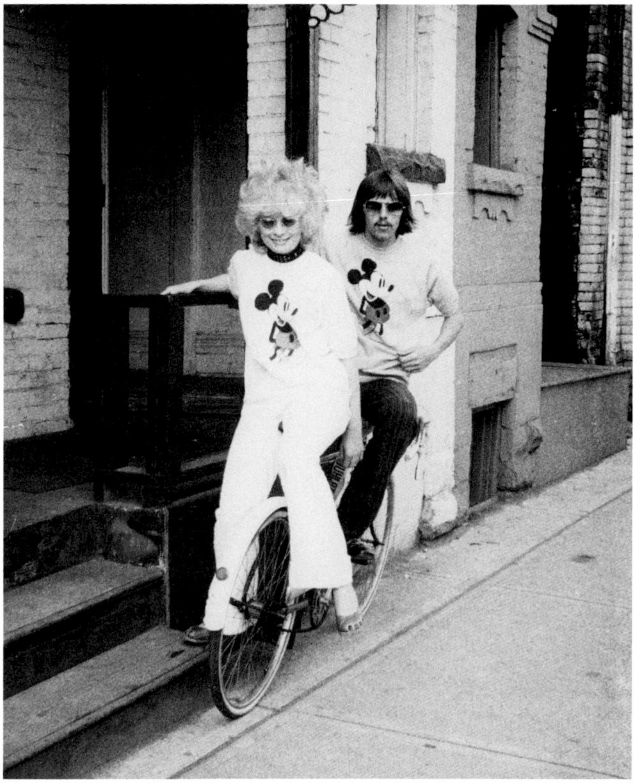

Mimi Paige et Felix Partz devant l'atelier de General Idea, 78 Gerrard Street, Toronto, ca. 1969

name. Then this process was repeated, but on a collective basis. It was the beginning of the myth in a way. Would you agree?

AA

I guess, yes. I'm not sure it happened in that order. It happened collectively first.

Felix

General Idea emerged from that, actually. I mean, we had been working separately on independent projects, which gradually started involving each other. Officially, and then non-officially, just living together, we started creating projects around the house that were collaborations without any framework or any name or any direction. And I think at some point they just sort of smacked together, where the working on each other's projects and the fooling around in the house sort of became the same thing. And then it became official.

Louise

So that's when you decided to name yourself General Idea?

Felix

Right.

AA

Well, when we decided, I guess, for that exhibition, I think it was June 1970, at the Nightingale Gallery, before it burnt down and then became A Space ... It was called *Concept 70*. They invited us to do an exhibition, I mean a piece, for that show, and the piece was called *Line Project*.

THE 1984 MISS GENERAL IDEA PAGEANT PAVILLION

DEPARTMENT | 1. THE SEARCH FOR THE SPIRIT OF MISS GENERAL IDEA

PAGE | PAGE

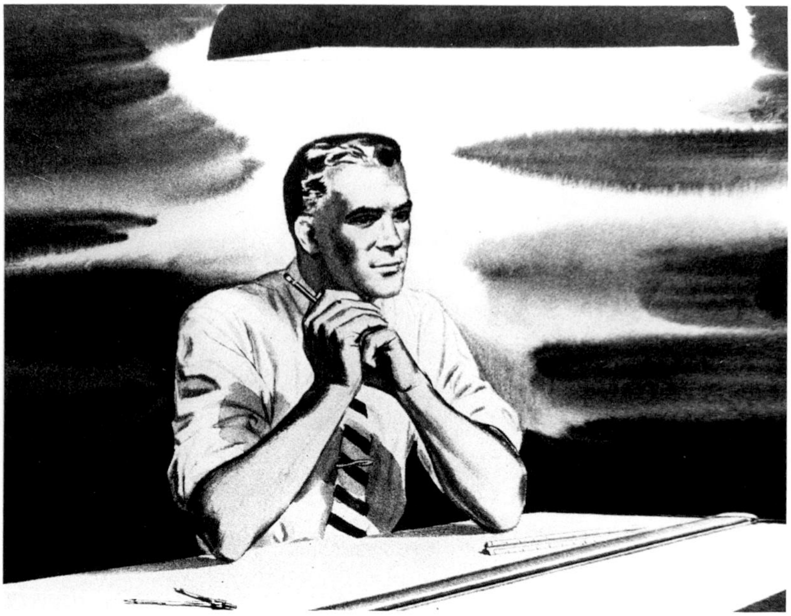

eadline

'GENERAL IDEA'

text

General Idea is basically this: a framing device within which
we inhabit the role of the artist as we see the living legend.
We can be expected to do what is expected within these bounds.
We are aware of the limitations of this and refer to it as
our Frame of Reference and act accordingly behind
the lines. Projecting our roles gives us some perspective
to start with so we can see clear to project
our frames frame by frame.

ADDENDA

PHOTO: General Idea
from Fortune Magazine

COPY NUMBER 1/2 1-001

LAYOUT DATE OCT 18 1975

SIGNATURE GENERAL IDEA

Showcard 1-001 'General Idea,' 1975

Felix

General Idea was the artist, I guess. The first time the name was used.

Louise

So were you, at that stage, AA Bronson, Felix Partz, and Jorge Zontal?

AA

No. No we weren't. I think at that time we were also just beginning to build up our "physical" presence. We would all go everywhere in a group, and with a big entourage, that was something we were definitely doing back then, through until the mid-1970s, I would guess. Our "arrival" would always be a sort of theatrical event.

Felix

Also, in the early days, I don't think that there was a definitive definition of who was General Idea. And for a long time, for a number of years, we purposely obscured who General Idea actually was, because we were involved with working and living with a variety of people. And everybody was seen as General Idea.

AA

And if somebody moved out, and another person came in, they became General Idea.

Felix

And we endorsed that form of identity at that time.

Louise

So when did you take your other names then?

AA

Those emerged.

Felix

They sort of evolved, in a way. They are all individual stories. Like when Jorge arrived in Toronto, because he was Venezuelan, and he had this name, Jorge, which is not his real name to start with. When he arrived in Canada it was translated into George, because it was simpler to deal with. And I can remember that his mother used to phone from Caracas, and ask for Jorge. Which, as I said is not his real name! So, she was already playing a game, and so we started calling him Jorge, in our bad pronunciation, instead of George. And so he became Jorge. And then the 'Zontal' was added at a later date.

AA

Not that much later. It was Ken Coupland who added it, because he found—I think it was a Jamaican record called *I just want to be horizontal*. And it was sort of kidding Jorge for being lazy and always sleeping late in the mornings. And so he started calling him horizontal: "Jorgezontal."

Felix

I should say that we were also involved in that whole mail art network. And just because of the nature of that correspondence, people were assuming personas, let's call them pen names, and developing quite elaborate mythologies around these pen names. So it was plugging into all that. And in some cases people would have a variety of names, depending on …

Louise

The moment?

Felix

Not necessarily the moment, but who they were corresponding with. I know that Jorge had other names. If you had a specific streak of correspondence with one person about some type of thing, you might have assumed a completely different identity. People had all these sub-identities. I think Jorge had one called "Lana Banal."

Louise

At some point you started to give meaning to General Idea. As you said, at the beginning there was no meaning attached to the term, and it was not even just the three of you. And I think it was you, AA, at some point, who said it gave a "general idea" of what you did. At other times, your name was discussed by others, or perhaps even by yourselves, in military or even corporate terms. Would you add anything to that, today, in retrospect, or in terms of what you're doing now?

Felix

When we were talking earlier about the origins of General Idea, and how we purposely disguised who was General Idea, I guess it was partially because we weren't quite sure who General Idea was, and through working together over a number of years it became quite clear, that Jorge, AA, and myself were the actual ongoing core members of General Idea, and the ones who were most involved in the project. It became clear at some point, that our obscuring who General Idea was, was becoming a problem. There were some very odd problems, for example, a lot of people thought that we lived in Vancouver. We'd constantly be faced with that; I guess it was a combination of factors—there was a lot of activity in Vancouver, and our sensibility was non-Toronto at the time.

Louise

Was the Western Front Society[2] existing at that point?

Felix

It was evolving, yeah.

AA

We were closely involved with the same group of people at the time, so we were being confused with them all the time. And people would think that they were part of General Idea. Even now, there are still people who think that General Idea are from Vancouver. It's amazing. Or that Michael Morris[3] is part of General Idea.

Felix

It's easy to understand the confusions in a way, but at some point we decided to do almost like an advertising campaign, that was to define who General Idea was, visually, and, talk about General Idea, talk about working together and that type of thing, so it was sort of an explanation of who we were, what our project was, and, what we were doing, and what we had done.

Louise

How did you do it, visually?

Felix

Well, it was presented in our work, as videotapes. *Pilot* (1977) was definitely establishing the identity. It was divided into three parts—essentially each one of us hosted a part. It was done in *FILE Megazine*[4] in a lot of cases.

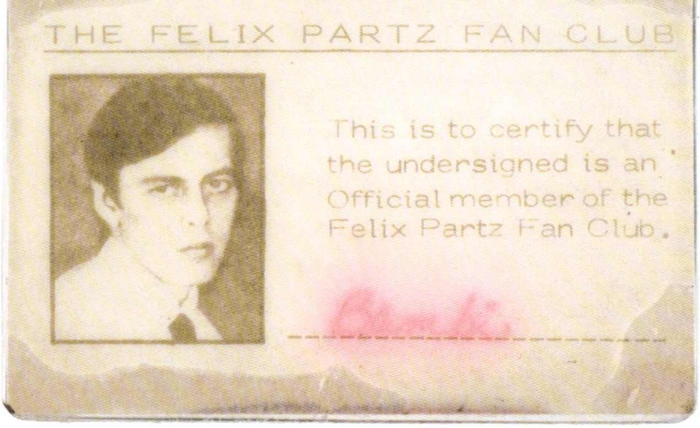

The Felix Partz Fan-Club, 1977

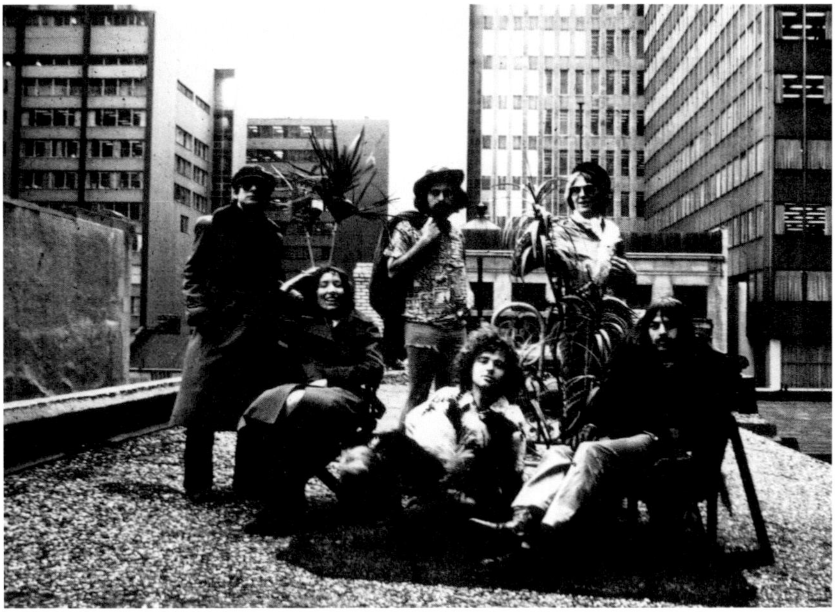

General Idea and friends on the roof of 87 Yonge Street, Toronto, ca. 1970

AA

And even in our gallery shows. We did a lot of self-portrait pieces—they were called "The Three Men Series"—pieces involving images of three men. Some were found images and some were images of us, but we were really trying to identify ourselves as a group of three men.

Felix

And things like the "Glamour"[5] article played the part of the manifesto. It was a matter of putting together all the components necessary to, I guess, market a group. Which had never been done before. We didn't really have any role models for how to do that, because people were, and still are, used to dealing with individual type of situations. In addition, a lot of time was needed to establish a credibility. When we initially started working, a lot of people were hesitant to get involved with us on a commercial level, because of the fact that "groups never stay together." So we had to establish a very strong foundation.

Louise

Was it difficult to establish this kind of working relationship between the three of you? You clearly have very distinct personalities. Was there a point when you felt that you were starting to feel comfortable as a working group, or as a collective?

Felix

I think that there were different stages. One very difficult thing to deal with in a group situation—because people are used to deal with individuals—is that they're so inquisitive as to who does what, "Who drew that?" "Who's idea was that?" etc., etc., that I think in the early days there were a lot more upfront ego problems. For example, if a newspaper reporter happened to talk to AA about a General Idea project, then all the emphasis would be on AA. And I think initially that was difficult for us to deal with and we had to be very careful about that. I don't think that that's a problem anymore.

AA

In the beginning we didn't have a strong identity as a group. But I do think that even by 1971, when we were working on *The 1971 Miss General Idea Pageant*, there was a definite working relationship between the three of us specifically. And a continuing commitment was established, by that time. We actually began *FILE* in early 1972, but we began working on it as a project, putting together the idea and trying to raise the funds in late 1971. So that's already quite early. And that seems to me a very ambitious thing to do as an artist's project in those times, given the nature of funding at the time. And also when you actually look back at our lifestyle, and what we were—this sort of "crazy" group of people, living together.

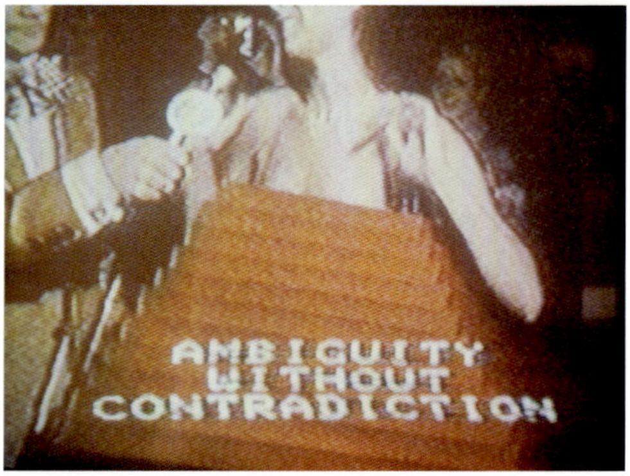

Going Thru The Motions, 1975

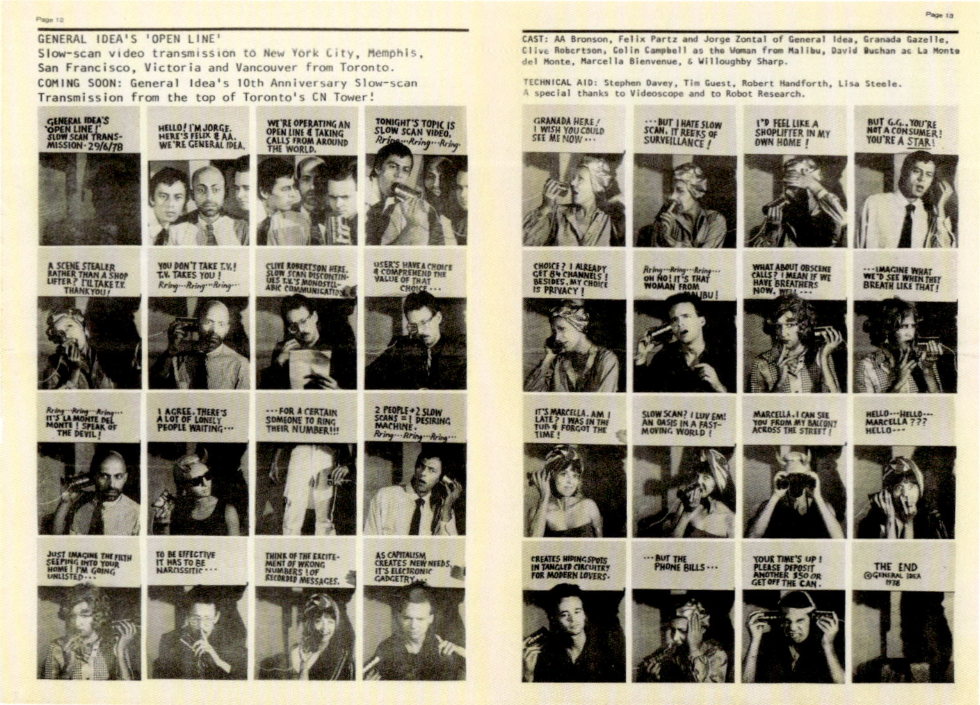

Open Line (Slow-Scan Transmission), 1978

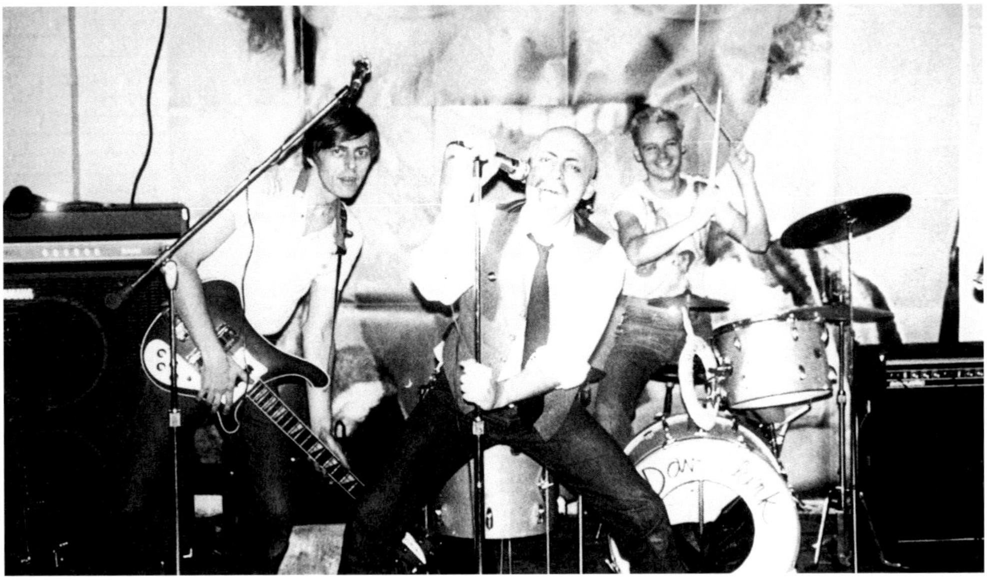

General Idea, 1977

There had to be a firm working relationship for that to happen at that point.

Felix

Also in 1971, what happened was that we established the whole "1984" project, which was a conceptual project, but was also in reality a commitment to working together for 13 years. And in retrospect that was practically like a marriage ceremony.

Louise

Yes, it must have been a bit frightening too?

Felix

Well, it was. 1984, at that time, was arbitrary in a sense, because we were just playing off of the mythology. So it could have been five years in advance, in reality, or it could have been 50 years in advance. It just happened to be 13 years in advance. We made the commitment that we were going to work on this project until 1984, and then the whole structure started evolving. The pageant fitted in, and the "Pavillion," and *FILE*, and so on and so on. The whole thing started rolling on this fake foundation. A commitment, so it's not a "fake," but a conceptual commitment.

Louise

Times change, of course, and so do you feel that you still function under the same kind of terms of reference as when you began? Or have things evolved?

AA

There have been shifts. First of all, in terms of our relationship, we've been together for so long that there is, as we usually say, a sort of group language that has evolved. And we're able to work, in a way, more independently than we were before. For example, it's possible for us to be in two cities, and still continue. The work can proceed more out of a group mind, rather than the three of us having to sit around a table and discuss every detail. At least that's the way I see it.

Felix

I think that there has been a shift in emphasis, though, in the last little while. I don't know when it happened, but now, rather than putting a lot of energy into working together, we're putting a lot of energy into figuring out how we can, individually, work within General Idea, and fulfill our own individual destinies. Taking advantage of our own individual interests and skills, without being limited by the General Idea context. So, the General Idea context is continually being tugged and pulled and what-have-you, to accommodate—and part of that is being practical about living in two different cities. But it's also a maturity. We've gone through periods where General Idea has felt like a straight jacket. We were so busy trying to project a group identity, that it was difficult to transgress that. More recently, we became less worried about transgressing, and more worried just that it makes sense. We don't want to end up as a group show. We want to maintain the individual artist as General Idea. But on the other hand, to allow for the …

AA

Individual eccentricities!

Louise

The people that were part of General Idea, the larger group, where did they come from? Were they graduates from Ontario College of Art? What were, broadly, people's backgrounds?

AA

I don't think there were any other people with an art background.

Felix

There were a lot of people who were in the creative field. There was an actor. There was Granada[6] who was working at the film co-op at the time. So there were these connections to the film world in Toronto. We had interior designers living with us. We had …

AA

A drag queen, for a while.

Felix

Not a drag queen, AA! A diva with a five octave range … or whatever it is. It was quite a hodge-podge. We were sort of "cultural refugees," I think. With a strong sense of alternative lifestyles and a vision of the culture. Sort of outsiders, in a sense.

Louise

So was it linked somehow with the idea of the commune?

AA

I don't think it was, consciously, linked with the idea of the commune, but I had come out of that sort of background—I was involved with a commune that produced an underground newspaper, and had a store, and so-on, in Winnipeg, before I came to Toronto. But, I don't think it was consciously that, it was much more free-form than that. It was more like us and our friends.

Felix

Of course we were aware of the whole commune thing, and in a certain sense, being "naughty" General Idea, we positioned ourselves in opposition to that, to the "back to the earth commune." General Idea was on Yonge Street, in the financial district.

AA

We tried to be a glamorous commune!

Felix

Yeah, everyone staggering around in high-heels and makeup, and all dressed-up all the time, as opposed to running around barefoot in the woods. On the other hand, we did have dealings with a lot of people who were involved in that other—let's call it aesthetic! And so we always positioned ourselves as having that immaturity—being "bratty" among those who can appreciate it, because the outside world wasn't sure what we were doing.

Louise

With what you took from popular culture, like the pageant, or *LIFE* magazine, you created the structure, and then filled it with your own content.

AA

Filled it with other people's content; not with the mass media's content, but with that of other artists. In fact it's an integral part of the work, that other people's work was included in our work. That's something I think that we've come to accept. Not that we necessarily want to do a lot of that, but in fact it was similar to appropriation. It was another strategy, or another method, that remains to be really defined in the larger art world.

Louise

I think you came in contact with Roland Barthes' *Mythologies* in around 1972 when it was translated into English. Was that an important moment for you, when you first read that?

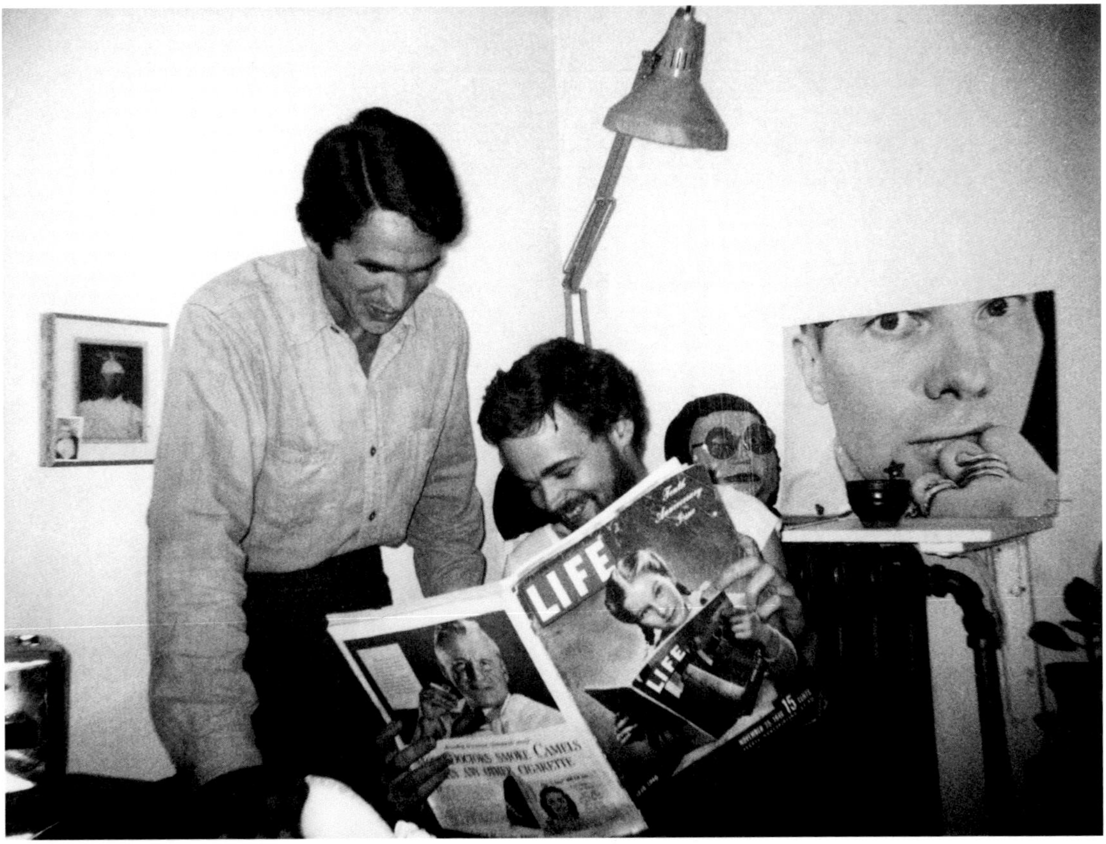

AA Bronson with Eric Metcalfe [a.k.a. Dr. Brute], ca. 1973

AA

I don't think we read it until later than that. I think that we didn't read it until maybe 1974.

Felix

But there was a lot of reading going on at that time—Lévi-Strauss, William Burroughs … there have been lots of literary traditions, or connections, in our work.

AA

And also, I personally had a big background with communications theory. So there was a fairly heavy-duty theoretical background that we never consciously tried to illustrate in our work, but it was always there.

Louise

So Barthes' writing didn't hold any special kind of place.

AA

Well, it did in that the "Glamour" article is a response to the major essay of Barthes' book. And what the "Glamour" article proposes is that glamour is to mythology what mythology is to reality. That was our definition of glamour. I think what captured our imagination with that particular book was his writing style, his ability to popularize his notions. In a way he was the first person since Marshall McLuhan who had been able to do that. And some of Marshall McLuhan's early writings do very similar things.

Louise

Like *The Mechanical Bride*. It's interesting, when you think back in retrospect, which books have played sort of an important role, but it's not always for the reasons people tend to assume, or it's a sort of recognition for activities or popular culture, generally—finding a similarity, in terms of what interested you. But your use of it was very different.

Felix

Even just thinking in terms of someone like William Burroughs and *Naked Lunch*, people think of it more as stylistic, because it's this sensational sex and drugs. But *Naked Lunch* creates this sort of "global myth." It all takes place in this sci-fi reconstructed world; it's a whole construct. It was influential on that level, as well as the clever phrases, and lingo, and imagery, and what-have-you. It was also a way of seeing the world.

Louise

The 1960s was a period in which fundamental questions about the nature of art, or the art system, and the role of the artist were raised and challenged. Your own decision to form a collective is a denial of the notion of the artist as individual genius.

Felix

Come to think of it, there would have been another big group influence—rock-and-roll. Which, in the mid-to-late 1960s, was obviously the alternative or underground scene, the major cultural manifestation. And it was—although there were individuals—a lot of bands. I think that was the strongest role model. Suddenly, it was possible to have people with individual personalities, working as a group, and they had cultural mobility, and they were plugged into contemporary culture, dealing with contemporary issues.

Louise

That's really interesting, because when you think of all you did afterward, the model of the rock band seems to make more sense. Because in the art world, this kind of glamour, those "high moments," just don't exist. Although they do for movie stars or rock stars.

Felix

In a way, it was taking that glamour, and that influence, and that importance, and

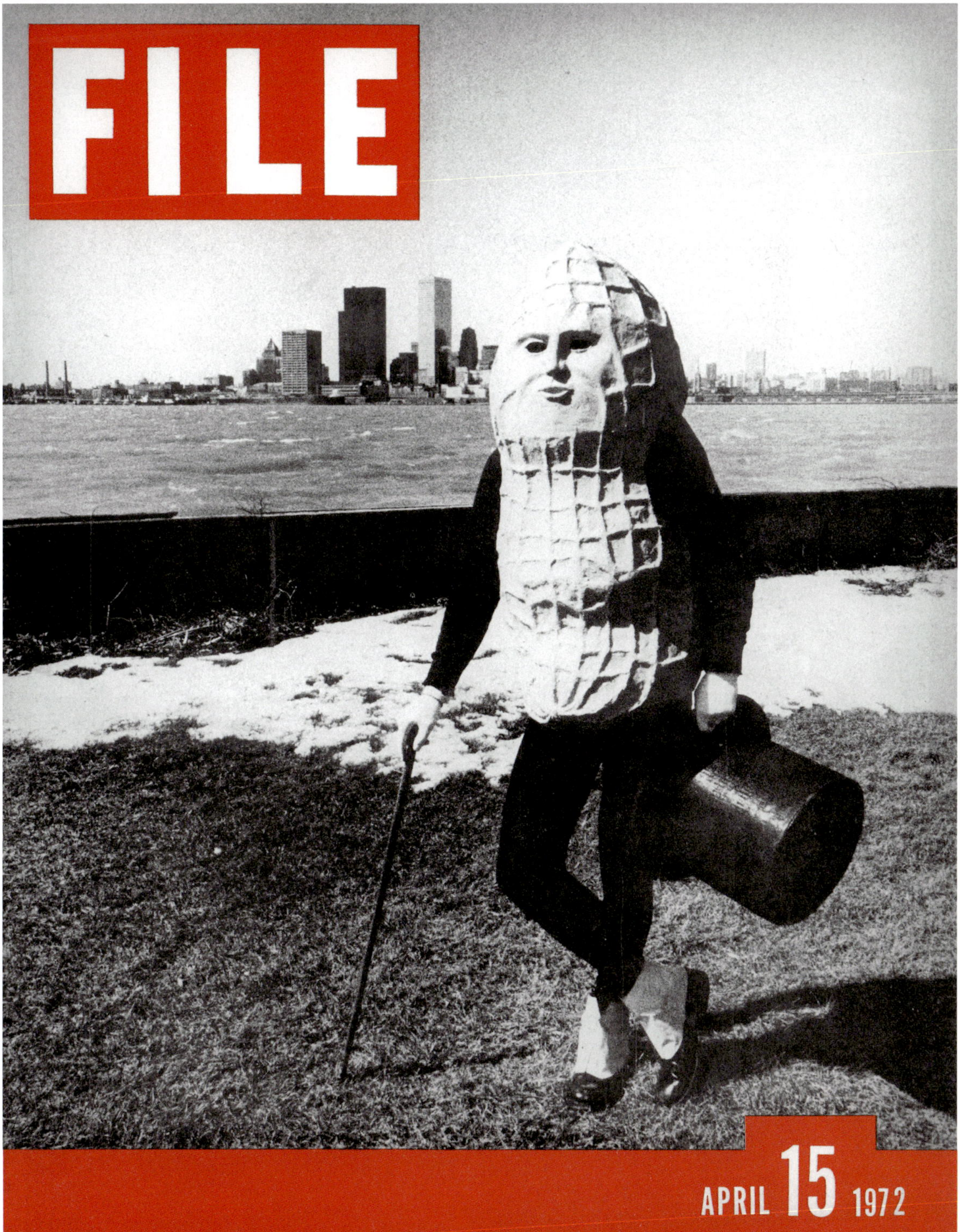

Mr. Peanut Issue, vol. 1, no 1, April 15, 1972

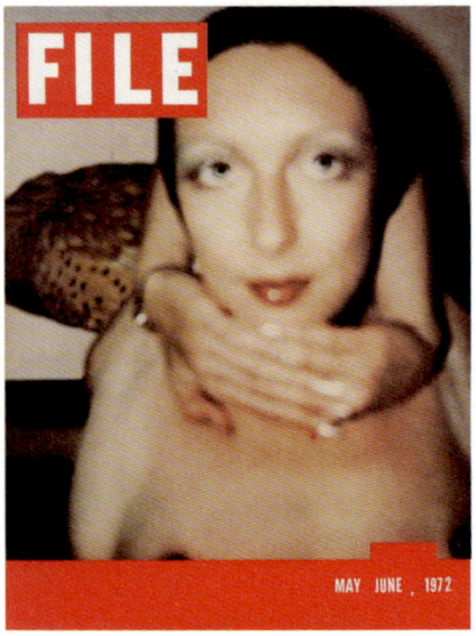

<u>Manipulating the Self Issue</u>,
vol. 1, no. 2 & 3, May–June 1972

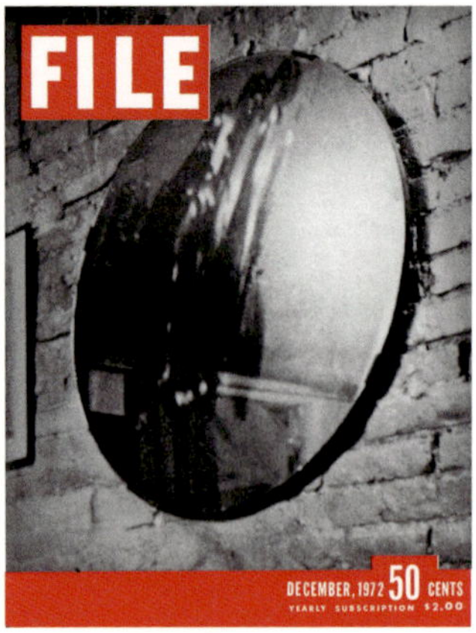

<u>Eye of the Shadow Issue</u>,
vol. 1, no. 4, December 1972

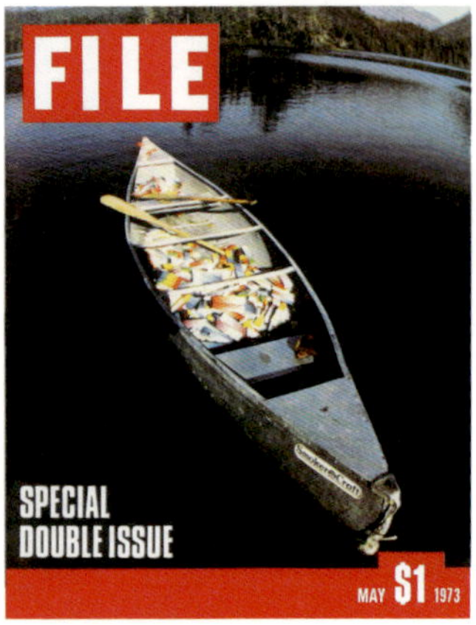

<u>Special Double Issue</u>,
vol. 2, no. 1 & 2, May 1973

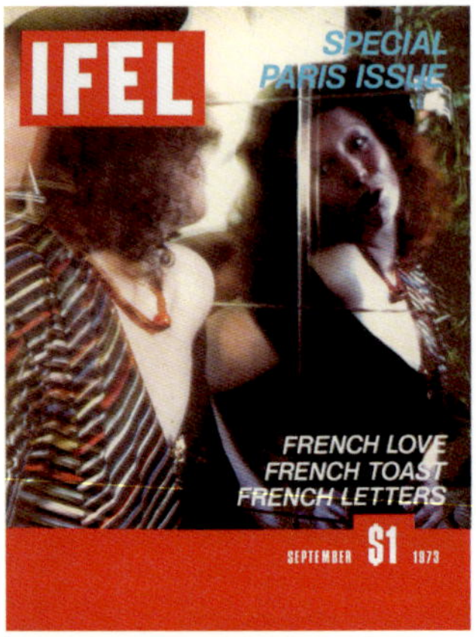

<u>IFEL Special Paris Issue</u>,
vol. 2, no. 3, September 1973

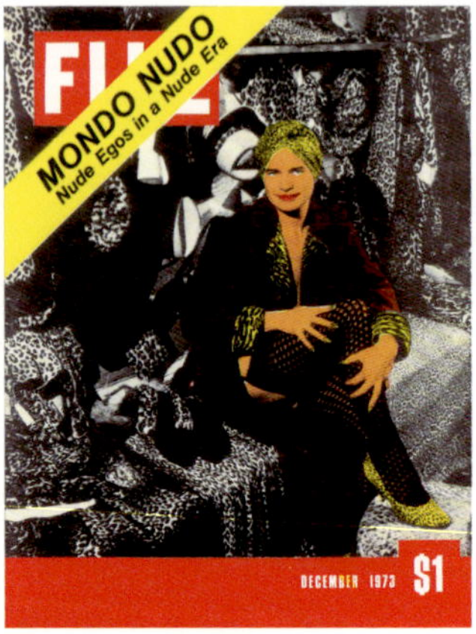

<u>Mondo Nudo Issue</u>,
vol. 2, no. 4, December 1973

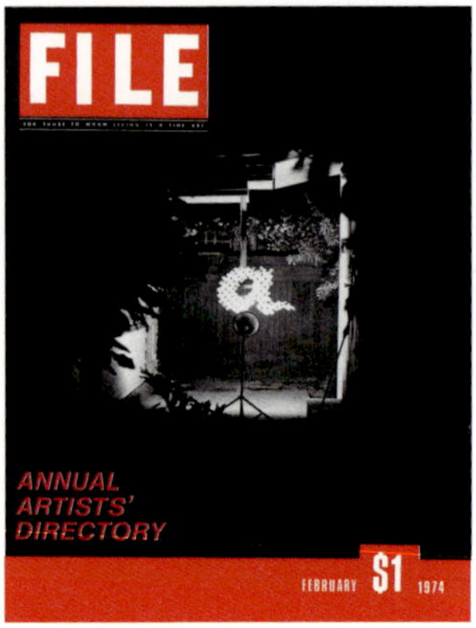

<u>Annual Artists' Directory Issue</u>,
vol. 2, no. 5, February 1974

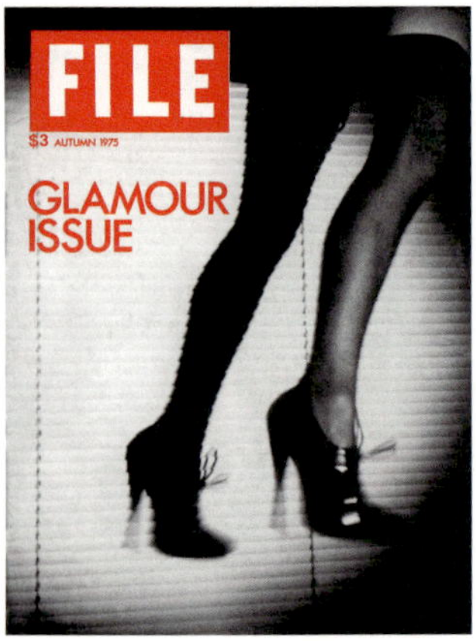

<u>Glamour Issue</u>,
vol. 3, no. 1, Fall 1975

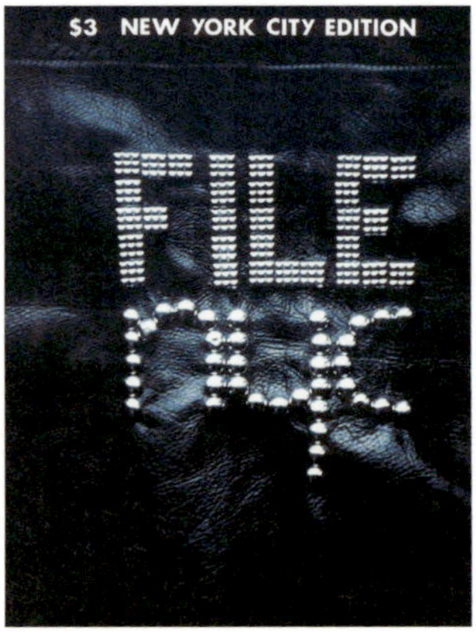

<u>New York City Edition Issue</u>,
vol. 3, no. 2, Spring 1976

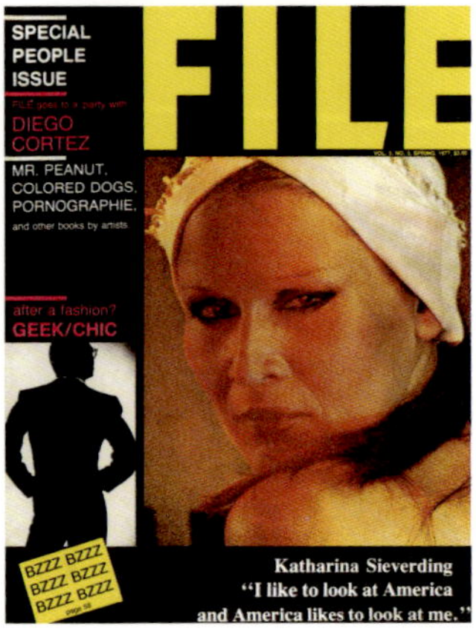

<u>Special People Issue</u>,
vol. 3, no. 3, Summer 1977

The 1984 Miss General Idea Pavillion is basically this: a framing device for accommodation. A terminal in which to rest the case of open and closed frameworks. A superstructure of containment formats like walls framing the theater of operations.

Showcard 4-001, The 1984 Miss General Idea Pavillion, 1975

The Frame of Reference
is basically this:
a framing device within
which we inhabit the role
of the general public,
the audience, the media.
Mirrors mirroring mirrors
expanding and contracting
to the focal point of view
and including the lines
of perspective bisecting
the successive frames
to the vanishing point.

Showcard 5-001, The Frame of Reference, 1977

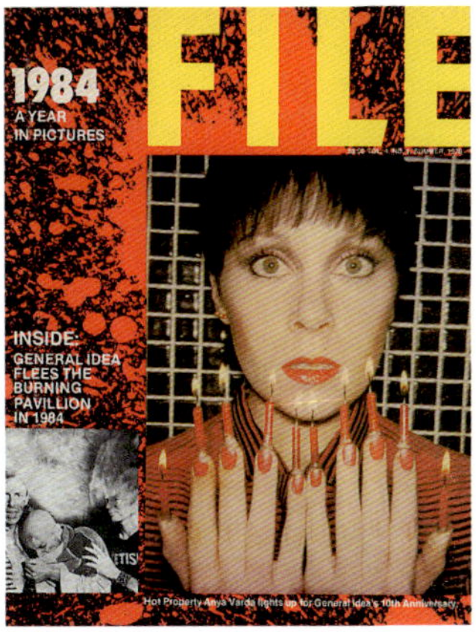

1984 A Year in Pictures Issue,
vol. 4, no. 1, Summer 1978

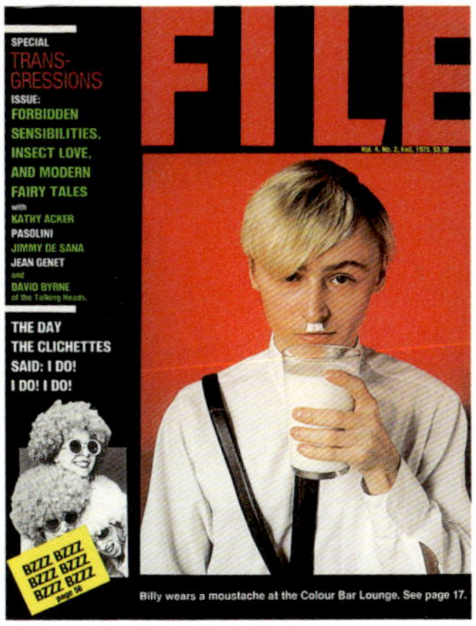

Special Transgressions Issue,
vol. 4, no. 2, Fall 1979

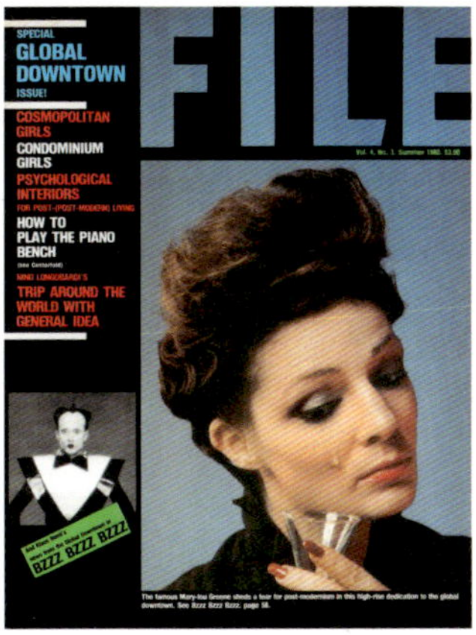

Special Global Downtown Issue,
vol. 4, no. 3, Summer 1980

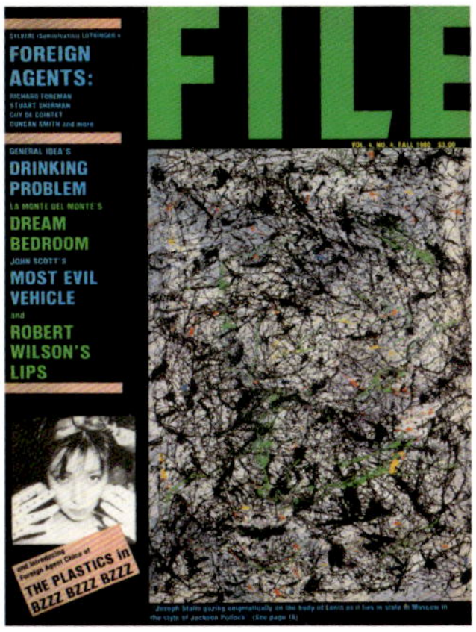

Foreign Agents Issue,
vol. 4, no. 4, Fall 1980

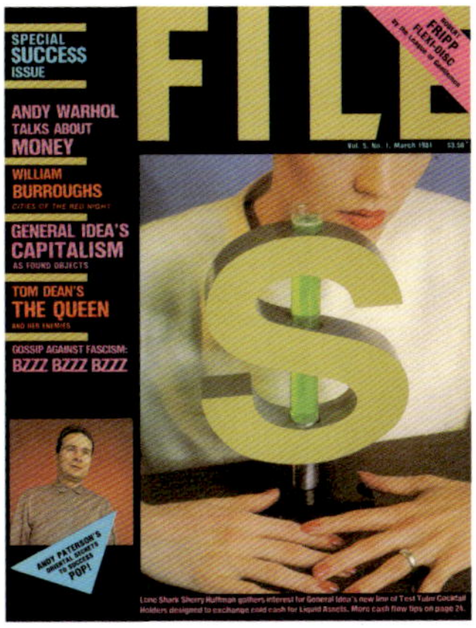

Special $ucce$$ Issue,
vol. 5, no. 1, March 1981

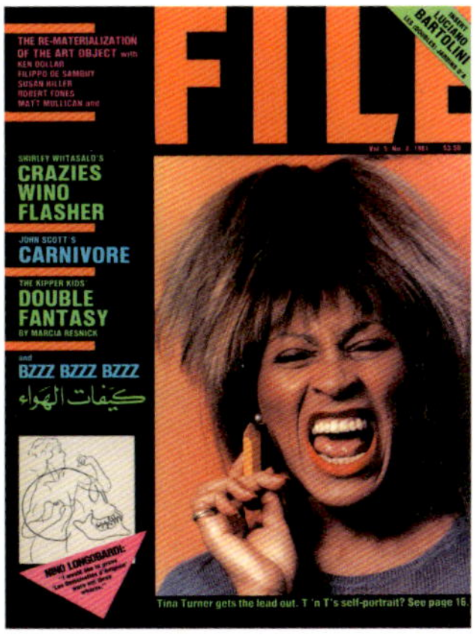

The Re-materialization of the Art Object Issue,
vol. 5, no. 2, Fall 1981

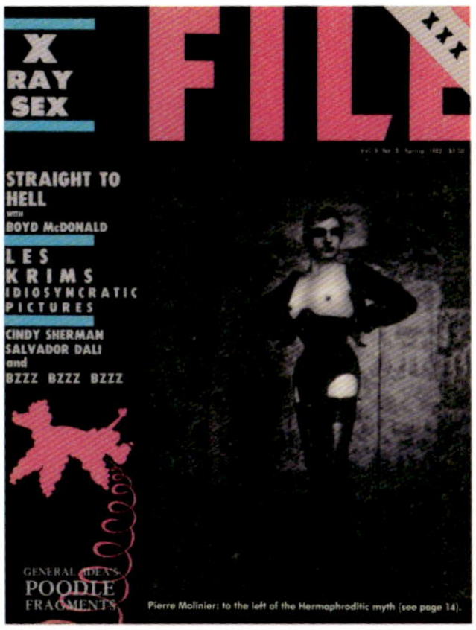

X Ray Sex Issue,
vol. 5, no. 3, Summer 1982

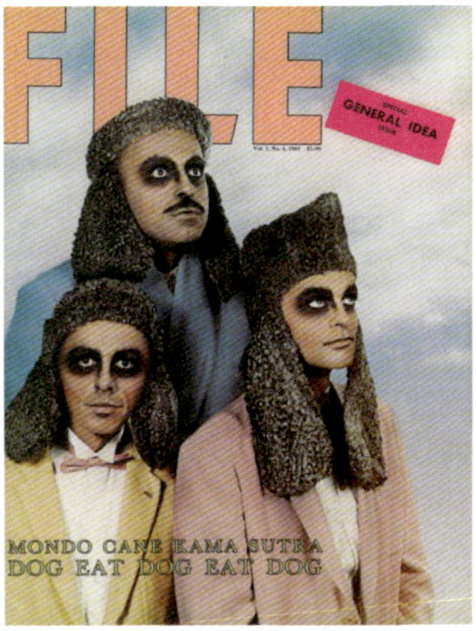

Special General Idea Issue—Mondo Cane Kama Sutra,
vol. 5, no. 4, 1983

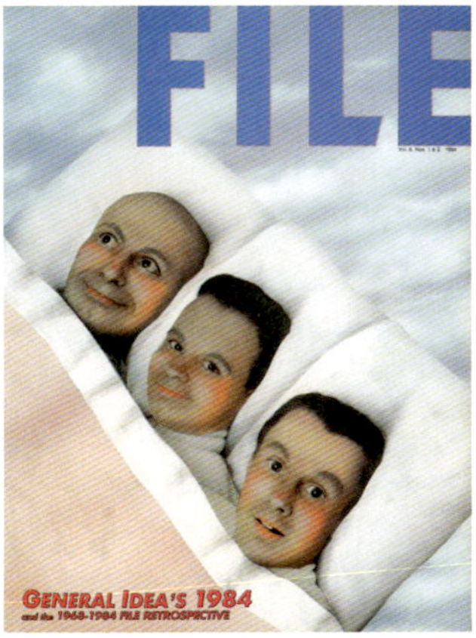

General Idea's 1984 and the 1968–1984, FILE Retrospective Issue,
vol. 6, no. 1 & 2, 1984

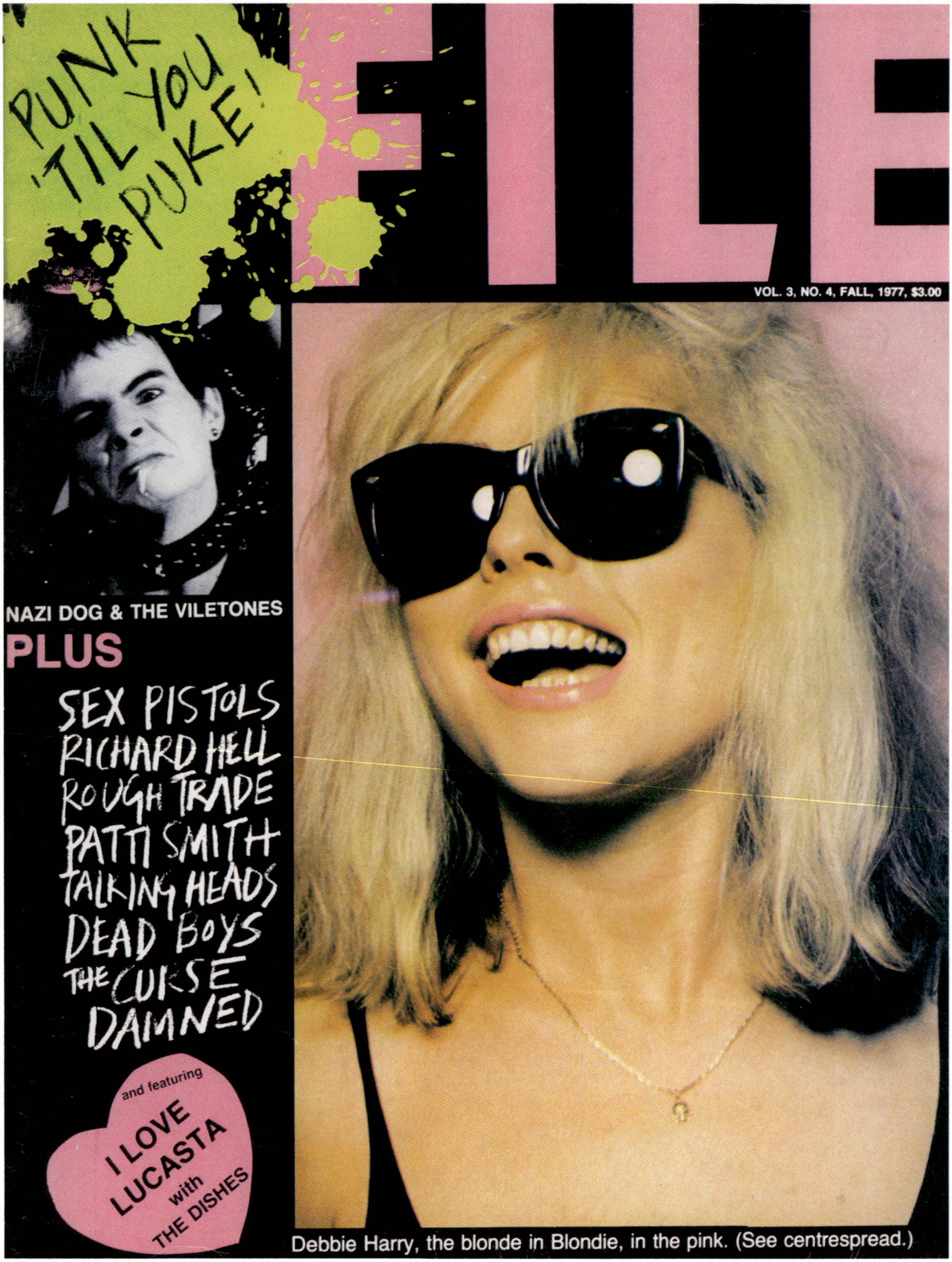

Punk 'Til You Puke ! Issue, vol. 3, no. 4, Fall 1977

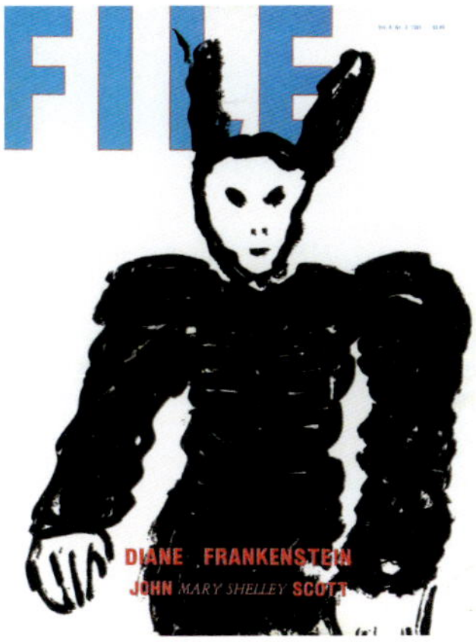

<u>Diane Frankenstein Issue</u>,
vol. 6, no. 3, 1985

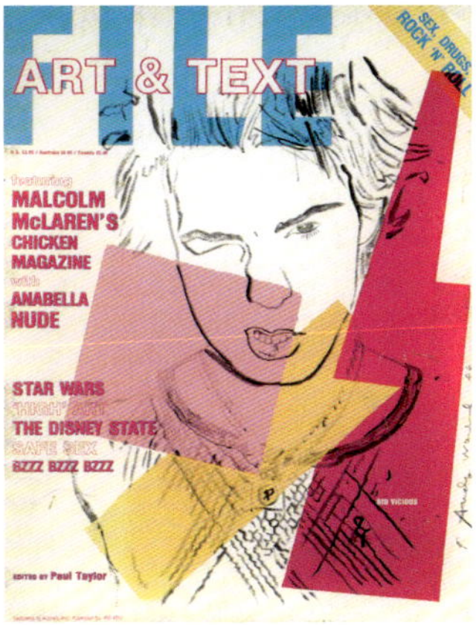

<u>Sex, Drugs, Rock 'N' Roll and Art & Text Issue</u>, <u>FILE</u> no. 25 and <u>Art & Text</u> no. 22, 1986

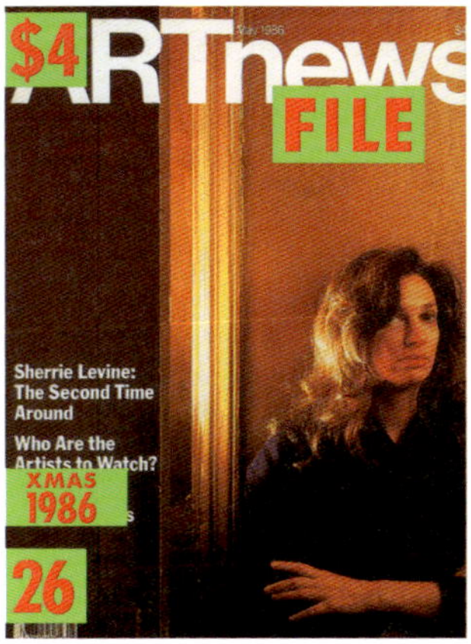

<u>Artnews Issue</u>,
no. 26, Christmas 1986

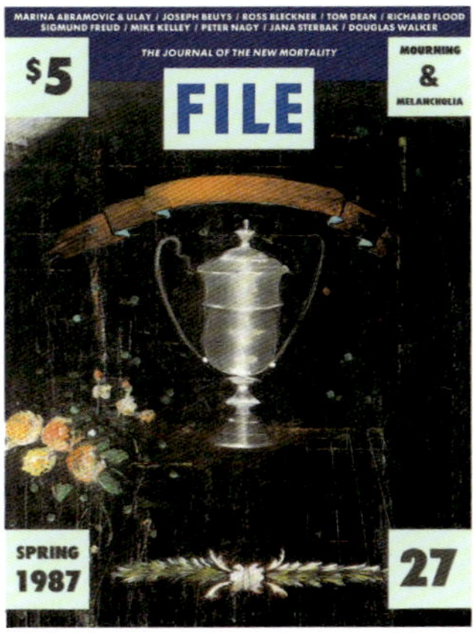

<u>The Journal of the New Mortality Issue</u>, no. 27, Summer 1987

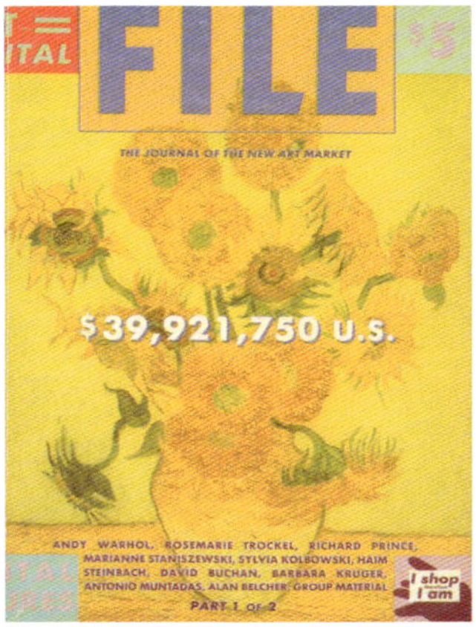

<u>The Journal of the New Art Market Issue</u>, no. 28, 1987

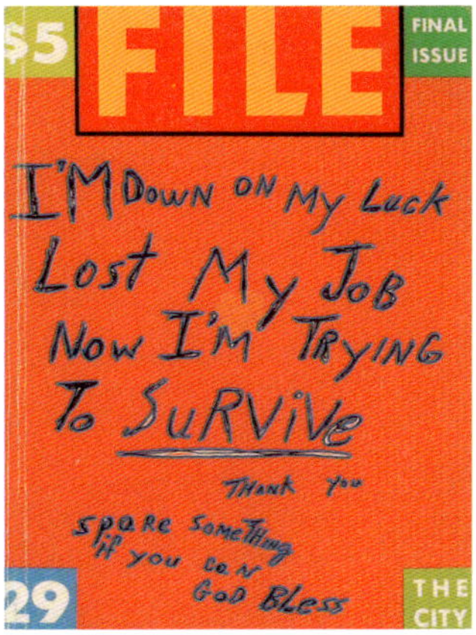

<u>Final Issue, The City Issue</u>,
no. 29, 1989

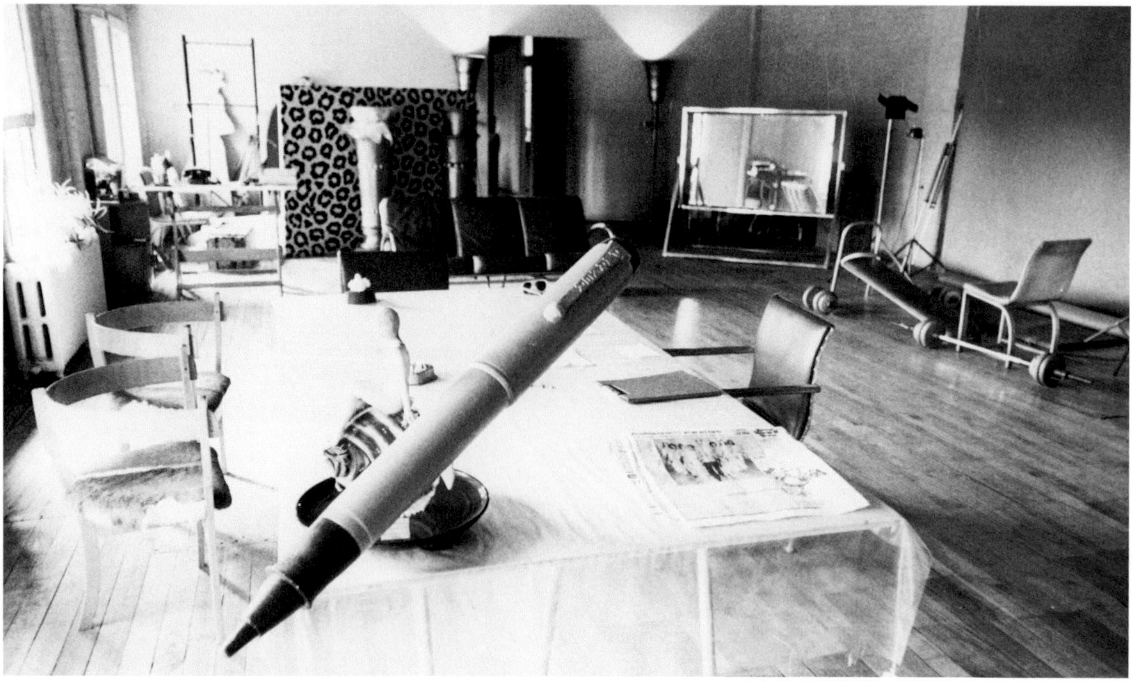

General Idea Studio, 136 Simcoe Street, Toronto, ca. 1977

stuffing it down the art scene's throat. Or stuffing it down our own throats. And it's odd, because we haven't done much work that has had any relationship to rock-and-roll. We've done things like this in *FILE*, but I can only think of one portrait in which we happen to have a rock band setting up in our studio where we had our photographs taken, pretending to play guitars and stuff like that, but we've never taken on that persona in the same way that we've posed like architects, or we've posed like babies, or poodles. I don't know why we've stayed away from the rock band. Although that *Nightschool* portrait (1989) that we did is obviously influenced by heavy metal.

AA

My own involvement in the underground newspaper scene from the 1960s was probably some sort of influence too, in terms of that group activity. And that was something I really loved doing.

Felix

Plus networking too.

AA

Yeah, exactly what I was going to say. It was a real networking activity, where we were closely in communication with probably 25 or 30 other publishers, and then not so closely connected to maybe another hundred more, over and above that. We all received each other's publications, and there was lots of trading back and forth of material, and we were in touch a lot with the Coach House Press. And the Coach House Press had been quite a visual influence on me. So it was interesting how many Canadian influences there are there—Marshall McLuhan, The Coach House Press, N.E. Thing Company.

Louise

I think that the late 1960s was a period when every system was challenged, thinking of political systems, the educational system, even the art system. But, it seems to have started earlier with the art world. It was also a time when authority, in all its form, was being examined. Do you feel that you come out of this context?

AA

I would say yes, absolutely.

Felix

And right from the beginning, we saw the beauty pageants as a critique. It was our examination of the existing art world. There was all the parody aspect—but it was quite obvious that it operated like that. It was a questioning of the process by which masterpieces are created, or validated, or selected, and worshipped. This came out of a questioning of the structures of the culture that we were living in at the time.

Louise

I'm still quite intrigued by Miss General Idea. Do you want to talk about your relationship with her?

AA

When did we first meet her?

Felix

I know when I first met her. Maybe it's easier to look at it on a practical level, like the first pageant, in 1970, which in many ways was our first real project, and the entire thing evolved in the process of working. We had a context, which was a festival of underground theater in Toronto. I think they invited Jorge to do a performance. And in fact he did a performance that we were involved in, which was based on a Gertrude Stein text. He had been officially invited to do something, and I think there maybe had been some other loose offer, "And if you would like to do anything else, just let us know." And by that point, we had just started working together.

AA

It was in August 1970, only two months after the show at the Nightingale Gallery.

Felix

Yes. And so, somehow, Miss General Idea as a concept was born. I can remember the initial fantasies were that it was going to be a parade. And so it was, "revolving" around Miss Honey, who was Miss General Idea 1970. There were all these fantasies of Miss Honey, sitting in the back of the convertible, waiting, going down Yonge Street, going to the St Lawrence Centre. It actually evolved into a sort of mini awards ceremony, which took place in the lobby, quite impromptu. But it had a sizable audience, for a lobby audience. And it was quite an elaborate little "costume epic." With a set, with ten thousand gladiolus that we'd gotten from some funeral home! It was quite nuts, and everyone was quite mystified as to what was going on. Because it looked quite real, Miss Honey was quite a good actress. The whole concept evolved, to actually doing it. And I guess it was a very important step for us, because it started the whole thing in, the whole relationship to time, the process. And then, of course, we had two other women at the time that

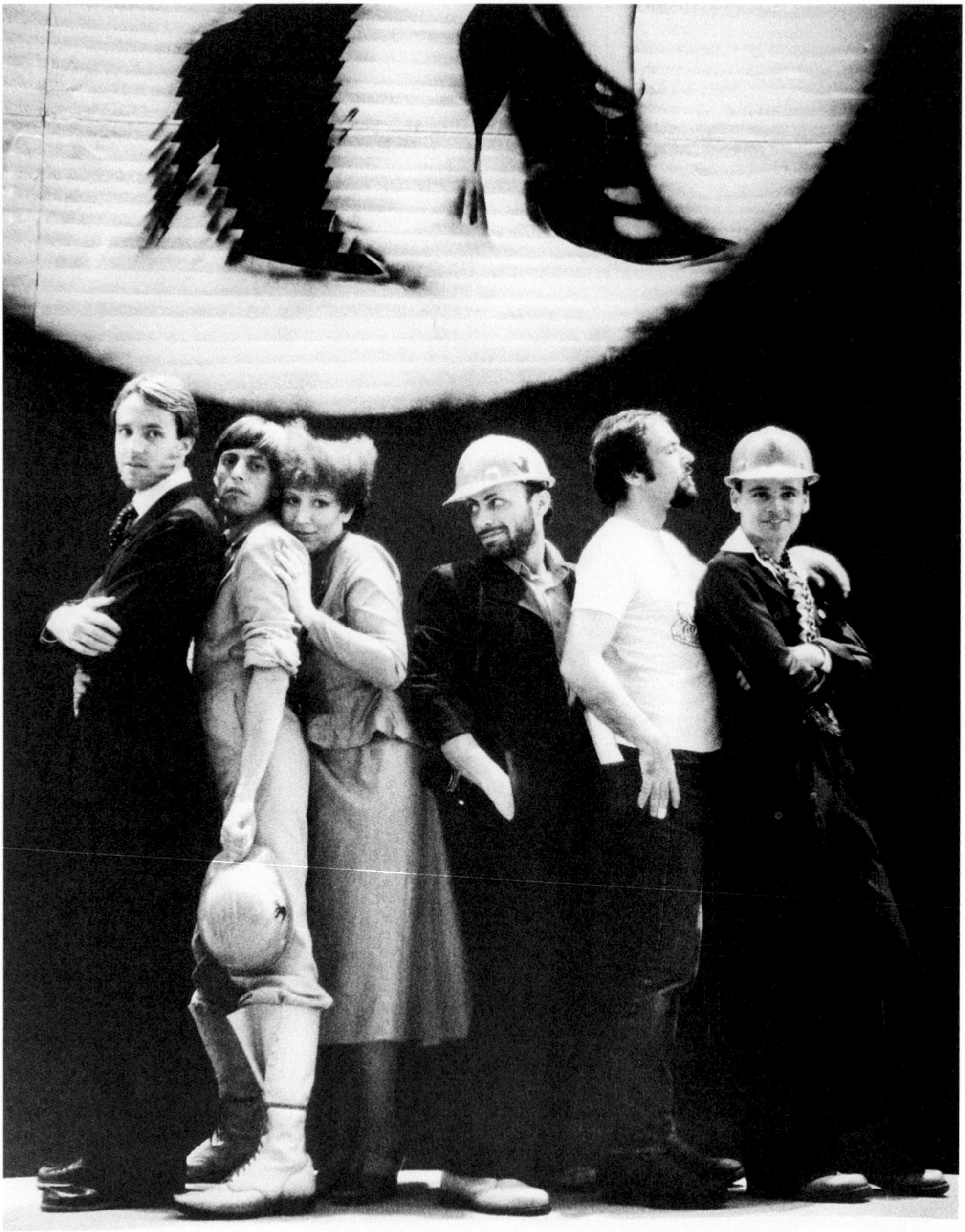

Robert Handforth, Felix Partz, Granada Gazelle, Jorge Zontal, John Dowd, and AA Bronson, Going Thru The Motions performance, Art Gallery of Ontario, Toronto, 1975

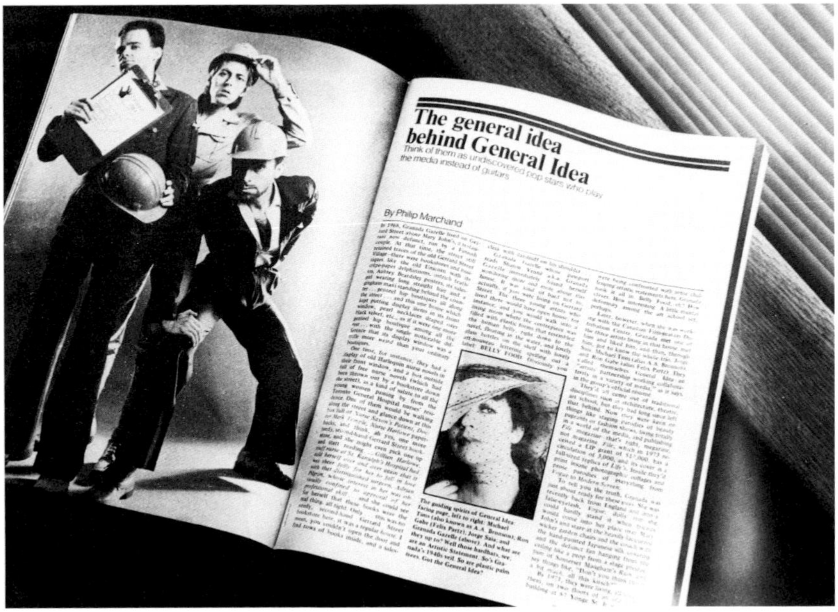

"The general idea behind General Idea," Toronto Life, November 1975

lived with us, who were jealous that Miss Honey was being selected as Miss General Idea. So, our diplomatic solution to the problem was to make Granada Gazelle Miss General Idea 1969, and she got to hand over her crown to Miss Honey, and Mimi Paige got to be the first Miss General Idea 1968. Which pre-dated our actual start, but this has now become the sort of official date.

Louise

Was there an event for Miss 1968?

AA

No, nor for 1969. The whole thing was backdated.

Felix

And in 1970 we ended up asking us the question of what's going to happen in 1971. So we had the other pageant, and then it became—well, what's going to happen in 1972, and by that point we just completely blew it up into 1984. One little thing led to the other. And all of a sudden we were trapped in this thirteen-year project!

Louise

But Miss General Idea became much more mysterious, and ambiguous. You deliberately started blurring the lines, didn't you?

AA

I think you're referring to the spirit of Miss General Idea!

Louise

So what was the spirit?

Felix

Quite elusive. We refer to it as the "muse." Miss General Idea, the spirit of Miss General Idea, is sort of an elusive image. So all the images are rather out of focus, or fleeting. In a more material way, Miss General Idea became the "art object." So it became "the next art object." It wasn't the painting you just finished, it was the one you were just about to start. So it was always that sort of sense of anticipation.

AA

Obviously the whole idea of Miss General Idea is also ironic. Some women have actually taken offense at our use of it, which surprises me because it seems to me that it's so clearly in fact critical. And it becomes quite clear in the performances, I think. But there is the whole political level to the term as well.

Felix

Which was partially being naughty I guess, too. Because, at that time, the beauty pageant had become an icon, a sort of feminist icon, it was like the brassiere, or something. The beauty pageant was definitely "out"! And so even fooling around with it a bit was problematic. We've always been intrigued by those problematic areas.

Louise

It's often difficult, when something is identified as being problematic, for people to see the humorous side of it, or even utilize this process. I guess I'm intrigued, because she was a form for you to project into. And there's a notion of desire there, isn't there, as well? In terms of every male has a feminine side, every woman has a masculine side. There seems to be that kind of element, as well, in it. Was there?

Felix

It seems to me, in retrospect, that the Miss America or whatever is like a vastly degraded form of the goddess. And in a way, that's what we were picking up on. It consequently does represent the inspirational, and in a way the feminine side of one's nature. In its most elusive form. With Conceptual art, that idea became completely outmoded, and being bad boys we took it back again. We decided to incorporate the idea of inspiration rather than reject it. Only we incorporated it in the form of the spirit of Miss General Idea.

Louise

I notice that, especially in the early years, not much was said about the fact that you're gay. So did you see, or did you talk about your practice as a gay practice in the early years?

AA

No, I don't think we did.

Felix

No, never. I don't think that we ever disguised it, but I think that there was some encouragement from some people to do that, and we always resisted it. And I think it was explicit, in a political sense, because of fears of marginalization. We didn't want to be pigeonholed as that—as opposed to being afraid that somebody would find out. I think it was more of a strategy, at that time. We've never discussed it together.

Louise

You thought it would be too limiting, in terms of exhibition opportunities, and so on.

AA

It just didn't seem interesting. For somebody to write about us that way would have been fine, and probably interesting. But we weren't interested in presenting ourselves that way. It just seemed to be beside the point, in a way.

Louise

Do you see your practice now as a gay practice?

AA

It's hard to know what that would be.

Felix

Yes, it's such an enormous kettle of fish. Is there a gay sensibility? In fact, in another interview we did, we were dealing with talking about being Canadian.

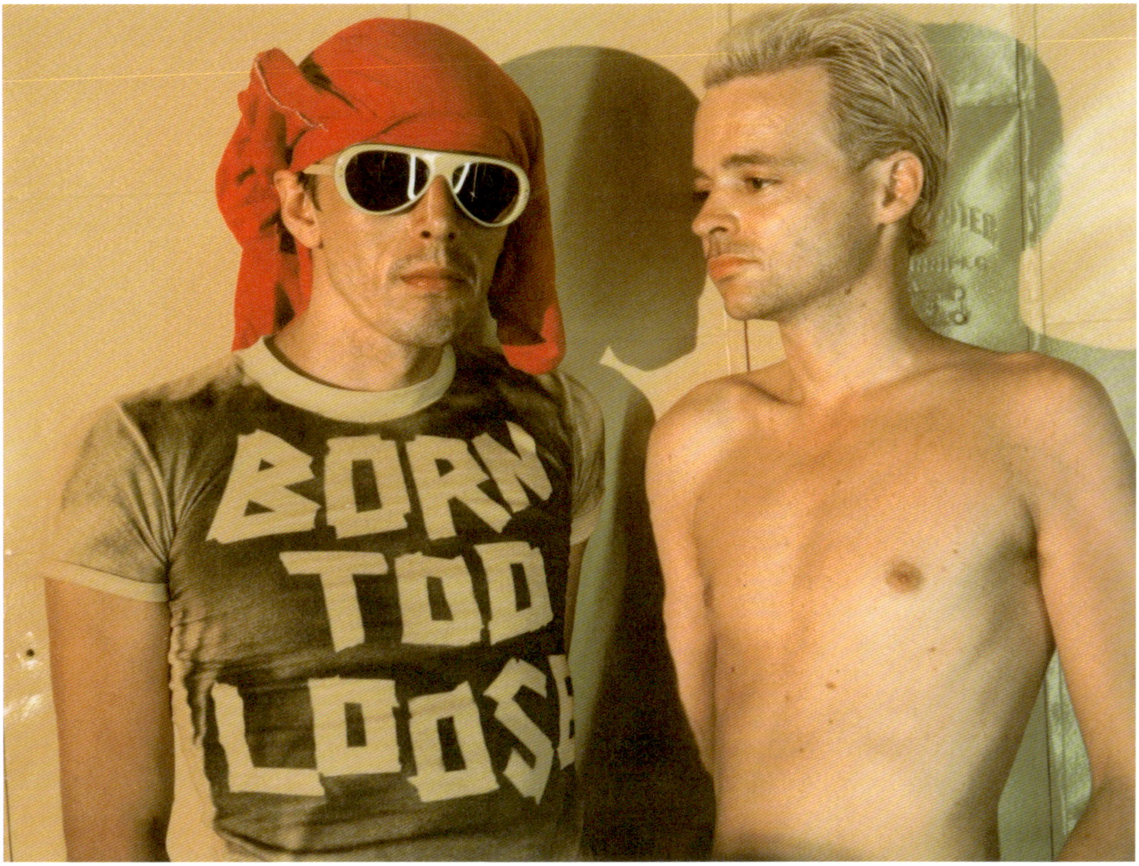

Felix Partz & AA Bronson, ca. 1978

Jorge

It's much worse than being gay!

Felix

It has similarities, in an odd sort of way, to being gay. Being Canadian in North America is like, well, you're not a visible minority, within the continental context, but you are definitely …

Jorge

Not an American.

Felix

You have a secret. You're not an American. And it's sort of similar, in a way, to being gay. You "pass," because—I don't know what, you've got legs, and you can walk, and you have a color, and what-have-you. So you're "normal," but you have this secret. The positions are interesting to speculate about, it's like being an outsider. You become this sort of observer, which forces you into this position of being critical, and observing, and ironic about it, because you are outside what's supposedly the mainstream.

AA

If I think back to our history, when there was this problem with censorship of *The Body Politic* issue, we did a performance; we've been fairly explicit in those situations.[7] There were also the *Mondo Cane Kama Sutra* paintings (1984) …

Felix

Hundreds of things, lately.

AA

Does that make it specifically gay work? That's always an unanswered question.

Louise

I guess it's more in terms of the question of how you see yourselves, and the speculation about it. Some people now position themselves clearly in that way. Certainly it would have been very unusual, when you began, for anyone to position themselves specifically as being gay. As you said, you would marginalize yourselves automatically by doing so, making it almost impossible to function because the scene was much more conservative at that time.

Jorge

I have no problem with the political end of it; I don't mind when politics come to the scene, the gay side of politics, but when it interferes with the practice I don't know. It's like always saying in lectures, "I'm politically correct in my private life, but not in the work." I don't think the work has to be politically correct all the time, it's boring. But in my personal life, I'm perfectly politically correct, always!

AA

That's good to know!

Louise

That's probably the most complex question these days! Political correctness. It's a tough one.

AA

I think in a way that our work could be seen more as antipatriarchal, than gay. Which is similar, but different. It's involved with a whole stream of thought.

Jorge

There are a lot of gay patriarchs around, but that's a whole other story.

Felix

The actual sex of Miss General Idea has never really been accurately determined either.

AA

No. It's a sexless identity, but with a feminine nature, obviously.

Felix

One aspect of General Idea and gayness was the issues involved with the "poodle."

Jorge

Oh yeah! For that show in Alma Quebec,[8] we did this poster with poodles. There was this woman who worked at the gallery. the issue of "gay" came up, and she said, "Well, I assumed you were gay, because of the poster."

Felix

It's hard to discuss it because it's such a complex layering. But I mean, in a sense, it was self-portrait, and so the poodle is standing in for us, but I think one of the primary interpretations, for ourselves, of the poodle, was that it's a "gay" image. There are these other interpretations of people's associations with the dog, but we saw it as "the gay hair-dresser's companion." Like our relationship to the beauty pageant, it was obviously politically naughty at that time—the projected image of the gay as the poodle. It's starting to change a bit. That was politically incorrect—frilly, concerned with it's personal appearance, and sophisticated, and all those gay clichés. On a certain level, for us that was a "gay" project. It was a way of examining that image.

Jorge

The poodles were the painters that were coming out in the late 1970s. Because we saw them as the poodles of the dealers, and the poodles of the market place. Our ideas before that were much more independent of the market place. So we thought of a lot of those poodles were portraits of the German and Italian painters that were coming out, "Zee Poodles."

AA

There were other layers. I was just thinking about how, actually, when you start to talk about the poodles, the imagery in many ways becomes more explicit as we go along. There are things that could be questioned, like the whole *AIDS* project. Most people would assume that means we're gay.

Louise

From that point on, after the poodles, do you see divisions in your work?

Felix

In a sense. At that point, even with the poodles, it was sometimes hard to contextualize what they were. Before that things had been very specific: it was a cocktail lounge; it had been a boutique; it had been the covering for a window, etc. All of a sudden, we were introducing things that could only be seen as decorative elements. As we wrote in a *FILE* editorial, it was the re-materialization of the "art object."[9] Another period was *Shut The Fuck Up* (1985), which is definitely like a manifesto for us, and I think this was a period in which we decided that we were going to drop the constant explanation and contextualizing of everything, and that's when we moved into the pavilion. It was like fantasizing about building this pavilion, and then deciding, "no, we're not going to build this pavilion, it's going to be destroyed." And I think that we are now "working" in the pavilion: the gallery, museum, whatever. Public sphere is the pavilion.

AA

The big division spans 1984 to 1986—when we did our big retrospective that toured.[10] It put us in a position where it was as if we were dead and looking back at our past. And I think that was a difficult point for us.

Felix

We had made this commitment to work together until 1984. So here was 1984, we were involved in this retrospective, but also in the conclusion of a project. Or was it? And also during that time, the whole New York experience started too, it was the start of another phase.

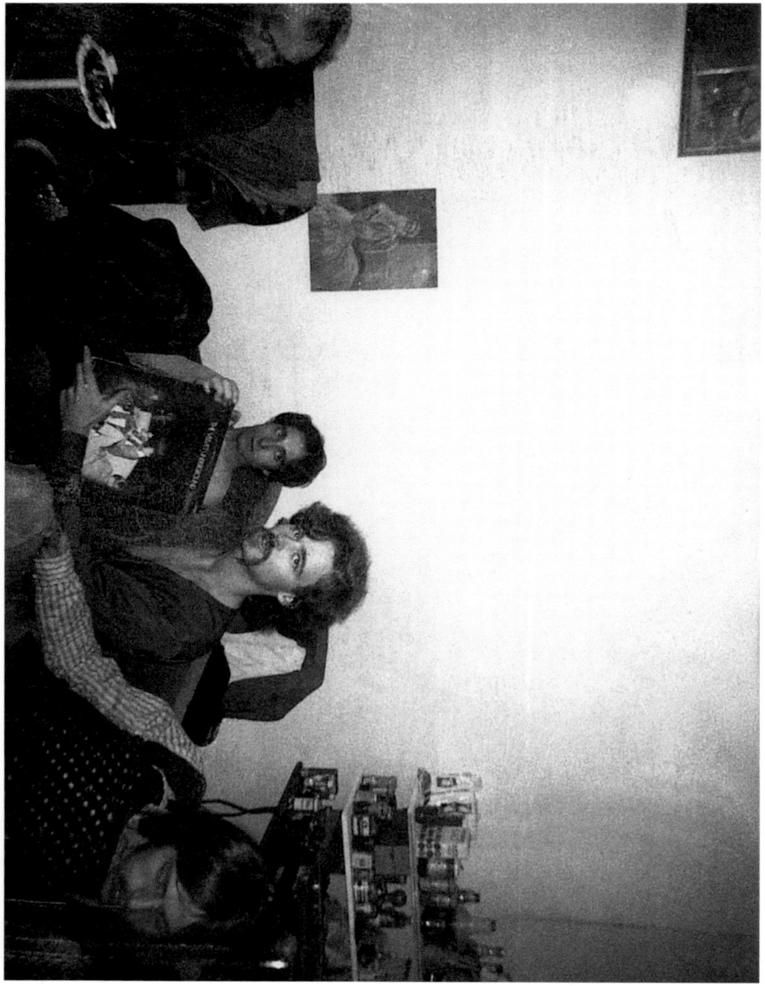

<u>Self-Portrait (Velvet Underground)</u>, 1969

Jorge Zontal, 1978

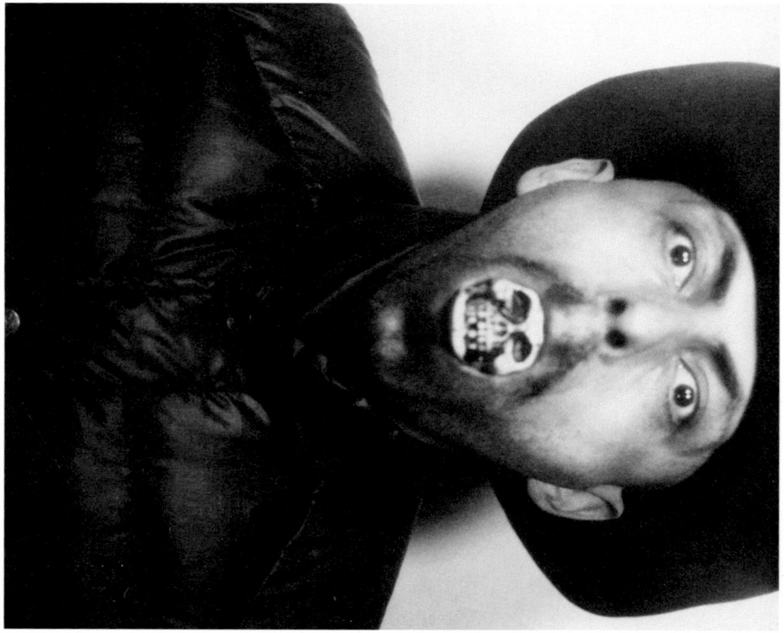

AA

Well, *The Armoury of the 1984 Miss General Idea Pavillion* happened in 1986.[11] And that still feels quite part of everything that happened prior to 1984, in terms of the actual work. But in terms of our mental position at that time, we were already a leap ahead of that. In the work that comes after that, there is no evident relationship to the whole idea of the pageant or the pavilion at all. There are a couple of years with the "Copyright" signs and consumer-based objects and the "Pasta Paintings." And then the *AIDS* projects. The first painting was in the summer of 1987, but the first poster project wasn't until the end of 1987. They almost have a life of their own, they're not really a period, they could go on forever, in a way. They're self-generating to a certain point. We must have done at least 40 projects using that image.

Felix

It was like a research and development period. And that seemed to then emerge again into another whole series of major projects.

Louise

Your strategy was one of ironic distance. Or you used different kinds of strategies. In other words, the content became as fictitious and idealized, if you talk in terms of a fictitious art scene. There's a sort of idealistic level in this, as in the world of stardom that you created. Is that correct?

AA

There was a strong narrative component to the work that was based on reality, but was also heavily fictionalized. Idealized is maybe a better word. It was like projecting the future into the present.

Louise

With works like *Fin de siècle* (1990) and the *AIDS* project, there seems to be a reversal in your strategy. Earlier on, with works like the pageant, or *FILE Megazine*, you drew from popular culture to address art issues or the artistic condition. Now, many works are based on art historical precedents, yet seem to focus on more socially based concerns. Is that the way you see it?

AA

I don't know whether it's the way we see it or not. I'm not sure if it's a description of the process, but it seems to be a description of the artworks that result.

Jorge

We've certainly looked good to have a social content!

AA

Yeah, and we've gotten very involved in references to other artist's work. I'm not quite sure how that came about.

Felix

Well, to go back to what we were talking about earlier, when I said that there had been that editorial in *FILE* about the re-emergence of the art object, we said at that time, in that editorial, that everything seemed to be floundering, in a sense, because the object had disappeared, the market had disappeared. I think this came out of our mid-1970s stay in New York. They were searches for new forms, new contexts to plug into. And people were looking at rock-and-roll. Lots of people involved in sort of bands and sort of clubs. Night club performances, da da da da, magazines, all that sort of stuff. So it was all this, artists looking at other media. Plugging into videotapes, and plugging into this, and plugging into that. And I think that we realized at some point that the art scene had become another one of those, it had become part of the media, it was no longer an esoteric little back water, it was, in a certain sense, out there competing.

Jorge

Especially in Europe.

Felix

Especially in Europe. And then here, when the money started hitting, it became quite hard to distinguish in some cases between *Artforum*, and *New York Magazine*. They were covering the same territory. So the art referencing started becoming much stronger. We felt more confidence in it, partially because of Europe, because you're often dealing with people who have more knowledge, historically. And we were interested in Fontana and Klein …

Louise

Do you see material like this as sort of a museum from which you can pull some references?

Felix

I think it became like an index. On a practical level, that was one of the impetuses for the Art Metropole Archive,[12] because often when you go out, and try and find information on someone, there's nothing. It's easier in Europe, in a lot of cases, even to find out about American artists. In Toronto, try to go out and find something on Piero Manzoni, good luck! Even on Yves Klein, a major name, there's not much around.

AA

Not all the work that we've been producing has these referential aspects. Like the whole *Nightschool* project doesn't specifically refer to anyone. And for that matter, the pills …

Jorge

Larry Poons![13]

Felix

I think that things moved in and out of focus. Sometimes they're very explicit, and at other times, like the pills, could possibly reference an Yves Klein. Rose, IKB, and gold, that type of thing. But in a way it's an applied reference. So things move off like that. Part of it is our interest in other artist's work, and a way to deal with one of those bug-a-boos of being an artist, which is influence. It's stylistic influence, and we're quite upfront about it when we are influenced by somebody. It's not influence, I don't think that's the word.

AA

It's more like a dialogue, to tell you the truth, even though it's been something in the past, in many cases.

Felix

When we dealt with the whole Yves Klein thing, and *Shut The Fuck Up*, some people thought that was a bit tasteless, but I felt it was a dialogue. I thought that we were getting revenge for what they did to Yves Klein![14]

Louise

It's like an act of recognition.

AA

Well, as Indiana says in this magazine article that just arrived, "Well, it's what I would have done if I'd been approached to do something for an AIDS charity." But, there's an interesting one there too, because he doesn't like the "D." I was proposing that we give the project back to Indiana, and say to him, "If you wanted to do an AIDS project, and you don't like the 'D,' why don't you take it, and tune it, and we'll put it out again as a Robert Indiana project."

Louise

You should do that.

Felix

I think we should, actually, it would be interesting.

Louise

Are there other aspects of your work that

you'd like to talk about, that you feel have changed. Not really fundamentally changed, but there are some shifts?

AA

It's like continuing again after a hiatus. In terms of our original strategies, we seem to be returning to these major installations, which we haven't done for a while, and multiples, and so on. The pills are made using a mass-production process; the replication process. It's almost like printing a magazine. *One Year of AZT* (1991), with 1,825 identical pills, is really like a printing press. They silkscreen a sheet of plastic, and then punch out the pill. This seems to be a return to our original way of working, but in terms of much more "defined" projects, rather than one overall project. Before the work was one big narrative; now each project is much more self-sufficient. That's partially because of New York, because in New York people don't have the energy or the time to work out the overall picture of what you're doing, they just want to look at one object and understand it instantly.

Louise

When you used the image of the poodle, there was a rationale behind that. Now you're using the image of seals. Is there a rationale for using that?

AA

There are various ways of looking at that piece. One of the interesting things about the seals, first of all, is that they are like an image of Canada—the scandal of Canada, internationally speaking, the so-called slaughter of baby seals. In fact, the baby seals are killed the same way the cows are killed; they have to be hit between the eyes. It's not particularly "slaughter." And in fact there is an overpopulation so the government has had to put a price on their heads, to encourage the reduction of the number of seals. It's some issue about whether or not they're eating all the fish, and so on and so forth. The point is that environmentally it's a very ambiguous issue. Secondly, the sea of Styrofoam. Styrofoam is, on the one hand, completely permanent; once it's made, it's there forever. On the other hand, it's the only

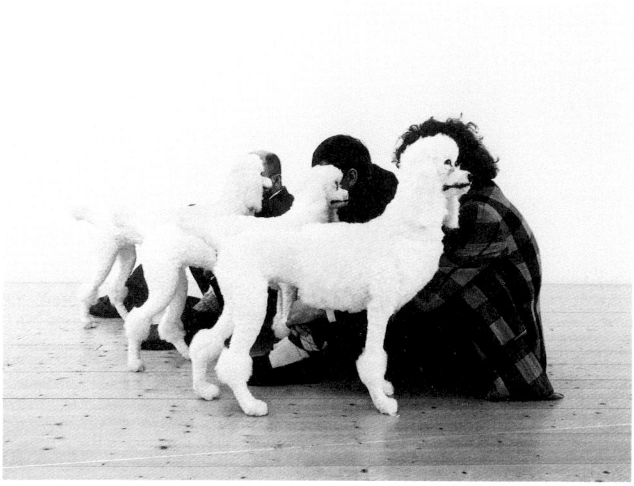

General Idea at the Centre d'Art Contemporain, Geneva, with the poodles of the XXX (bleu) performance, 1984

plastic that can be recycled. So it also has an ambiguous, environmental issue attached to it. But in a way, both of those issues are red herrings, because ultimately the piece also operates as a sort of self-portrait. And I guess obviously it's a portrait as victim. But it's also, because of the two issues I just mentioned, quite ambiguous.

Felix

I think it relates on some other level to the "marketing" of victims. And then it becomes a reference to the whole *AIDS* project. In a way the baby seals have been successful in their campaign to not be killed because of their visuals. They have been marketable as victims. And it's one thing that you become aware of with the AIDS situation, too—how unmarketable it is. That's something that we're dealing with as well. That it's much easier to market the slaughter of baby seals than it is to market the deaths of homosexuals, drug-users, whatever, and other deviants!

Louise

The *AIDS* paintings are all very strong images.

Felix

I think that maybe this refers back to something else we were talking about originally, about our whole relationship to projecting ourselves as "gay artists," and our attempts not to marginalize ourselves. I think that our *AIDS* project—which has been criticized, because it hasn't been so overt or explicit—was intentionally designed to avoid most of the issues of sexuality, or "gay-ness." It was just the word. And that would allow the word to travel in the popular media culture further than because we were aware of that discrimination.

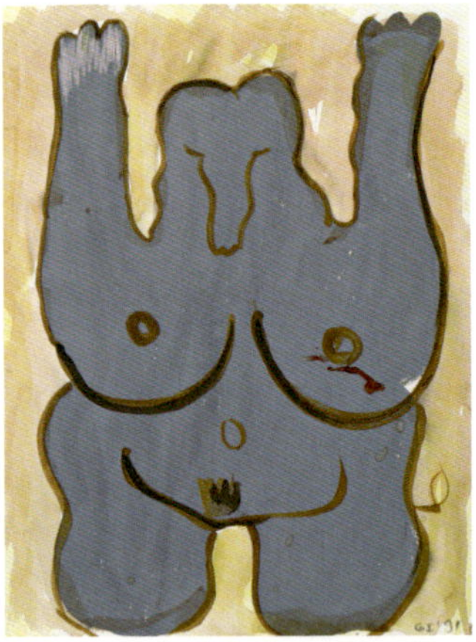

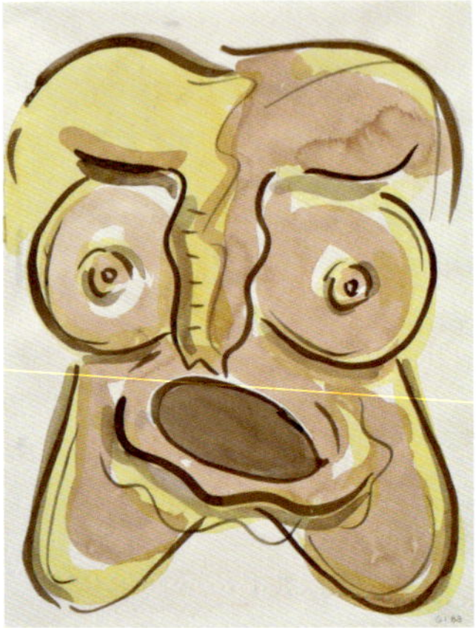

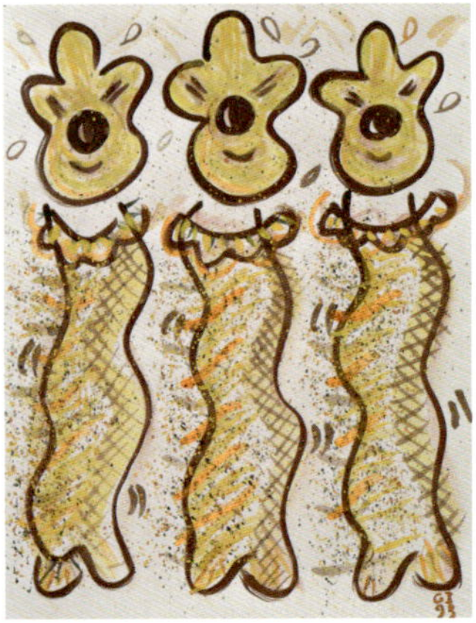

Jorge Zontal, Untitled, 1991

“Think of them as undiscovered pop stars who play the media instead of guitars.”
Philip Marchand, Toronto Life, November, 1975.

Showcard 5-009, The General Idea Behind General Idea, 1977

We wanted an ingredient that wasn't too easy to get, a bit expensive with a mythology to match. We looked for a sense of altered consciousness, blended with infantile repression. Above all, it had to be associated with money and sex. The result is a drink that pops the corks from cultural fetishes. We call it "The Champagne Experience."

Showcard 2-089, Consenting Cocktails, 1979

Louise

Do you feel that the pills will function in the same way?

Felix

I think they can be more insidious, in a way, because it causes people to interpret them. And in some cases they'll be more explicitly related. Some will be more explicitly AZT. The first series that we're going to do in the multiple format will be color-wise. The same as the *AIDS* posters: red, green, and blue. This will be their only connection. In fact, we talked about them as being placebos, not pills. They're not cure-alls, they're only little pleasers. Little helpers.

1 This unpublished interview took place in New York on July 26, 1991, three years before the deaths of Felix Partz and Jorge Zontal in 1994. Louise Dompierre is the president of the Art Gallery of Hamilton, Ontario. It was edited by Frédéric Bonnet for this publication.

2 Founded in 1973, and devoted to poetry, visual and living arts, the Western Front Society is one of the first Canadian artist-run interdisciplinary artistic centers.

3 Michael Morris, born in 1942, is one of the players in the artistic scene in Vancouver in the 1960s and 1970s. Influence by Fluxus and the European avant-guarde, in 1966 he became the curator at the Vancouver Art Gallery and at the Centre for Communications and the Arts of the Simon Fraser University. In 1969 he founded, with Vincent Trasov, Image Bank, a network of information and idea exchange between artists. He is one of the founders of the Western Front Society.

4 Created in 1972, FILE Magazine became FILE Megazine in 1975.

5 General Idea, "Glamour," in FILE Megazine, "Glamour Issue," vol. 3, no. 1, Toronto, Autumn 1975, p. 20–33.

6 Granada Gazelle, one of the first members of General Idea.

7 See Elisabeth Lebovic's essay "Gender 'Trouple'" in this volume.

8 Caniche à la mode, an exhibition held in 1984 in Alma, in Québec.

9 General Idea, "Editorial," in FILE Megazine, vol. 5, no. 2, "The Re-Materialization of the Art Object Issue," Toronto, Autumn 1981, p. 17.

10 See Jean-Christophe Ammann, "The Life and Work of Miss General Idea," in this volume.

11 The Armoury of the 1984 Miss General Idea Pavillion, traveling exhibition, Albright Knox Art Gallery, Buffalo; 49th Parallel, New York; University Art Gallery, California State University, Northridge;Long Beach Contemporary Arts Museum, Houston; Setagaya Art Museum, Tokyo.

12 Established in Toronto in 1974 by General Idea, Art Metropole was one of the first Canadian art centers managed by artists. Art Metropole's role was to collect, catalogue, and preserve artistic production of the Conceptual art movement and the documentation that went with it. The collection was donated to the National Gallery of Canada in 1999.

13 Born in 1937, Lawrence Poons is an abstract painter affiliated with Op art in the 1960s, due to his paintings of circles and ovals (which often look like pills) on colored backgrounds.

14 See Frédéric Bonnet, "Setting the Stage: Back to Reality!" in this volume.

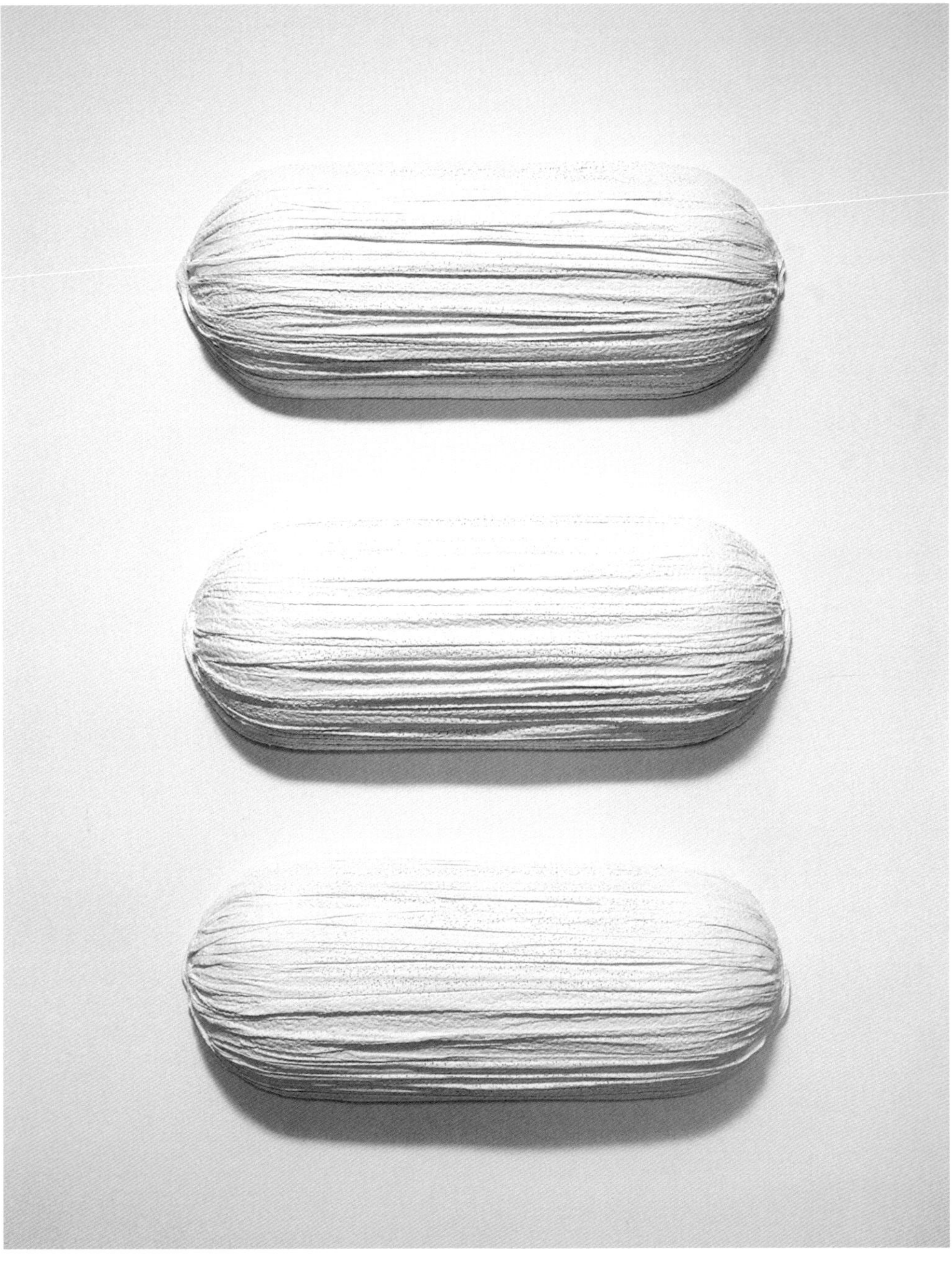

Achrome (Manzoni), 1993-1996

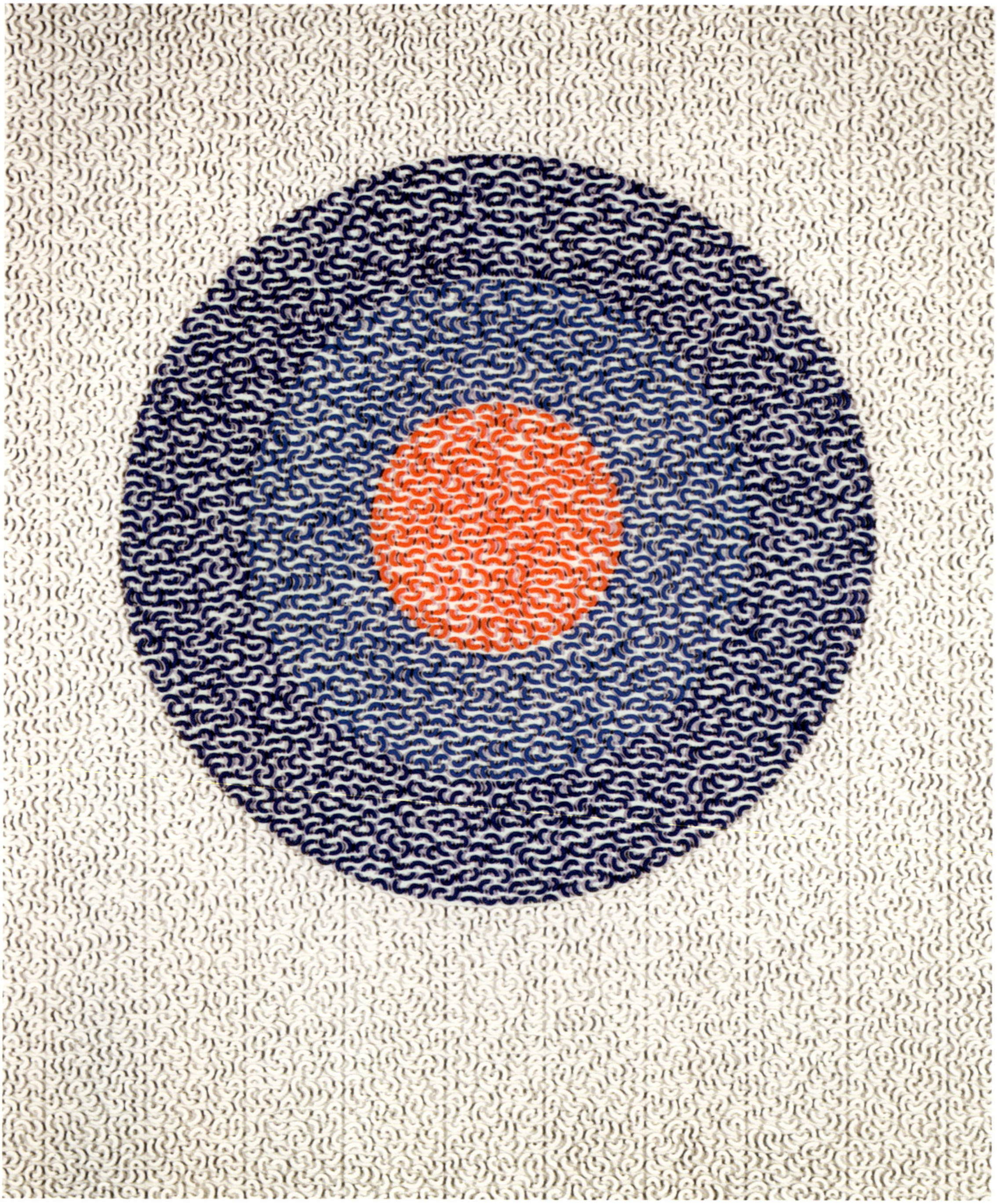

Untitled (Vantage), 1986

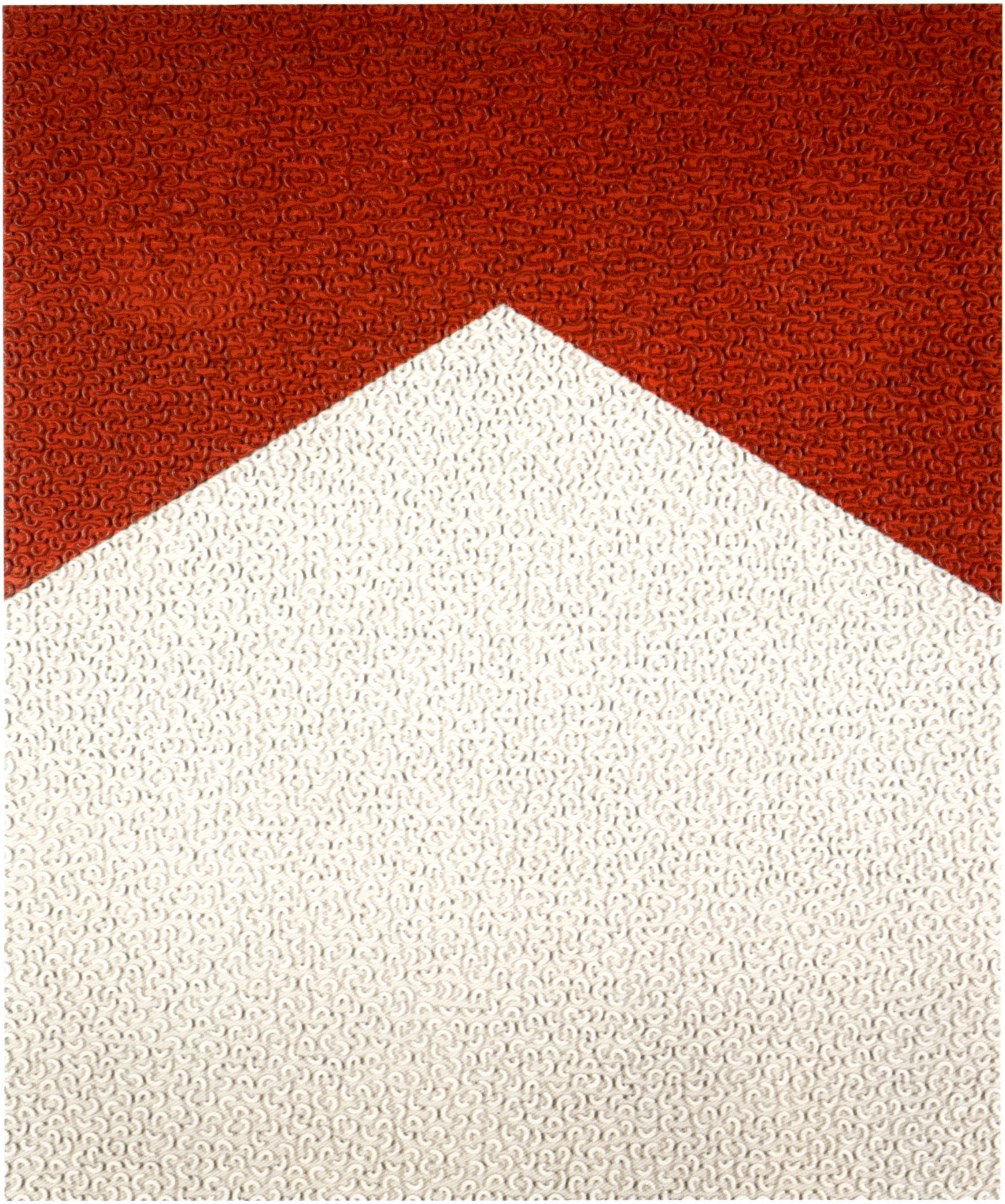

Untitled (Marlboro), 1985–1986

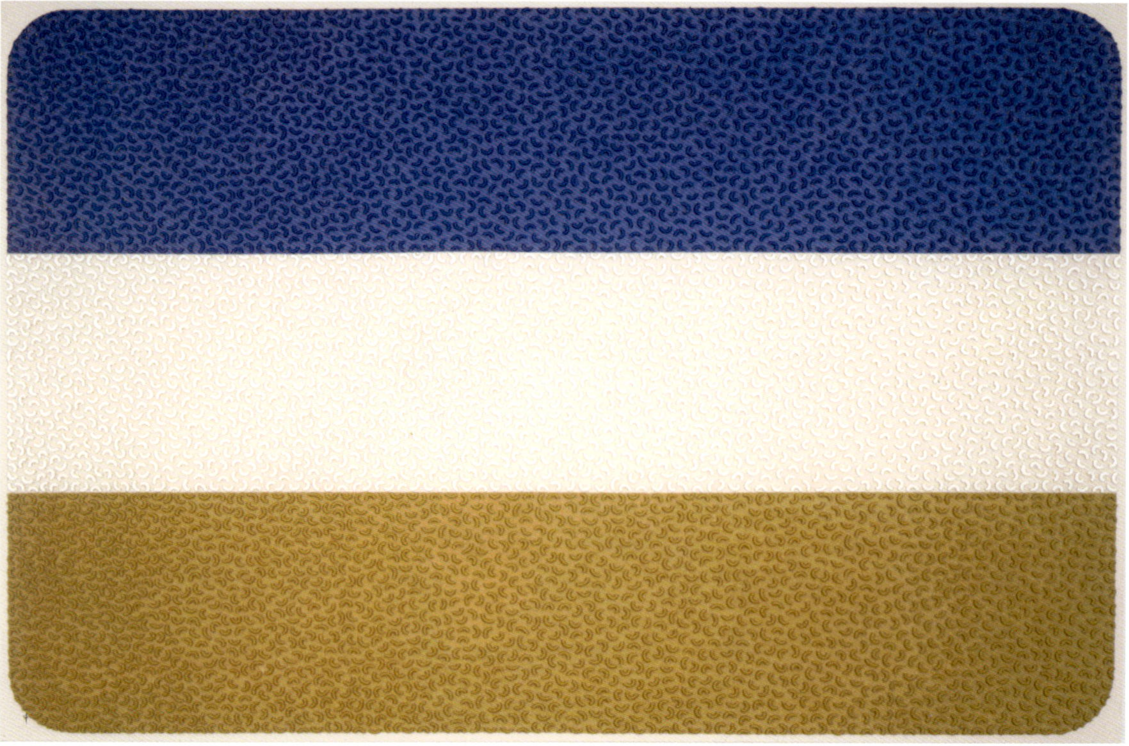

Untitled (Visa), 1986

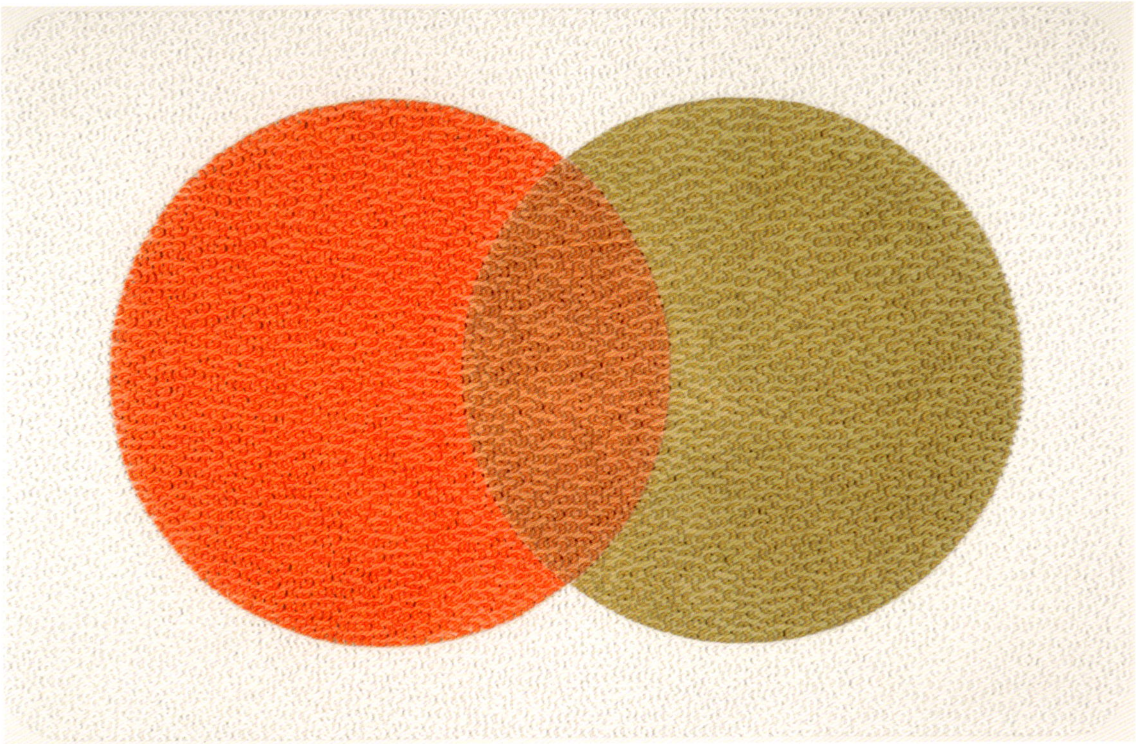

Untitled (Mastercard), 1985–1986

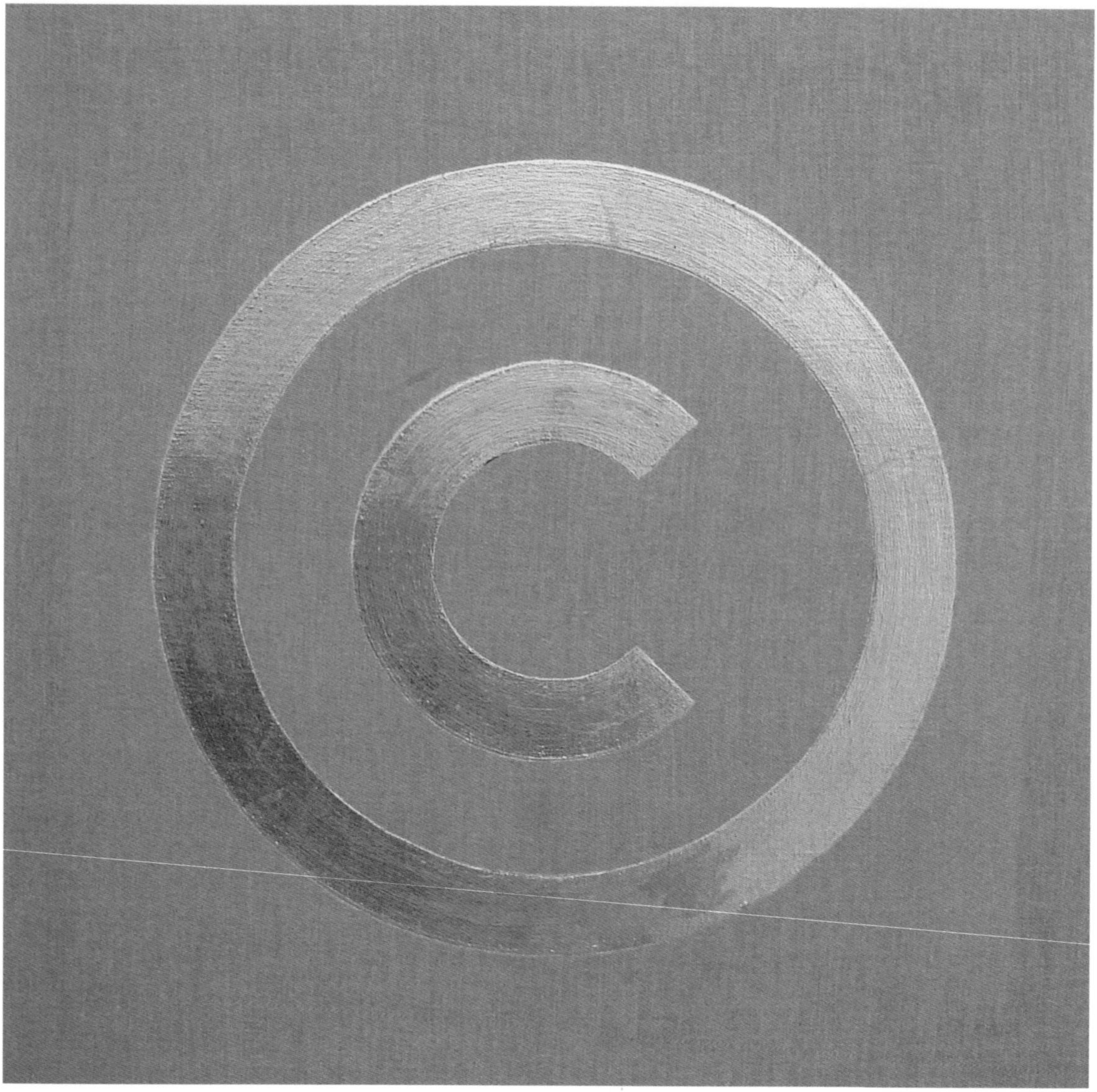

Copyright (Blue) #3, 1987

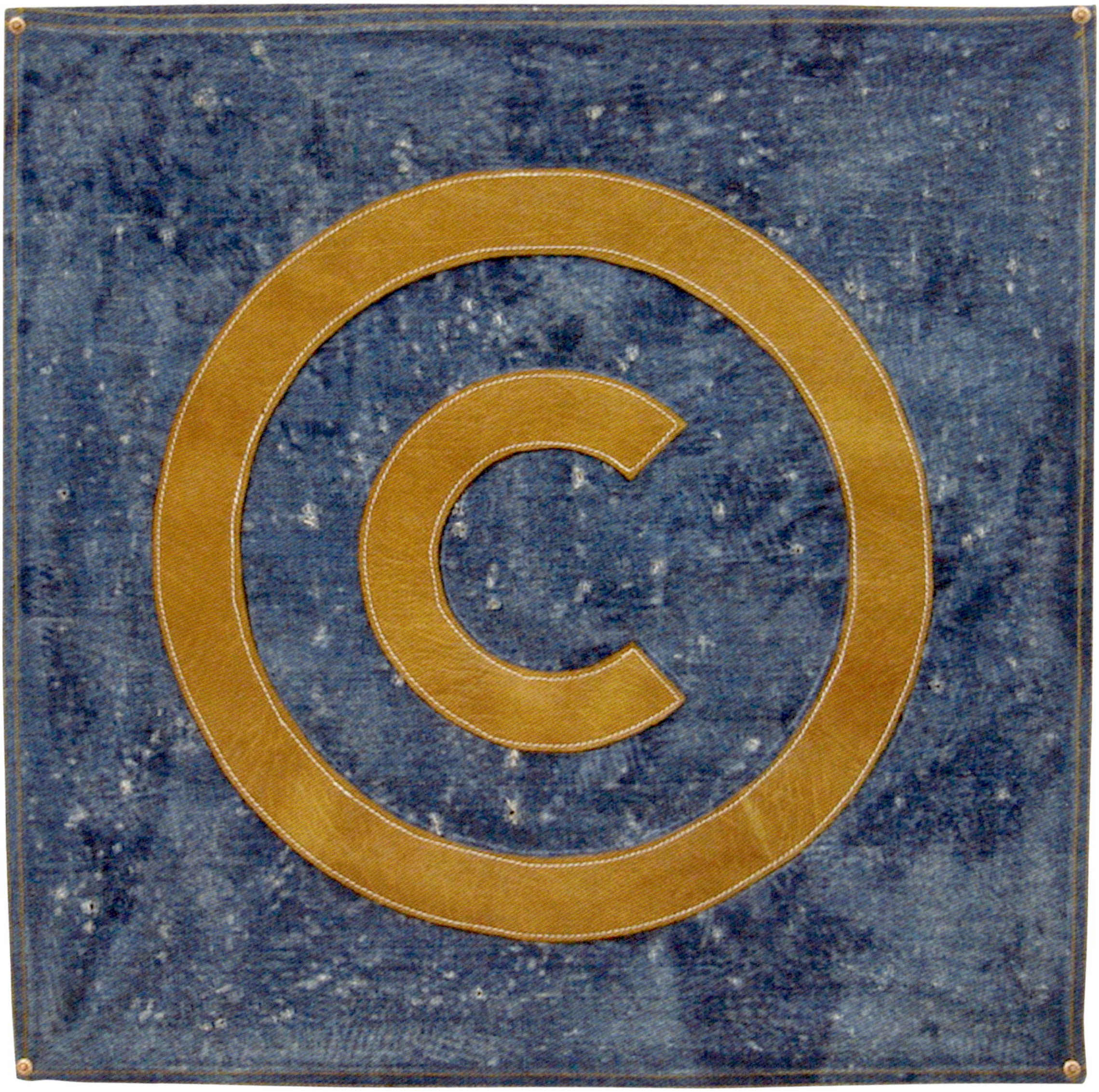

Leather and Denim Copyright #4, 1987

Atomic Blast #3, 1986

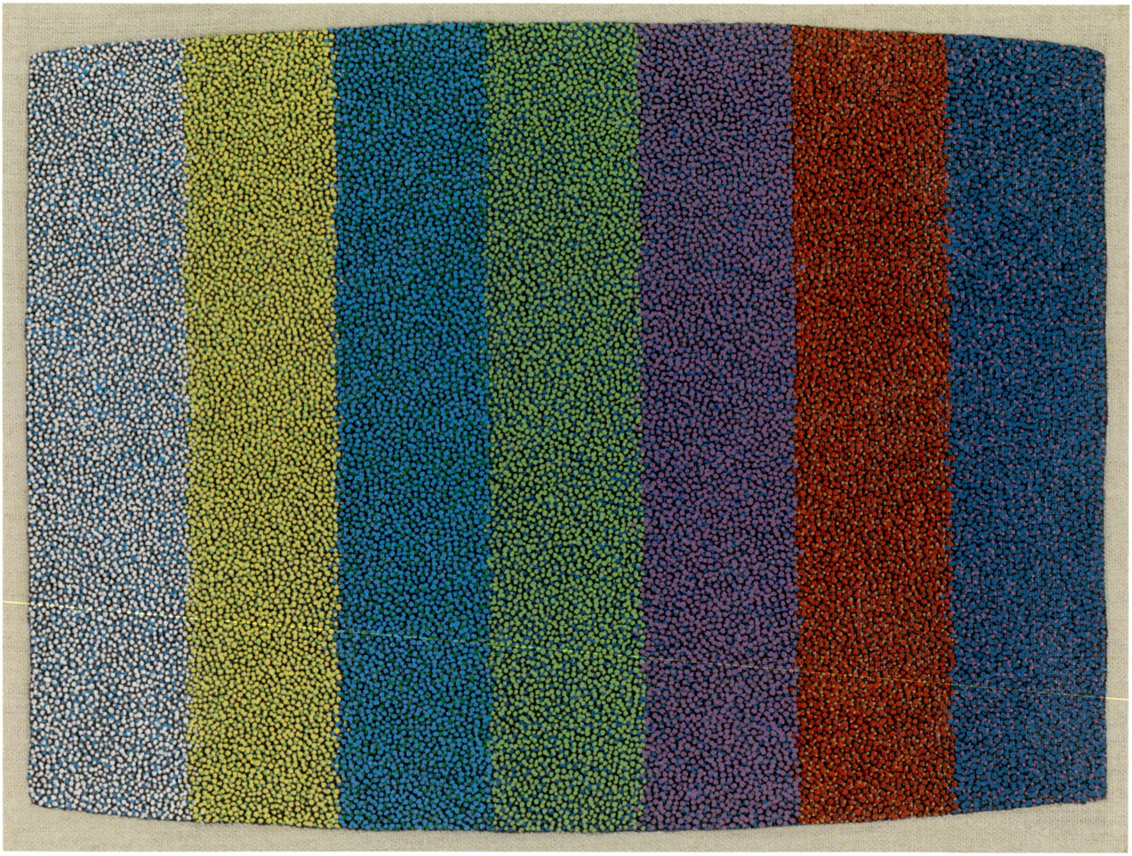

Trinitron #6, 1987

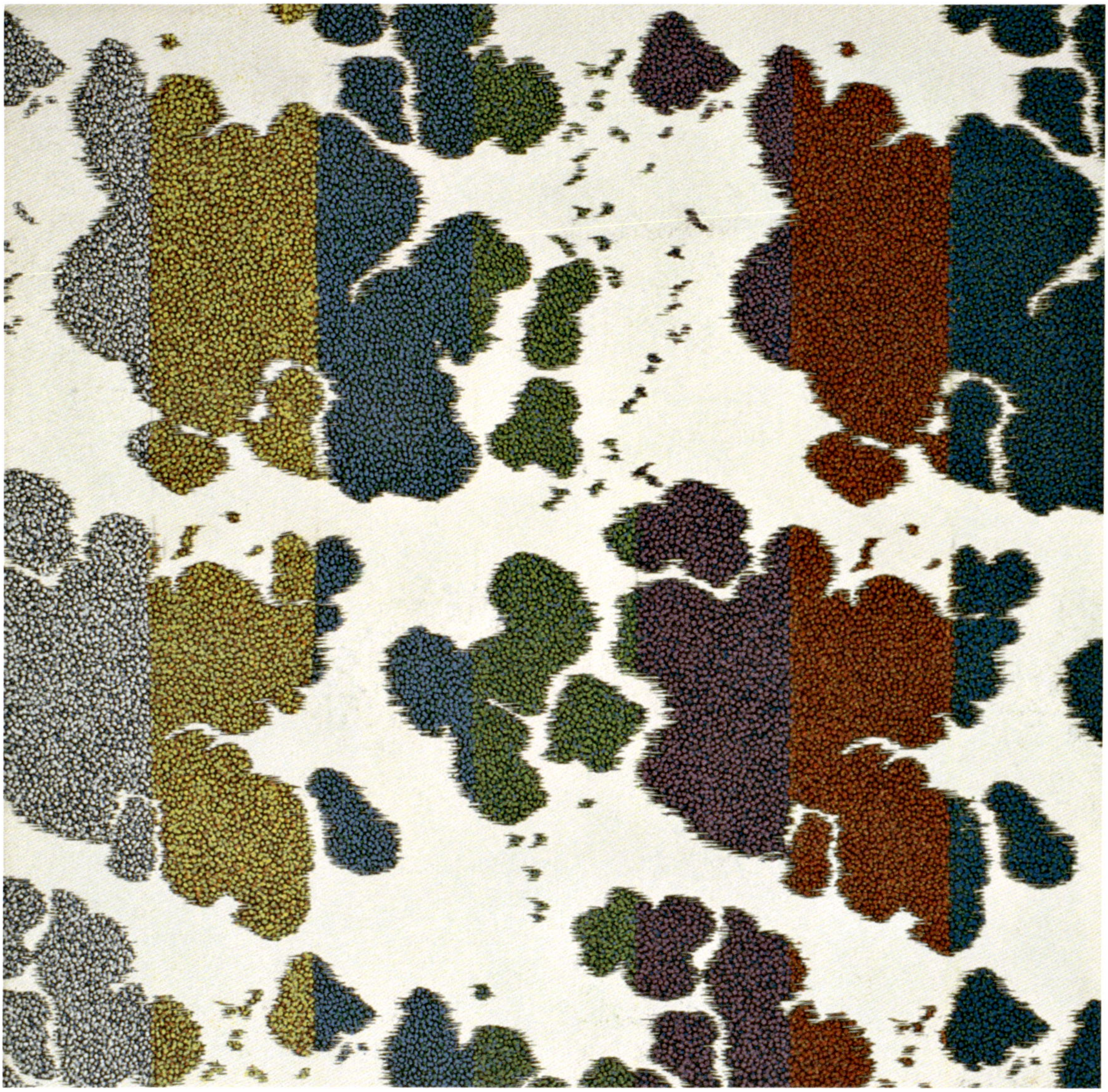

Ponytron #3, 1988

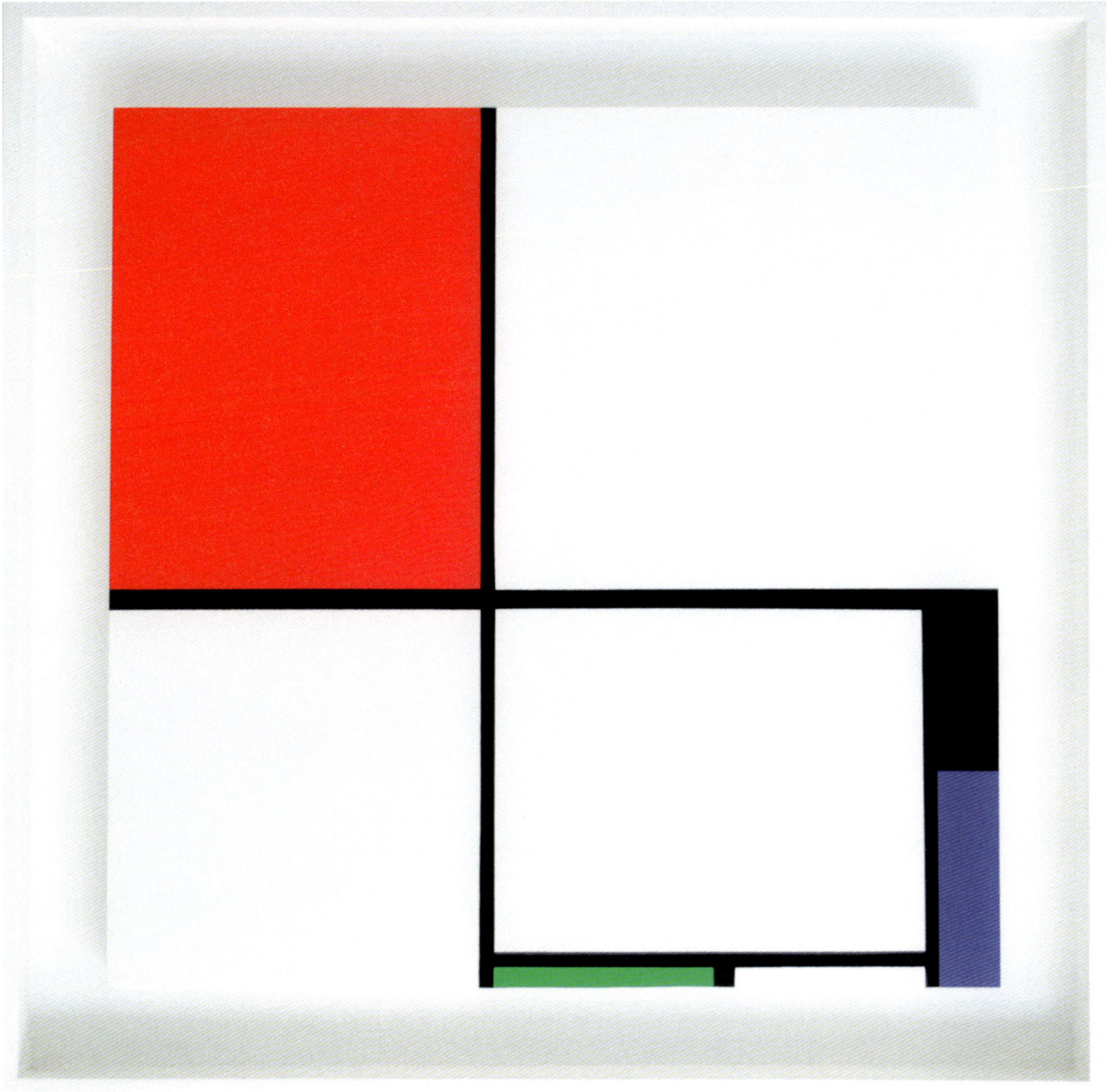

Infe©ted Mondrian #6, 1994

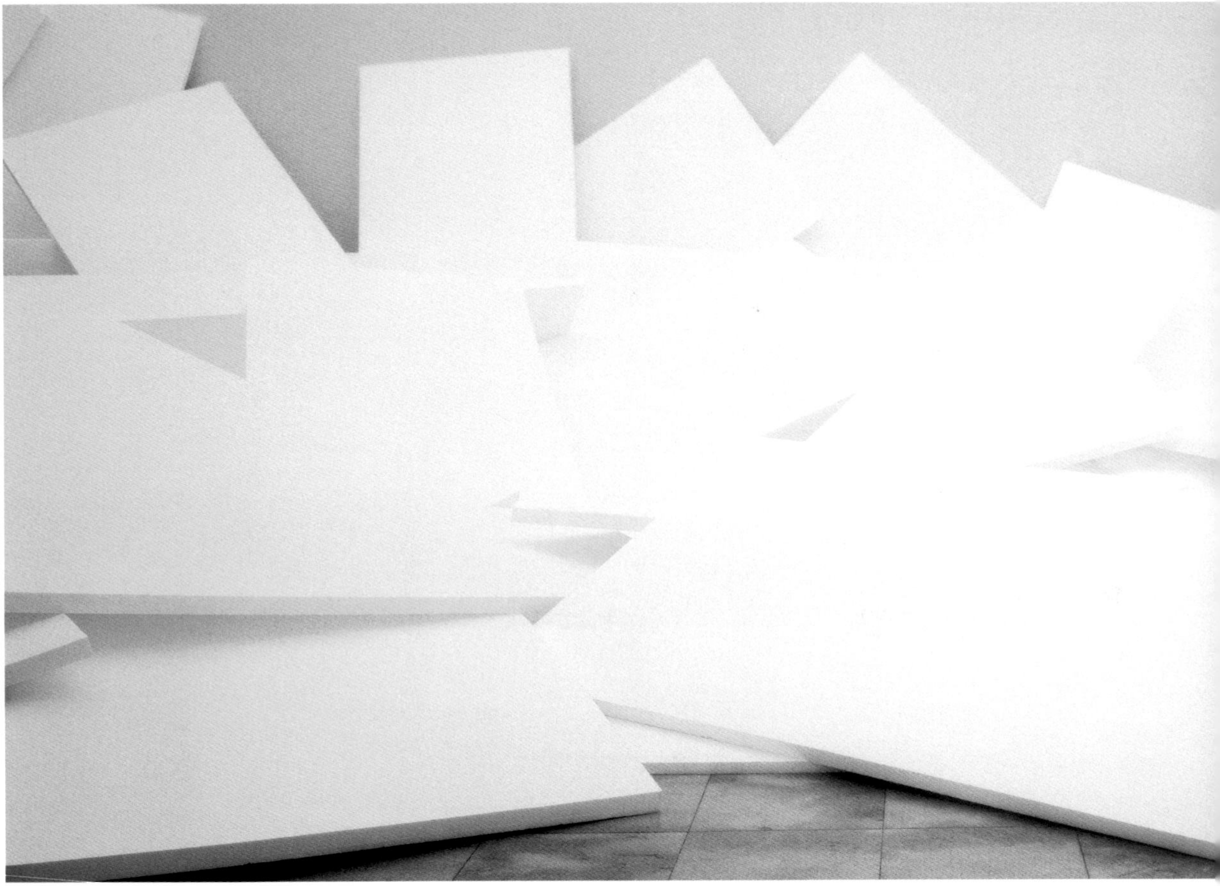

Fin de siècle, 1990

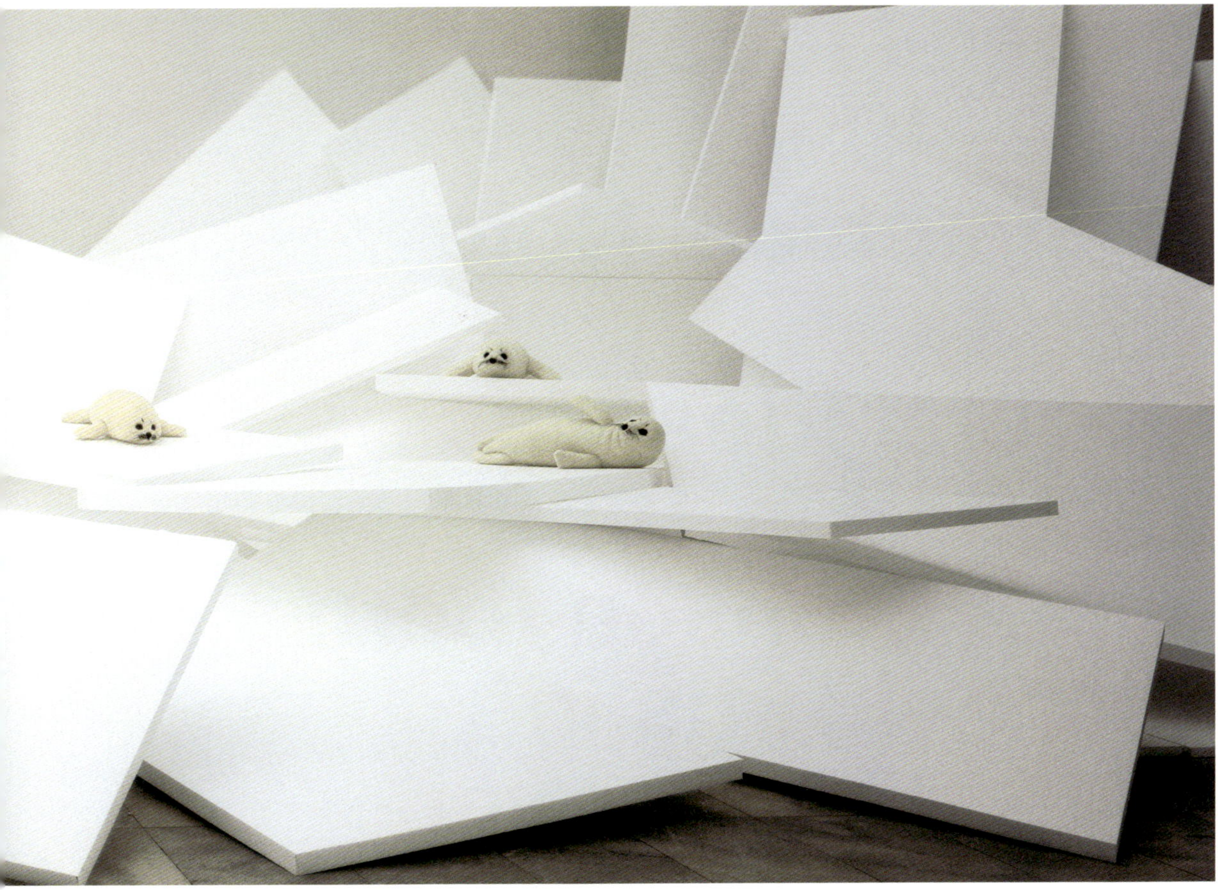

General Idea, 1969–1994 Biographical Note

General Idea was founded in 1969 by AA Bronson (born Michael Tims in 1946 in Vancouver, British Columbia, Canada), Felix Partz (born Ronald Gabe in 1945 in Winnipeg, Manitoba, Canada), and Jorge Zontal (born Slobodan Saia-Levy

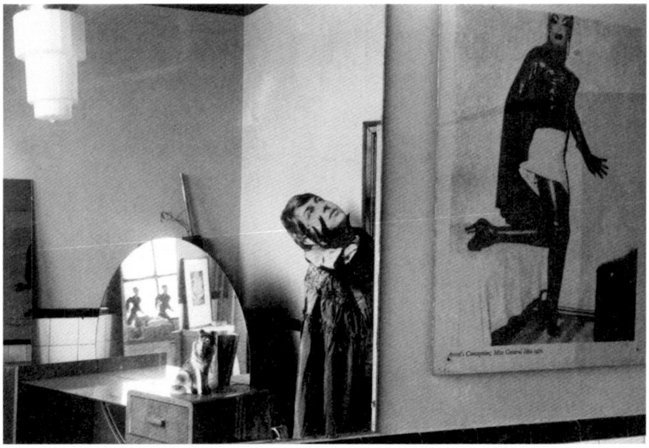

General Idea Studio, 241 Yonge Street, Toronto, 1974

in 1944 in Parma, Italy). Although the legend generated by the group cites 1968 as the year of conception—the antedated year given for the crowning of Mimi Paige as Miss General Idea—it was only in 1969 that the three founding members, then the driving force behind a large art collective that notably included Granada Gazelle, Danny Freedman, and Mimi Paige, produced their first joint works. They came from different backgrounds—Felix had done painting, sculpture, and performance art, Jorge was a photographer, filmmaker, and performance artist, while AA ranged from architecture, photography, and performance to publishing (via The Loving Couch Press)—but all three were active on the alternative art scene in Canada in the late 1960s. The founding of General Idea was inspired, as was that of Image Bank (another Vancouver-based collective close to General Idea), by their experience of Intermedia, an arts organization founded in Vancouver in 1966.

In 1969 Felix, AA, and Jorge moved into 78 Gerrard Street in Toronto (along with Mimi Paige and Danny Freedman). It was their first shared studio, which doubled as a public venue where they presented their first show, *Waste Age*, in October (all the while continuing to produce their final solo works). That same year they gave their first collective performances, *Laundromat Special #1* and *Match My Strike*. Other early public outlets included La Galerie B in Montreal, A Space, the Art Gallery of Ontario, St Lawrence Center for the Arts, and the Carmen Lamanna Gallery in Toronto.

From 1970 to 1974 they worked out of 87 Yonge Street, simultaneously a studio and a meeting place for numerous Canadian and international artists; then, in 1974, they moved to 241 Yonge Street. There, that same year, they founded Art Metropole, an organization designed to collect, conserve, and publish artist's books, multiples, and sound and video works, as well as to assemble hard-to-find documentation on contemporary art and artists (www.artmetropole.com).

During the period 1969–1978, General Idea basically produced conceptual,

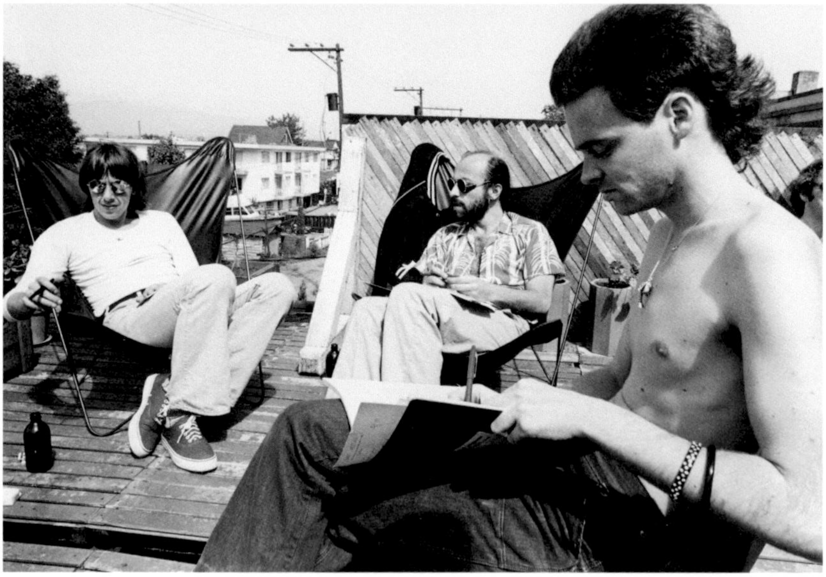

General Idea, Western Front Society, Vancouver, 1974

ephemeral works: installations, environments, mail art, films, and theatrical events, notably centered around their invented creature, Miss General Idea, and around the fiction of the *1984 Miss General Idea Pavillion,* for which substantial video and photographic documentation survives. In April 1972, General Idea founded *FILE Megazine*, a magazine conceived, designed, and edited by the trio. Twenty-six issues appeared before publication ended in 1989.

In 1975, a performance titled *Going Thru The Motions*, presented at the Art Gallery of Ontario, summed up their output of preceding years and signaled a new period of creativity based on a return to the making of objects. One of the crucial events of this period was the 1977 destruction of the *Pavillion,* for which General Idea then created "ruins," leading to years of "archaeological" works. Alongside projects related to the *1984 Miss General Idea Pavillion* with its artifacts and *Boutique* from which they sold their many multiples, Felix, AA, and Jorge turned out several sets of works that brought them growing recognition (including the *Colour Bar Lounge,* the *T.V. Dinner Plates,* a series of self-portraits, the "Pasta Paintings, " and the "Copyright Paintings").

From the mid-1970s up to the late 1980s, General Idea exhibited its developing work internationally, notably in the United Kingdom, the Netherlands, France, Italy, and Switzerland (where the trio had its first European show, at the Galerie Gaëtan in Geneva in 1976, and where in 1984 it presented one of its most famous performances, *XXX (bleu),* at the Centre d'Art Contemporain, also in Geneva).

Major exhibitions during this highly productive period of recognition, when the group became a key player on the contemporary scene (figuring in the Canadian pavilion at the Venice Biennale in 1980 as well as in Documenta in Kassel in 1982, 1987, and 1997), included: in 1979, *Colour Bar Lounge*, Stedelijk Museum (Amsterdam), *Test Tube*, de Appel (Amsterdam); in 1980, the inaugural presentation of their boutique, *The Boutique from the 1984 Miss General Idea Pavillion*, Carmen Lamanna Gallery (Toronto); in 1984–1985, a traveling show titled *The 1984 Miss General Idea Pavillion*, Kunsthalle Basel (Basel), Stedelijk Van Abbemuseum (Eindhoven), Art Gallery of Ontario (Toronto), and the Museum of Contemporary Art (Montreal); in 1986–1987, a traveling show entitled *The Armoury of the 1984 Miss General Idea Pavillion*, Albright Knox Art Gallery (Buffalo), 49th Parallel (New York), University Art Gallery, California State University (Long Beach), Contemporary Arts Museum (Houston), and Setagaya Art Museum (Tokyo); in 1988, *Test Pattern: T.V. Dinner Plates from the 1984 Miss General Idea Pavillion*, SPIRAL, Wacoal Art Center (Tokyo); in 1992-1993, a traveling show entitled *General Idea's Fin de siècle*, Württembergischer Kunstverein (Stuttgart), Centro de Arte Santa Mònica (Barcelona), Kunstverein (Hamburg), The Power Plant (Toronto), Wexner Center for the Visual Arts, Ohio State University (Columbus), and San Francisco Museum of Modern Art (San Francisco); in 1994, *General Idea: Drawings 1989–1994*, Stedelijk Museum (Amsterdam), and *One Year of AZT/One Day of AZT*, National Gallery of Canada (Ottawa).

This last show was part of the *AIDS* project that ran between 1987 and 1994, after General Idea had moved to New York in 1986. The countless manifestations of this polymorphous project in North America and Europe—exhibitions, public commissions, urban events, production of multiples, etc.—represent the group's final period of creativity. The deaths in 1994 of Felix Partz and Jorge Zontal from AIDS put an end to the trio's activities. AA Bronson has subsequently pursued a career as a solo artist, all the time continuing to promote awareness and recognition of General Idea's contribution to the contemporary art scene.

Clément Dirié

Translated from the French by Deke Dusinberre.

For a complete list of multiples and of General Idea's solo and group shows, as well as a bibliography of monographic publications and articles and a list of public collections holding works by General Idea, see: http://www.aabronson.com/art/gi.org.
The General Idea archives are held at the Library and Archives of the National Gallery of Canada, Ottawa.

General Idea is represented by Galerie Frédéric Giroux (Paris), Esther Schipper Galerie (Berlin), and Mai 36 Galerie (Zurich).

Bibliographic note

- For an in-depth study of General Idea's early years, see: The Search for the Spirit: General Idea 1968–1975, exh. cat., Art Gallery of Ontario, Toronto, 1997.
- For a catalogue raisonné of General Idea's multiples, see: General Idea Editions: 1967–1995, Blackwood Gallery, Mississauga, 2003.
- For a complete reprint of FILE Megazine, see: FILE Megazine: General Idea (Complete Reprint), 6 volumes in a box, JRP|Ringier, Zurich 2008.

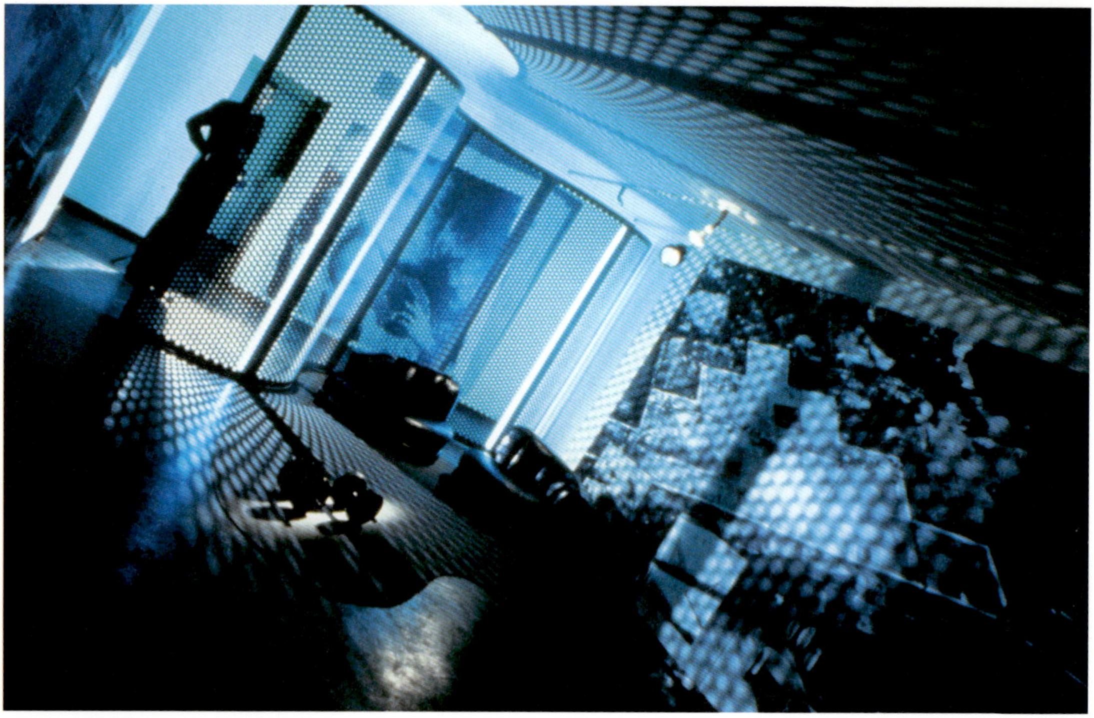

Reconstructing Futures, 1977

Khroma Key Klub: The Blue Ruins from the 1984 Miss General Idea Pavillion, De Vleeshal, Middelburg, 1985

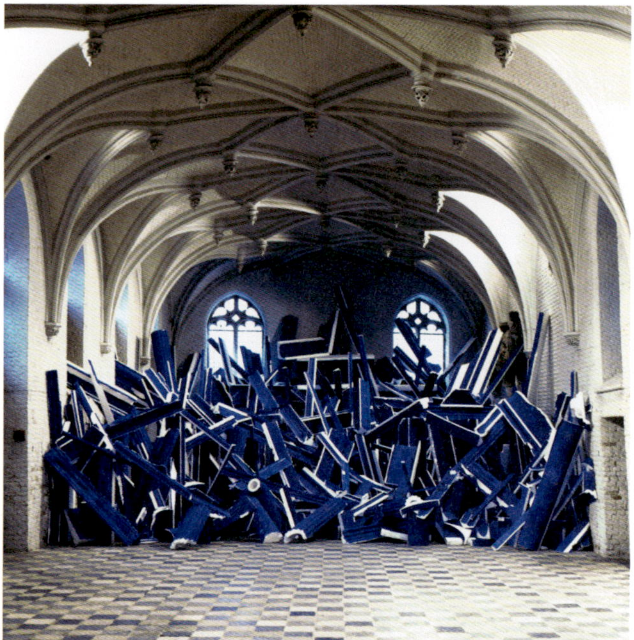

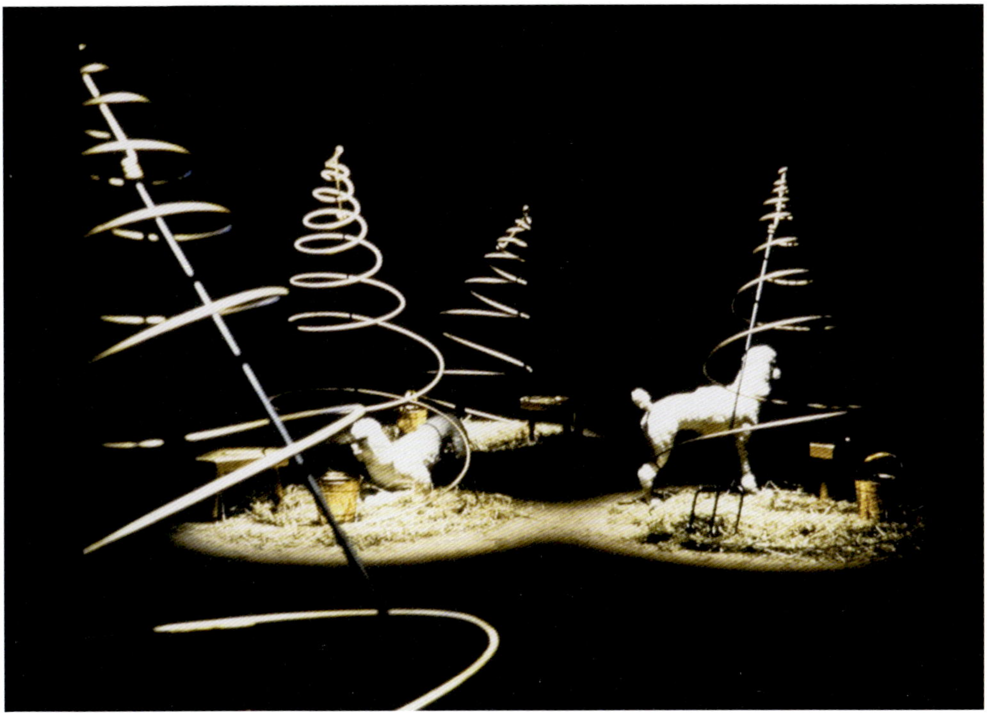

P Is For Poodle (The Milky Way from the 1984 Miss General Idea Pavillion), Akademie der Kunst, Berlin, 1982

Monday, Wednesday, Saturday, 1984

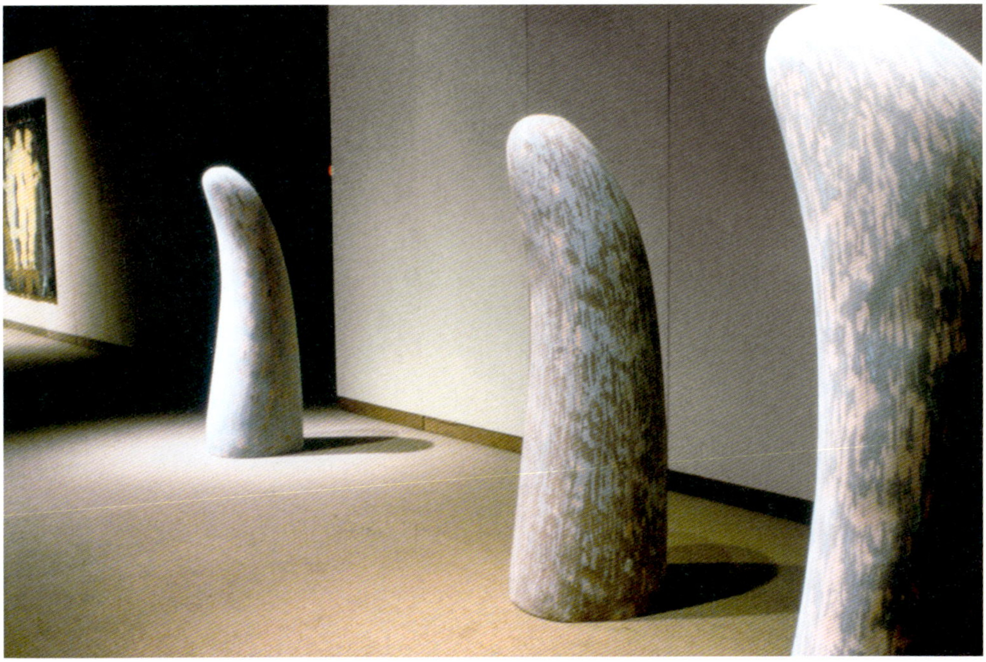

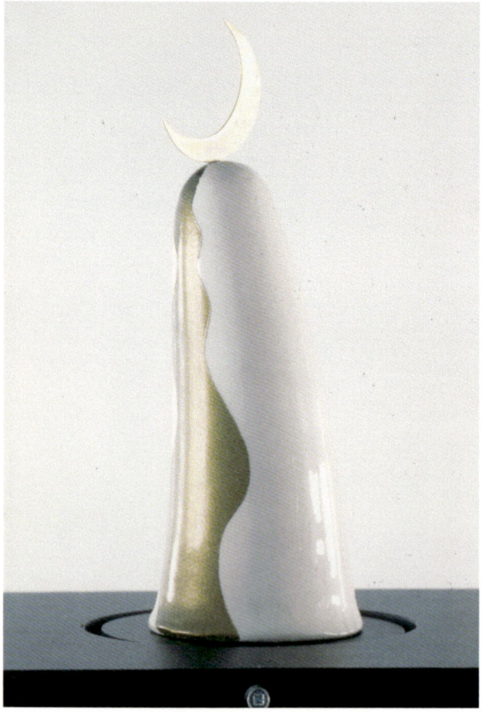

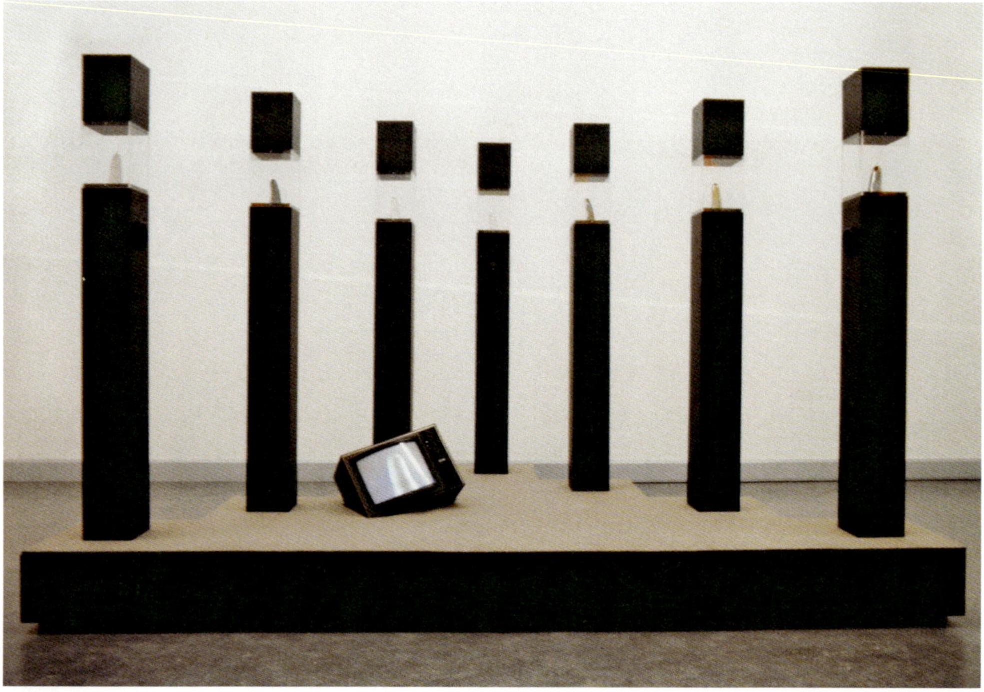

<u>Cornucopia: Fragments from the Room of the Unknown Function from the 1984 Miss General Idea Pavillion</u>, 1982
(Top: detail)

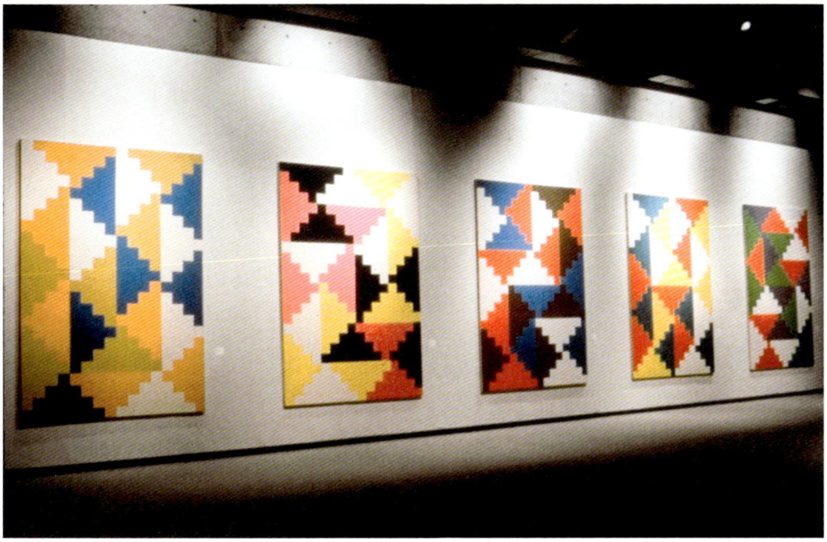

"Ziggurat Paintings," 1968–1969, The 1984 Miss General Idea Pavillion, Art Gallery of Ontario, Toronto, 1985

V.B. Gowns and "Ziggurat Paintings," The 1984 Miss General Idea Pavillion, Art Gallery of Ontario, Toronto, 1985

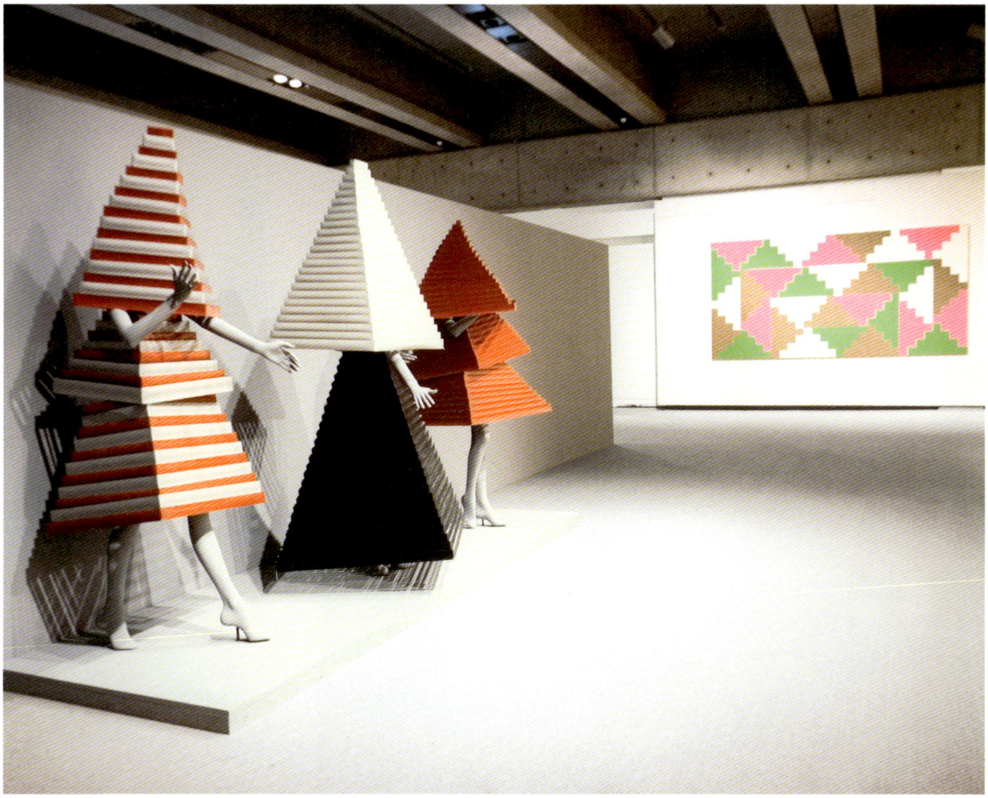

White AIDS, 1993

AIDS, 1988–1990, Fodor Museum, Amsterdam, 1990

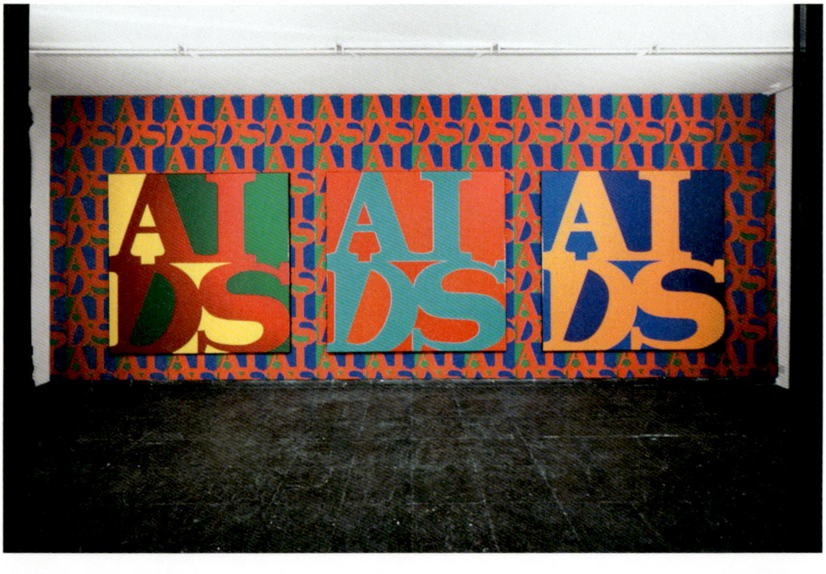

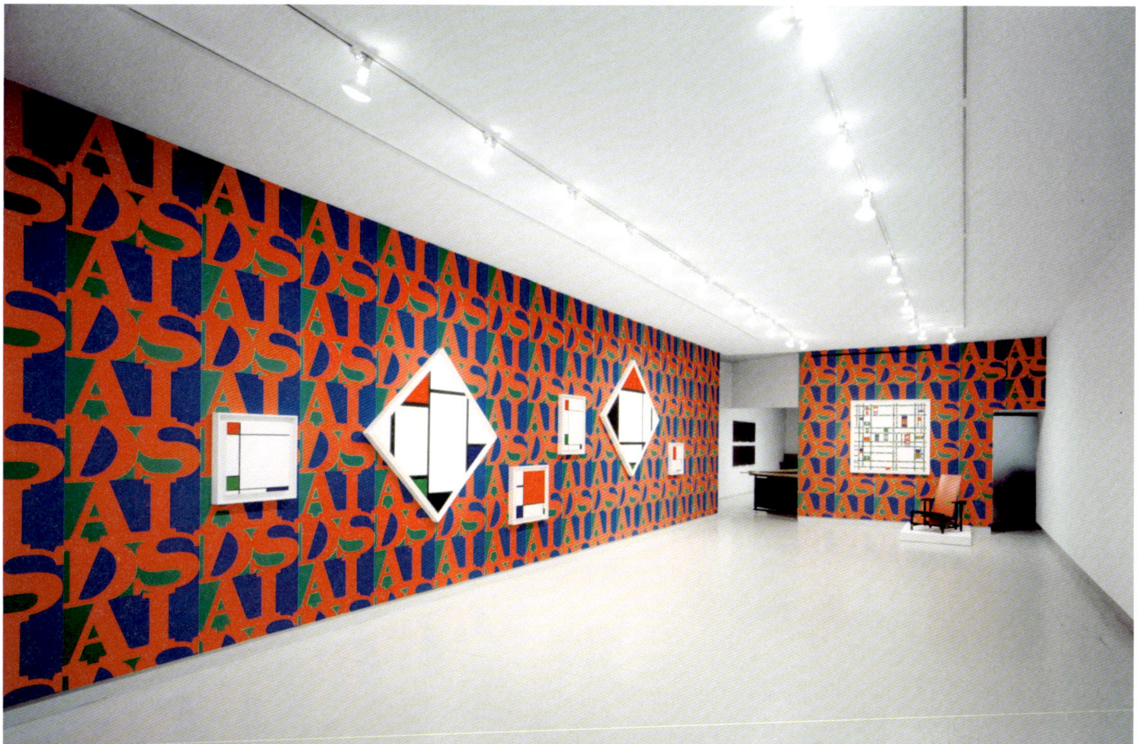

Infe©ted Mondrian, 1994, on AIDS Wallpaper, 1990; Infe©ted Rietveld, 1994, S. L. Simpson Gallery, Toronto, 1995

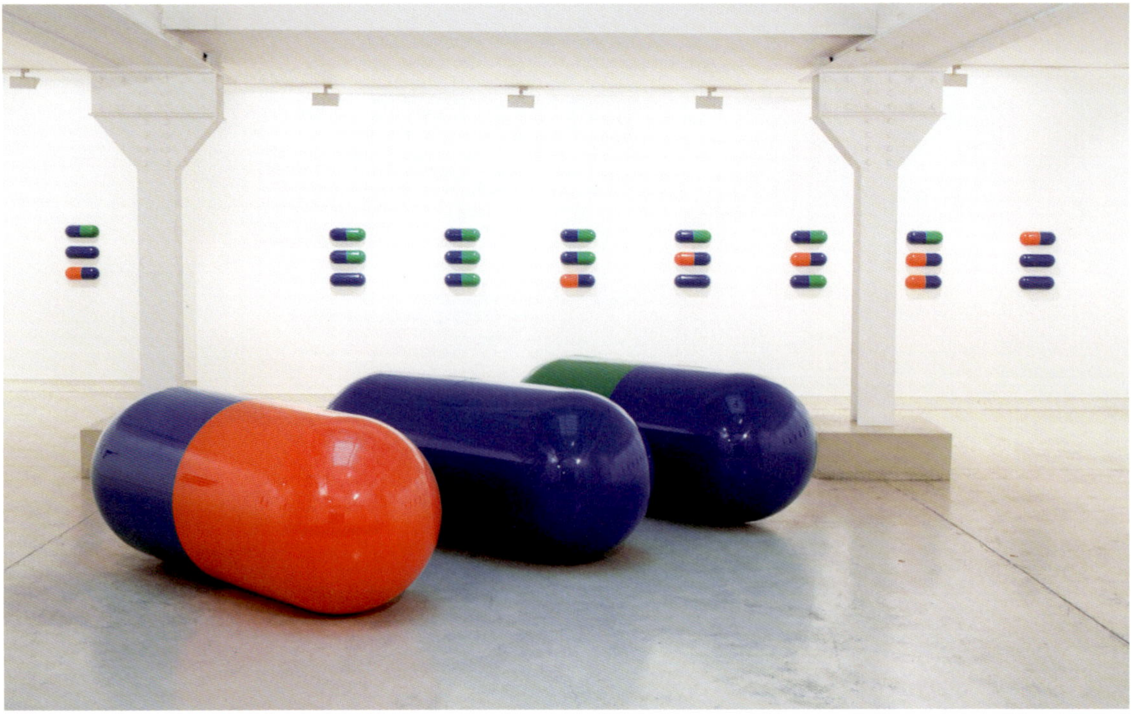

Blue (Cobalt) PLA©EBO [a.k.a. Blue (Mazarine) PLA©EBO], 1992

One Day of AZT, 1991; One Year of AZT, 1991

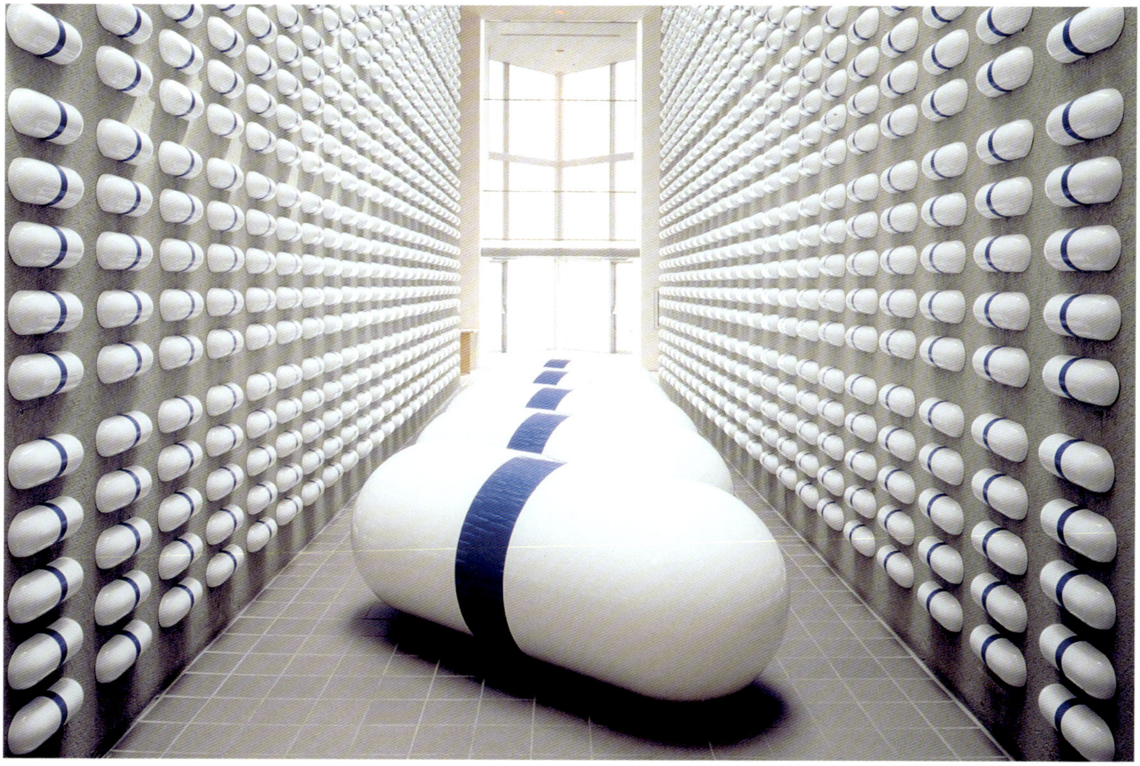

Pla©ebo (Helium), 1992

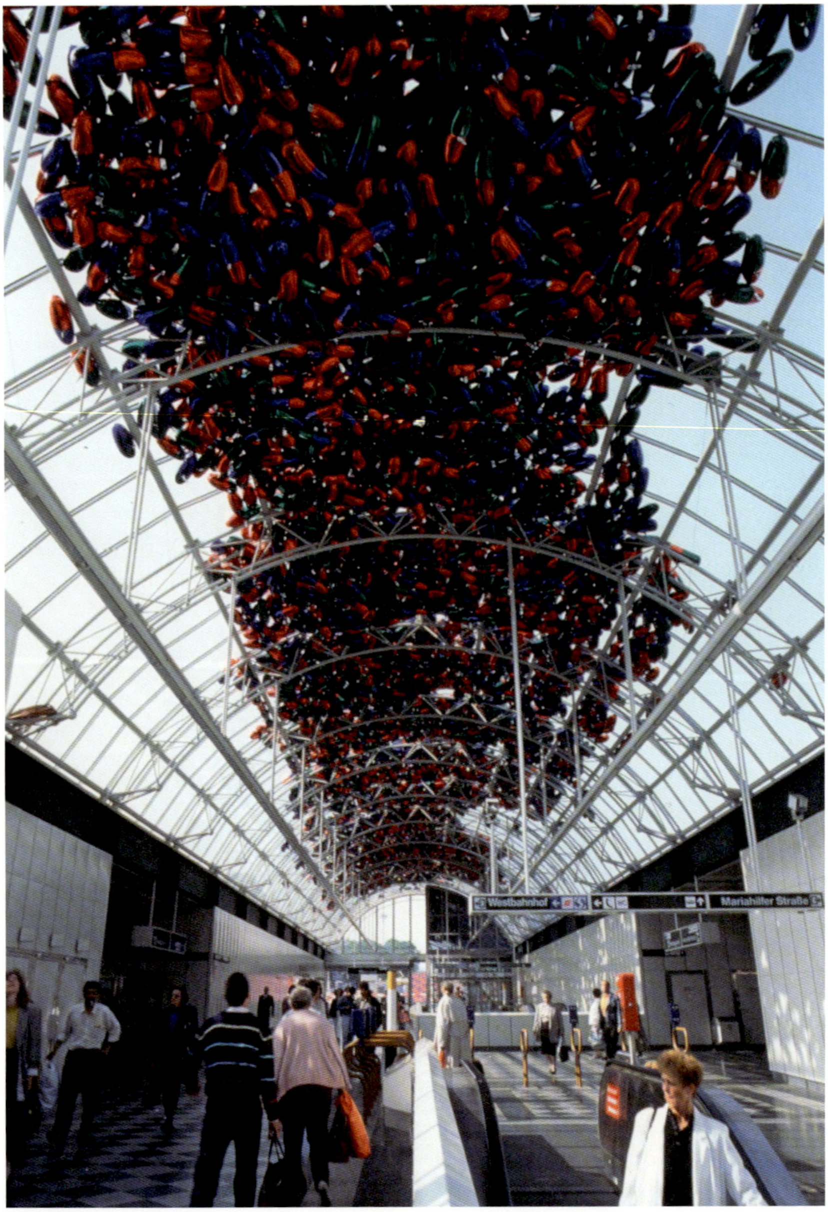

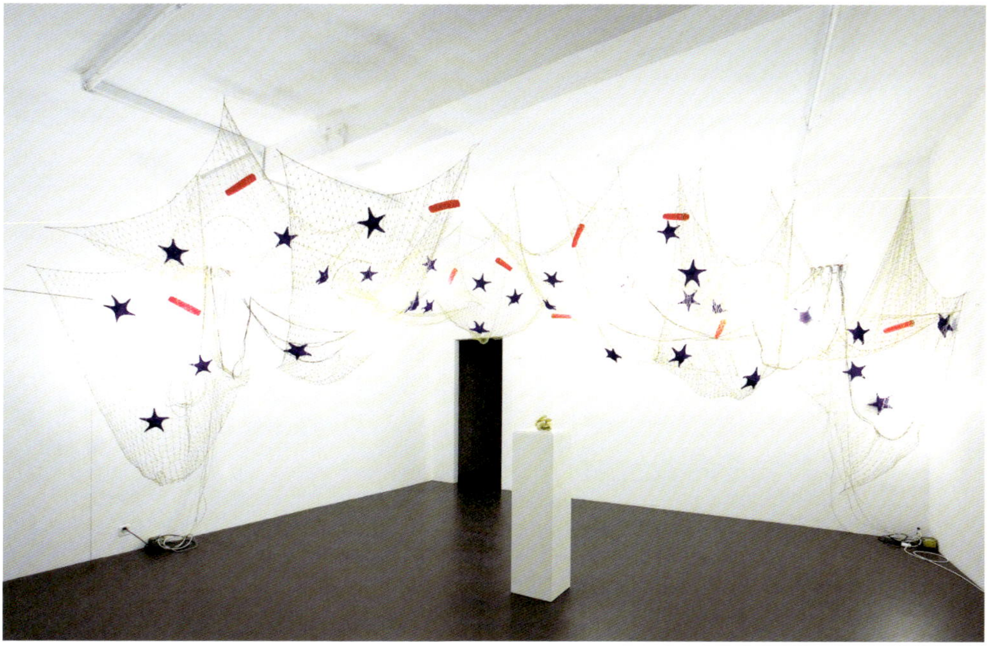

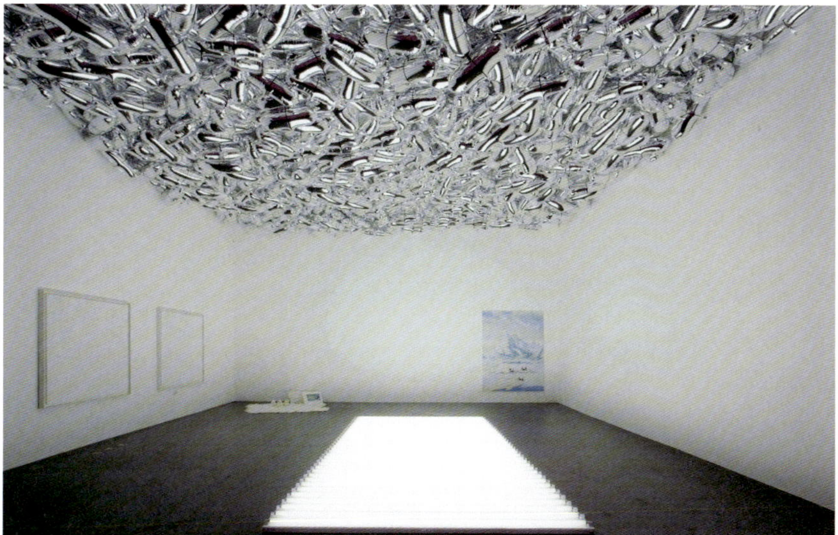

Exhibitions views General Idea: Found Formats and
General Idea Editions 1967–1995, Kunsthalle Zürich, Zurich,
2006–2007
(Top: Fruits de mer, 1992–1994)
(Bottom: Magi© Bullet, 1992; Magi© Carpet, 1992)

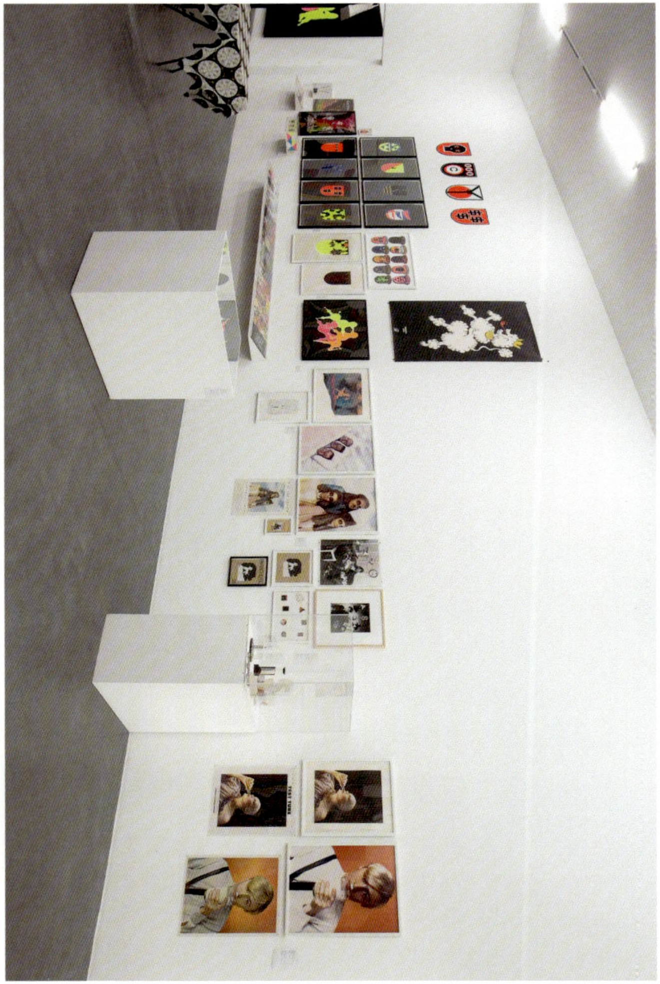

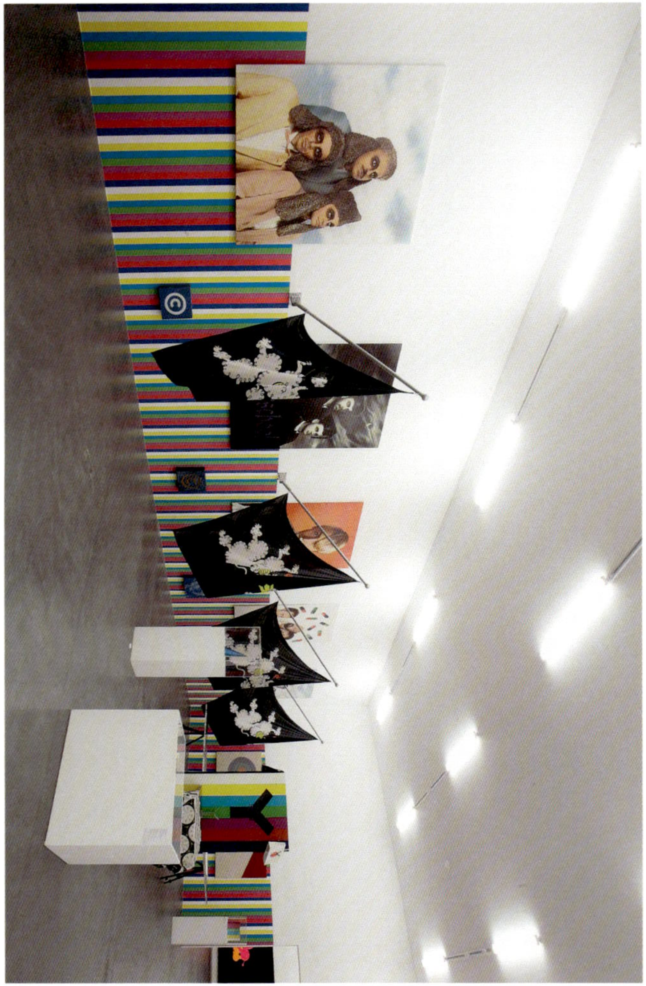

Exhibitions views General Idea: Found Formats and General Idea Editions 1967–1995, Kunsthalle Zürich, Zurich, 2006–2007

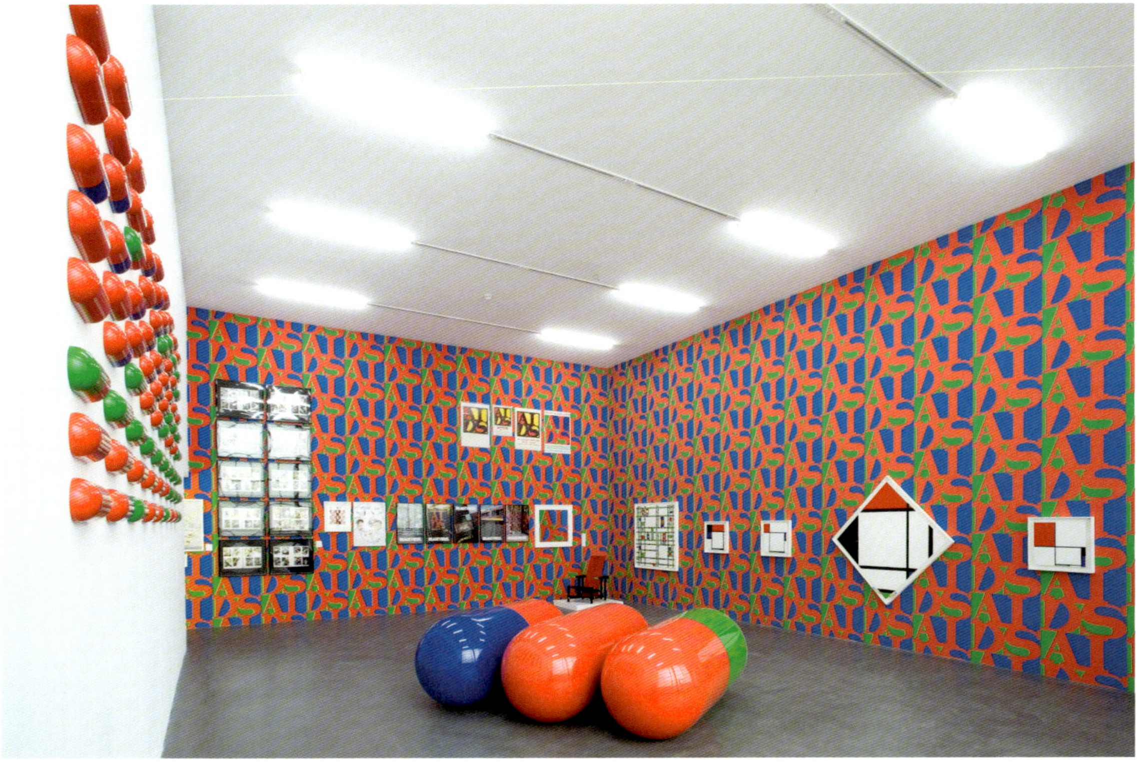

List of Works Reproduced

Except for the mention [n.e.] [for works not exhibited], the works reproduced in the publication figured in the exhibition Haute Culture: General Idea. A Retrospective, 1969–1994, organized by the Musée d'Art moderne de la Ville de Paris from February 10 to April 30, 2011.

Pages 218–221 list the works exhibited at the Musée d'Art moderne de la Ville de Paris and not reproduced here.

1 Rodney Werden
Portrait of General Idea, 1974
Gelatin silver print: 39.8 × 50.2 cm
Collection General Idea, Toronto/New York

10–11 Double page spread, "Glamour," FILE Megazine, "Glamour Issue," vol. 3, no. 1, Autumn 1975, p. 20–21
[p. 7: detail]

13 AIDS posters, 1987–1988 [n.e.]
Screen-print on paper: 68.4 × 68.5 cm
Installation view, streets of San Francisco

14 XXX [bleu], 1984
Installation resulting from a performance
Acrylic on canvas and poodle mannequins, three canvases: each 493.5 × 296 cm, overall installation: 350 × 988 × 143.5 cm.
Collection Art Gallery of Ontario, Toronto. Gift of Sandra Simpson, 1993
Installation view, Art Gallery of Ontario, Toronto, 1985

15 What Happened—The 1970 Miss General Idea Pageant, 1970
Left: among the contestants, Danny Freedman and Mimi Paige, in their bear costumes on the staircase of the St Lawrence Centre for the Arts, Toronto
Right: Miss Honey demonstrates her talents at the telex machine

16 Letter of Invitation [signed by Granada Gazelle, Miss General Idea 1969], 1971
Typescript, pink letterpress on paper: 25.5 × 20.3 cm
Part of The 1971 Miss General Idea Pageant Entry Kit, 1971
Assorted ephemera mounted on board, with glass protection: 102 × 76.5 cm
Collection Carmen Lamanna, Toronto

The 1971 Miss General Idea Pageant Programme, 1971
Offset pamphlet, 16 p. plus cover, black and white reproductions, 25.5 × 16.5 cm
Self-published edition of 500, unnumbered and sometimes signed

17 The 1971 Miss General Idea Pageant Entry Kit, 1971
Items:

[Bottom left] The Miss General Idea Gown, found cellulose acetate "taffeta" dress with embroidery: 30.5 × 23 cm [folded]; 117.5 × 55 cm [unfolded], affixed with 2-color letterpress thermographic tag: 13.3 × 10.4 cm

"The 1971 Miss General Idea Pageant," screen-printed card folder with pink letterpress title 30.5 × 23 cm, containing the following items:

- "Reworked newspaper article featuring the Miss General Idea Gown," gelatin silver print: 25.5 × 20.2 cm
- "Miss Honey Miss General Idea 1970," gelatin silver print with autograph: 25.5 × 20.2 cm
- The 1970 Miss General Idea Pageant, offset pamphlet, 12 p. plus embossed cover, black-and-white reproductions, edition of approximately 50, some signed, unnumbered; self-published: 11.5 × 11.5 cm
- "Entry form with rules and application form," offset, screen-print, perforation on paper: 19.6 × 42 cm
- "Acceptance card," pink letterpress on folded card and pre-addressed return envelope: 8.5 × 11.5 cm
- General Idea Business Card, pink letterpress on card: 6 × 9.3 cm

Collection General Idea, Toronto/New York

Middle:
"The 1971 Miss General Idea Pageant: Canadian National/Canadian Pacific Telegram from Dr. Venus to General Idea," 1971
Typescript, ink, rubber-stamp, on offset form, 14 × 21.6 cm
General Idea Archive [Projects Series 1968–1971], on loan to National Gallery of Canada Library and Archives, Ottawa

Right:
The 1971 Miss General Idea Pageant Poster, 1971
Offset on paper, 101.6 × 66 cm
Collection General Idea, Toronto/New York

18 The 1971 Miss General Idea Pageant, 1971 [n.e.]
Judges arrive at the Awards Ceremony: from left to right, Michael Hayden, Daniel Freedman, Mimi Paige, Michael Morris, David Silcox, Mimi Silcox, Dorothy Cameron, and Ronald Bloor

20 Pilot, broadcast notice, TV Ontario, April 1, 1977 [n.e.]

21 Invitation card to General Idea's Luxon V.B., exhibition at Carmen Lamanna Gallery, Toronto, 1973–1974 [n.e.]
Luxon V.B., 1973 [n.e.]
Site-specific installation
Double-sided mirror slats fitted to canvas and metal Venetian blind apparatus, dimensions variable
Installation view, Carmen Lamanna Gallery, Toronto

Luxon V.B. with Sandy Stagg and the Hand of the Spirit, 1973–1974 [n.e.]

22–23 Lux-on, 1974
Screen-print with silver pencil on paper: 46.5 × 57.8 cm
Edition of 45 plus APs
Collection Art Gallery of Ontario, Toronto. Gift of AA Bronson, 1998

24–25 Painting Drawing Sculpture
[a.k.a. No Mean Feet],1976
Gelatin silver prints: overall 76×204 cm
[4 panels assembled]
Courtesy Stampa Galerie, Basel

27 Untitled [Sandy Stagg Models the Miss General Idea Shoe and the Hand of the Spirit Against the Backdrop of Luxon V.B.], 1973–1974
Gelatin silver print, 43.2×27.9 cm
Courtesy Esther Schipper Galerie, Berlin

No Mean Feet, 1973–1974
Gelatin silver print: 27.9×43.2 cm
Courtesy Esther Schipper Galerie, Berlin

28 Collage from photographs of V.B. Gowns, ca. 1977 [n.e.]

29 Production shot during filming of Pilot, "V.B. Gowns take to the ski slope," Lake Louise, Banff, 1977 [n.e.]

30 Going Thru The Motions, 1975 [n.e.]
Performance view, Walker Court, Art Gallery of Ontario, Toronto, 1975

31 Felix Partz models V.B. Gown #3 at City Hall, Toronto, ca. 1975–1977 [n.e.]
Gelatin silver print: 25.4×20.3 cm

33 Floor Plan for 1984 Folding Chairs for the Pavillion, 1974 [n.e.]

34–35 V.B. Gown against the skyline of Calgary, 1977 [n.e.]

37 Nightschool, 1989
Chromogenic print [Ektachrome]: 95.3×76.2 cm
Self-published, edition of 12+1 AP, signed, numbered, and with the inscription "Nightschool" on the back
Courtesy Mai 36 Galerie, Zurich

38 P Is For Poodle, 1983–1989
Lacquer on vinyl: 200×160 cm
Edition of 3+1 AP
Courtesy Galerie Frédéric Giroux, Paris
Here: chromogenic print [Ektachrome], 76.2×63.5 cm

39 Baby Makes 3, 1984–1989
Chromogenic print: 76.2×63.5 cm
Collection Fonds national d'art contemporain [CNAP], ministère de la Culture et de la Communication, Paris-La Défense

41 Fin de siècle, 1994
Lacquer on vinyl: 225×150 cm
Courtesy Galerie Frédéric Giroux, Paris
Here: chromogenic print [Ektachrome]: 79×55.7 cm
Self-published, edition of 12+3 AP, signed and numbered

43 Playing Doctor, 1992
Chromogenic print: 76.2×55.3 cm
Self-published, edition of 12+3 AP+1 HC, signed and numbered
Collection General Idea, Toronto/New York

44–45 Reverie, 1985
3 parts, chromogenic print: each 66×152 cm
Collection McCarthy Tétrault LLP, Toronto

47 Pascal, "chanteuse extraordinaire," performs at The 1971 Miss General Idea Beauty Pageant, Walker Court, Art Gallery of Ontario, Toronto, 1971 [n.e.]

48 Showcard 4–032 Test Model 2, 1977
Chromogenic print, felt pen, and screen-print on paperboard, 45.7×35.6 cm.
Edition 1/2: Art Gallery of Ontario, Toronto, gift of Vivian and David Campbell, 1994

The Katimavik, a giant inverted pyramid, towers above the other structures that comprised the Canada pavilions at Montreal's Expo '67. [n.e.]

50 Going Thru The Motions, 1975 [n.e.]
Performance view, Walker Court, Art Gallery of Ontario, Toronto, 1975

51 General Idea with the Light-On Mirror, 1971 [n.e.]
With one or several mirrors, General Idea reflects a luminous form on furniture, landscapes, vehicles, and people. These actions are the subject of a photographic and video documentation

Light On [Double Mirror], 1971 [n.e.]
Offset on card, recto and verso: 9×14 cm
Edition of approximately 500, some signed, unnumbered
Published by Fine Arts Gallery, University of British Columbia, Vancouver, and National Gallery of Canada, Ottawa

General Idea's Headquarters, Toronto [Light On], 1971 [n.e.]
Set of 2 panels, each panel composed of 3 black and white photographs on masonite: each 20.3×25.4 cm [work #11]

52–53 Canvas Weaving, 1970
A project by Felix Partz
A big canvas is cut in strips; these are woven on the floor, and then hung on the wall
8 gelatin silver prints mounted on 4 panels: each 16.9×11 cm [overall: 67.6×11 cm]
Here: detail, two pannels
Courtesy Esther Schipper Galerie, Berlin

56 Manipulating the Self, 1971
Offset pamphlet, 20 p. plus cover, black and white reproductions, with photocopies of 2 interior pages: 21.5×13.8 cm
Edition of 500, some signed and unnumbered, published by The Coach House Press, Toronto
Collection General Idea, Toronto/New York

Towards an Audience Vocabulary, 1978 [n.e.]
Tele-Performance Festival sponsored by the Fifth Network/Cinquième Réseau, held at Masonic Temple, Toronto [the audience performs the "gasping" gesture, as per General Idea's request]

57 Club Canasta, 1972
14 letters, photocopy, and colored pencil on paper: each 28.5×21.7 cm
6 gelatin silver prints, 16.4×24 cm each
2 tables with audiotapes and documents: each 80×125 cm [H: 85 cm]
Courtesy Galerie Frédéric Giroux, Paris; Mai 36 Galerie, Zurich; Esther Schipper Galerie, Berlin

Bottom, left to right:
Club Canasta, FILE's Filathon Telephone Canasta Party ["Rules of the Game/Technical Data"], 1972 [n.e.]
Club Canasta, FILE's Filathon Telephone Canasta Party [Participants at CBC Radio studio], 1972 [n.e.]

58–59 Untitled [Mail Art Project], 1969
Mail art project by AA Bronson
Set of 8, offset on card: each 10.7×7 cm
Self-published, unsigned, edition number unknown
Collection General Idea, Toronto/New York

60 Dear General Idea, if I live to be a hundred I'll never forgive myself for ... , 1973
Set of 2, offset on bond paper: each 28 × 21.5
Self-published, edition of about 100, unsigned and unnumbered
Collection General Idea, Toronto/New York

61 Skyportraits Chain Letter Project, 1969
Typescript, felt pen on paper: 13.3 × 21.6 cm
Self-published, unsigned, edition number unknown
Collection General Idea, Toronto/New York

Jorge avec Girdle—Evidence of Body Binding, 1970
A project by Jorge Zontal
Gelatin silver print postcard: 13,8 × 8,8
Collection General Idea, Toronto/New York

Jorge sans Girdle—Evidence of Body Binding, 1970
A project by Jorge Zontal
Gelatin silver print postcard: 13.8 × 8.8 cm
Collection General Idea, Toronto/New York

62–63 Family Resemblances, 1972
7 p., pink card cover with plastic binding and handwritten title "Family Resemblances," rubber-stamped "SWEEPING GENERALITY" on front cover and "CANADIAN COMPANY" with a maple leaf pattern on the back cover, 7 gelatin silver prints: 12.8 × 17.8 cm [framed with facsimile prints]
Collection General Idea, Toronto/New York

64 Exposé—A Video Device, 1971
Closed-circuit video installation: black and white, silent, dimensions variable
A monitor is installed in front of the men's toilets of the museum and plays a recording of the empty toilets. A "ghost" camera is installed in the toilets, giving the impression of a surveillance system
Here: invitation card for Exposé, A Space, Toronto, July 1971
Collection General Idea, Toronto/New York

65 Off Hand Photo-Booth Hands, 1969–1970 [detail]
A project by Felix Partz linked to his first solo exhibition in Toronto in 1970, including, notably, a series of "Hand Paintings," or "Paintings made by hand," now destroyed
Two parts:
a. set of 4 black and white photo-booths photographs mounted on card;
b. photography on paper [of sheet a.]: each 20.1 × 16 cm
Collection General Idea, Toronto/New York

66–67 The Hoarding of the 1984 Miss General Idea Pavillion, 1975
Three panels, groove and shellacked plywood with pine nails, chicken wire, wooden support: 246.4 × 366 × 10.2 cm [overall]
Three "cut-outs," plywood:
35 × 44 cm, 44.5 × 34.3 cm, 42.5 × 30.5 cm
Collections General Idea, Toronto/New York [main part] and Carmen Lamanna, Toronto [three elements]

Pavillion Construction Hoarding, 1975
Diazotype on acetate over plywood, 49.2 × 88.6 cm [framed]
Edition of 5, stamp-signed and numbered, incomplete edition
Edition 2/5
Collection Art Gallery of Ontario, Toronto. Purchased with the support of Wintario, 1976

69 Artist's Conception: Miss General Idea 1971, 1971
Screen-print on paper: 101.5 × 66 cm
Self-published multiples on different supports, signed and unnumbered
Collection General Idea, Toronto/New York

70 / 72 Ruins of the 1984 Miss General Idea Pavillion, 1977 [n.e.]
Site-specific installation and performance, rubble, chalk, and other elements: approx. 91.44 × 39.01 meters
Installation views, Kingston, Canada

70 The 1984 Spirit of Miss General Idea Vehicle, 1973
Offset postcard, recto: color, ballpoint pen, felt pen; verso: felt pen; 10.1 × 15.2 cm
Found object, lacquered metal, rubber, 1.5 × 10.3 × 3.5 cm
General Idea Archive [Projects Series 1972–1973], on loan to National Gallery of Canada Library and Archives, Ottawa

71 Luxon Louvre [Ambiguity Without Contradiction], 1975
Diazotype and enamel on acetate, overpaper board, 69.6 × 151.1 cm [framed]
Edition of 5 + 1 AP, stamp-signed and numbered, incomplete edition
Edition 1/5: Collection Art Gallery of Ontario, Toronto. Purchased in 1987

73 Miss General Idea Glove Pattern [Form Follows Fetish], 1975
Diazotype on acetate, craft paper: 45 × 67.3 cm
Edition of 5, stamp-signed and numbered
Collection Carmen Lamanna, Toronto

74 The Armoury of the 1984 Miss General Idea Pavillion, 1985–1990
Installation of 40 paintings
Acrylic and fluorescent acrylic and metallic leaf on wood panel;
10 large panels: each 152 × 121.5 cm,
30 small panels, each 50.8 × 40.6 cm
Collection Art Gallery of Ontario, Toronto. Gift from the Volunteer Committee Fund, 1990
Here: installation view, Setagaya Museum, Tokyo, 1987

75 Rude Awakening, 1982
Gelatin silver print: 57 × 50.5 cm
Self-published, edition of 10, 5 produced, unsigned and unnumbered
Courstesy Stampa Galerie, Basel

76 Ghent Flags, 1984
3 flags, screen-print on nylon: each 200 × 200 cm
Edition of 50, unsigned and unnumbered, published by the Museum Van Hedendaagse Kunst, Gand
Collection General Idea, Toronto/New York
Here: installation view, roof of the Musée d'Art contemporain de Montréal, Montreal, 1985

Tuscany Poodles—Fragment With Trees, 1984
Acrylic on plaster: 26 × 37 cm
Private collection, Paris, courtesy Galerie Frédéric Giroux, Paris

The Unveiling of the Cornucopia: A Mural Fragment from the Room of the Unknown Function in the Villa dei Misteri of the 1984 Miss General Idea Pavillion, 1982 [detail]
5 panels, enamel on plasterboard and plywood: each 244 × 122 cm [overall 244 × 610 cm]
Collection University of Lethbridge Art Collection, Lethbridge, purchased 1986 with funds provided by the Canada Council Special Purchase Assistance Program

Pavillion Poodle Fragments, 1983–1984
Installation, various elements, aniline dye on plaster: dimensions variable
Collection General Idea, Toronto/New York

77 The Dr. Brute Colonnade [Dominant Imagery], 1975
Diazotype and enamel on acetate over craft paper, 65.5×119.2 [framed]
Edition 1 of 5 [not all produced]
Collection Art Gallery of Ontario, Toronto. Purchase, 1987

Proposed Seating Arrangement [Form Follows Fiction], 1975
Diazotype and enamel on acetate over card, 99×202 cm [framed]
Self-published, edition of 5, stamp-signed and numbered
Edition 3/5: Collection Art Gallery of Ontario, Toronto. Purchased in 1987

Double Ziggurat Maze from the 1984 Miss General Idea Pavillion, 1984–1985 [n.e.]
Graphite on graph paper, 43×28 cm

79 Post Mortem, 1985
Acrylic, fluorescent acrylic, metallic enamel on wood: 152. 4×122×3.2 cm
Collection Art Gallery of Ontario, Toronto

81 Passion Over Reason, 1986
Acrylic, fluorescent acrylic on wood: 40.6×50.8×3.2 cm
Collection Art Gallery of Ontario, Toronto

83 The Juggler, 1985
Acrylic, fluorescent acrylic, metallic enamel on wood: 152. 4×122×3.2 cm
Collection, Art Gallery of Ontario, Toronto

85 Marital Triangles: A Psychological Presentation of Extra-Marital Affairs, 1984
Found offset book collaged with trimmed color postcard on cover: 32 p., 21.3×14 cm
Self-published, edition of 6, signed and numbered
Collection General Idea, Toronto/New York

86 Press Release—Orgasm Renewal Project, 1972
Offset and rubber-stamp on bond paper, 27.9×21.6 cm
Self-published, unsigned, edition number unknown
Collection General Idea, Toronto/New York

87 "Three Heads are Better," double page spread, FILE Megazine, "1984 A Year in Pictures Issue," vol. 4, no. 1, Summer 1978, p. 14–15

89 General Idea's Dominant Dream, 1978 [n.e.] [detail]
Installation in 4 parts:
a. 1 gelatin silver print mounted on masonite: 38.1×23.5 cm;
b. 1 chromogenic print mounted on triangular-shaped masonite, aluminum construction: 19.7×45.1 cm;
c. 1 chromogenic print mounted on triangular-shaped masonite, aluminum construction: 19.7×45.1 cm; d. 1 chromogenic print mounted on triangular-shaped masonite, aluminum construction: 19.7×45.1 cm
[overall: 243.8×139.7 cm]

Playing the Triangle, 1979
Installation in 4 parts, 3 black and white photographs, each mounted on triangular-shaped masonite, aluminum construction: each 19.7×45.1 cm; one metal musical triangle, overall installed: 243.8×139.7 cm
Collection Massimo de Carlo Arte Contemporanea, Milan

91 Menage A Trois, 1978
Offset pamphlet, 22 p. plus cover, black and white reproductions: 26.7×20.4 cm
Edition of 500, some signed, unnumbered
Published by Art Metropole, Toronto
Collection General Idea, Toronto/New York

92 Orgasm Energy Chart, 1970
Offset on bond paper, 43×27.8 cm
Here: instruction sheet, 6.2×24 cm
Self-published edition of approx. 100, unnumbered and unsigned
Collection General Idea, Toronto/New York

93, 94 Orgasm Energy Chart, 1970–1971
6 completed forms, offset, graphite, colored pencil, ink, rubber-stamp, felt pen on bond paper, each 43×27.8 cm
Here: two versions
General Idea Archive [Projects Series 1968–1971], on loan to National Gallery of Canada Library and Archives, Ottawa

95 Process of Elimination, 1988–1991
Acrylic, enamel and copper leaf on canvas: 259×259.2 cm
Collection Art Gallery of Ontario, Toronto. Gift of Sandra Simpson, 2001

96 Evidence of Body Binding, 1971–1972
Installation, 15 gelatin silver transparencies mounted in fluorescent stainless steellight boxes: each 20.3×30.5×8.6 cm [installation size variable]
National Gallery of Canada, Ottawa. Purchased 1973

97 Nazi Milk, 1979–1990
Lacquer on vinyl: 200×160 cm
Edition 3/3: private collection, France, courtesy Galerie Frédéric Giroux, Paris
Here: chromogenic print [Ektachrome]: 76.2×53.3 cm
Self-published edition of 12+3 AP+1 HC [2007], signed and numbered

98 Dick All, 1993–2001
Handblown glass: 16×7 cm [diam.]
Edition of 26+2 AP, signed and marked A to Z, produced by Éditions Florence Loewy, Paris
Collection General Idea, Toronto/New York

99 Bondage, 1987
Black satin ribbon with silver hot-foil stamping: 1.5 cm wide, 22.86 meters per roll
2 prototypes for an edition never produced
Collection General Idea, Toronto/New York

100 An Evening with the Maids, 1969
Poster conceived for the presentation of Jean Genet's play, Les Bonnes, at the Théâtre Passe Muraille, Toronto, August 1969
Gelatin silver print: 87.6×85 cm
Inscriptions: "Mimosa, Divine and Darling" and "The Golden Mink"
Edition of 100, numbered and not signed
Collection Jim and Susan Garrard, Battersea, Canada

103 Three Graces: Mural Fragment from the 1984 Miss General Idea Pavillion, 1982 [n.e.]
Latex enamel on wood, 279.5 × 249 cm
Collection Vancouver Art Gallery, Vancouver Art Gallery Acquisition Fund

104–105 Lunatic Poodles Panels [Partial Reconsruction] from the Room of the Unknown Function in the Villa dei Misteri at the 1984 Miss General Idea Pavillion, 1982
2 parts, enamel paint, gelatin silver prints on wood; left panel: 45.1 × 53.8 × 2.4 cm, right panel 45.1 × 53.8 × 2 cm
[overall installed 45.7 × 114.3 cm]
Collection Helen Chapman, Toronto

The Unveiling of the Cornucopia: A Mural Fragment from the Room of the Unknown Function in the Villa dei Misteri of the 1984 Miss General Idea Pavillion, 1982
5 panels, enamel on plasterboard and plywood: each 244 × 122 cm [overall 244 × 610 cm]
Collection University of Lethbridge Art Collection, Lethbridge. Purchased 1986 with funds provided by the Canada Council Special Purchase Assistance Program

106 Mondo Cane [Wall Painting from the 1984 Miss General Idea Pavillion], 1982
Oil pastels and acrylic on canvas: 68 × 86 cm
Private collection, Basel

Eau d'Artifice, 1983 [n.e.]
Oil pastel and acrylic on craft paper, 109 × 88.6 cm [irregular shape]
Collection Art Gallery of Ontario, Toronto.
Gift of Lonti Ebers, 1999

107 Tableau Vivant, Natura Morta, 1983
Oil pastels and acrylic on canvas: 182 × 122 cm
Collection Carmen Lamanna, Toronto

108–109 Représentation Confusé, 1981–1994
Enamel, latex on five vertical wood slats [each approx. 83 × 23.5 cm], metal mending plates, wood molding pieces, on recto and verso: 184.8 × 117.5 cm
Collection General Idea, Toronto/New York

110–111 Baby Makes 3, 1984
Fluorescent acrylic on canvas: 122 × 173 cm
Collection Carmen Lamanna, Toronto

112–117 Mondo Cane Kama Sutra, 1984
Set of 10, fluorescent acrylic on canvas: each 243.8 × 304.8 cm × 10 cm
Courtesy Galerie Frédéric Giroux, Paris; Mai 36 Galerie, Zurich; Esther Schipper Galerie, Berlin

119 Antic Across the Atlantic Scrapbook, 1972 [n.e.]
Page from scrapbook, hand-stitched white cotton cover over hand-assembled, with green yarn, sheets of white glossy paper, rubber-stamps: 19.5 × 24.5 × 7 cm [approx.]

120 General Idea Studio/Art Metropole, 241 Yonge Street, Toronto, 1974 [n.e.]

121 AIDS [Lottery Ticket], 1989
3 parts, offset on paper, each 10.6 × 16.2 cm
Unsigned, edition number unknown
Produced by Arbeitsgemeinschaft deutscher AIDS-STIFTUNGEN, Bonn
Collection General Idea, Toronto/New York

122 The Boutique from the 1984 Miss General Idea Pavillion, 1980
Installation, counter in the shape of dollar sign, constructed of galvanized metal and Plexiglas, containing various multiples, prints, posters and publications, 153 × 335 × 260 cm
Collection Art Gallery of Ontario, Toronto. Gift of Sandra Simpson, 1998

125 Jockey Short Shopping Bag, 1991–1998
Altered Jockey-brand undershorts, machine-embroidered label, offset postcard, title sheet [photocopy on paper], in zip-lock plastic bag, bag: 35.8 × 23.5 cm; undershorts: 77 × 40 cm [flat]
Edition of 100 + 20 AP, signed and numbered on embroidered label, produced by Texte zur Kunst, Cologne/Berlin
Collection General Idea, Toronto/New York

126–127 Colour Bar Lounge, 1979
Aluminum, glass, color photographs and printed cards, wall unit: 63.5 × 377 cm, floor unit: 101.3 × 380 × 24 cm
Collection Art Gallery of Ontario, Toronto.
Purchase, 1981

128 Test Tube, 1979 [film stills]
Video, color, sound: 28:08 min.
Courtesy General Idea, Toronto, and distributed by Netherlands Media Art Institute, Montevideo/Time Based Arts, Amsterdam

Test Pattern: T.V. Dinner Plate, 1988 [n.e.]
Porcelain plate, 22.5 × 30 × 1.5 cm

129 Magic Palette, 1980
Found object of anodized aluminum cups on chromed-metal palette, softcover book with tipped-on chromogenic print, in plastic box with gold hot-foil stamping: 5.1 × 19.7 × 14.6 cm
Collection General Idea, Toronto/New York

130–131 Test Pattern: T.V. Dinner Plates from the Miss General Idea Pavillion, 1988
Installation, 432 porcelain plates, each 22.9 × 30.5 cm [each panel 274.3 × 365.8 cm; [overall installed: 274.3 × 1280 cm]
Collection General Idea, Toronto/New York
P. 130 and 131 bottom: General Idea in front of Test Pattern: T.V. Dinner Plates from the Miss General Idea Pavillion, 1988 [n.e.]
Installation view, SPIRAL, Tokyo, 1988

132–133 The Boutique from the 1984 Miss General Idea Pavillion, 1980
Installation, counter in the shape of dollar sign, constructed of galvanized metal and Plexiglas, containing various multiples, prints, posters, and publications, 153 × 335 × 260 cm
Collection Art Gallery of Ontario, Toronto. Gift of Sandra Simpson, 1998
P. 133: Carmen Lamanna in the Boutique

134 AIDS, 1987
Acrylic on canvas: 183 × 183 cm
Private collection
Courtesy BFAS Blondeau Fine Art Services, Geneva

135 AIDS [Cadmium Orange Light], 1988
Acrylic on canvas: 243.7 × 243.7 cm
Collection Art Gallery of Ontario, Toronto

136 AIDS [Lascaux Green Light], 1988
Acrylic on canvas: 243.7 × 243.7 cm
Collection Art Gallery of Ontario, Toronto

137 AIDS [Permanent Rose Deep], 1988
Acrylic on canvas: 243.7 × 243.7 cm
Collection Art Gallery of Ontario, Toronto

139 White AIDS #6, 1993
Gesso on canvas: 154 × 154 cm
Private collection, France, courtesy Galerie Frédéric Giroux, Paris

140 AIDS [Gold], 1987
Acrylic, gold leaf on canvas, 77.5 × 77.5 × 3 cm
Collection Katharina Faerber, Geneva

141 AIDS Stamps, 1988
Offset on perforated paper: 25.5 × 21 cm
Self-published edition of 200, signed and numbered
Collection General Idea, Toronto/New York

142 AIDS [Nauman], 1991 [n.e.]
Installation, 2 free-standing walls, the inside walls papered with AIDS Wallpaper, each 315 cm high × 13 m long, placed at 75 cm at one end and so as to converge at the distance of 25 cm apart [outside of walls are finished as much as possible to match the gallery walls], 3 fluorescent tubes with fixture

143 AIDS [Project for Amsterdam Trams], 1990 [n.e.]
Screen-print on adhesive-backed vinyl [each 62.1 × 62.9 cm], produced for the advertising panels of seven trams of the Amsterdam Transit Authority

AIDS [Project for Seattle Arts Commission], 1991 [n.e.]
Intervention, poster [screen-print on adhesive-backed vinyl: 61 × 223.5 cm], installed on the advertising panels of 34 metro buses of Seattle, King County Metro Transit, 1–28 August 1991
Commissioned for the public art project In Public: Seattle 1991 of the Seattle Arts Commission, Seattle

144 AIDS, 1989
Lacquered metal: 200 × 200 × 100 cm
Courtesy Galerie Frédéric Giroux, Paris; Mai 36 Galerie, Zurich; Esther Schipper Galerie, Berlin
Here: installation view, Dialogues de Paix/Dialogues of Peace, Palais des Nations, Geneva, 1995

145 AIDS, 1989 [n.e.]
Study for a sculpture

146–147 AIDS, 1989 [n.e.]
Computer generated animation [30 sec.] broadcast from the Spectacolor lightboard, One Times Square, New York

149 Mimi Paige and Felix Partz at General Idea Studio, 78 Gerrard St. West, Toronto [n.e.]

150 Showcard 1–001 General Idea, 1975
Gelatin silver print, felt pen and screen-print on paperboard, 45.7 × 35.6 cm
Edition 1 of 2: Art Gallery of Ontario, Toronto. Gift of Vivian and David Campbell, 1994

152 The Felix Partz Fan Club, ca. 1977
Photocopy on card in plastic laminate, 6.5 × 9.5 cm
General Idea Archive [Projects Series 1968–1971], on loan to National Gallery of Canada Library and Archives, Ottawa

153 General Idea and friends on the roof of 87 Yonge Street, Toronto [n.e.]

154 Going Thru The Motions, 1975 [n.e.]
Photogram of the film made during the performance

Open Line [Slow-Scan Transmission], 1978
Slow scan video, black and white, silent, with audio components: 6:01 min.
Collection General Idea, Toronto/New York
Here: extract of documentation from Video Guide, Vancouver, September/October 1978, p. 12–13

155 General Idea, 1977 [n.e.]

157 AA Bronson with Eric Metcalfe [a.k.a. Dr. Brute], ca. 1973 [n.e.]

159–163 FILE Megazine, 1972–1989
Groups of 26 issues: 22 numbers, 35.5 × 28 cm; 4 issues 25.4 × 18 cm
Collections General Idea, Toronto/New York and Frédéric Giroux, Paris

164 General Idea Studio, 136 Simcoe Street, Toronto, ca. 1977 [n.e.]

166 Team from the performance Going Thru The Motions, Art Gallery of Ontario, Toronto, 1975 [n.e.]
Left to right: Robert Handforth, Felix Partz, Granada Gazelle, Jorge Zontal, John Dowd, and AA Bronson

167 "The general idea behind General Idea," Toronto Life, November 1975 [n.e.]
Gelatin silver print: 25.4 × 20.3 cm
Collection General Idea, Toronto/New York

169 Felix Partz & AA Bronson, ca. 1978 [n.e.]

172 Jorge Zontal, 1978 [n.e.]
Black and white photo-booth photograph

Self-Portrait [Velvet Underground], 1969
Polaroid, black and white photograph, 8.6 × 10.7 cm
General Idea Archive [Projects Series 1968–1971], on loan to National Gallery of Canada Library and Archives, Ottawa

175 General Idea at Centre d'Art Contemporain, Geneva, with poodles from XXX [bleu], before the performance, 1984 [n.e.]

176 Jorge Zontal
Each: Untitled, 1991
Gouache and watercolor on pages of sketchbook, 35.7 × 26.8 cm
Collection General Idea, Toronto/New York

179 Achrome [Manzoni], 1993–1996
3 parts, plaster bandage on wood, each 25.4 × 61 × 12.7 cm
Private collection, Switzerland

180 Untitled [Vantage], 1986
Acrylic, pasta on canvas, 121.9 × 101.6 cm
MUDAM [Musée d'Art Moderne Grand-Duc Jean], Luxembourg

181 Untitled [Marlboro], 1985–1986
Acrylic, pasta on canvas: 121.9 × 101.6 cm
MUDAM [Musée d'Art Moderne Grand-Duc Jean], Luxembourg

182 Untitled [Visa], 1986 [n.e.]
Acrylic, pasta on canvas, 101.6 × 152.4 cm
MUDAM [Musée d'Art Moderne Grand-Duc Jean], Luxembourg

183 Untitled [Mastercard], 1985–1986 [n.e.]
Acrylic, pasta on canvas, 101.6×167.6 cm
MUDAM [Musée d'Art Moderne Grand-Duc Jean], Luxembourg

184 Copyright [Blue] #3, 1987
Gold leaf on ultramarine ground on linen: 53.3×53.3 cm
Courtesy Galerie Frédéric Giroux, Paris

185 Leather and Denim Copyright #4, 1987
Leather on denim, copper rivets: 61×61 cm
Courtesy Galerie Frédéric Giroux, Paris

187 Atomic Blast #3, 1986
Enamel on canvas: 91×76 cm
Private collection, Paris, courtesy Galerie Frédéric Giroux, Paris

188 Trinitron #6, 1987
Enamel and acrylic on linen: 23×31×7.6 cm
Private collection, Zurich

189 Ponytron #3, 1988
Pony skin vinyl on stretcher: 38.1×38.1×7.6 cm
Collection General Idea, Toronto/New York

191 Infe©ted Mondrian #6, 1994
Acrylic on Gatorboard: 56×56 cm
Collection Franco and Barbara Noero, Turin, courtesy Mai 36 Galerie, Zurich

192–193 Fin de siècle, 1990 [n.e.]
Installation consisting of: a] 3 facsimile Harp seal pups constructed of acrylic fake fur, plastic eyes, whiskers, nose, and straw; life size; b] minimum of 300 sheets of expanded polystyrene [EPS]; each sheet no less than 1×2 m, overall dimensions variable
Private collection, Turin

195 General Idea Studio, 241 Yonge Street, Toronto, 1974 [n.e.]

196 General Idea at the Western Front Society, Vancouver, 1974 [n.e.]

198 Reconstructing Futures, 1977 [detail] [n.e.]
Installation consisting of seven elements: overall installed 2.74×4.32×10.17 m
Collection National Gallery of Canada, Ottawa

Khroma Key Klub: the Blue Ruins from the 1984 Miss General Idea Pavillion, 1985 [n.e.]
Site-specific installation, scenic paint on found Styrofoam objects: approx. 4×10×10 m
Installation view, De Vleeshal, Middelburg, 1985

199 P Is For Poodle: The Milky Way From the 1984 Miss General Idea Pavillion [a.k.a. XXX], 1982–1983
Installation with performative/theatrical/audio elements, in 8 units:
Unit 1: 3 facsimile standard poodle constructed of acrylic fake fur, plastic, straw: a. 81×82×21 cm; b. 45×89×33 cm; c. 78×62,5×28 cm
Unit 2: 5 spirals, painted steel with interior steel trident fork [each 169×26×2 cm, each with small spotlights installed on top: each 152.4×121.9 [diam.] cm
Unit 3: 5 milking stools, wood with metal-leaf gilding: each 31.5×44×50 cm
Unit 4: 5 brass buckets: each 20.5×26.4 [diam.] cm
Unit 5: 3 sound machines in wood boxes with rotating speaker [15×15×31 cm]: each 30.5×61×61 cm
Unit 6: 3 audiocassette recorders and 3 tape cassettes [original audio components but upgraded to contemporary standards]
Unit 7: 1 bale of hay
Unit 8: screen [composed of 3 panels of painted aluminum]: overall installed 239×307 cm with one ultra-violet light, one theater spot
Audio: 3 cassette tape decks, 3 audiotape loops
Overall installed 152.4×1219.2×1829.8 cm [variable]
Collection Carmen Lamanna, Toronto
Here: installation view, OKanada, Akademie der Kunst, Berlin, 1982

Monday, Wednesday, Saturday, 1984 [n.e.]
Set of 3 elements, acrylic-tinted plaster on core of polyurethane foam block and expandable polyurethane foam: approx. 185.4×53.3×61 cm, 188×63.5×50.8 cm, 180.3×53.3×40.6 cm
Collection National Gallery of Canada, Ottawa

200 Cornucopia: Fragments from the Room of the Unknown Function in the Villa dei Misteri of the 1984 Miss General Idea Pavillion, 1982 [n.e.]
Top: Detail of one of the rotating ceramic "cornucopia" elements of the video installation, composed floor display module, 7 display stands with Plexiglas boxes, each with kinetic element and each with a ceramic sculpture; monitor; videotape
Bottom: 7 ceramic sculptures sculptures en céramiques, highlights in gold and silver, each 16×7 cm, presentation module with video and mobile elements, 244×427×244 cm
Collection: San Francisco Museum of Modern Art, San Francisco

201 "Ziggurat Paintings," 1968–1969 [n.e.]
Installation view, The 1984 Miss General Idea Pavillion, Art Gallery of Ontario, Toronto, 1985

V.B. Gowns and series of "Ziggurat Paintings" [n.e.]
Installation view, The 1984 Miss General Idea Pavillion, Art Gallery of Ontario, Toronto, 1985

202 White AIDS paintings, 1993 [n.e.]
AIDS, 1988/1990
AIDS [Cadmium Orange Light]; AIDS [Lascaux Green Light]; AIDS [Permanent Rose Deep], each acrylic on canvas 243.7×243.7 cm on AIDS Wallpaper
Installation view, Fodor Museum, Amsterdam, 1990
Collection Art Gallery of Ontario, Toronto. Don de Robert and Lynn Simpson in 1997

203 Installation view, series of "Infe©ted Mondrian Paintings" [1994] on AIDS Wallpaper [1990] with Infe©ted Rietveld [1994]
Installation view, S. L. Simpson Gallery, Toronto, 1995

204 Blue [Cobalt] PLA©EBO [a.k.a. Blue [Mazarine] PLA©EBO], 1992
Installation, 3 units, fiberglass, enamel: each 85×213.3×85 cm
Collection Fonds national d'art contemporain [CNAP], ministère de la Culture et de la Communication, Paris, on loan to the Musée d'Art moderne de la Ville de Paris
Installation view, General Idea, Galerie Montenay, Paris, 1992

205 One Day of AZT and One Year of AZT, 1991 [n.e.]
a. Installation, 5 parts, fiberglass and enamel: each 85.0×213.3×85.0 cm
b. Installation, 1,825 parts, vacuum-formed styrene with vinyl: each 12.7×31.7×6.3 cm
Collection National Gallery of Canada, Ottawa [a and b]
Installation view, General Idea's Fin de siècle, The Power Plant Art Gallery, Toronto

206 Pla©ebo [Helium], 1992 [n.e.]
Installation, [variously recorded as 4,500 or 4,800 helium-filled printed mylar balloons]: each 25 × 65 × 25 cm [inflated]
Installation view, Expanded Art, Wiener Festwochen [General Idea work at U-Bahn Station U6-Westbahnhof, Europaplatz], Vienna, 1992

207–209 Installation views General Idea: Found Formats and General Idea Editions 1967–1995, Kunsthalle Zürich, Zurich, 2006–2007 [n.e.]

224 General Idea's rubber stamp, 1971 [n.e.]

List of Works Exhibited and not Reproduced

[Chronological Order]

- Carmen, 1968–1969
Fluorescent acrylic and latex on canvas: 192.4×381 cm
Collection Art Gallery of Ontario, Toronto. Gift of Robert and Lynn Simpson, 1997
- Granada, 1968–1969
Fluorescent acrylic and latex on canvas: 301×202 cm
Collection Art Gallery of Ontario, Toronto. Gift of Robert and Lynn Simpson, 1997
- Burning Ziggurats, 1968–1969
A project by Felix Partz
Set of 4, gelatin silver print [each 9×12.5 cm] mounted on black photo-album paper, with 3-hole punch marks: 28×21.5 cm
General Idea Archive [Projects Series 1968–1971], on loan to National Gallery of Canada Library and Archives, Ottawa
- Portrait of General Idea, 1969–1970
Collage: 21.1×12.1 cm
Private collection, Paris, courtesy Galerie Frédéric Giroux, Paris
- Mondo Drag, 1970
Set of 2,
a. recto and verso, typescript, ballpoint pen, felt pen, graphite on paper: 30.5×21.5 cm;
b. recto and verso, typescript, graphite on paper: 30.5×21.5 cm
General Idea Archive [Projects Series 1968–1971], on loan to National Gallery of Canada Library and Archives, Ottawa
- What Happened—The 1970 Miss General Idea Pageant, 1970
2 gelatin silver prints mounted on card, both mounted on bond paper, with telex print-out, ballpoint pen: 30.5×21.6 cm [overall]
[photograph a.: 12.3×18.2 cm, photograph b. 12.4×18.2 cm]
1 gelatin silver print mounted on card, both mounted on bond paper, with telex print-out, ballpoint pen: 30.5×21.6 cm [overall]
[photograph: 18×12.2 cm]
Collection General Idea, Toronto/New York
- The 1971 Miss General Idea Pageant Documentation, 1971
Installation consisting of 17 elements:
A. Contestants:
Set of 13, black and white and chromogenic prints on board
a. Victoria Barkoff [by Shulim Rubin], black and white photograph on board: 76.3×101.9 cm
b. Michaele Berman [by Rex Raglan], black and white photograph on board: 76.3×101.9 cm
c. Susan Bunny [by Art Rat], chromogenic print on board: 76.3×76.3 cm
d. Janis Campbell [by GI], black and white photostat on board: 101.8×76.3 cm
e. Margaret Colemen [by Jim Lang], black and white photograph on board: 101.9×76.3 cm
f. Marcel Dot [by Vincent Trasov], black and white photograph on board: 101.9×76.3 cm
g. Anne Elliott [by Doug Elliott], black and white photograph on board: 76.3×101.9 cm
h. Tina Miller [by Rodney Werden], black and white photograph on board: 76 3×76 3 cm
i. Myra Peanut [by Michael Morris], black and white photograph on board: 101.9×76.3 cm
j. Tess Tickle [by Doug Barry], black and white photograph on board: 101.9×76.3 cm
k. Jane Vasey [by Rex Raglan], black and white photograph on board: 101.9×76.3 cm
l. Dr. Venus [by Dr. Brute], black and white photograph on board: 101.9×76.3 cm
m. Marnie Wright [by Harold Wright], black and white photograph on board: 101.9×76.3 cm
B. Granada Gazelle, Miss General Idea 1969 Displays the Entry Kit
Black and white photograph on board: 76.3×101.9 cm
C. Portrait of Granada Gazelle, Miss General Idea 1969
Black and white photograph on board: 101.9×76.3 cm
D. The 1971 Miss General Idea Pageant [Artscanada]
Set of 3 panels, black-and-white photographs on board: each 101.9×76.2 cm
Collection Carmen Lamanna, Toronto
- Documentary clip of The 1971 Miss General Idea Pageant, 1971
Excerpt, video, black and white and color, sound, 9:55 min
[Clip from General Idea's High Profile, 1978, video, black and white, color, sound, 47:20 min.]
Collection General Idea, Toronto/New York
- Double Mirror Video [A Borderline Case], 1971
Video, black and white, sound, 5:50 min
Courtesy General Idea, Toronto, and distributed by Netherlands Media Art Institute, Montevideo/Time Based Arts, Amsterdam
- General Idea Business Card, 1971
Letterpress on plastic-coated yellow card: 6.6×10.6 cm
Collection General Idea, Toronto/New York
- Shoe Journal, 1971/2007
A project by Jorge Zontal
Offset publication, 64 p., black and white reproductions plus hand-bound simulated leather cover, foil stamped, with letterpress insert: 15.6×10.9 cm
The publication was finally bound in 2007
Collection General Idea, Toronto/New York
- Find Granada in the Palm Trees, 1972
Set of 6 gelatin silver prints, each: 7×20.2 cm [sight]
Collection General Idea, Toronto/New York
- Manipulating the Self [a.k.a. Manipulating the Scene], 1973
Offset color lithograph on paper, 73.7×58.4 cm
Edition of 65 plus APs
Edition 40/65: Collection Art Gallery of Ontario, Toronto. Purchase, 1974

- The Miss General Idea Shoe, [found ca. 1973]
  Set of 2, patent leather, metal: men's North American size 9 ½
  General Idea Archive [Performance Props Series], on loan to National Gallery of Canada Library and Archives, Ottawa
- Luxon V.B., 1973
  Pen and ink on paper, 49.5 × 63.5 cm
  Collection Carmen and Claire Colangelo, Unionville
- The Hand of the Spirit, 1973–1974
  Clear Plexiglas cut-out on Plexiglas rod handle, 19.5 × 22.8 cm
  Courtesy Esther Schipper Galerie, Berlin
- Blocking, 1974
  Video, color, sound: 17:00 min
  Produced by Western Front Film & Video, Vancouver
  Courtesy General Idea, Toronto and distributed by Netherlands Media Art Institute, Montevideo/ Time Based Arts, Amsterdam
- V.B. Gown #5, 1975
  3 parts, enamel plating on aluminum with steel chain in three parts, top: 76.5 × 43.7 × 50.8 cm, middle: 60.5 × 47 × 52 cm, bottom: 102 × 57 × 69 cm
  Collection Art Gallery of Ontario, Toronto. Gift of Fern Bayer, 1995
- Showcards Series, 1975–1979, organized in 5 categories:
  1. The Search for the Spirit of Miss General Idea
  2. The 1984 Miss General Idea Pageant
  3. Miss General Idea 1984
  4. The 1984 Miss General Idea Pavillion
  5. The Frame of Reference
  Collection Art Gallery of Ontario, Toronto. Gift of Vivian and David Campbell in 1994
  Edition 1 of 2, with several APs, except no. 5–027 to 5–044: courtesy Esther Schipper Galerie, Berlin
  All: Chromogenic print or gelatin silver print [marked below as CP or GSP], felt pen and screen-print on paperboard, 45.7 × 35.6 cm
- 1–001 General Idea, 1975
  CP
- 1–004 Haute Culture, 1975
  GSP
- 1–007 Brilliant in its Vacancy, 1975
  GSP
- 1– 009 Battle Plans, 1975
  CP
- 1–010 Hushed Voice Over, 1975
  CP
- 1–016 Close-up Of The Hand Of The Spirit, 1975
  CP
- 1–018 It Was At One of Those Late Sessions in the Small Hours, 1975
  CP
- 1–019 Concentrated Vision, 1975
  CP
- 1–021 Under Construction, 1975
  CP
- 1–023 Audience Instruction, 1975
  CP
- 1–029 Cultural Imperialism, 1975
  GSP
- 1–031 Working on it, 1975
  CP
- 1–034 The Spirit of Research, 1975
  GSP
- 1–042 Image Load, 1975
  CP
- 1–046 The Colour Bar, 1975
  GSP
- 1–055 Fashion Note, 1975
  CP
- 1–057 Fashion Note, 1975
  CP
- 1–063 He's Got Her Nerve, 1977
  CP
- 1–071 The Artist Constructs a Model, 1977
  GSP
- 1–072 The Artist Constructs a Social Model, 1977
  GSP
- 1–073 The Artist Constructs an Artists' Model, 1977
  GSP
- 1–074 The Artist Constructs a Scale Model, 1977
  GSP
- 1–075 The Artist Constructs a Fashion Model, 1977
  CP
- 1–076 Right Hand Man, 1977
  GSP
- 1–077 Single Image Reflex, 1977
  GSP
- 1–078 Three Heads are Better, 1977
  GSP
- 1–079 Three Men, 1977
  CP
- 1–080 Group Decisions, 1977
  GSP
- 1–084 Fascism and Anarchy Join Hands to Create a Work of Art, 1977
  CP
- 1–090 Dedication & Inspiration, 1977
  CP
- 1–101 Pavillion Applause Machine, 1977
  CP
- 1–102 Now Appearing in Galleries of The World, 1978
  CP
- 1–104 Oedipal Triangle, 1979
  GSP
- 1–105 Menage A Trois, 1979
  GSP
- 1–106 An Animated Trio, 1979
  GSP
- 1–109 Three Blind Artists, 1979
  CP
- 1–110 The Geometry of Inspiration, 1979
  CP
- 1–111 Untitled, 1979
  CP
- 1–112 Giving the Audience A Hand, 1979
  CP
- 1–113 Cultural Struggle, 1979
  CP
- 2–001 The 1984 Miss General Idea Pageant, 1975
  GSP
- 2–006 At Home, 1975
  GSP
- 2–010 Being an Object, 1975
  CP
- 2–011 Urban Armour for the Future, 1975
  CP
- 2–012 Volumes for Voyeurs, 1975
  CP
- 2–023 Voice Over, 1975
  GSP
- 2–026 GRANADA [Animal growls from a hidden tape recorder], 1975
  CP
- 2–030 Voice Over, 1975
  GSP
- 2–035 Voice Over, 1975
  GSP
- 2–042 AA Bronson, 1975
  GSP
- 2–043 Felix Partz, 1975
  GSP
- 2–044 Jorge Zontal, 1975
  GSP
- 2–045 It Was At One of Those Late Sessions in the Small, 1975
  CP
- 2–050 Some Sort of Cultural Parasite, 1977
  GSP
- 2–052 The Tyranny of the Myth of the Individual Genius, 1977
  GSP

- 2–054 Escalating Costs, 1977
  CP
- 2–057 Pumping Irony, 1977
  CP
- 2–069 ∆ The Graduated Cock, 1979
  CP
- 2–070 O Slice of Life, 1979
  CP
- 2–071 □ Father Knows Best, 1979
  CP
- 2–072 Audience Vocabulary: Laughter, 1979
  CP
- 2–073 Audience Vocabulary: Standing Ovation, 1979
  CP
- 2–074 Audience Vocabulary: Booing, 1979
  CP
- 2–075 Audience Vocabulary: Sleep, 1979
  CP
- 2–076 Audience Vocabulary: Gasp, 1979
  CP
- 2–077 Audience Vocabulary: Panic, 1979
  CP
- 2–078 Playing the Triangle [Note: To Play the Triangle, You Need a 4th Element], 1979
  GSP
- 2–079 Playing the Triangle [Note: To Play the Triangle, You Need a 4th Element], 1979
  GSP
- 2–080 Playing the Triangle [Note: To Play the Triangle, You Need a 4th Element], 1979
  GSP
- 2–089 Consenting Cocktails, 1979
  GSP
- 2–090 Good Sports, 1979
  CP
- 2–096 Maximize Transparency, 1979
  CP
- 3–001 Miss General Idea 1984, 1975
  CP
- 4–001 The 1984 Miss General Idea Pavillion, 1975
  GSP
- 4–003 Conestipation, 1975
  GSP
- 4–011 Luxon V.B., 1975
  GSP
- 4–018 Are you saying that the Pavillion will be composed of decentralized sites?, 1977
  GSP
- 4–021 Note the Ziggurat Configuration, 1977
  GSP
- 4–022 Just Another Fetish Object, 1977
  EC
- 4–023 Aerial Viewpoint, 1977
  CP
- 4–031 Test Model 1, 1977
  EC
- 4–032 Test Model 2, 1977
  EC
- 5–001 "Frame of Reference," 1975
  CP
- 5–009 "The General Idea Behind General Idea," 1979
  EC
- 5–010 Self-Portrait, 1977
  EC
- 5–011 Audience Rehearsal, 1979
  CP
- 5–013 "Their Hearts Belong to DADA," 1977
  EC
- 5–014 Fantasy Architecture, 1977
  EC
- 5–023 "Great Canadian Art Tragedy," 1977
  EC
- 5–027 LIFE is Dead, but FILE Goes On, 1977
  EC
- 5–028 General Idea and the Cultural Cliché, 1977
  EC
- 5–029 A Truly Illuminating Exhibition, 1977
  EC
- 5–030 Canadada Fragments, 1977
  EC
- 5–031 Three New Magazines, 1977
  EC
- 5–032 Opinion, 1977
  EC
- 5–033 At the Galleries, 1977
  EC
- 5–034 Getting It All Apart, 1977
  EC
- 5–035 Des Potins a la Torontoise, 1977
  EC
- 5–036 General Idea, 1977
  EC
- 5–037 Toronto, 1977
  EC
- 5–038 D—For Different, 1977
  EC
- 5–039 Art, 1977
  EC
- 5–040 Correspondence Art, 1977
  EC
- 5–041 Vision of 1984, 1977
  EC
- 5–042 Luxon V.B., 1977
  EC
- 5–043 These Bands are Weirder Than You, 1977
  EC
- 5–044 Une Thématique de Clichés, 1977
  EC
- Pilot, 1977
  Video, color, sound: 28:56 min.
  Courtesy General Idea, Toronto, and distributed by Netherlands Media Art Institute, Montevideo/Time Based Arts, Amsterdam
- Untitled [XXX], 1981
  Enamel on wood panel: 32 × 25 cm
  Collection Angelo and Orienda Caranci, Toronto
- Cornucopia, 1982
  Video, black and white, sound, 10:06 min.
  Produced by Western Front Film & Video, Vancouver
  Courtesy General Idea, Toronto, and distributed by Netherlands Media Art Institute, Montevideo/Time Based Arts, Amsterdam
- Three Leashed Poodles with Cornucopia [Mural Fragment from the 1984 Miss General Idea Pavillion], 1982
  Pastel, enamel and graphite on paper: 58.5 × 77.4 cm
  Collection Art Gallery of Ontario, Toronto. Purchase, 1983
- Three Poodles with Honeymoon [Mural Fragment from the 1984 Miss General Idea Pavillion], 1982
  Pastel, enamel and graphite on paper: 58.5 × 77.4 cm
  Collection Art Gallery of Ontario, Toronto. Purchase, 1983
- Three Poodles with Cocktails [Mural Fragment from the 1984 Miss General Idea Pavillion], 1982
  Pastel, enamel and graphite on paper: 58.5 × 77.4 cm.
  Collection Art Gallery of Ontario, Toronto. Purchase, 1983
- Jorge Zontal's drawings series, 1984–1992
  50 drawings on paper or on sketchbook paper, mixed media: colored pencil, watercolor, feltpen, pastel chalk, graphite, market and gouache according to the drawing, used together or alone
  Each drawing: 35.7 × 26.8 cm except La Toilette, 1984, 20.1 × 27.8 cm, and Untitled, 1984, 31.7 × 25.5 cm
  All: Untitled except La Toilette, 1984, The Sniffles, 1989, Welt War in dem Antlictz der Geliebten 1 [White], 1989, Now You See It, 1990, and Industrial Strength/Wake Up Daddy, 1991
  Collection General Idea, Toronto/New York

- Water Babies: Prototype Tile for the 1984 Miss General Idea Pavillion, 1984
  3 elements, dye and acrylic on plaster and plastic: 28 × 84.5 cm
  Collection General Idea, Toronto/New York
- Bottle-Neck Entrance for the Pavillion: Rotating Doors of the Future, 1984
  Graphite, colored pencil on graph paper: 29.5 × 42.1 cm
  General Idea Archive [Projects Series 1984-1991], on loan to National Gallery of Canada Library and Archives, Ottawa
- Ziggurat Maze Project, 1984–1985
  Graphite on paper: 113.5 × 113.8 cm
  Collection General Idea, Toronto/New York
  Courtesy Esther Schipper, Berlin
- The Firewall, 1985
  Aniline dye on plaster cast tiles with acrylic on plaster on plywood: 243.8 × 457.2 cm [overall]
  Collection Carmen Lamanna, Toronto
- Shut the Fuck Up, 1985
  Video, color, sound, 14:07 min
  Courtesy General Idea, Toronto, and distributed by Netherlands Media Art Institute, Montevideo/Time Based Arts, Amsterdam
- Leather and Denim Copyright #1, 1987
  Leather on denim, copper rivets: 38.1 × 38.1 cm
  Courtesy Galerie Frédéric Giroux, Paris
- Copyright [Collector], 1987
  Bleach on denim: 38.1 × 38.1 cm
  Courtesy Galerie Frédéric Giroux, Paris
- Copyright [Curator], 1987
  Bleach on denim: 53.3 × 53.3 cm
  Courtesy Galerie Frédéric Giroux, Paris
- Trinitron #1, 1987
  Enamel and acrylic on linen: 23 × 31 × 7.6 cm
  Private collection, Zurich
- Trinitron #3, 1987
  Enamel, acrylic on linen: 22.9 × 30.5 × 7.6 cm
  Collection General Idea, Toronto/New York
- Trinitron #9, 1987
  Enamel, acrylic on linen: 22.9 × 30.5 × 7.6 cm
  Collection General Idea, Toronto/New York
- AIDS, 1988
  Graphite, ink, gouache on paper: 37 × 28 cm
  Collection General Idea, Toronto/New York
- AIDS, 1988
  Graphite, ink, gouache on paper: 37 × 28 cm
  Collection General Idea, Toronto/New York
- AIDS, 1988
  Graphite, ink, gouache on paper: 37 × 28 cm
  Collection General Idea, Toronto/New York
- AIDS, 1988
  Pencil, ink, gouache, gold leaf on paper: 37 × 28 cm
  Private collection, Paris, courtesy Galerie Frédéric Giroux, Paris
- Black Trinitron #3, 1989
  Enamel and acrylic on linen: 23 × 31 × 7.6 cm
  Private collection, Paris, courtesy Galerie Frédéric Giroux, Paris
- Black Trinitron #4, 1989
  Enamel and acrylic on linen, 23 × 31 × 7.6 cm
  Courtesy Galerie Frédéric Giroux, Paris
- Imagevirus [Posters], 1989
  Chromogenic print: 76 × 50.4 cm
  Collection General Idea, Toronto/New York
- Imagevirus [Times Square], 1989
  Chromogenic print: 76 × 50.4 cm
  Collection General Idea, Toronto/New York
- Imagevirus [Hamburg], 1991
  Chromogenic print: 76 × 50.4 cm
  Collection General Idea, Toronto/New York
- Imagevirus [Amsterdam], 1991
  Chromogenic print: 76 × 50.4 cm
  Collection General Idea, Toronto/New York
- Imagevirus [New York Subway], 1991
  Chromogenic print: 76 × 50.4 cm
  Collection General Idea, Toronto/New York
- AIDS Wallpaper, 1990
  Site-specific installation of serigraph wallpaper: roll 68.6 × 4.6 [diam.] cm; unrolled: 457 × 68.6 cm
- The End of the [Western] World, ca. 1993–1994
  A project by Felix Partz
  Graphite, felt pen marker on paper: 28 × 21.5 cm
  Collection General Idea, Toronto/New York
- AIDS Ring, 1993–1996
  Sterling silver ring in black velvet-covered jewelry box, title card [photocopy on vellum], in white card box; box: 7 × 6 × 4.5 cm; ring size 10
  Collection General Idea, Toronto/New York

This book is published on the occasion of the exhibition Haute Culture: General Idea. A Retrospective, 1969–1994, curated by Frédéric Bonnet and organized by ARC/Musée d'Art moderne de la Ville de Paris (February 11–April 30, 2011), in association with the Art Gallery of Ontario, Toronto (July 16, 2011–January 1, 2012).

Exhibition

Musée d'Art moderne de la Ville de Paris
11 avenue du Président Wilson
F–75116 Paris
www.mam.paris.fr

The exhibition in Paris was supported by Air Canada and Air Canada Cargo.

AIR CANADA

AIR CANADA CARGO

Art Gallery of Ontario
317 Dundas Street West
Toronto ON M5T 1G4
www.ago.net

AGO

The Art Gallery of Ontario is partially funded by the Ontario Ministry of Culture. Additionnal operating support is received from the Volunteers of the Art Gallery of Ontario, City of Toronto, the Department of Canadian Heritage, and the Canada Council for the Arts.

Contemporary programming at the AGO is supported by the Canada Council for the Arts

Canada Council for the Arts

Acknowledgments

The two institutions would like to thank first and foremost AA Bronson for his great commitment toward the project; without him, the exhibition and the publication would not have existed.

Our gratitude goes to all the lenders, institutions, galleries, and private collectors for their generous contribution to the exhibition:

National Gallery of Canada, Ottawa, Marc Mayer; University of Lethbridge Art Gallery, Lethbridge, Josephine Mills; Centre National des Arts Plastiques, département Fonds National d'Art Contemporain, Paris-La Défense, Richard Lagrange; MUDAM, Luxemburg, Enrico Lunghi; Galleria Massimo De Carlo, Milan; Galerie Frédéric Giroux, Paris; Mai 36 Galerie, Zurich; Esther Schipper Galerie, Berlin; Galerie Stampa, Basel; BFAS Blondeau Fine Art Services, Geneva; Lionel Bovier; Angelo & Orienda Caranci; McCarthy Tétrault LLP, Toronto; Helen Chapman; Katharina Faerber; Jim & Susan Garrard; Collection Carmen Lamanna; Nicolas Libert & Emmanuel Lenoir; Franco & Barbara Noero; Ringier Collection; Beatrix Ruf; as well as to those who wished to remain anonymous.

Our thanks go to
Fern Bayer for her undisputable knowledge and commitment, to the authors for their contributions, as well as to all those who helped this project to be realized:

Philip Aarons & Shelley Fox Aarons, Heather Anderson, Ann Adachi, Joke Ballintijn, Colette Bargas, Tamiko Barker, Kathleen S. Bartels, Gilles Beaujard, Alison Beckett, Katia Blanchard, Marie-Eve Bouillon, Mathieu Briand, Jessica Bright, Stéphanie Buccker, Belma Buljubasic, Sophie Caimano, Cyndie Campbell, Massimo De Carlo, Jessica Castex, Anne Cartier-Bresson, Carmen Colangelo, Sylvie Corréard, Catherine Couturier, Jill Cuthbertson, Philippe Davet, Christelle Demoussis, Morgane Desailly, Clément Dirié, Josée Drouin-Brisebois, Edouard Duval, Lonti Ebers, Jane Edmundson, Marie-Noëlle Farcy, Laurent Fetis, Barbara Fischer, Sandrine Frieden, Margaret Haupt, Kathrin Heimburger, Tony Izaacs, Ursula Krinzinger, Benjamin Lafore, Marc Leboiteux, Christophe Lebrun, Jean-Philippe Leclair, Lucie Linhart, Gareth Long, Florian Luedde, Dominique Martos-Levif, François Michaud, Elena Micheluzzi, Olivier Millagou, Philip Monk, Maria Naula, Jean-Christophe Paolini, Brian C. Pel, Maya Pfeiffer, Sherry Phillips, Mathieu Pronovost, Frédéric Queffelec, Holly Robbins, Geneviève Saulnier, Angeline Scherf, Pierre-Emmanuel Schimdt, Elizabeth Smith, Jordan Sonenberg, Sandy Sparks, Gilli Stampa, Jill Sterrett, Maria Sullivan, Kim Svendsen, Lucie Taboulot, Elena Tavecchia, Hélène Tiberi, Kim Tomczak, Laurent Torlay, Fabienne Vernet, Fiona Vianello, Marcia Vissers, Robert Wainstein, Michael Williams, Frédérique Yourath, Theus Zwakhals.

Publication

Editor
Frédéric Bonnet

Editorial Coordination
Lionel Bovier & Clément Dirié

Copy-Editing
Clare Manchester

Translations from the French
Deke Dusinberre (Frédéric Bonnet, Biography);
Madeleine Aktypi (Elisabeth Lebovici)

Design
Gavillet & Rust

Assistance
Vincent Devaud and Mathias Clottu

Typeface
Genath + Antique by François Rappo
(www.optimo.ch)

Cover
Front: Nazi Milk, 1979–1990
Chromogenic print: 76.2 x 53.3 cm
Collection of General Idea, Toronto/Canada

Back: Self-Portrait with Objects, 1981–1982
Gelatin silver print: 35.6 x 27.7 cm
Collection Canadian Museum of Contemporary Photography, Ottawa

Photo Credits
Stefan Altenburger, Zürich/Kunsthalle Zürich: p. 112–117, 188, 207–209; Shigeo Anzai: p. 74, 126b, 129; Art Gallery of Ontario: p. 70b, 96, 100; Murray Ball: p. 155; Robert A. Barnett: p. 47, 50; Mary Canary: p. 166; Centre d'Art Contemporain, Geneva: p. 175; Bill Cotter: p. 48; Jane Edmundson: 104–105b; Galerie Frédéric Giroux, Paris: p. 76h+g, 139, 184, 185, 187, 204; Galerie Stampa, Basle: p. 24–25; General Idea: cover and p. 10–11, 13, 14, 15, 16b, 17 (not b/d), 18, 21, 22–23, 27, 31, 33, 37, 38, 39, 41, 43, 51, 55, 56, 57, 58–59, 60, 61, 62–63, 64, 66–67, 69, 70h, 71, 72, 73, 75, 76 (not h/g), 77, 79, 81, 83, 85, 86, 87, 89g, 91, 92, 95, 97, 98, 99, 103, 104–105h, 106, 107, 108, 110-111, 119, 120, 122, 123, 125, 126h, 130–131, 132–133, 140, 141, 143, 146–147, 149, 150, 154, 159–163, 164, 167, 169, 172, 176, 180, 181, 182, 183, 189, 192–193, 198, 199, 200, 201, 202b, 203, 224; Tohru Kogure: p. 128; Roland Krauss: p. 206; Peter McCallum: p. 109; Massimo De Carlo Arte Contemporanea: p. 89d; National Gallery of Canada Library and Archives: p. 93–94, 145, 154; Cheryl O'Brien: p. 44–45, 205; Paul Oberst: p. 51h; Jim Panou: p. 16h, 17bd, 20, 65; Elke Town: p. 153; Rodney Werden: p. 1; Zindman/Fremont: p. 134, 135, 136, 137.

Color Separation and Print
Musumeci S.p.A., Quart (Aosta)

Printed in Europe

Published by

JRP|Ringier
Letzigraben 134
CH-8047 Zurich
T +41 (0) 43 311 27 50
F +41 (0) 43 311 27 51
E info@jrp-ringier.com
www.jrp-ringier.com

ISBN 978-3-03764-162-0

(French edition available from Paris-Musées:
ISBN 978-2-7596-0147-9)

JRP|Ringier books are available internationally at selected bookstores and from the following distribution partners:

Switzerland
Buch 2000, AVA Verlagsauslieferung AG, Centralweg 16, CH –8910 Affoltern a.A.
buch2000@ava.ch, www.ava.ch

France
Les presses du réel
35, rue Colson
F–21000 Dijon
info@lespressesdureel.com
www.lespressesdureel.com

Germany and Austria
Vice Versa Vertrieb
Immanuelkirchstrasse 12
D–10405 Berlin
info@vice-versa-vertrieb.de
www.vice-versa-vertrieb.de

UK and other European countries
Cornerhouse Publications
70 Oxford Street,
UK–Manchester M1 5NH
publications@cornerhouse.org,
www.cornerhouse.org/books

USA, Canada, Asia, and Australia
D.A.P./Distributed Art Publishers
I55 Sixth avenue, 2nd Floor
USA–New York, NY 10013
dap@dapinc.com, www.artbook.com

For a list of our partner bookshopsor for any general questions, pleasecontact JRP|Ringier directly at info@jrpringier.com, or visit our homepage www.jrp-ringier.com for further information about our program

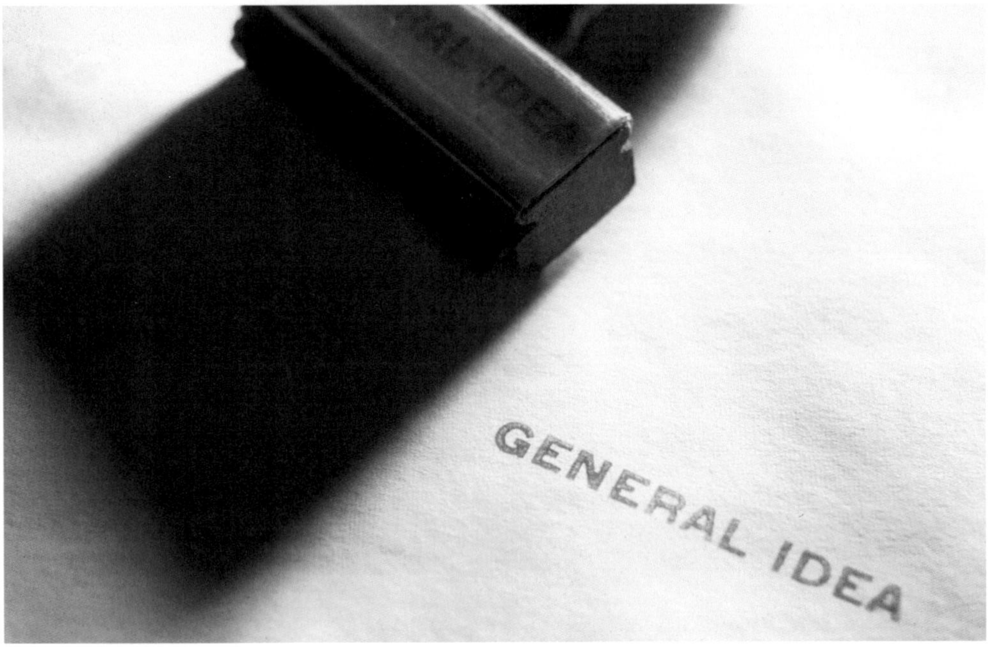
GENERAL IDEA